ALLEN TATE AND HIS WORK
Critical Evaluations

ALLEN TATE
AND HIS WORK
Critical Evaluations

~~~~~~

Edited with an introduction by
RADCLIFFE SQUIRES

UNIVERSITY OF MINNESOTA PRESS ■ MINNEAPOLIS

© Copyright 1972 by the University of Minnesota.
All rights reserved.
Printed in the United States of America
at Napco Graphic Arts Inc., Milwaukee, Wisconsin.

Published in the United Kingdom and India by the Oxford University
Press, London and Bombay, and in Canada
by the Copp Clark Publishing Co. Limited, Toronto

Library of Congress Catalog Card Number: 78-167297

ISBN 0-8166-0627-7

Contents

III THE NOVELIST

IV THE POET

ALLEN TATE AND HIS WORK
Critical Evaluations

Introduction

by RADCLIFFE SQUIRES

In the Princeton University Library repose thousands of letters written to Allen Tate over a period of more than forty years. The letters come from the great hierophants of modern letters as well as from obscure acolytes. And it is a strange thing: from the letters of the famous and the obscure alike—and with almost no letters of Tate's own composition—a consistent essence of a person emerges. One becomes conscious first of Tate's kindness and generosity to others. Then he sees that this generosity is inseparable from moral action. Finally he sees that both the generosity and the action are entirely disinterested. That is because Allen Tate has always conceived of the profession of letters as a service to something more important than self. We can read nothing of Tate's properly, not even his letters, unless we know this truth. An awareness in others of Tate's serious and dispassionate objectivity has, I think, inspired an equally serious and dispassionate criticism of his work. This book is an occasion for bringing some of that criticism together.

(John Orley) Allen Tate was born on December 19, 1899, in Winchester, Kentucky. His ancestry, primarily English, Scotch-Irish, and Irish, combines the settled values of a Tidewater culture with the impulsive energies of pioneers who pushed to the frontiers of Kentucky and Tennessee. Though as a child Allen Tate made the usual friendships and engaged in the common sport of children, he knew, without knowing how, that his life would have to take a course different from that of his young friends. Somehow he would have to distinguish himself through spirit and mind. He wrote a few poems at an early age, but he put no stock in them. And in adolescence he was drawn to music rather than literature. Yet when it became clear that his talent for the

3

violin was not remarkable, he abandoned his ambition for, though not his love of, musicianship. Then, in 1918, unsure what his career should be, he entered Vanderbilt University where his two elder brothers had studied.

At Vanderbilt he came under the benevolent influence of two of his teachers, Walter Clyde Curry and John Crowe Ransom, as well as Donald Davidson; with them he helped to found in 1922 a poetry magazine, *The Fugitive*, which almost overnight became internationally famous. Soon Merrill Moore and Robert Penn Warren joined the Fugitive group. The fortnightly meetings were spirited and heady, and Allen Tate who had had only a mild interest in literature when he entered Vanderbilt became a tenacious devotee.

In the space of a few years *The Fugitive* printed some of Ransom's finest poems and a few of Tate's most promising early poems. These poems and others that he published in *The Double Dealer*, a New Orleans journal, brought him a letter from a fellow poet, young Hart Crane, then as unknown as Tate. Crane observed that Tate's poems reminded him of T. S. Eliot's. Since Tate's work has throughout his career reminded readers of Eliot's, it is interesting to note that at this time Tate had not read Eliot's poetry at all. Of course, as a result of Crane's letter, he did read Eliot's verse and shortly became a passionate advocate of his work. Indeed, his advocacy often brought him into conflict with Ransom and Davidson.

The Fugitive ceased publication in 1925, but even before that unhappy event, Tate had loosened his ties with the group. In 1924 he married Caroline Gordon and moved to New York City where for the next few years he earned a living by writing reviews and doing hack editorial work. He also, however, wrote his first important poems, his first major essays, his biography of "Stonewall" Jackson, as well as part of his biography of Jefferson Davis. His first volume of poetry, *Mr. Pope and Other Poems*, was published in 1928. And his circle of literary friends grew to include Louise Bogan, Léonie Adams, Kenneth Burke, Malcolm Cowley, Katherine Anne Porter, Hart Crane, Mark Van Doren, and Edmund Wilson. By all standards his career was beginning well, yet there was an irony. He had come to New York in order to test his talent and to prove it in a world larger than Vanderbilt. But no sooner was he established in the city than he hated it and began to meditate nostalgically on the South. This represents a consistent pattern in Tate's life: he has always been drawn toward an international ideal of culture, yet he has also always been drawn back to his native ground.

Temporarily sick of the city, in the winter of 1925 he and Caroline shared a farmhouse with Hart Crane at Patterson, New York. Here Crane worked on a section of *The Bridge*, and Tate wrote "Ode to the Confederate Dead." The poem brought Tate fame, but it also tyrannized his career, for, though he subsequently wrote finer poems, the "Ode" tended to become the poem most often associated with his name. Although it perfectly expressed his despair about modern man's introversion, his "dissociation of sensibility," Tate's thought did not cease with these Eliotesque themes, and in later life he tended to reconsider and revise these views.

In 1928 Tate received a Guggenheim Fellowship and with Caroline and their young daughter Nancy went abroad. In England he met and established lifelong friendships with Herbert Read and T. S. Eliot. In France he saw a good deal of the people who frequented Sylvia Beach's bookstore and Gertrude Stein's apartment. With Ernest Hemingway he went almost every Sunday to the bicycle races at the Velodrome d'Iver, a fact which Hemingway slyly reminded him of years later in a letter. Yet the profoundest friendships he made in Paris were with Ford Madox Ford and John Peale Bishop, both of whom he had met earlier in New York. Ford placed before Tate a model of the complete man of letters. Bishop's and Tate's work possess a similarity of subject matter and method. They sometimes wrote "companion pieces" to each other's poems. Until Bishop's death in 1944 they maintained a steady correspondence. The letters are remarkable for their mutual sincerity and sympathy.

Tate did not write very many poems in Paris, but several of them reflect the fact that, just as in New York, his separation from the South intensified his thinking about his tradition. After finishing his life of Jefferson Davis, he returned, early in 1930, to an America where the Great Depression had just begun and where he found himself soon embroiled in the movement that came to be known as "Southern Agrarianism."

Upon his return to America, Tate moved into an antebellum house near Clarksville, Tennessee. The location brought him close once again to his Fugitive friends, John Crowe Ransom and Donald Davidson

in Nashville and Robert Penn Warren in Memphis. Nor was he too
distant from Andrew Lytle, then living in Monteagle, Tennessee.
(Lytle, later to become a distinguished novelist, qualifies as a Fugitive
by having published a poem in a late issue of the magazine.) These
gentlemen, who as Fugitives had entertained doubts about the state of
Southern culture, banded together to "defend" the South against the
calumnies heaped upon it as a result of the Scopes trial at Dayton.
They made their enemy the faceless technology of Northern industrialism to which they attributed the evils of abstraction, despotism, dehu-
manization, cultural deprivation, and economic imperialism. These,
at least, were the primary targets of their symposium *I'll Take My
Stand*, published in 1930. A second symposium appeared six years later
under the title *Who Owns America?* After that the movement declined
and finally died with the advent of World War II. Southern Agrarianism never had much of a following and received more rude hilarity
than serious analysis. Perhaps the hilarity was deserved; certainly it is
true that Agrarianism could offer little more than subsistence farming
as an antidote to industrialism. Still, if we were to substitute today
certain terms such as "ecology" and "quality of life" for the near
equivalents the Agrarians employed, we might be tempted to think the
movement was simply ahead of its time. Be that as it may, Southern
Agrarianism tended to crystallize Tate's ideas about modern life. It
bolstered his contempt for Irving Babbitt's Neo-Humanism, just as it
strengthened his hatred of positivism. Furthermore, by reason of the
movement's concern with Southern culture, it enhanced his consciousness of his personal present and his historical past. It intensified his
"sense of history." As a result his poetry turned more certainly toward
an attempt to link personal experience with mythical or historical
incident, as we see in his "Sonnets of the Blood" or in "The Mediterranean." His remarkable novel, *The Fathers* (1938), also brays in the
mortar past and present, tradition and modern chaos, for although it
is set during the Civil War, the hero is premonitive of an American of
the twentieth century.

   In 1934, nagged by debts, Tate doubted his ability to live as a free-
lance writer and took a job at Southwestern College in Memphis, Tennessee. Unhappy there, he left Memphis in 1936, but after a year in
Clarksville, he took a position at the Woman's College of the University of North Carolina at Greensboro. From 1939 to 1942 he was a resi-

dent fellow in the Creative Arts Program at Princeton University. During these years his reputation as a critic soared with the publication of his first two collections of essays, *Reactionary Essays* (1936) and *Reason in Madness: Critical Essays* (1941). But he found it increasingly difficult to write poetry. When, however, his appointment at Princeton terminated in 1942 he spent that fall and the following winter and spring at Monteagle, Tennessee, writing only poetry. It was one of his most productive periods, culminating in the sardonic but majestic masterpiece "Seasons of the Soul." "Sardonic" and "majestic" do not go readily together, yet in this poem they merge. For Tate's view of man's fate seems an annotation on the acrid myth of the bronze man that our first technologist, Daedalus, made to defend Crete against the invasions of the Sardinians. This creature had the habit of squeezing his victims in arms that had been rendered furnace-hot by fire. In such a relentless embrace the helpless Sardinians died as they stared into a fixed metallic smile which, if we may believe etymologists, gave us the word "sardonic." On the other hand "Seasons of the Soul" may claim to be "majestic" because we see that Tate was redeeming his growing interest in Dante by shifting his thematic concern from "failure" toward "vision."

In 1943, at the urging of his friend Archibald MacLeish, Tate served as the first consultant in poetry at the Library of Congress, where he inaugurated the Library's series of poetry recordings. In the following year he assumed the editorship of *The Sewanee Review*, a position he held until 1946. During his tenure *The Sewanee Review* became one of the most important literary quarterlies in the English-speaking world. From 1946 to 1948 Tate was an editor for Henry Holt and Company and after that until 1951 he taught at New York University. The year 1950 is significant for Tate's conversion to Roman Catholicism and for his beginning to write a long poem in terza rima. To date only three parts of the poem have been published, but even as parts they intimate a grandeur scarcely known in modern poetry; and one of the parts, "The Swimmers," achieves a clarity and beauty beyond anything Tate had done before.

The next year, 1951, is also significant, for it marks Tate's acceptance of a professorship in English at the University of Minnesota. This appointment was the first academic position with tenure ever offered this eminent man of letters. He taught at Minnesota until his retirement in 1968 when, with his third wife, the former Helen Heinz, he returned to live in Sewanee, Tennessee. These years at Minnesota were years of public triumph. He made lecture tours throughout Western Europe and in India. He was awarded numerous honorary degrees, including one from the University of Oxford. Among many other honors he was awarded the Bollingen Prize for Poetry for 1956. Brandeis University honored him with its Medal for Poetry in 1961; the Dante Society of Florence awarded him its Gold Medal the following year; in 1964 he was elected to the American Academy of Arts and Letters and in the next year to the American Academy of Arts and Sciences.

Allen Tate merited the public honors; in fact, had merited them long before they came. Before he was twenty-six he had written one of the permanent poems of his century. Before he was thirty he had written an indispensable essay on Emily Dickinson. Before he was forty he had written a novel that over the years not only has justified the early praise it received but has come to seem better and better.

The last three divisions of this volume of essays take cognizance of the astounding diversity of Allen Tate's achievement. But in a last analysis the divisions are an Aristotelian nicety, an arbitrary convenience. His work is really all of a piece. It has all derived from the same energy, the same insights. It has all had a single aim. When I try to explain that aim I am drawn toward a quaint analogy or a metaphor whose coordinates are very distant from each other. There used to exist in elementary courses in physics an apparatus intended to instruct students in principles of pressure. Consisting of a sealed jar nearly filled with liquid, it had some provision for pumping air into the space at the top. As the air pressure was increased, from the bottom of the jar would rise a little imago—an ivory-colored homunculus, one thought at first. Then, as it rose higher one saw that it was a representation of a medieval Satan. The synergy of Allen Tate's poetry, fiction, and essays has had the aim of applying pressure—think of his embossed, bitterly stressed lines, his textured metaphors—until it brings up before our eyes a blanched parody of the human figure, which is our evil, the world's evil, so that we begin to long for God. That has seemed to him a worthwhile task to perform for modern man threatened by such fatal narcissism, such autotelic pride that he is in danger of disappearing into a glassy fantasy of his own concoction. We shall need his help for a long time to come.

I. THE MAN

In Amicitia

by JOHN CROWE RANSOM

The poet, the thinker, the public figure, the whole man—Allen Tate's personality is greatly distinguished in our time. It goes back partly to his inheritance; and maybe to his luck in having been born under a benign constellation. And what other causes of distinction might there be? There is one at least; he could earn it.

But Tate entered upon his scene at a time when its intellectual climate was particularly distraught and uncertain; or it may be that our own time will always seem more desperate than previous ones have been. At any rate I will try to sketch some of the intangibles in the background against which he emerged. When we consider the here and the now, we observe many fine minds which belong to the specialist thinkers, to the scientists; who know what they are doing, and are admirable in their profession. Their thinking pertains to "l'ordre des actions," the phrase which Valéry underlined in order to distinguish the grand physical scientist in Descartes from the somewhat muddled metaphysician; to the order of action, which is primary. And there is a bigger and better kind of mind, or at least a kind more comprehensive and more imaginative, which is flooded with metaphysics and a precarious but passionate concern for "last things." Specifically, minds of this sort exercise themselves with religious dispositions, and the equally metaphysical "judgment of taste," as that appears in poems and fine arts. Religion offers a faith to go by; professing it though we cannot prove it, and adhering to it by stubborn, slogging will, but reinforced by the rites and disciplines of the religious institution and the

EDITOR'S NOTE: Reprinted from *The Sewanee Review*, 67:528–39 (Autumn 1959), copyright © 1959 by The University of the South, by permission of the author and publisher. Brief deletions of remarks relating to the occasion for which the essay was prepared have been made.

11

company of the congregation of believers, we can order the conduct
of our lives in that dignity to which human creatures seem to aspire.
And the arts? They have no institutional organization; but they offer
individual masterpieces of the imagination which represent our life
lifted momentarily into impossible perfections of taste; the moments
are miraculous but their epiphanies are spontaneous and separate,
not fit for systematic faith. Which is better? Evidently we can do pretty
well with either; with a system of mysteries embraced by faith, or a
profusion of arts bringing fresh mysteries every day. Election may be
said to be according to the natural habit or temperament of the mind.
But there cannot but be a little of both temperaments in us all. And
something of the scientific temperament too; for we must have it to
make our livelihood; and we respect its powers when we observe the
labors of the professional scientists, perhaps intricate beyond our understanding, which make the job so much easier for us. But here are three
kinds of mind at once; one is scientific, and two are metaphysical. The
two are at war instantly against the scientist when he denies the necessity of metaphysics; but the two have somewhat the character of alternatives, and are fully capable of contending with each other. The mind
of our society, and even the individual mind, is divided within itself,
and torn by opposed interests which it cannot harmonize.

And now for our proper subject. Allen Tate's mind is exceptional
in its harmony, and we will note its characteristic decisions as we go
along. His personality is as whole and undivided, and it is as steady,
as it is vivid. Allen would readily have found his role in the Golden
Age of Hellenism, or in classical Rome, or the Elizabethan Renaissance. All the powers of the mind engaged at once in the great figures
of those ages. And if he had been of middle age in Virginia during the
Civil War, he would have been a statesman, or a warrior, and he would
have retired like General Lee afterwards to the university, but in the
role of poet in residence. Yes, and if it had been fated—and even in
this age it may be fated, in view of the religious establishment which
survives so resolutely from "the age of faith"—Allen would have been
a theologian and a poet in those Middle Ages when there was a sort
of closure of the whole mind under the religious prescription. There
was not in theory any division within that mind. It was not necessarily
contemplated that the right hand would have to be jealous of the free-

dom of the left hand. And here I take the right hand as standing for religion, and the left hand as standing for poetry and literature.

But I must explain. I am thinking of an old book which describes and rates all the human virtues. It is a sort of pagan bible, and as a student I used to repair to it now and then even of my own volition, and still do; it is the *Nichomachean Ethics* of Aristotle. In this treatise friendship is regarded as the sum and crown of the common single virtues. In its highest form Aristotelian friendship requires both intellectual and moral maturity; its best exercise is when two well qualified friends talk long and fruitfully together with perfect understanding. But the fact is that Allen's personality was always more harmonious than mine, and unfolded more surely and happily. At twenty his mind was further on its road than mine when I had passed thirty. So it has not been an equal friendship; not according to the specifications of Aristotle. But I will elect not to make too much of the irregularity; it may not have mattered a great deal. To the best of my knowledge there has been an excellent understanding between us for more than thirty years; and I have felt as pleased and comfortable in his company as in any which I have been offered. Perhaps in more of those thirty years than not we have met no oftener than two or three times the whole year long. But when we met we started talking where we had left off before.

Mr. Tate is an eminent figure now, but when I first met him he was exposed to certain of the ignominies of youth, and one of them was to be registered in my freshman writing course at Vanderbilt. I have not known another in that low predicament who came and stayed with his colors flying so high. He had a native sense, or at least a very early sense, of being called to the vocation of literature, and he had decided to start his writing at the top. It was my rule to follow old pedagogical custom and prescribe elementary exercises to the freshmen, but he would have none of that. He wrote essays about the literary imagination, with corollary excursions into linguistics and metaphysics; they were slightly bewildering to me in more ways than one. But I would not have stopped him if I could; he was a step beyond my experience, but I figured that perhaps he had really discovered a way to the top which might be worth knowing. It would consist in assuming topographically the terrain where the top writers seem to inhabit, and plunging with all one's might into the current of ideas and language within which they moved so splendidly. And so, exactly so, the method proved out in his case a little while later.

He was never what we call an imitative writer. But his early writing was eclectic, and had literary resources which were not the property of our region at that time. Whether poetry or prose, it was done in the consciousness of a body of literature which was unknown to his fellow students, and to my faculty associates and myself, unless it was by the purest hearsay. A new literature had made its brilliant beginnings, and there were advanced journals and books which were full of it if we had looked. Besides the part which was indigenous to our language, there was the literature of nineteenth century France, which after the necessary lag was being imported in volume. Allen in his student days was reading Baudelaire and Mallarmé. If I am not mistaken, he was already quoting de Gourmont on the "dissociation of ideas"; that destructive feat of genius which simply abandons the familiar image when it is dying, that is to say when its power has weathered away though it is the image under which the idea once offered its lovely face; and that vital sequel when the teeming imagination is required to take hold of the idea again and find for it another incarnation in a fresh image; for all things pass. But I am grateful to Allen even more for introducing me to the critical essays of Mr. T. S. Eliot in *The Sacred Wood,* and to his poems; in that order. I believe Allen must have just graduated from the university when the time came for him to write to me, with as much agitation as I ever knew him to register, about a new work called *The Waste Land.*

As champion of the new literature—though ever so fastidious in his elections—among people who did not know anything about it, and were as likely as not to resist it when they were made to know, Allen had a mission in Tennessee which he was ten years discharging, during his intermittent residence among us. Because he was young, and in his address as polite and charming as he was firm, we scarcely noticed that we were being instructed.

I will make comment upon the two "movements" of the Nashville writers with whom Allen was associated during the 'twenties of this century, which happened to be his own twenties too. Then for conclusion I will comment more diffidently upon a later action which he took alone, when the Vanderbilt friends were far away and not in touch.

The Fugitive group got out a small quarterly of verse under that name for four years, but the Saturday night meetings had been going as early as 1920, two years before publication began. We published for a good reason; in order to see ourselves in print. It is hard for a poet to reach the peak of his talent without the benefit of a deadly and objective self-criticism, as well as the outside criticism too, such as we incurred when we exposed ourselves nakedly in the cold and ugly print of *The Fugitive*. It gave us pretty much the service we had wanted of it. But after that stage, when the poet's verse has attained to some technical proficiency, there is still the hard and embarrassing effort to find his own personal voice. This seems to be accomplished best within the intimate group whose members read their poems to each other, after which they all begin to talk. It was just barely possible to govern our heated talk by the parliamentary rule of one speaker at a time. Eventually we discovered how different we were individually, and how reputable it appeared for us to profess our own special identities if we could find them. Tate was one of the younger members, but in our meetings and publications he came unerringly into his poetic identity. For I suppose that since this period it has been so distinct that he can hardly have uttered a passage of twenty words which has not been recognizable as in its author's voice.

There is another note which his literary biographers might be well advised to take of the Fugitive period. In those many sessions he became confirmed for us as a critic whose quick unstudied judgment of a poem possessed authority. If it was protested, as was likely, he was able, by a process of thought so earnest and careful that it almost became visible, to make the unconscious grounds conscious; and as reasons they were valid. His judgment was a thing earned as well as natural, coming out of a study of the range of the poetic power which was total, insofar as it could be for a critic of his age, therefore responsive to the power or the failure of power in the poem at hand. I think we all coveted his judgment of our poems as being the most instant, and about the best, that we were going to find; for I know that I did; and there was as much profit to be taken when it was unfavorable as when it was favorable. But to couple the first impression of a writing immediately with finality and decision is the indication of what Mr. Blackmur calls the executive power; that is, the capacity to carry on the business of literature, and for example to run a literary journal, or to make anthologies. Both these professional areas of his later career were prefigured then.

And now the Agrarian movement, at the other end of the decade. Tate and I have had up the subject in our conversations often, without falling into that entire solemnity which has sometimes been attributed to the Agrarians. When I think of our making of the book as a behavior, it looks to me from here sometimes like an escapade; like the last fling of our intellectual youth. But that does not stop me from remembering that behind our black smoke there was red fury, which I can recover very quickly. The personnel of the group was not the same as that of the other group, but fiery Davidson was in it, and Warren, enlisting *in absentia* from Oxford, and Lytle our honorary Fugitive, and Tate and myself. We had another round of tremendous sessions going over the principles and the tactics of the essays we were promised to deliver severally to the book. Perhaps there was only this hollowness, that like gentlemanly conspirators in a movie we tended very kindly to conceal from each other the fact that individually we had no expectation of throwing up such a dyke as would turn a historic tide from overflowing our region as it had submerged the others in the land. We were engaged upon a war that was already lost. Historically, we were behind the times. But we were right in thinking that the times were bad, and even in thinking they were desperately bad, inasmuch as they have only worsened since. But even during our agitation the economy had become so enterprising that it was not serving our needs quite so much as it was meddling with our tastes. Everybody was involved in it without knowing how it had come about; the bankers, the producers, the middlemen, the consumers; as if to ensure the entire collapse of the public taste. When the book was out, there was applause from many nice Southerners, and it came from the heart, but not without being a calculated risk inasmuch as they had to feel sure that it was not going to affect their business, nor anybody else's business; all businesses being involved together. Only a poor and ineffectual remnant of Southerners still carried on the old agrarian economy, and that was not by choice. By this time we were asserting reluctantly that the prevailing economy determines the culture, though it had been Marx who had made the grand play with that idea.

Tate joined in all such talk as this; and now some significant comment relating it to his career. The easy first comment is to say of course

that Tate's essay was magnificent (as mine certainly was not). Having
come into his mature poetic style, it was now that he exhibited his
mature prose, and before his thirtieth year; Sir Philip Sidney had not
gone faster. I think of his Agrarian essay as a fighting prose flowing
with supple elegance and deadly in its ironic aim. And the second and
harder comment. Tate played a leading part again in the conversations, poring over his Southern history in the meantime, and eventually he found a new major thesis to cover all his preoccupations. It was
a sort of cultural or anthropological thesis, which I have heard expressed like this: "Mr. Tate does not accept the modern world." And
this is accurate in its intention, though the form is negative. Underline
modern, and by logical conversion we obtain the positive, which might
go something like this: "What Mr. Tate accepts is the ordered and
individual way of life which obtained in the Western economy before
the industrial revolution developed into mass production." I admire
his position very much, for it is a reasoned conservatism. A complete
and intelligent conservative, who is in literature and not in politics nor
in business, is invulnerable; he is greatly honored as a monument to
the past, but as a monument he is not expected to play a part in
"*l'ordre des actions.*" And ever after the Agrarian movement I believe
that Tate and I conducted our lives in much the same fashion; in a
free society we assumed the right to live simply and to keep company
with friends of our own taste, and with increasingly unpopular books
in the library. We lived in an old-fashioned minority pocket of the
culture, so to speak. It has done us no material harm. For there are the
educational institutions, with pockets of "humanities," whose interest
has identified itself increasingly with ours; there are the publishers,
who are culturally neutral; and as for the public platform, Tate conducts himself so ably there that his adversaries are beguiled even while
they are being flayed. Tate does not expect the old order to be patched
up and restored to power. The new economic forces have made a fatal
breach in the continuity of our national culture, and realizing this
Tate could not be like Dryden, who at the end of his own troubled
seventeenth century required his actors in the *Secular Masque* to sing,

> 'Tis well an Old Age is out,
> And time to begin a New.

Dryden did not know what trouble was; his words do not mean to us what they meant to him. Our New Age seems to have lost those marks of a culture which go with a metaphysical taste and to have lapsed into something like a sprawling and unformed barbarism. So I have often recited Tate's position with full accord. And yet at other times in my inconclusive way I have had a small persistent hope, perhaps a forced hope, in considering that the new barbarians are of our own breed and country, our friends, perhaps even our children, and surely must be destined to erect a new culture though they will have to start all over again at the bottom to discover its new forms. I have talked about their potential, and watched for and sometimes approved a few cultural signs as they appeared. That was an anthropological line of my own; Tate has known it of me and suffered it. And my hope is not likely to be justified in my time nor even in his.

Allen's next decisive step was to enter the Roman Catholic Church. A short time earlier he had remarked to the late Philip Rice, a friend to us both, that something he had observed led him to think Ransom was about to have a conversion. It was generous to attribute to me a capacity for bold decision which I do not have, and which with more justice I have imputed to him. But the new decision did not surprise me greatly nor for long. I quickly made the entry in the unwritten book which I keep of Allen's career.

I am sorry to have to say that in our later conversations—we have never discussed it. He would have known that my approval was there, though it was tacit. But he may have thought that the conversation would have to be much more extensive than I knew; that because of our distance geographically I had not quite kept up with his intentions. My comment can only be what I would have said in a conversation which never took place.

It is shameful that my sense of the Roman Church, like that of so many Protestants, is remote; that I lack any intimate acquaintance with its governance and ritual, or even with certain of its especially friendly and magnanimous priests. I can only recite the common knowledge. For all practical purposes it is the oldest body in Christendom, and the most numerous. It speaks many tongues, and its mission to all sorts and conditions of mankind has been deeply studied over many centuries, and the most eminent men have entered into its communion in most centuries. It has made its peace with Caesar and the political power; and I would have said that it has made its peace with modern science and its corollary the economic power. Such things need saying when we are thinking of the Roman Church as the strictest of the Christian bodies in asserting its religious authority.

But has not the Roman Church made its peace also with the pagans of the antique world, and those who inhabit the present outer world, whose "natural religion" was the best that could be expected of them, lacking access to Christian theology? And does not the natural religion of the pagans bear a close relationship to the miraculism of poetry and other arts in our own world? I come back to what I was saying earlier, and confess that my regular piety is that of a pagan, or a primitive, and that my regular theology is something improvised to suit the literary occasion. I say this out of professional feeling. It seems in order to say it because my profession and Allen's have been the same profession; we are of the literary estate.

I will even add a little more emphasis. Not long ago I was pleased to see a remark made by Valéry in one of his more informal essays, to the effect that there were occasions when he felt himself "lulled . . . with a metaphysic which is naive and mixed with myth"; and the context indicated that out of this sort of experience issued his poems. I would like to couple to the word "metaphysic" the word "miraculism," though it is redundant, in order to make his description of the genesis of poetry as full as possible. And a miraculism of an elevated or noble sort plays constantly over the imagery or configuration of Valéry's verse; while in Allen's own verse it plays too, and is even bolder.

So Allen would have joined the Church for the right reason; in order to profess the faith. And I witnessed the zeal and devotion of the new convert. Religion is so imperative for a society that those of us who do not profess it are glad when our friends do.

But there may have been multiple reasons. The biographer might risk a construction upon his action which would put it precisely into place in his literary career. Allen accepts the old order and the unified life, but the historic instance which he first cited was only the nearest one; the Southern tradition in these United States. That had its defects, and from a world view it was too local or provincial. He found a world order more to his purpose in a Church which has an imperial name, and retains from the Middle Ages its immensely careful yet liberal Scholastic theology.

That is not quite all. Surely the power of the Roman Church must be concerned with the general lapse of taste, as an effect accompanying the failure of morality? The emphasis of the Church is upon morality, but the incidence of its authority is many times more immediate and larger than that of the arts, whose emphasis is only upon taste, that is, upon the order and beauty which we find and make in the natural world. Here is the great authority of the Church, and even if the Church with severe economy might prefer to stick to its primary mission, which is to save men's souls, that would mean from my present point of view to change their lives. And perhaps Allen knew it, and in a time of crisis which is as desolating as a war, at least a cold war, may have chosen simply to join in that mission, on the understanding that people's tastes might be elevated eventually and necessarily but indirectly. Who would not be for that?

Allen Tate: A Portrait

by MARK VAN DOREN

It was Allen Tate who brought me Hart Crane's poems, just as it was he who made me sit down in his basement on Bank Street and listen to Phelps Putnam's "Hasbrouck and the Rose"; I can still hear his soft, very intelligent voice intoning two of the lines:

> In Springfield, Massachusetts I devoured
> The mystic, the improbable, the Rose.

Allen, who as one of the Fugitives of Tennessee—more specifically, as one of those wits for whom John Crowe Ransom at Vanderbilt Univer-

EDITOR'S NOTE: Reprinted from Mark Van Doren's *Autobiography* (Westport, Conn.: Greenwood Press, 1968), pp. 156–58, by permission of the author and publisher. The selection here is from the middle of chapter 4.

sity was the Ben Jonson of his time, counseling and comparing notes
with them in a responsible, professional way—had learned to be generous with the work of others, would have been generous in any case,
for that was his nature. He thought I was generous to him because I
published "Mr. Pope" and other brilliant poems of his. But I found
him singularly generous to me; which was gratifying, because his
critical instrument had the finest razor edge, and he could decapitate
with it a person or a poet he despised.

He and his wife, the novelist Caroline Gordon, were spending the
winter of 1925–1926 in the same house with Hart Crane, near Patterson, New York. From there Allen came to town one day to have lunch
with me, and our talk ran among so many subjects, and so easily and
eagerly, that he wrote me after he went back: "I get very little 'literary
conversation,' and I miss it. . . . There are few persons these days
who do not mistake obsessions, missions, remedies, and purposes for
ideas. . . . To hear you speak as you did of Wordsworth was worth,
in itself, a trip to town; there aren't ten people in America who have
that feeling for *literature*. . . . Finally, let me be self-conscious and
offer excuses for a long letter in this age of 'hurry.' But, you see, I am
still very young and retain my enthusiasms; 'letters' are not yet a routine, they are still a passion. But I am almost afraid to tell you that I
am just twenty-five; the fact might shake some of the confidence which
I very gratefully feel you have in me."

This was the first of a great many letters Allen was to write me over
the next thirty years. And it was the last one that was the least self-
conscious. In November, 1929, he began one from Paris, where he had
gone on a Guggenheim fellowship: "Dear Mark. But who is he? Mark
Van Doren? It seems to me that I knew him long ago, and even cherished much affection and esteem for him, in the days before I wrote
him a letter that went months unanswered. Ah, I have him placed at
last. He is the scholarly looking poet who always looks as if . . . he
were going to say grace, but says instead damn. He also looks as if he
had never been interrupted, but constantly expects to be. He also has
a plan for every minute of the year—which rouses Tate to envy not
great enough to stimulate imitation, because plan would bore him to
death. He prefers to be harried, never quite caught up."

The Tates moved to New York the next year after Patterson and
lived on Bank Street, where Dorothy and I made the acquaintance of

their infant daughter Nancy; at that age she addressed our infant son as "Charlie Fandory." We also met their literary friends, who then, as always since, were legion; once we brewed with them a barrel of wine and called it sherry. Allen's reviews of my own poetry were on the whole the most interesting ones it had. They were generous and yet judicious, with expressed or implied reservations that seemed to come out of an age-old occupation with the art; and they were written as if I were a complete stranger to him, as when he put on his critic's robes I was. He and Caroline did not stay long in New York, and after they left we missed them. We were to see more of them in time; and for many years these warm, bright letters came from Allen. They were of course intermittent, as he had accused mine of being. In his own case the reason, I sometimes thought, was a trait which everyone had noted in him: readily enthusiastic, he could as readily be bored. He would change in an instant from a child who remembered nothing to an old man who remembered everything, and suddenly, like the soul in Emily Dickinson's poem, would close the valves of his attention. I have said of him since:

> He was the soonest friendly,
> But then the soonest tired.

Always, however, he could be the child again to whom everything and everybody was brave and new.

Allen Tate: Upon the Occasion of His Sixtieth Birthday

by ANDREW LYTLE

It was John Ransom who introduced me to Allen Tate. I was at Yale working with George Pierce Baker (where I learned what a scene was) and he wrote me there and gave me his address in New York. So I owe to John Ransom, among other things, a long and cherished friendship. It could be said that I owe him my wife, since it was Tate who some years later introduced me to her. But in this kind of sorites where does gratitude end? It neither begins nor ends, for friendship cannot afford to measure the occasions for its uses nor mark too narrowly the moments of communion. Certainly all this was in the future. Yet the future may be no more than the suspension of what is always present, awaiting the moment, the seeming accident in which it finds its substantial form. In the Old West of Tennessee and Kentucky people of like interest and station were bound to know each other, or at least know the stories of common friends whose personalities were interesting enough for gossip or tales. I'm sure I must have played with Tate at Monteagle, and Nicholson Springs was only a few miles from Estill Springs. And who can say it was not the tone of Captain Beard's voice reciting poetry upon the verandah of the summer boarding house at Estill, pausing only long enough to call to his wife,

EDITOR'S NOTE: Reprinted from *The Sewanee Review*, 67:542–44 (Autumn 1959), copyright © 1959 by The University of the South, by permission of the author and publisher. Brief deletions of remarks relating to the occasion for which the essay was prepared have been made.

"Maria, Maria, the hogs are in the yard," which marked the little boy
with the enormous head?

At any rate the day I presented myself at the basement entrance of
27 Bank Street I was met with a severe and courteous formality—it
was as if the eyes reflected but did not see what was before them. Later
I came to recognize this as a mask to keep the world at a distance,
because of the artist's necessity to be saved interruptions while at work;
or merely to save himself boredom, which he cannot hide. I learned
this necessity for withdrawal in his house, as I learned that the artist's
discipline is almost its only reward. Once a caller asked for Katherine
Anne Porter at this same address and was received with grave decorum
and told, with a bow, "The ladies of this house are at the riot in Union
Square." The bow, as well as the words, was a conscious emphasis upon
the irony of his situation, the common situation of the artist living in
New York, belonging to no cliques, and demanding that the profession
of letters be accepted as a profession. He, more than any other writer,
has upheld this professionalism of letters. This attitude is obviously
more French than English and is, I feel, unique in the English-speaking world, at least to the extent he carried and carries it. Ford Madox
Ford had this sense of himself as a writer, but he would have claimed
not England but Europe for his habitation. Tate would see Europe
for what it is historically, as it relates to our common inheritance. To
hold this position has not been without its price. I have at times
thought that he had advanced himself into tactically untenable positions, or used too much force upon what seemed only an outpost
engagement. But in a rearguard action, after the campaign and, indeed, the cause is lost, strategy and tactics become one and the same
thing; that is, "no bulge," as General Forrest called it, can be allowed
to the enemy as your force retreats, lest all be swept into oblivion.

Every serious writer has one subject, I believe, which he spends his
life exploring and delivering as fully as he may. Tate's subject is simply what is left of Christendom, that western knowledge of ourselves
which is our identity. He may be classed as a religious writer, and that
from the very beginning. The literary historian is likely to see his
work as the best expression of the crucial drama of our time. "We've
cracked the hemispheres with careless hand!" Does language more
poetically describe the plight of western civilization? He has many
voices: verse, biography, criticism, essay, even fiction—but one lan-

guage and one subject. In rereading him I was surprised to find that, even as a young man, especially a young man in the 'twenties, he saw the religious doubt, the failure of belief, as crucial. In the same way he accepted the South's defeat not as a private or local affair but as the last great defense in a going society of those values, particularly human, we know as Christian. Even in the earlier verse such as "Causerie" and "Last Days of Alice" the ironic complaint derives from and hangs upon this ambiguity of belief. In *I'll Take My Stand* it was his essay which argued the religious position. The diversity and range, certainly in the verse, can be seen in the manner he divides his collected poems into sections. Early pieces are put by the latest, but the book opens with the larger treatments of his position, the historical and cultural past, not as background but as vision immediately related to the poet and all others now living. The first section opens with "The Mediterranean" and closes with the "Ode to the Confederate Dead." The final irony of the sound of nature's soughing of the leaves serves for a transition to the other parts of the book.

Behind Allen Tate lies a body of work anyone would be proud to call a life's work. And yet there is time for it to be only the great body which awaits its crown. Ours is the immortal generation. And how do I know it? I know it with my aging eyes which see now, at last, that it is not we who are getting older, but the young who are getting younger, smoother-cheeked, more innocent-eyed, so that it is a marvel to find that the sounds they are making are words, perhaps language even.

Two Winters with Allen Tate and Hart Crane

by MALCOLM COWLEY

I n June, 1924, Allen Tate was making one of his first visits to New York. He had been exchanging letters with Hart Crane, for whom I had recently found a job at Sweet's Catalogue Service, where our desks in the copywriting department stood side by side, and it was Hart who introduced him to most of my friends. I had forgotten the circumstances of my own meeting with Allen until he mentioned them in a letter. There was a party, he says, in the Greenwich Village apartment of Jimmy Light, a director of the Provincetown Playhouse. "I remember," the letter continues, "that I appeared neatly dressed in a dark suit, carrying a preposterous walking stick and wearing a Phi Beta Kappa key. I was completely unsophisticated. You were already a man of the world—had been to France and known the Dadaists, etc. You remarked, 'We no longer wear our Phi Beta Kappa keys.' And you picked up somewhere an old stick—not a cane—and carried it the entire evening."

That is Allen's story, not mine, for I didn't feel then like a man of the world, and he never impressed me as being an innocent. I thought, then or later, that he had the best manners of any young man I had known, in America or France. I thought he used politeness not only as a defense but sometimes as an aggressive weapon against strangers.

EDITOR'S NOTE: Reprinted from *The Sewanee Review*, 67:547–56 (Autumn 1959), copyright © 1959 by The University of the South, by permission of the author and publisher. The original title, "Two Winters with Hart Crane," has been changed by the author for this volume.

But he couldn't have been aggressively polite to me that evening, in spite of my jibes, and we must have arranged to meet again at Hart Crane's on the following Tuesday.

That second meeting I do remember, and I even found the date of it in a letter: June 24, in the late afternoon. Hart had recently moved to Columbia Heights, in Brooklyn, where he had rented a back room with a magnificent view of Brooklyn Bridge. After exclaiming at the view, we talked about poetry. Hart gestured, as always, with a dead five-cent cigar and declaimed against the vulgarity of Edgar Poe. Seeing a volume of Poe on the shelf, I opened it and read "The City in the Sea":

> While from a proud tower in the town
> Death looks gigantically down.

Hart exclaimed that it was good to hear a poem read aloud. We left his room, all three of us talking excitedly, and wandered through streets lined with red-brick warehouses until we came to the end of a scow at the end of a pier at the Brooklyn end of the bridge. There we sat talking, more slowly now, while we looked across the river at an enormous electric sign—WATERMAN'S FOUNTAIN PENS—and all those proud towers beyond it with the first lights flashing on. Suddenly we felt—I think we all felt—that we were secretly comrades in the same endeavor: to present this new scene in poems that would reveal not only its astonishing face but the lasting realities behind it. We did not take an oath of comradeship, but what happened later made me suspect that something vaguely like that was in our minds.

It must have been late in the summer that Allen moved to New York. William Slater Brown was there too, a former ambulance driver who had come close to dying of scurvy in a French military prison, after spending some weeks with his friend E. E. Cummings in the detention station that Cummings called the Enormous Room. Bill had lately married one of my high-school friends, Sue Jenkins, who was editing a pulp-paper magazine called *Telling Tales*. Allen soon became her assistant, at a salary that couldn't have been much more than thirty dollars a week, then the beginning rate for assistant editors. Matthew Josephson, who had been the editor of *Broom*—for no salary whatever, in the last months of the magazine—was now a customer's

man in Wall Street; and even Kenneth Burke had deserted his New
Jersey farmhouse to spend a winter in the Village. That was the good
winter, or so I have always thought of it, when we met after work in
the Poncino Palace to drink hot rum toddies at the kitchen table,
and when we had dinner together perhaps twice a week at John
Squarcialupi's restaurant on Perry Street. We were all of the same
age, and we felt invulnerable.

At the time we were planning the first (and last) issue of an angry
little magazine to be called *Aesthete 1925*, and that gave a sort of direction to the dinners, with contributions to be argued about and poems
to be read aloud, but soon the meetings would dissolve into anecdotes
and horseplay. Kenneth Burke was the noisy analyst of human fol-
lies, including his own. Hart made more than his share of the jokes,
laughed louder, if possible, than anybody else, and drank more of
John Squarcialupi's red wine. Later in the evening, however, he
might be as morose as a chained bear in a Russian tavern scene. There
were times when he upset a bottle of wine on the tablecloth, pushed
back his chair, and plunged out of the door without saying a word.
Allen stayed to the end, always, and we found that his politeness was
mingled with comic inventions and pure impishness.

Although I saw him often that winter, I still knew very little about
him. I knew he was writing good poems because he read some of them
aloud at Squarcialupi's, as Hart read some of his "Voyages." I knew
he was married, but I didn't meet his wife till the winter was over;
Sue Brown told me that her name had been Caroline Gordon and
that she was a newspaper woman from Tennessee. I didn't know where
Allen himself was born (except that it was somewhere in the South),
or how he was educated (except for the Phi Beta Kappa key, which
he had stopped wearing), or anything about his family. I didn't even
know his full name until twenty years later, when I went to see the
Tates and for the first time found a calling card tacked to the door:
John Orley Allen Tate. But who were the Orleys and the Allens, and
who were the Tates of an earlier generation? We never asked such
questions, immersed as we were in the absolute pastlessness of life in
New York. Everybody we met had come from somewhere else, it didn't
matter where. Everybody was young, everybody was poor, almost everybody was writing poems, and nobody seemed to have relatives.

But some of us must have had relatives in the background, for one of them died that winter and left Bill Brown a small legacy. By combining it with a big mortgage, the Browns bought an abandoned farm in the hills seventy-five miles north of Greenwich Village; it was what we all wanted to do. Although we didn't read Emerson, we had the Emersonian dream of establishing ourselves in some untouched Concord not too far from the city, but closer to the wilderness, where we could write in the morning, roam the hills in the afternoon, and sometimes gather in the evening round the fire in a chunk stove. We all visited the Browns, and most of us felt that they had found the right neighborhood.

The Tates made their bold move in the autumn of 1925. They couldn't buy a farmhouse, not having received a legacy, but they rented eight semifurnished rooms from a country neighbor of the Browns. Her name was Mrs. Addie Turner, and she was a grass widow of sixty who lived with her aunt in a barnlike house half a mile from the Browns' cottage by a path that wound through overgrown fields. As compared with the cottage it had conveniences: a pump in the kitchen, a mailbox outside the door, and a telephone less than a mile away. The rent for the rooms she didn't use was only ten dollars a month, but I wondered how the Tates were going to keep warm and pay for their groceries. Much later Allen told me that while they were living at Addie Turner's the monthly income of the family—mostly from book reviews—was less than a hundred dollars. Fortunately potatoes were cheap that year, and Allen warmed himself twice, in Thoreau's phrase, by sawing and splitting his own wood.

They were living as cheaply as possible in order to buy time. For Caroline it was time to finish a novel, the second she had attempted. Allen had no such definite project—at least he didn't speak of one— and I think he was trying to preserve something precious to poets; Scott Fitzgerald called it an "inner hush," but it is closer to being an inner monologue, an intermittent stream of words directed to an inner audience, which silently approves the words or demands that they be repeated and revised. Sometimes new conceptions or magical phrases occur in the midst of the monologue, and then it is time to write them down, to work over them patiently, to shape them into a poem. But I know Allen felt, as I did too, that real poems did not come from a deliberately chosen subject; they had to be waited for; they could not be willed into being. The problem was how to achieve a continual readiness to accept and shape the poems when they did appear, while refusing to commit oneself to any lesser and time-consuming purpose such as earning more money, for example, or eating meat every day.

In the midst of their poverty, the Tates were planning to solve Hart Crane's financial problem and thus make it possible for him to finish the long poem he had been talking about for nearly three years. By the late autumn of 1925, Hart had left Sweet's Catalogue Service and was dependent on the small sums he could borrow from friends. The Tates invited him to share their living quarters. He would need very little money, they told him; there would be no distractions from writing, and he would have a big room to himself. Hart accepted their offer after trying vainly to find a job, but before he took the train to Patterson, New York, which was the nearest station to Addie Turner's, there was a dramatic change in his fortunes. He wrote to the financier Otto Kahn, asking for the loan of a thousand dollars to help him write *The Bridge*, and Kahn—after consulting with Waldo Frank and Eugene O'Neill—not only gave him the money but promised him another thousand if he needed it. Hart finally reached the Turner house on Saturday, December 12, after several nights of celebration. Instead of being despondent and emptyhanded, he arrived with liquor, fancy groceries, a new pair of snowshoes, and extravagant plans of work for the coming year.

Considering the strongly marked personalities of all three writers, and the cramped quarters in which they were living—only three of the eight rooms could be heated above freezing—and considering the difference in economic status, with Hart now spending three times as much on himself as the Tates were spending together, anyone might have predicted that his visit would end in a quarrel; the proof of good will on both sides is that everyone lived in comparative harmony for nearly four months of a hard back-country winter. There is a pretty full record of those months in *The Letters of Hart Crane*, which of course should be read with the understanding that the letters present only one side of the story. For two or three weeks Hart was happy putting his room in order and collecting his old and new books in one place for the first time in years. January proved to be colder than usual, even for the hill country along the Connecticut border, and he complained of chillblains from sleeping alone in a frigid room. He said that his hands were so stiff from chopping wood that he could scarcely hold a pen, but nevertheless he was "at work in an almost ecstatic mood" on the last or "Atlantis" section of *The Bridge*. Downstairs at the kitchen table, Caroline was typing away at her novel hour after hour. Allen was meditating poems as he tramped through the woods with a single-barreled shotgun called the White Powder Wonder; once he shot a squirrel. Hart finished a draft of "Atlantis" toward the end of the month and made a hasty visit to his mother in Cleveland. Soon after his return the deep snows fell and the Turner house was as effectively isolated as a lighthouse on a Maine island. There were six weeks when the mailman couldn't get through and when Hart used his snowshoes to carry the mail from the farmhouse with a telephone. Still everything was harmonious because everyone was working. Hart had started on the first section of *The Bridge*; then he formulated a new scheme for the whole cycle of poems. "One's original idea has a way of enlarging steadily," he said, "under the spur of concentration on minute details of execution."

The trouble with that sort of minute concentration is that it can be continued only for a certain time. The trouble with back-country winters is exactly opposite; they go on and on without consulting the calendar. Hart had finished his new outline for *The Bridge* by the middle of March and had summarized it in a letter to Otto Kahn, but snow was still falling at the end of the month. When it melted at last, the roads were deep in mud, and the Turner house was as effectively isolated as it had been in February. For the first time Hart's letters assumed a querulous tone, now that he found himself incapable of working. "A life of perfect virtue, redundant health, etc.," he said, "doesn't seem in any way to encourage the Muse, after all. . . . I drone about, reading, eating and sleeping." But Hart was never able to drone about for days on end. He would feel a sudden need to unburden himself, or would think of a funny story that had to be told, and a moment later he would come bursting into the room where Allen was trying to finish a review; or else he would clump across the kitchen while Caroline was puzzling over a difficult scene, and then, if he was greeted with something less than heartfelt warmth, he would clump back to sulk in his study. There had to be an explosion, and it came in the middle of April, before the first spring weather. After that the only communication between "Mr. Crane's part," as Addie Turner called his two rooms, and "the Tates' part" was by means of notes slipped under doors.

Hart left Patterson at the end of the month, met Waldo Frank in New York, and sailed off with him to the Isle of Pines. The Tates stayed in the Turner house all summer and raised a garden. Then, having been offered a basement flat on Perry Street, they went back to the place where money had to be spent, but where it was a great deal easier to earn.

I am not trying to tell the whole story of the literary friendship between Allen and Hart, but merely to clarify two or three episodes that certain commentators have misrepresented. At those points the record has to be put straight, and I suppose that is my responsibility as much as anyone's, since I watched the story as it unfolded. After the winter in Patterson the next episode was the acceptance for publication of Hart's first book of poems, *White Buildings*. Allen played a part in the publisher's decision, perhaps not so great a part as Waldo Frank and Eugene O'Neill, Hart's older friends, but still decisive when the moment came.

Not long before Hart came to Patterson, Frank had strongly recommended his poems to Horace Liveright, who was Frank's own publisher. Liveright, who made most of his decisions without reading manuscripts, said that he would take the book if O'Neill would write a foreword. Gene promised most unwillingly to write it, but months went by while Hart besieged him with letters, with explanations of what the poems meant, and still the foreword wasn't produced. "I like the poems," Gene kept saying, "but I don't know why." The situation became more complicated when Liveright finally read the manuscript, took a violent dislike to it, and went back on his bargain. It required the best efforts of O'Neill and Jimmy Light on a week-end party, and of Waldo Frank in business hours, to make him change his mind again, but still he insisted on the introduction, and still Gene was unable to write it.

At this point—it was in June, during Hart's stay on the Isle of Pines —Allen heard about the difficulty and solved it by an act of disinterested friendship. He wrote an introduction to *White Buildings*, showed it to O'Neill, and offered to let Gene sign it so as to meet the publisher's stipulation. Gene admired the introduction, but wouldn't put his name to it; "Anybody could see I didn't write that," he said. He went back to see Liveright, as Frank also did, and between them they persuaded him to publish *White Buildings* with Allen's introduction, for which, incidentally, there was never any talk of payment. Gene's final promise was to write a blurb for the jacket. After some further months of cogitation, he produced twenty-nine words that deserve to be quoted as a masterpiece of well-meaning incomprehension. "Hart Crane's poems," he said, "are profound indeed—seeking. In them he reveals, with a new insight, and unique power, the mystic undertone of beauty which moves words to express vision."

Hart received his contract at the end of July. Until that time his visit to the Isle of Pines seemed to have been wasted, but suddenly he found himself in a mood of exaltation. "Hail Brother!" he wrote to Waldo Frank. "I feel an absolute music in the air again, and some tremendous rondure floating somewhere. . . . The news of Allen Tate's generosity refreshed me a great deal; truly beautiful of him." For the next six weeks Hart poured out one grand poem after another, including more than half of *The Bridge* and all the best sections except "The River"; among the productions of those weeks were "Proem," "Ave Maria," "Cutty Sark," "Three Songs," "The Dance," and "The Tunnel," all pouring out together while Hart went skipping from one section to another "like a sky-gack or girder-jack" and said that he felt "as though I were dancing on dynamite." In the midst of his excitement he received a galley proof of Allen's introduction and found that it was "clever, valiant, concise and beautiful." Their friendship was renewed from that moment and lasted till Hart's death, though they would never again try the experiment of spending a winter in the same house. But the experiment was by no means a failure, and one can see that the months of "perfect virtue, redundant health, etc.," in Addie Turner's house were the preparation for Hart's amazing outburst of genius. Without those months—and without Allen's generosity—his *Bridge* might never have been built.

Visiting the Tates

by ROBERT LOWELL

April 1937—I was wearing the last summer's mothballish, already soiled white linens, and moccasins, knotted so that they never had to be tied or untied. What I missed along the road from Nashville to Clarksville was the eastern seaboard's thin fields chopped by stone walls and useless wildernesses of scrub. Instead, plains of treeless farmland, and an unnatural, unseasonable heat. Gushers of it seemed to spout over the bumpy, sectioned concrete highway, and bombard the horizon. Midway, a set of orientally shapely and conical hills. It was like watching a Western and waiting for a wayside steer's skull and the bleaching ribs of a covered wagon.

My head was full of Miltonic, vaguely piratical ambitions. My only anchor was a suitcase, heavy with bad poetry. I was brought to earth by my bumper mashing the Tates' frail agrarian mail box post. Getting out to disguise the damage, I turned my back on their peeling, pillared house. I had crashed the civilization of the South.

The Tates were stately yet bohemian, leisurely yet dedicated. A schoolboy's loaded twenty-two rifle hung under the Confederate flag over the fireplace. A reproduced sketch of Leonardo's *Virgin of the Rocks* balanced an engraving of Stonewall Jackson. Below us, the deadwood-bordered Cumberland River was the color of wet concrete, and Mr. Norman, the token tenant, looked like slabs of his unpainted shack padded in work-clothes. After an easy hour or two of regional anecdotes, Greenwich Village reminiscences, polemics on personalities, I began to discover what I had never known. I, too, was part of a

EDITOR'S NOTE: Reprinted from *The Sewanee Review*, 67:557–59 (Autumn 1959), copyright © 1959 by The University of the South, by permission of the author and publisher.

legend. I was Northern, disembodied, a Platonist, a puritan, an aboli-
tionist. Tate handed me a hand-printed, defiantly gingersnap-thin
edition of his *The Mediterranean and Other Poems*. He quoted a
stanza from Holmes's *Chambered Nautilus*—"rather beyond the flight
of your renowned Uncle." I realized that the old deadweight of poor
J. R. Lowell was now an asset. Here, like the battered Confederacy, he
still lived and was history.

All the English classics, and some of the Greeks and Latins, were at
Tate's elbow. He maneuvered through them, coolly blasting, rehabili-
tating, now and then reciting key lines in an austere, vibrant voice.
Turning to the moderns, he slaughtered whole Chicago droves of slip-
shod Untermeyer Anthology experimentalists. He felt that all the
culture and tradition of the East, the South and Europe stood behind
Eliot, Emily Dickinson, Yeats and Rimbaud. I found myself despising
the rootless appetites of middle-class meliorism.

Tate said two things this afternoon that at once struck me as all
but contradictory and yet self-evident. He said that he always believed
each poem he finished would be his last. His second pronouncement
was that a good poem had nothing to do with exalted feelings of being
moved by the spirit. It was simply a piece of craftsmanship, an intelligi-
ble or *cognitive* object. As examples of cognitive objects, Tate brought
forward Mr. Norman, the hand-printed edition of *The Mediterranean,*
and finally a tar-black cabinet with huge earlobe-like handles. It was
his own workmanship. I had supposed that crafts were repeatable
skills and belonged to the pedestrian boredom of manual training
classes. However, something warped, fissured, strained and terrific
about this cabinet suggested that it would be Tate's last.

I came to the Tates a second time. Ford Madox Ford, the object of
my original visit, was now installed with his wife and secretary. Already, their trustful city habits had exhausted the only cistern. On the
lawn, almost igniting with the heat, was a tangle of barked twigs in
a washtub. This was Ford's Provençal dew-pond. The household
groaned with the fatigued valor of Southern hospitality. Ida, the colored day-help, had grown squint-eyed, balky and aboriginal from the
confusion of labors, the clash of cultures. Instantly, and with keen,
idealistic, adolescent heedlessness, I offered myself as a guest. The
Tates' way of refusing was to say that there was no room for me unless
I pitched a tent on the lawn. A few days later, I returned with an olive

Sears-Roebuck-Nashville umbrella tent. I stayed three months. Every other day, I turned out grimly unromantic poems—organized, hard and classical as a cabinet. They were very flimsy. Indoors, life was Olympian and somehow crackling. Outside, Uncle Andrew, the calf, sagged against my tent sides. I sweated enough to fill the cistern, and breathlessly, I ached for the conviction that each finished poem would be my last.

Like a torn cat, I was taken in when I needed help, and in a sense I have never left. Tate still seems as jaunty and magisterial as he did twenty years ago. His poems, all of them, even the slightest, are terribly personal. Out of splutter and shambling comes a killing eloquence. Perhaps this is the resonance of desperation, or rather the formal resonance of desperation. I say "formal" because no one has so given us the impression that poetry must be burly, must be courteous, must be tinkered with and recast until one's eyes pop out of one's head. How often something smashes through the tortured joy of composition to strike the impossible bull's-eye! The pre-Armageddon twenties and thirties with all their peculiar fears and enthusiasms throb in Tate's poetry; imitated ad infinitum, it has never been reproduced by another hand.

Our Cousin, Mr. Tate

by HERBERT READ

I have known and admired Allen Tate for a long time. When we first met (it was in London) the *Criterion* was newly born, and I think it was at one of our regular editorial gatherings that a visitor from overseas, perhaps introduced by Uncle Tom, was invited as a guest and remained for ever a friend. My title is not altogether facetious—my paternal great-grandmother was a Jane Tate, descendant of a Jacobite fugitive from Scotland, and it is not inconceivable that Allen's father came from the same loyal stock. But there are other grounds of sympathy—an agrarian background in our childhoods, and a natural sympathy with organic patterns of life and feeling:

> Maryland Virginia Caroline
> Pent images in sleep
> Clay valleys rocky hills old fields of pine
> Unspeakable and deep.

Such circumstances make us both romantics, but I think we have been romantics who have maintained the necessity of reason. One has only to recall those Arnoldian "touchstones" which Allen Tate gave in his essay on "Tension in Poetry" to see the romanticism openly confessed —not one of these touchstones could conceivably be given as an example of classical precision or elegance. The whole concept of "tension," central to much of Allen Tate's thought, is a romantic concept. The classicist ideal is not tension, but serene security.

EDITOR'S NOTE: Reprinted from *The Sewanee Review*, 67:572–75 (Autumn 1959), copyright © 1959 by The University of the South, by permission of the publisher and the author's literary executor, David Higham Associates, Ltd., London. Brief deletions of remarks relating to the occasion for which the essay was prepared have been made.

Allen Tate has suffered the common fate of poets in our age, and
has given much of his time and energy to exposition, to teaching and
to criticism. It has been and continues to be an extraneous work of the
highest interest—I know of no critic, in America or elsewhere, who in
our time has combined such sensitivity with such severity, or who has
so happily married an aesthetic judgement to an ethical judgement.
His critical work is replete with such antitheses, neatly applied; and
though they may all reduce to one or two fundamental distinctions,
such as that between the will and the imagination (or more fundamentally still, that between the head and the heart), nevertheless what
is criticism but such a multiplication of refinements, applied with
subtlety to whatever matter is in hand?

I am not instructed in the hierarchies of American criticism, but I
have never seen Allen Tate in the battle-dress of one of its factions,
and I imagine that he cannot easily be classified. That, to me, is the
mark of a sound critic, forever dwelling in uncertainties, forever qualifying categorical logic with intuitive *finesse*. I think it is a characteristic to his credit that although he has voluntarily accepted the
rigors of a dogmatic faith, he has never sought to subordinate his criticism to morality. Perhaps he has never confused morality with religion, or faith with belief. He knows that Satan, if put to it, could
write his own *Paradise Lost*.

I am speaking too much of the critic and too little of the poet; but
that is always easier. I hate to turn an analytic mind on to the poetry
of my contemporaries. We are all engaged on a common front, against
the Unknown, culling syllables to express the same truth about a
shared experience. If I glance sideways at Mr. Tate (or at my other
friends such as Mr. Eliot or Mr. Muir) I lose some of the tension I
should be striving for in my own verses. But naturally, one's glance
does occasionally stray from the immediate task, and then I admire
this metaphysical athlete beside me: I like the stance he has taken up
and the clean way he uses his tools. Not a stroke misguided, nor any
useless sacrifice of the electric energy. The action is graceful, nervously
rhythmic, but long sustained. I cannot imitate it, though I may envy
it. The man is no bungler: he has been apprenticed to the best masters. As he works he strikes sparks from the hidden stones, and these
illuminate the movements he makes. A tedious metaphor, perhaps,
but appropriate to the author of those profound essays on the Sym-

bolic and the Angelic Imagination. Allen Tate knows that poetry survives and has meaning for survival only to the extent that it is and remains a symbolic language. In an Introductory Note to his translation of the *Pervigilium Veneris* (one of the few translations that exist in their own poetic virtue) he suggested that this great poem of antiquity is trying to tell us (with contemporary philistines in mind) that the loss of symbolic language may mean the extinction of our humanity. This is perhaps the most urgent note in Allen Tate's poetry, and the purpose of his criticism. He has had many forces working against him, in American civilization (which is merely the perfection of the frustrations we all suffer) and in American academies (which are advanced posts of our desolate rationalism), but the protest cannot be ignored.

Others, no doubt, have commented on the affinity which Allen Tate bears to Edgar Allen Poe, but I might perhaps draw attention to one remark, in the essay on Poe in *The Forlorn Demon,* which might stand for the author of that essay no less truly than for its subject. It is there suggested that "in the history of the moral imagination in the nineteenth century Poe occupies a special place. No other writer in England or the United States, or, as far as I know, in France, went so far as Poe in his vision of dehumanized man." In that respect Poe was prophetic: the vision has now become a harrowing reality, and the rôle of the prophet must change. I am not sure whether in our tragic predicament Allen Tate places most reliance on poetry or on prayer, and perhaps he would say they are the same thing.

But, as he said in the essay on "The Angelic Imagination," "the human intelligence cannot reach God as essence; only God as analogy. Analogy to what? Plainly analogy to the natural world; for there is nothing in the intellect that has not previously reached it through the senses." Poe refused to see nature and was therefore doomed to see nothing. "He has overleaped and cheated the condition of man." Such angelism of the intellect has not been Allen Tate's. He has, on the contrary, always embraced the condition of man, and his work as a whole moves towards the reconciling image, knowing

> There is no civilization without death;
> There is now the wind for breath.

Allen Tate

by JOHN HALL WHEELOCK

Allen Tate's vigor and quick energy, which give such force and liveliness to all his thinking and writing, have enabled his rather spare frame to retain its alert and tireless youthfulness throughout years of work and achievement that would have taken their toll of one less spirited. For Allen Tate is that phenomenon rare in our day, a man of letters. Even more so than Mr. Eliot, another contemporary man of letters, he has been active in many branches of literature. I tend, naturally perhaps, since it is my own field, to regard him first of all as a poet. Yet his work as a critic, a writer on the philosophy of literature, as a biographer and historian, as a novelist, and, more recently, as an anthologist, is impressive. He has not as yet, to the best of my knowledge, written a play, but I should not be surprised to learn that he had one up his sleeve.

Another aspect of Mr. Tate's work and career that seems to me to have given both of these a distinction quite singular in our day is the almost classical balance of the point of view he has brought to bear on confused issues, more especially in the fields of poetry and of criticism. This is not to imply that he has been outside the movement which, in our time, has had so great an influence on the course of criticism and of poetry itself. Quite the reverse, as we all know, has been the case. He has been active in that movement, in the forefront of it, and has had a part in its determination. But in the thick of it he has never lost his head or lost sight of those values which remain,

EDITOR'S NOTE: Reprinted from *The Sewanee Review*, 67:577–78 (Autumn 1959), copyright © 1959 by The University of the South, by permission of the author and publisher. Brief deletions of remarks relating to the occasion for which the essay was prepared have been made.

if I may coin a word, moveless throughout all movements. For this, he doubtless has his thorough grounding in the great literatures of the past, at least partly, to thank. There is such a thing as being so truly sophisticated, if one must use the word, as to enjoy immunity to all so-called sophistication, the fads, foibles and novelties of the moment, that actually are anything but new. Yet a thorough grounding in what has been done in the past would not, of itself, have been enough without an imaginative perception of what is relevant to the present. Mr. Tate's poetry represents, to my mind, an achievement that could only have come about through the happy and inspired coincidence of these two uncommon qualifications. In that poetry, contemporary sensibility finds embodiment in forms that are timeless.

This balance of perception, of judgment, of taste is exerted by a true poet throughout the entire structure of a poem, from the grand scheme down to the smallest detail. I recall the occasion when I showed Allen a poem on which I had just finished work and how unerringly he put his finger on a word there that seemed to say what I meant and yet was somehow, I knew, wrong. Not only did he put his finger on it, but he told me why it was wrong and, best of all, proposed a substitute word of almost identical sound-value. In the lines describing the song of a wood-thrush,

> The fountains of the sun
> Are in that tiny jet
> Of song, so clear, so cool . . .

the word, "tiny," is wrong because of its tone—the word has trivial or even humorous connotations out of keeping with the tone of the poem. Allen's proposed substitute, "twining," greatly improves the poem and is a more accurate description, both of a wood-thrush's song, which consists of three interwoven notes, and of the turning, twisting streams of water that make up the jet of a fountain. I am immeasurably grateful to him for the gift of that word.

Allen Tate as a Teacher

by WARREN KLIEWER

It is not accidental, I think, that Allen Tate has been a teacher as well as a writer, for our time makes that demand of many writers: teaching is better than starving. But Mr. Tate is, it seems to me, more than a writer-turned-teacher, a literary craftsman who made the best of the accidents of economic necessity. For the idea of professionalism of the man of letters is a theme running throughout all his written work, and his teaching partakes of that same professional attitude, evidenced partly in the fact that he has been a co-editor of two first-rate anthology textbooks. For the purposes of this essay, then, I should like to ignore Allen Tate's poems and essays, his fiction, his biographies, his studies of social matters in the South; I shall discuss only the way in which he brought his experience of writing and of the practice of criticism to the problems of teaching university students how to read, understand, and talk about poems, and I shall assume that such a study, even if it necessarily oversimplifies his subtle reasoning, will show Mr. Tate's teaching to be an integral and consistent part of the creative work of a professional man of letters.

One aspect of Mr. Tate's thinking became clear because of the classroom situation. It was necessary for him to explain his fundamental assumptions about the relationships between poetry and things outside the discipline. The first of these assumptions is one which, I suppose, we all make but almost never express: that some form of poetry has existed in all civilizations and that there is a close connection between a civilization and its poetry. Poetry does not exist without a

EDITOR'S NOTE: Reprinted from *Descant*, 7:41–48 (Autumn 1962), by permission of the publisher.

relationship to a civilization, nor can the people speaking a language be civilized unless the language has a poetry. This assumption sounds neither startling nor new. It certainly is far more cautious than the Victorian substitution of art for religion, and the assumption may be startling only when a moral conclusion is derived from it, namely that the state of civilization depends to some degree on the good state of literature.

The first assumption is based on another and is related to a third. Mr. Tate assumed in much of what he said that "thought cannot be separated from language." That is, not only do our thoughts—the content of a poem—determine which words we will choose, but also the words determine the thoughts. Form and content, vehicle and tenor, language and thought or feeling or meaning, therefore, may be distinguished from each other so that they may be considered separately, but they may be considered only as two aspects of the same thing. Poetic language cannot be thought of as pretty adornment of commonplace ideas, nor can we think of poetic language as having "captured" an idea or feeling, as if the idea were a bird that had been caught in a linguistic net, for as a matter of fact, the idea or feeling did not exist before these particular words were put together in this particular order. And so, because of the connection between language and thought, Mr. Tate was able to approach poetry through its language—or more specifically, through rhetoric and its bases, grammar and logic.

It was in this context that he defined rhetoric as "the study of the full language of experience, not the specialized languages of method": a definition directly related to a third assumption of Mr. Tate's thinking. Although civilization has never been perfect, it has never been more imperfect than it is now, and it shows every sign of becoming worse. There was a time—a great age though not a Golden Age—when things were better, an age like the age of Dante, that time when civilization gave to a poet a complete and coherent system of beliefs which the poet could use, knowing that his audience shared them and would understand what he was writing about. For the handicap is too great if the poet finds it necessary to create his own system of beliefs, as did William Butler Yeats, before he can begin writing his poems. This assumption of the value of the body of beliefs shared by both poet and reader can be found throughout Mr. Tate's critical work—in the recent essay, "The Symbolic Imagination: The Mirrors of Dante," as well as in the very early essay, "Emily Dickinson" (1932), in which the critic comments that the poet needs a thorough "discipline in an objective system of truth" and that the second necessary condition prior to writing a poem is the poet's "lack of consciousness of such a discipline."

These three relationships, then—between the poet and audience by way of a coherent body of beliefs, between language and thought, and between poetry and civilization by way of language—united Mr. Tate's teaching and his formal criticism by being the assumptions underlying both. But ordinarily the relationships were only implied, for the whole body of his criticism demands that theory and criticism be subordinate to the literary text and that the reader must proceed as quickly as possible to the particular literary work. In order to do this, he had developed a method of analysis based on medieval biblical exegesis, which resulted in four levels of meaning.

This method began with the critic's looking for the answers to several simple, fundamental questions: "Where?" "When?" "What?" and "How?" These are not unusual questions. They are the questions one may ask about any trivial piece of gossip, the questions a good journalist attempts to answer in the first sentence of a news story. But a poem is not a news story, and there is another question which can be asked about a poem: "Why?" Of course, one cannot ask all these questions at once; there must be some order. And so Mr. Tate would ask the question which was relevant to the particular poem he was talking about, and the other questions would be suggested by the first.

Let me illustrate. These questions suggested four levels or components of a poem. If you ask the questions "Where?" or "When?" of a poem, you are asking about a literal level. You are asking about the location, the place where the action of the poem is occurring. On this literal level you discover the concrete details. For example, when you ask "Where?" and "When?" about Thomas Hardy's "Channel Firing," it becomes clear that the speakers of the poem are in their graves and that the action takes place during a time of war.

Analysis of the literal level of the poem leads naturally to discussion of the grammar and to the analyses of the literal meanings of words. For example, in the line, "Let me not to the marriage of true minds," Mr. Tate would attempt to discover what the word *let* meant at the time when the poem was written. And analyses of meaning lead to questions of metrics, for obviously the stresses and rhymes affect the grammar of the sentence.

The second level of a poem is sought by asking the question "What?" This is the level of logic, or the allegorical level. On this level of the poem the reader discovers the "meaning," that part of the sense which can be paraphrased in prose. For example, when you are reading Marvell's "To His Coy Mistress," you discover very quickly that the structure of the poem is based on a syllogism which can be paraphrased: "if we had all the time we needed, then we could afford to delay our pleasures. But we have only a short time. Therefore, let us take our pleasures immediately." It is obvious that this paraphrase is not the whole meaning but only its basis, for the fallacy of the syllogism, interacting with the satirical elements of the third section of the poem, creates another dimension of meaning which cannot be paraphrased. But it is clear that the syllogism is part of the meaning.

Of any action we may ask how it happened, and this question leads to Mr. Tate's third level or third component of a poem: the tropological or dramatic level. On this level we discover the action which is taking place, the mode of the poem, the moral change. On this third level exists, for example, the action of John Donne's love in "The Canonization" when the mode of the poem rises from the sensuality and playfulness of the beginning to the expression of sanctified love at the end of the poem. On this level exists also the reversal of fortune and the realization of guilt by Oedipus. This third level is the level of rhetoric, which Mr. Tate defined in this context as "the study of human intercourse through language."

At this point I should like to emphasize something which, I am sure, you have already noticed. The first level of the poem was named the level of grammar, the second the level of logic, and the third the level of rhetoric. I should like to refer back to Mr. Tate's assumption that language is inseparable from thought and feeling, and to suggest that in this relationship lies the solution to a common critical dilemma. For although one could approach poetry through the feeling of the poem, this approach is at best fuzzy and vague, and to approach a poem through the thought also leads one to the distortions of subjectivism. In an attempt, then, to find an objective basis for studying poetry, and a basis which moreover was firmly grounded in tradition, Mr. Tate chose the medieval distinctions of language which were contained in the Trivium. He studied a poem through verbal analysis.

But there is a fourth question to be asked: "Why?" The answers to this question lead to the fourth level, and the anagogical level, the spiritual meaning of the poem. This fourth level is the level of teleology; the answer to the question "Why?" is the purpose or end of the poem. The fourth level involves the ultimate and complete realization of all the complex elements: Mr. Tate always insisted that to the component names the term "dynamic" should be added; for all of these levels, the language and details, the meaning, and the moral change, are constantly interacting.

The difficulty of giving an example to illustrate the anagogical level is obvious, for Mr. Tate contended that it was the whole business of literary criticism to explore this most difficult of all levels, the anagogical meaning. An illustration of his definition would occupy an entire long critical essay in itself. But I think I can make a negative allusion to it. Mr. Tate pointed out that part of the difficulty of understanding Hart Crane's poetry lies in the poet's attempt to reach the anagogical level without going through all the intervening steps. In a poem such as "Voyages" there is nothing for the reader to comprehend as a preliminary or tentative meaning. Certainly there are concrete details in the poem, but beginning with section II the relationships among these details are so different from those of the world outside the poem that we cannot take them to be literal descriptions. There is no logical or rational organization, no character going through an action or being acted upon. A reader can only do as Hart Crane himself did: he must leap directly to the spiritual meaning of the poem.

This, then, is an outline of the critical method which Mr. Tate used. It is necessary for me to point out that the method was never presented as a complete system. For both the assumptions stated earlier in this paper and the method of explication were kept in the background where they would not obscure the poem, and Mr. Tate would use only as much of either as was necessary to understand a particular work. My presentation of his critical system is retrospective and is my interpretation of its coherence: his system, since it subordinated itself to the poems, was necessarily expounded in a fragmentary form. It was the poem itself that determined which fragment was to be used. As I suggested above, one must begin with the anagogical level when approaching Hart Crane. With a dramatic monologue by Browning one begins with the third level, the level of moral change. With an imagist poem one begins by asking the literal questions about the time, the place, the concrete details. With a poem like "To His Coy Mistress" one begins by examining the logical structure. The important thing, however, is that though the system is seen only in parts and fragments, it never loses its coherent integrity. It is a complete whole which does not need to be revised whenever the reader approaches a new poem.

The parts have been illustrated above; in illustrating the coherence of the critical method—and doing this in a particular way, namely by looking at one of Mr. Tate's own poems from the point of view of his system—I think I can suggest a further extension of my thesis that the genres of Mr. Tate's work exist together as integral parts of a single whole. For the system which I have outlined does describe rather accurately the components of at least one of his poems, "Aeneas at Washington."

As frequently happens with Mr. Tate's poems, the title leads the reader directly to the literal meaning of the poem, in this poem naming the speaker and the place and hinting at the time. But this title does even more: it economically alludes to the second, allegorical level of meaning, suggesting to the reader that he is dealing with a man who has survived a destroyed aristocratic civilization and who is contemplating the capital city of the dominant democratic. Examining this second level of meaning and thus expecting to find hints of more universal meanings, the reader will also notice such things as the descriptions of the countryside in the third strophe—details which sound not like the Troy we know about but, curiously enough, like Kentucky. The third level of meaning is indicated by the speaker himself, Aeneas, who describes the extent of the dramatic change. In the first line he remembers seeing violence; in the final line he names the action: "I thought of Troy." The first three levels, then, are clear in "Aeneas at Washington." To the extent that the poem is successful, one cannot paraphrase the fourth level of meaning, the anagogical level. But I think I can point to its existence by commenting on one of the particularly fine qualities of the poem. The first three levels of the poem conclude and come together in the understated clause describing the speaker's purpose: "what we had built her for." The literal situation, the allegorical meaning, and the dramatic action become fused into one, and their dynamic inter-relationships are demonstrated. This in itself evokes the suggestion of anagogical level. But it is even more appropriate that the anagogical meaning, the level of teleology, is neatly paralleled by a clause stating purpose on the other three levels.

Therefore, in retrospect it is clear to me that Mr. Tate's poetry, his criticism, and his teaching are coherent. But it was this same coherence which aroused my doubts when I first confronted the body of critical essays, the vast and inclusive esthetic theory, and the precise, structured methodology. And I hope that by now you have also begun to question Mr. Tate's critical machinery. Just as he criticized other all-too-complete critical systems, so I also began to ask whether he had not overwhelmed the poem with a theoretical system. The thought, the language, and the form had been accounted for. Where was the emotion? I know, of course, that to some extent I was asking the wrong question: a reader's searching a poem for an emotion is like an anatomist's searching a cadaver for the soul. And yet we speak of emotion in relation to poetry. It seemed then—and I was by no means the first to raise this objection—that Mr. Tate's system had achieved its completeness by excluding emotion.

The unannounced and unexplained answer came one day: the emotion is, of course, not in the poem at all but in the reader, and is aroused when the reader in some way partakes of the reality which the poem refers to. Of course, this makes the poem an "emotionless" symbol, but it does not imply a lack of emotion in either the poet or the reality symbolized by the poem. But more important than the truth of this simple distinction is that Mr. Tate never bothered to explain: though he may have done so inadvertently, he dramatized. For on the day when he was to discuss Tennyson's "Tears, Idle Tears," Mr. Tate—the great explainer, the great theorizer, the great systemizer —made an unexpected apology: "I must apologize for my reading of this poem. I have never been able to read all the way through the poem without getting tears in my eyes, and there are times when I almost lose my voice trying to read it. I don't know why I feel this poem so deeply. Perhaps it's because the poem is vague. Someone once told me that the poem is totally unlike anything I have ever written or ever will be able to write. That may be the reason." He broke off his introduction, and he gave the poem a more dignified and profound reading than I have ever heard given to any other poem. This was, I thought, not an inadequate comment. For the inexplicable emotion had caused the system to open out into the total experience of poetry.

An Encounter in Florence

by PIER FRANCESCO LISTRI

translated by Radcliffe Squires

It is said that, along with Ezra Pound, Allen Tate is the greatest of living American poets. Born in Kentucky in 1899, this son of the American South is an essayist, a novelist, and a professor as well as a poet. His cultural world is double-stitched. One thread secures him to Europe, the other to the defeated South, so that his poetic imagination redounds with an exquisite metaphysics blended with generals, region, and the Confederate flag. Within this farrago, however, we can discern a great intellectual (after the model of Eliot who for a time constituted his god on earth), encumbered with a weighty tradition, fixed in his illustrious position of an authentic conservative, and favored (O rare occurrence) with an inexhaustible sense of irony.

It was in Florence—through which Tate passed unnoticed by the world and fêted only by a handful of Italian poets gathered for dinner atop the hill of Fiesole—that I met this extraordinary master in all his diversity. At the State University I had been accustomed to two

EDITOR'S NOTE: Reprinted from *La Nazione*, 22 July 1970, by permission of *La Nazione*.

sorts of poets. There were the poet-bards, old not only in years but in the passions as well, perfectly cast for the role of reading official orations in the Campidoglio in honor of new presidents: one thinks of Robert Frost's homage to Kennedy. Or else there were those young and wild poets who delight in dishonoring the Stars and Stripes and who, like Allen Ginsberg, wander, scruffy and dazed with drugs, about the Old World, declaiming poetry spiteful to their fatherland.

Tate plays neither role; on the contrary, he embodies a solitary alternative which for Europeans is provocative: he is a magisterial poet perpetually discomfited by the global power of his country. Yet his quarrel, unlike that of the younger poets, affects no wild rage. Rather, it is a profound murmur which gives an inkling of something even deeper—a stone dropped into a well to measure the depths of an abyss.

No, Tate's rebellion has nothing of the surly whine of the contemporary world. Armed only with the grandeur of his despair and the grandeur of his language, he is exposed to the scornful incomprehension of his younger colleagues. Furthermore, that lofty rationality which governs his poetic discourse (a discourse simultaneously politic and civil) ultimately yearns to turn into a saving spirit of conciliation. Hence, it is necessary to guard against abandoning his private "global war," all fused with the matériel of his folkloric Southern arsenal—slavery, regionalism, agrarianism—and embroidered with ballads about generals and battles.

We come now to the heart of the matter. In a world preoccupied with collectivism, Tate's poetry is dramatically tensed to defend individualism. In a rather leaden society governed by a myth of science, his poetry conducts a fearless campaign against science, producing from that irony a measure both musical and fabulous. In an apathetic, agnostic period he is not ashamed to recommend a Christianity to be lived as intellectual anguish. (Tate became a Catholic when he was fifty.) One has to admit that rarely does America produce a personality that is persuasive chiefly because it is out of joint with the times.

Italian culture has slighted Tate. A few scattered poems have appeared in reviews or in such anthologies as merit more than a quick glance. In 1959 a selection of his essays was translated by Nemi D'Agostino, while his one novel, *I Padri*, appeared five or six years ago on the shelves of our libraries—but little enough of his dozen collections of poetry and his numerous books of criticism and essays that over the years have accumulated as his "works." Today, however, a publisher's announcement of an important and representative collection of Tate's poetry, chosen by the author himself and masterfully translated by Alfredo Rizzardi (*Ode ai caduti confederati et altri poesie*, Milano 1970), encourages one to share with the Italian reader a stimulating encounter with the voice of Allen Tate . . .

Tate always responds willingly to "vast" questions: *The state of poetry in America?*

"The young poets of my country," he says, "so intensely occupied with their own sensations, seem extremely subjective. Actually, they are the choral leaders of the very system which they denigrate. They do not know how to propose any 'truth,' but prefer to deal in terms like 'value,' taken from the language of economics . . . it is only about anarchy that they are really very subjective!"

The relationship between the cultures of America and Europe?

"Yes," he answers, "there is indeed a school that would like to break completely with the old continent. And that is fatuous. We derive from Europe and we owe her almost everything. The American intellectual still very much needs Europe."

A diagnosis of the position of the poet in society?

"The position of the poet in the western world is difficult. Certainly, the total loss of civil, religious, and cultural standards, the violent break with tradition are apocalyptic omens. These catastrophes could not but constitute the substance of our poetry. And the only way of a genuine, though limited, credibility . . ."

We speak about the "credibility" of the poet in America today. "I answer that," Tate says and extends a quivering tongue, "with a statistic. In the last ten years a population of two hundred million has bought only six thousand copies of my books of poetry. That seems to me the answer to your question!"

Still, Tate is serene. He knows there is no solution; only that the engagement is exacting. His metaphysical side speaks primarily of the apocalypse: "If modern civilization has fallen into decadence there can be no abstract solution. The poet," he observes, "being the only one who can fully render an account should be made the final arbiter between this civilization and the past."

Isn't that asking a lot?

"Irony," he murmurs, "is our unique music . . ."

A Dove

by BREWSTER GHISELIN

Twenty-five years ago, when Allen Tate and I were teaching at a writers' conference in northern Utah, we met in the dark dawn to go fly-fishing in one of the nearer canyons. At that hour no breakfast was available, not even coffee, and the substitute we drank, cold Coca Cola dispensed by a machine in the bleak basement of the dormitory, was not very agreeable. When a few minutes later we passed through town we found it black and still as midnight. The only breakfast we then could look forward to was delayed till the sun was high. We built a fire on a spit of cobblestones under native cottonwoods, threaded our trout on a skewer of fence wire, and ate saltless flesh made savory by the crisped skin and a light dusting of ash.

There was conversation, but all I recall of it came on the drive back: first some discussion of attitudes toward fishing, then, at my remark that I had given up hunting at eighteen, Tate's story of his own renunciation of hunting, after finding a mourning dove he had shot, dying outspread against the earth, a drop of blood forming in the corner of each of its eyes. Because he told no more than this, I was free to imagine how the man with his cooling gun leaned to pick up the bird.

One who has never held a dove in his hand can scarcely grasp all the reality of the image: bird-hot body firm in grey-brown iridescent plumage, pointed tail, pink legs and feet, rounded head and deft beak, near its base the bright eyes. I do not suppose Tate saw this familiar image suddenly haloed in meaning that transmuted it into symbol. I infer that he was not rapt away beyond the occasion, but that it

EDITOR'S NOTE: Reprinted from *The Michigan Quarterly Review*, 10:229–30 (Autumn 1971), by permission of the publisher.

remained immediate in all its natural substance and order. Yet there can be no doubt that for him, even more inevitably than for me in his recounting, the moment more vivid than the illuminations of Audubon glowed in an embrace of meaning in which symbols were elemental.

The dove, shot from the air, dying, and dead in the hand, was nested in significance, cradled in projections of light. Unabsolved from its relations with the instant world, unextricated from nature—it was dead and subject to be eaten—it was nevertheless transfigured.

In the circumstances of our conversation, only a few words were necessary for evocation. Simply by the tact of his silence, Tate made it apparent that understanding was to be reached through "command" (as he had written in his essay "The Hovering Fly") of "the imaginative power of the relation of things": through apprehension of the object within the context of a fully human vision of the substance and order of reality. The significance of the death of the bird was realized through that mode of cognitive vision later to be called by Tate "symbolic imagination" and described as serving "to bring together various meanings at a single moment of action." Thus the bleeding dove was involved for us in a rich nidus of meanings, powerfully of the classic and Christian traditions though not of these alone. Brief representation of "an action in the shapes of this world" gave the "fullest image" of an insight, unity comprising "infinite strands of interconnection," implications complex and "deep as life itself," of the kind that Tate has seen converged and fused in certain works of literature, as in exemplary passages of Donne and Dante and in the fully rendered action of *Madame Bovary* and some other fiction in which, as he argues, "the novel has at last caught up with poetry."

Descriptions of any such realization can never be more than approximate. Even if it were feasible to name and examine all the symbolic referents implicit in the image of the fallen dove—the oak grove of Dodona, the chariot of Aphrodite, the waters of the Jordan, some lines of the *Commedia*, trecento paintings of the Trinity, the Annunciation, the Crucifixion, and countless more—and to show how in force and meaning each is intricated with all through sequences of association, analogies, ironies, and to suggest how they constellate and cluster into one order and single glow, the account would fail because it would not keep intact the original insight. As Allen Tate has pointed out in an early essay, "form is meaning." Since the unity of insight is that of a single configuration, the precise meaning of any form can be realized only directly, in the integrity of its whole aspect. In analysis, it cannot be presented, it can only be represented—often usefully, always imperfectly—in atomistic terms which in fragmenting it confront us with fragments, from which if we desire to return to it we must turn away.

For the figure of the part, in the degree to which it is fully attended to, assumes dominance and displaces all other figures and dispels their effects. This displacement is observable in any figure brought to focus in awareness: it pre-empts the field of attention. Simple but compelling illustration of this phenomenon is available in those gestalts that permit formation of alternative images, one image or the other, but not both together, as a white circle on black can be viewed either as a disk on black ground or as a hole framed in black, but not as both disk and hole simultaneously.

Such demonstrations show that forms are constituted ultimately in subjective realizations determined by the way the structured substance (always of specific potentialities) is used. When structural aspects or elements of a form perceived in its unity are discriminated and separately considered—and so brought independently to focus—the form falls apart in successive fixations of attention, and thus the meaning too falls apart. Its perspectives are resolved into others and the energies at play in their realization are diverted to other paths or dispersed altogether. In the narrower psychic syntheses thus engendered, the unitary life is frustrated. Those who lose the original synthesis in this fashion can recover it, if they will. But others less capable of imaginative vision, who may never have grasped the whole, or who can do so only vaguely, will tend to take the inferior figures of meaning for substance and essence.

These observations may return us to the dove in the hand and the man grasping a body of flesh and meaning interdictive of death.

II. THE ESSAYIST

A Note on the Vitality of Allen Tate's Prose

by FRANCIS FERGUSSON

In "The Man of Letters in the Modern World," Allen Tate writes, "He [the man of letters] has an immediate responsibility, to other men no less than to himself, for the vitality of language." And he proceeds to suggest what "vitality of language" means: "the rediscovery of the human condition in the living arts." This is, of course, a counsel of perfection, never to be followed with complete success. But it haunts Allen Tate, and his best critical work has as much of this authentic life as any prose now being written.

Consider, for example, this paragraph from *The Forlorn Demon* (1953). He is explaining his title, a phrase from a poem perhaps by Poe:

To the question, What would attract the attention of demons if they lost interest in us? we have no answer at present; nor can we guess how different their personalities seem to them; perhaps every demon is sure that he is unique. Poe was certain all his life that he was not like anybody else. The saints tell us that confident expectancy of damnation is a more insidious form of spiritual pride than certainty of salvation. The little we know of hell is perhaps as follows: it promptly *adjusts* and *integrates* its willing victims into a standardized monotony, in which human suffering, its purpose thus denied, begins to sound like the knock of an unoiled piston. A famous literary critic predicted years ago that our poetry would soon echo the rhythms of the internal

EDITOR'S NOTE: Reprinted from *The Sewanee Review*, 67:579–81 (Autumn 1959), copyright © 1959 by The University of the South, by permission of the author and publisher.

combustion engine, and he produced a short verse-play to prove it. I take it he meant that poetry would no longer move to the rhythms of the heart, which are iambic or trochaic, depending on whether the ear picks up the beat at the diastole or the systole, with occasional fibrillations and inverted T-waves to delight the ear and to remind us of the hour of our death. The rapidity of a piston reminds us of a machine which can temporarily or permanently break down; but it can be exactly duplicated and it cannot die. To this god, I believe, we owe our worship of *rapid* and exciting language, an idolatry that in one degree or another is the subject of most of these essays.

The vitality of this paragraph is produced by very complex tensions within and between "demon," "damnation," "the rhythm of the heart," and the god of the machine. Is the writer a demon, or does he have a demon who makes him (like Poe) unique and totally alone? Would it be spiritual pride to say so too confidently, a version of that "standardized monotony" which is hell? Hell we have all about us, in our mechanized world; real poetry moves to the rhythm of the heart, delighting the ear and reminding us of death. So we might weave back and forth within the paragraph, responding in many ways to its balanced stresses and strains. The elements are made present to the imagination without loss of mystery. And together they define a human condition, and a life-seeking motive which appears to have small hope of success.

There is a further tension in the paragraph which accounts for its light tone and the anticlimactic movement of the whole: that between the writer and his audience. The writer steps forth like an urbane but remorseful lecturer; he accepts his obligation to answer, as well as he can, a crucial question. The explicit question with which he begins is partly a joke, not the main matter in hand; but it leads, on the bias, to the real question, which is deep as hell. It is, in fact, too deep for us: let us turn, quite lightly, to "the subject of most of these essays."

Most of the elements which compose this paragraph are old-fashioned. The writer's acceptance of his obligation to his audience, the assumption that he owes them both scrupulous thought and wit; his polite reliance upon their intelligence, are foreign to our time and place. Poe's romantic despair, bits of the classic Christian scenario, are made to interact with the gasoline engine. Questions historical and metaphysical throb at every point, but are never mentioned. And it would be silly, in this context, to impose the heavy-handed question of the "ontological status" of the elements in play.

When Richard II, having renounced the crown, smashes his mirror to destroy the "brittle glory" of his face, Bolingbroke, terribly embarrassed and out of his depth, remarks,

> The shadow of your sorrow hath destroyed
> The shadow of your face.

To which Richard replies,

> 'Tis very true, my grief lies all within,
> And these external manners of laments
> Are merely shadows to the unseen grief,
> That swells with silence in the tortured soul.
> There lies the substance.

Richard speaks for all poets and all writers and artists who try to represent the human condition. But when the "shadows" of language are cast by a real experience, the language has some share of that vitality which Allen Tate seeks. His own best prose has it; we can ask no more of any writer.

The Criticism of Allen Tate

by MONROE K. SPEARS

Like Jonathan Swift, Allen Tate means to vex the world rather than
divert it; he hopes to break through the reader's complacent in-
difference, make him aware of his predicament, and force him to
take sides. Since I assume that Mr. Tate achieves his purpose, and that
most readers of this review[1] will already admire him or dislike him, I
shall spend no time in general praise of his career. Mr. Tate is, as critic,
essentially a polemicist, an aggressive and sometimes truculent warrior
who for more than twenty years has conducted a skillful defensive
action. Believing that the best defense is an offense, he has given no
quarter to any in whom he detects, under whatever disguise, allegiance
to the Enemy—the reigning tyrant, Positivism. Though I do not come
to praise Tate, I am not attempting to bury him, for the *corpus* of his
criticism here displayed is still fresh and lively. But the appearance
of this collection, together with many other omens, does seem to mark
the end of a campaign. The cause that Mr. Tate champions has probably won as much territory as it is likely to obtain without a change of
strategy; and it is time now for a consolidation of gains, a check of
casualties, a re-grouping of forces. In the hope of aiding in this necessary task, I shall devote my review to analysis of the ideas and assumptions upon which his criticism is founded. There is plenty of comment
on Tate, but most of it is controversial and partial; a reasonably objec-

EDITOR'S NOTE: Reprinted from *The Sewanee Review*, 57:317–34 (Spring 1949), copyright © 1949 by The University of the South, by permission of the author and
publisher.
    [1] Of *On the Limits of Poetry. Selected Essays: 1928–1948*. By Allen Tate (Alan
Swallow Press and William Morrow & Co., 1948).

tive attempt to define the basic convictions underlying the various essays should, therefore, serve a useful function.

First, a note on the contents of this book. Mr. Tate is a severe critic of his own work, and he has collected here only a small part of his critical writing.[2] Specifically, the book contains five essays not published before in book form (but to be published separately this year as *The Hovering Fly*), and most of the contents of Mr. Tate's two previous volumes of criticism (three pieces from each of them are omitted). The essays are arranged in five sections. Those in the first concern the relation of literature to society, and define the functions of literature and criticism in an age dominated by Positivism; the fourth group consists of essays similar in approach, but dealing with the special problems of Southern society and literature. The pieces in the second division are general discussions of the nature of poetry and, more briefly, of fiction. The third section is composed of extended interpretations and evaluations of particular poets; the final group consists of shorter comments, written originally as reviews, on individual poets. The new essays reveal no important change in Mr. Tate's views, though they do seem to indicate a certain broadening of interest. In "A Reading of Keats," for example, Mr. Tate approximates "total" criticism, and of a Romantic poet; in "Techniques of Fiction" he deals with the novel; and in "The Hovering Fly" he ventures farther than usual into aesthetic theory. In the two last-mentioned pieces he substitutes for his usual blunt directness a more subtle and tentative style which is even, at times, reminiscent of Virginia Woolf. But, with these minor differences, the new essays fit naturally into place beside the old. Mr. Tate's criticism is remarkably homogeneous; his basic principles and methods have remained unchanged, as far as I can tell, from his first essay to his latest. In discussing his work, I shall therefore ignore chronology.

Mr. Tate's approach to criticism is refreshingly modest. Criticism, he holds, is a form of literature, since it tells us the meaning and value of concrete experience; but it is definitely not autotelic: its purpose is "the protection of that which in itself is the end of criticism"—creative

[2] See the checklist of Tate's works by Willard Thorp, *Princeton University Library Chronicle*, April 1942.

writing. The function of criticism is "to maintain and to demonstrate the special, unique, and complete knowledge which the great forms of literature afford us." (p. 8) It must instruct the reader in "the exercise of taste, the pursuit of standards of intellectual judgment, and the acquisition of self-knowledge." (p. 66) Its function, in thus creating a proper audience for imaginative writing, is highly important, especially in times such as the present; but it is distinctly subordinate. Mr. Tate's criticism fits his own definition: it is intended to educate the reader and guide him to an understanding of literature, and especially of modern poetry. To achieve this purpose, the negative task of preventing the audience from misunderstanding literature through expecting too much, or the wrong things, of it is now most urgent: "On reading my essays over, I found that I was talking most of the time about what poetry cannot be expected to do to save mankind from the disasters in which poetry itself must be involved. . . . Lessing says that poetry is not painting or sculpture; I am saying in this book, with very little systematic argument, that it is neither religion nor social engineering." (p. xi) For the most part, Mr. Tate aims at the limited objective of destroying popular misconceptions which distort or prevent the reception of poetry among its potential audience. Since he emphasizes this corrective function, he does not elaborate his positive demonstration of the value of literature, which is developed mostly by implication. All criticism, Mr. Tate believes, is limited and partial: there "are all kinds of poetry . . . and no single critical insight may impute an exclusive validity to any one kind." (p. 75) The critic "is convinced that the total view is no view at all, the critic not being God, and convinced too that even if (which is impossible) he sees everything, he has got to see it from somewhere." (p. 149) And his own criticism, he points out in his preface, is particularly unsystematic and incomplete: most of his essays are occasional, controversial, and comparatively brief; hence they represent opinion rather than any fully-developed theory. In the face of this disclaimer, to discuss Mr. Tate in terms of general principles may seem unfair or foolish. Yet even negative criticism must proceed from a coherent intellectual position if it is to be valid; and permanent value will depend upon the presence, by implication at least, of a satisfactory positive theory.

I

The central theme in Mr. Tate's criticism of society may be stated simply: the "deep illness of the modern mind" which he labels *Positivism* has deprived modern man of tradition and of the religion upon which tradition ultimately depends. Positivism (scientism, pragmatism, instrumentalism), assuming that all experience can be ordered scientifically, reduces the spiritual realm to irresponsible emotion, irrelevant feeling. Regarding action as an end in itself, and concerned only with practical results, it substitutes method for intelligence. It interprets history in terms of abstract concepts of natural law and quantitative differences (the historical method instead of the historical imagination); ignoring the concrete particularity of history, it compels no choice, no imaginative identification. Thus Positivism destroys tradition, and cuts man off from his past.

Against the Positivist spirit, Mr. Tate asserts the existence and value of tradition and of the individual intelligence. With T. E. Hulme, he assumes "a radical discontinuity between the physical and spiritual realms" (p. 4); "it is contrary to the full content of our experience to assume that man is continuous with nature." (p. 308) Only the traditional religious attitude is true to man's total experience. The form of society depends ultimately upon religion, for "the social structure depends on the economic structure, and economic conviction is still . . . the secular image of religion." (pp. 316-7) Mr. Tate illustrates through a horse-metaphor, much like Ransom's image of the World's Body: the Positivist sees only one half of the horse, the Irrationalist (Symbolist, Mystic) the other half; the religious imagination alone is aware of the horse as he really is. Abstracting the rational, predictable aspects of experience, and forgetting the other half of man's total experience—the concrete, unpredictable qualities which constitute the traditional awareness of evil—Positivism worships the false absolute of omnipotent human rationality. A society dominated by this demireligion which falsifies the nature of man and ignores its own failures, says Mr. Tate (invoking the concepts of *hubris* and *nemesis*), is "riding for a crushing fall," and it "will be totally unprepared for collapse. . . ." (p. 308) A traditional society depends upon a true religion of the whole horse.

The essence of tradition, Mr. Tate believes, is a harmony between man's moral nature and his economics, between his way of life and his way of earning a living. (p. 303) This harmony can best be achieved in an agrarian society: "Traditional property in land was the primary medium through which man expressed his moral nature; and our task is to restore it or to get its equivalent today." (p. 303) Modern man has lost not only the religious imagination with its Christian mythology, but also the historical imagination which, since the Renaissance, has furnished substitute myths through which men have dramatized themselves as Greeks or as Romans of the Republic; he is therefore unable to form any imaginative version of himself. Mr. Tate interprets the "Game of Chess" section of *The Waste Land* as a symbol of the "inhuman abstraction of the modern mind," deprived of both kinds of imagination: "It means that in ages which suffer the decay of manners, religion, morals, codes, our indestructible vitality demands expression in violence and chaos; it means that men who have lost both the higher myth of religion and the lower myth of historical dramatization have lost the forms of human action; it means that they are no longer capable of defining a human objective, of forming a dramatic conception of human nature. . . ." (p. 301)

Mr. Tate upholds Regionalism as one aspect of tradition. Dismissing the "picturesque regionalism of local color" as a by-product of literary nationalism, he defends true Regionalism: "that consciousness or that habit of men in a given locality which influences them to certain patterns of thought and conduct handed to them by their ancestors." (p. 286) Its opposite is Provincialism, whose horizons are geographically larger but spiritually smaller; Regionalism is limited in space but not in time, while Provincialism is limited in time but not in space. The provincial man "cuts himself off from the past, and without benefit of the fund of traditional wisdom approaches the simplest problems of life as if nobody had ever heard of them before." (p. 286) Provincialism is increasingly our ideal; in our secular Utopianism we think that we should "save" others with the gospel of world Provincialism, for we have forgotten the nature of man.

Mr. Tate's comments on the South constitute his most extensive specific application of these general ideas. Though the ante-bellum South was a traditional society, it failed, for two main reasons, to produce great literature. First, because it was an aristocracy (which is, like plutocracy, class rule), and its best intellectual energy therefore went into politics; second, because of slavery—not that slavery was immoral, but that the Negro was alien. "All great cultures have been rooted in peasantries," but the Negro was not a good root; the "white man got nothing from the Negro, no profound image of himself in terms of the soil." (p. 273) Considering Southern society generally, Mr. Tate finds the chief cause of its downfall in the lack of an adequate or appropriate religion. An agrarian economy, the South had "a non-agrarian and trading religion that had been invented in the sixteenth century by a young finance-capitalist economy" (p. 316), and Southerners developed no philosophy or body of doctrine of their own. This failure of the South to possess a "sufficient faith in her own kind of God," and not the Civil War ("the setback of the war was of itself a very trivial one"—p. 321), is responsible for her ultimate spiritual defeat, her present conversion from Regionalism to Provincialism.

Although I do not intend to quibble about specific points, and I certainly do not wish to revive extinct controversies, I feel that two general difficulties in Mr. Tate's view of society should be mentioned. In "Humanism and Naturalism" (*Reactionary Essays*; not reprinted in this collection) Mr. Tate argued that the Humanism of Babbitt and More "is obscure in its sources; it is even more ambiguous as to the kind of authority to which it appeals." The Humanists make literature a substitute for philosophy and religion; their Socratic method yields no absolutes, and ultimately they pursue morality for morality's sake. Mr. Tate concludes: "There should be a living center of action and judgment, such as we find in the great religions, which in turn grew out of this center. The act of 'going into the Church' is not likely to supply the convert with it. Yet, for philosophical consistency, this is what the Humanists should do. . . . The religious unity of intellect and emotion, of reason and instinct, is the sole technique for the realization of values." (*RE*, p. 139) With his usual candor, Mr. Tate makes no secret of the fact that he is himself unable to accept religious faith (pp. 288, 306); his own attitude would seem to exemplify what he calls, speaking of Bishop, "our modern unbelieving belief"—the "attempt to replace our secular philosophy, in which he does not believe, with a vision of the divine, in which he tries to believe." (p. 247) He is more logical and consistent than the Humanists in stating that the traditional view of human nature and the traditional society which embodies it are based ultimately upon religion, that religion is the core of the problem. But it is hard to see why Mr. Tate's criticism of the Humanists does not apply essentially to his own position. Lacking belief himself, he cannot derive authority for his values from religion, nor find any positive way of realizing them. In another essay not included in this volume, "Liberalism and Tradition" (*Reason in Madness*), Mr. Tate defends himself against such criticisms. Workability and truth, he points out, are not identical; belief is not to be confused with potentiality of fact: whether a traditional society is possible in the future is a question of fact, but that moral unity in such a society is "the highest good that men can seek to achieve" (*RM*, p. 212) is an imperative of reference. Similarly, the traditionist may believe that modernism is false without having, necessarily, any special positive beliefs; appealing to history, he is convinced that "man needs absolute beliefs in order completely to realize his nature," even though he himself, affected by the mental climate of his time, cannot accept absolutes. (*RM*, p. 206) But even the non-Positivist reader will ask (as does Mr. Tate in the Humanism essay) what can be done to attain these desirable values; and he will find no adequate answer. "Being from all salvation weaned" like the moderns in his poem "The Cross," Mr. Tate is, I think, driven unwillingly to set up false absolutes; and the attempt to posit moral unity and traditional society as absolute imperatives of reference is foredoomed to failure; for they can derive sanction and workability only from religion. Religion cannot take its sanction from tradition and moral unity considered as absolutes, although this seems to be Mr. Tate's conception; to strive to achieve a society in which belief will be possible is to begin at the wrong end. I am afraid that Mr. Tate's comment on the Humanists applies equally to his own social criticism: "The truth of their indictment, negatively considered, cannot be denied. But this is not enough." (*RM*, p. 113)

II

In literary criticism, according to Mr. Tate, Positivism dominates academic historical scholarship and sociological (he has in mind primarily Marxist) criticism. Critics of both these schools subscribe to the Doctrine of Relevance, which "means that the subject-matter of a literary work must not be isolated in terms of form; it must be tested (on an analogy to scientific techniques) by observation of the world that it 'represents.'" (p. 11) Assuming that literary works are not existent objects, but are expressive of substances beyond themselves, the Positivist cannot discuss the literary object in terms of its specific form; he can only "give you its history or tell you how he feels about it" (p. 56); he is either naturalistic or impressionistic. Refusing to judge, Positivists deny their moral nature and intelligence; substituting for them the historical method, they dissolve the literature into its history. The historical scholar defends himself by the hypocritical pretense that his work is a preparation for future criticism, just as Positivist social-planners ask us to look for reference not to the past, but to the future. Against these trends, Mr. Tate asserts the necessity of intellectual and moral responsibility toward both past and present: "We must judge the past and keep it alive by being alive ourselves; and that is to say that we must judge the past not with a method or an abstract hierarchy but with the present, or with as much of the present as our poets have succeeded in elevating to the objectivity of form." (p. 60)

Although Mr. Tate has occupied himself mainly with demonstrating that poetry is not what the Positivists variously take it to be—history, emotion, false science, propaganda, religion—he has always maintained positively that its true value is cognitive, that it gives us a unique, true, and complete knowledge (e.g., pp. 8, 47, 95, 113, 250). Usually, he rests his case upon simple assertion, with little explanation. The only systematic exposition of his theory of poetry that I have been able to discover is that in his early essay, "Poetry and the Absolute" (*Sewanee Review*, XXXV [1927], 41–52). Since his later remarks are more comprehensible in the light of this explicit statement, a brief summary of it will perhaps be useful. Both poet and philosopher, Mr. Tate argues, strive to construct a "portrait of reality" which will be absolute; but the poetic absolute, being "a function of subject-matter in interaction with a personality," is not single and unchanging like the metaphysical; it is capable of infinite recreations. The poetic absolute is achieved, created, in terms of form. The poet may come to terms with his experience through contemplating it in the created absolute of art; he constructs the possibility of this kind of absolute experience first of all for himself, but if the perceptions are perfectly realized, presented free of the disturbance out of which they have sprung, the poem will provide the same absolute experience for others. If, on the other hand, the poem is not completely realized, it presents an inferior and mixed experience like that of ordinary life; it may even increase the disturbance normally connected with such experience and do moral damage. Romantic poets produce poems that are absolute only in the sense that they have no connection with the practical, relative world:

> But Donne created a permanent focus of emotional reference out of the disorder of feeling started in him by frustrated love. He did not wish to discover an escape from emotion. . . . The world of "The Funeral" is a section of the known world. . . . But there is a particular quality of the poem that makes it wholly unlike the portion of the knowable world for which it stands; as a portion it is complete, it is finite. There is nothing beyond it; while in the current of ordinary experience the last consequent is always a fresh antecedent: the practical world of science has no dimensions, no frame, no form. "The Funeral" has form — completeness, finality, absolutism. And it is great art because its absolute quality is created out of the perceptions not of an easy, imaginable world, but of the accepted, common-sense world. (p. 42)

In the absolute poem, any original ulterior motive is absorbed and implicit in form, not explicit and didactic; only if the poet can accept his experience without too much intermediary rationalizing—which is not so much interpretation of experience as rejection of it—can he come to absolute terms with it. "For the perfectly realized poem has no overflow of unrealized action. It does not say that men ought to be better or worse, or as they are; it has no ulterior motives." (p. 44) The bad poem confronts the reader with the problem the poet should have solved for him; there is a diffusion of interest beyond the margins of the poem, and some extra-aesthetic activity is demanded. But great poets are absolutists; there is nothing beyond their poetry. Donne found the "ultimate value of experience to be its ordered intensification; and this is the sole value and meaning of poetry. He found this meaning in absolute form." (p. 45) This absolute quality, Mr. Tate concludes, explains the necessity for poetry: if the need of the mind for absolute experience could be satisfied adequately in ordinary experience, this experience, metaphysically defined and classified, would be sufficient; but only sentimentalists hope for a world absolute of this sort. Art alone provides absolute experience.

Perhaps Mr. Tate decided that the term "absolute" was misleading, for he does not use it in his later comments on the nature of poetry. These comments are, in other respects, entirely consistent with the earlier essay; in fact, two of the new essays in this collection seem to indicate a curiously specific return even to its terminology. "Techniques of Fiction" defines the "completeness of presentation," "fullness of realization" achieved by Flaubert, through which the novel caught up at last with poetry; the distinction is between "getting it [original purpose] all inside the book and leaving some of it irresponsibly outside." (p. 138) In "The Hovering Fly" the conclusion is that "we shall not know the actual world by looking at it; we know it by looking at the hovering fly." (p. 156: the fly, of course, symbolizes Art)

This aesthetic is obviously, in a sense, art for art's sake, and Mr. Tate does not disclaim the inevitable label. Discussing the kind of knowledge gained from poetry, he remarks:

It is not knowledge 'about' something else; the poem is the fulness of that knowledge. We know the particular poem, not what it says that we can restate. . . . I have expressed this view elsewhere in other terms, and it has been accused of aestheticism or art for art's sake. . . . There is probably nothing wrong with art for art's sake if we take the phrase seriously, and not take it to mean the kind of poetry written in England forty years ago. Religion always ought to transcend any of its particular uses; and likewise the true art for art's sake view can be held only by persons who are always looking for things that they can respect apart from use (though they may be useful), like poems, fly-rods, and formal gardens. . . . (p. 250)

This defense of poetry as knowledge, though effective controversial technique, seems to me ultimately dubious, for it depends on a semantic shift: Mr. Tate's *knowledge* which is about itself, proves nothing, explains nothing, and "has no useful relation to the ordinary forms of action" (p. 113) is certainly not *knowledge* in the Positivist or any ordinary sense. But the important point is that Mr. Tate seems to mean by *knowledge* precisely what he earlier termed *absolute experience*: the contemplation or vision or revelation of absolute truth sought usually in philosophy and religion. And this goes beyond art for art's sake; it suggests life for art's sake. In asserting that art, and only art, gives us this absolute knowledge, Mr. Tate seems to be doing (much more

subtly and intelligently) what he takes others to task for: making art
a substitute for religion. In order to understand Mr. Tate's scale of
values, however, we must examine his comments on the relation of art
to society.

III

Though Mr. Tate regards genuine poetry as autotelic and uncon-
cerned with action, he attributes to it an important, if indirect, moral
and social function. Poetry is above morality, but it assumes its existence: "a mind without moral philosophy is incapable of understanding poetry. For poetry, of all the arts, demands a serenity of view and
a settled temper of the mind, and most of all the power to detach one's
own needs from the experience set forth in the poem." (pp. 342–3)
Poetry belongs to the realm of contemplation, which is an end in itself,
and beyond—though not unrelated to—practical ethics: "perhaps the act
of contemplation after long exercise initiates a habit of restraint and the
setting up of absolute standards which are less formulas for action
than an interior discipline of the mind." (p. 317) Thus demanding and
encouraging contemplation, poetry has the indirect psychological function of counteracting over-emphasis on the will: ". . . poetry finds its
true usefulness in its perfect inutility, a focus of repose for the will-
driven intellect that constantly shakes the equilibrium of persons and
societies with its unremitting imposition of partial formulas. When
the will and its formulas are put back into an implicit relation with
the whole of our experience, we get the true knowledge which is
poetry." (p. 113) As this quotation implies, Mr. Tate sees the social
effect of poetry as essentially conservative: poetry is "the instinctive
counter-attack of the intelligence against the dogma of future perfection
for persons and societies"; it "tests with experience the illusions that
the human predicament tempts us in our weakness to believe." (p. 340)

Mr. Tate is, however, much more interested in the effect of society
on poetry than in the effect of poetry on society. His view is, with some
qualifications, deterministic; and its most extreme embodiment is the
concept of the "perfect literary situation." The perfect literary situation occurs when a tradition, a culture, is breaking up; the "poet finds
himself balanced upon the moment when such a world is about to
fall." (p. 209) The world order can then be assimilated to the poetic

vision, "brought down from abstraction to personal sensibility." In such an age the clash of powerful opposites "issues in a tension between abstraction and sensation"; the poet is able to fuse sensibility and thought, perceive abstraction and think sensation. (p. 204) "Only a few times in the history of English poetry has this situation come about, notably, the period between about 1580 and the Restoration." From the similar age in New England emerged two great talents, Hawthorne and Emily Dickinson; and the recent Southern renascence sprang from another such transition, on a lesser scale, as the South changed from traditional Regionalism to Provincialism. (p. 281) Poetry "probes the deficiencies of a tradition. But it must have a tradition to probe." (p. 208) The poet criticizes his tradition, puts it to the test of experience, compares it with something that is about to replace it.

The perfect literary situation is obviously not by any means the perfect situation for society as a whole; great art is produced not by traditional societies, but by the break-up of such societies. With his usual candor, Mr. Tate makes this conflict of values perfectly explicit; speaking of the moral aspect of Emily Dickinson's poetry, he says that it is "a magnificent personal confession, blasphemous and, in its self-revelation, its honesty, almost obscene. It comes out of an intellectual life towards which it feels no moral responsibility." (p. 213) "In Miss Dickinson, as in Donne, we may detect a singularly morbid concern, not for religious truth, but for personal revelation. The modern word is self-exploitation. It is egoism grown irresponsible in religion and decadent in morals. In religion it is blasphemy; in society it means usually that culture is not self-contained and sufficient, that the spiritual community is breaking up. This is . . . the perfect literary situation." (p. 208)

There would seem to be, in Mr. Tate's thought, a fundamental ambiguity, for his two goals—great art and a traditional society—ultimately conflict. And art is largely determined by society: tradition provides its myths, controlling ideas, unification of sensibility, apprehension of total experience; yet for its greatest stimulation it requires the disintegration of tradition. Mr. Tate, however, frequently implies that the two goals agree, when he is discussing social questions or modern poetry. The two problems involved—primacy of values and literary determinism—he never considers directly. My impression is that the aesthetic value is primary for Mr. Tate (though he does not want to change society only for the sake of art); as to literary determinism, the inconsistency results from his double purpose: he wishes to defend modern poetry, and at the same time use its defects as a basis for condemnation of the society which produced it; the first motive leads him to minimize the relationship between literature and society, and the second to emphasize it. Hence Mr. Tate's attitude toward contemporary poetry is curiously ambivalent.

Modern poetry, as Mr. Tate sees it, is the culmination of tendencies beginning at the Renaissance, and manifest in poetry since the Restoration. The loss of traditional religious and moral unity and the spread of Positivism have led the public to expect poets to give them new systems of belief; the poets, forsaking their proper function, have misguidedly attempted to do so. In "Three Types of Poetry" Mr. Tate describes the "heresy of the will," positive and negative Platonism (i.e., roughly, allegorical or optimistic acceptance of science, and "romantic irony" which rejects it and becomes escapist), which has ruined most poetry for the last 150 years; genuine poetry, in contrast, presents an imaginative vision of the whole of life, the vision itself being its own goal. In "Tension in Poetry" he puts essentially the same thesis into different terms, this time labeling the trouble the "fallacy of communication" which leads poets either to compete directly with science or to reject all claim to truth and reality. In technique, the two extremes manifest themselves as the Metaphysical (stressing extension, denotation) and the Symbolist (stressing intension, connotation); the greatest poetry is that of the center, achieving neither extension nor intension, but *tension*. Since the Restoration, the dramatic instinct has survived best in lyric poets; for, lacking any epos or myth, any "pattern of well-understood behavior," poets are unable to write longer works successfully. "With the disappearance of general patterns of conduct, the power to depict action that is both single and complete also disappears . . . the dramatic lyric is a fragment of a total action which the poet lacks the means to sustain." (p. 364) Modern poetry lacks *form*, in the larger sense in which Mr. Tate uses the term: "form is meaning and nothing but meaning: scheme of reference, supporting symbolism that ceases to support as soon as it is recognized as merely that." (p. 240) "In ages weak in form, such as our own age, theory will concentrate upon form, but practice upon the ultimate possibilities of language." (p. 239)[3] Our criticism, he remarks, is better than our poetry; the Elizabethans, in contrast, "wrote better than they knew." Having form in poetry, they concentrated in their (rudimentary) criticism upon propriety in language; we, lacking form, concern ourselves with it in criticism, but in poetry we try to compensate for deficiency in form by forcing language beyond its natural limits. The degeneration of public language provides further incentive for specialization of language: "today many poets are driven to inventing private languages, or very narrow ones, because public speech has become heavily tainted with mass feeling." (p. 76) Modern poets, because the Nineteenth Century used subject-matter badly, tend to be afraid of it and to try to do without it completely ("Poetry and the Absolute"). With the loss of tradition, of a common center of experience, specialization thus supplants a central view of life, and poetry becomes specialized aesthetic effects without formal limitations; distinctions of *genres* disappear; the arts tend to become geometrical and abstract. The novel, least formal of the arts, takes the place of epic and tragedy; lacking formal limitations and appealing to the ordinary sense of reality, it drives out the formal arts. The great problem of the modern poet is (since no substitute is ultimately satisfactory) to find a central source of form; and only Yeats, in Mr. Tate's view, has had much success in solving the problem. As John Peale Bishop represents, for Mr. Tate, the unsuccessful search for form, Hart Crane is the symbol of our spiritual life; his poetry "reveals our defects in their extremity." (p. 235) Crane ends the romantic era; by "attempting an extreme solution of the romantic problem Crane proved that it cannot be solved." (p. 237) He represents the narcissistic sensibility divorced from intelligence, relying upon "the intensity of consciousness, rather than the clarity, for his center of vision." This dissociation, because of our lack of an objective system of truth, a myth, a tradition, is characteristic of modern poets generally. (Again, Mr. Tate excepts Yeats, whom he seems to regard as a conspicuous exception to literary determinism, a great poet in spite of the defects of his age.)

Defending modern poetry against the charge of "difficulty," Mr.

[3] In his recent essay on Longinus *(Hudson Review,* Autumn 1948) Mr. Tate seems to abandon this distinction: modern criticism, he says, approaches form through the analysis of language (pp. 349, 354).

Tate asserts in one magnificent counterblast that the fault is not in the poetry, but entirely in the readers. The villain is Positivism, which, through modern education, has taught us that poetry is purely emotional; that reading, and education, are passive conditioning; that there is no such thing as intelligence or cognition. We are incapable of understanding *any* genuine poetry, not merely modern poetry: "If we wish to understand anything, there is only the hard way . . . we had better begin, young, to read the classical languages, and a little later the philosophers." (p. 128) In a more temperate discussion, he distinguishes two types of misguided readers: the innocent reader, who lives in the past, and the social reader, who lives in the future; both have their heads buzzing "with generalizations that they expect the poet to confirm—so that they will not have to notice the poetry. It is a service that the modern poet, no less amiable than his forbears, is not ready to perform; there is no large scheme of imaginative reference in which he has confidence." (p. xv) Loss of tradition makes modern poetry available to a more restricted group than was poetry of the past; only to the proper reader, "the critical reader," who is aware of the present, not in terms of abstractions, but of experience. Mr. Tate's considered judgment seems to be that the difficulty of modern poetry, as well as its grave limitations and deficiencies, is real, but that it is the result of historical circumstances for which the poets are not responsible and which they cannot escape. The implied moral is that if we do not approve of the poetry, we must change the society that made it what it is.

IV

Because Mr. Tate's criticism is intended as a corrective, a "reaction," and not as self-sufficient, many of his specific ideas and interpretations appear over-simplified or extreme when taken out of their controversial context. My concern has been, not to dispute any such matters, but to determine, as precisely as possible, just what Mr. Tate's essential position is. I do not know how completely these essays represent Mr. Tate's own philosophy; but they seem to reveal a fundamental inconsistency.[4]

[4] *Invitation to Learning*, radio broadcasts by Tate, Cairns, and Van Doren (Random House, 1941) presents Mr. Tate's comments on a wide range of subjects; but he suggests in it no solution to the difficulties with which I am concerned.

Unable to accept religion (but convinced of its necessity), Mr. Tate is driven to set up art and traditional society (or the moral unity to be attained within it) as absolutes; the two agree imperfectly, and are unreconciled. Mr. Tate's literary criterion is a rigorous one: most poetry lacks absolutism, and he is therefore occupied most of the time with explaining the failure of poetry in terms of its relation to society. Being a poet, he wishes to defend modern poetry (and the poetry of the past which is most like modern poetry); yet, largely on the evidence of the poetry, he condemns the society; and this dual purpose produces further ambiguities. Mr. Tate would probably say that only a Positivist would look to a literary critic for philosophy, and I hope that I have not appeared to do so; my point is only that the criticism would be more effective if the central ideas were clarified. Mr. Tate, who exhibits himself the self-knowledge he recommends, is aware that theorizing is not his *forte*; he omits from this collection the essays that deal most systematically with general ideas. I do not mean for a moment to suggest that Mr. Tate should set up as aesthetician or philosopher, instead of continuing to do what he does so admirably; but I think that we need desperately, at this stage of our criticism, a satisfactory general theory. Even Mr. Tate's inconsistencies, however, are valuable; because of his honesty and refusal to compromise, they reveal "our defects in their extremity."

Mr. Tate's character as critic may be illustrated by a brief comparison to other critics.[5] He is much like Yeats—from whom, apparently, he takes the key terms *abstraction* and *unity of being*—in his bitter hatred of science, which deprives him of religious faith; like Yeats, he undertakes his social and philosophical analysis with a motivation which I take to be basically aesthetic. Mr. Tate's general ideas, literary and social, are most like those of T. S. Eliot; the chief difference is that Mr. Eliot puts the position into explicitly religious terms and that his standard of values is therefore definite and unambiguous. Yvor Winters, like Mr. Tate, upholds a position ultimately religious without religious sanction, but otherwise there is little similarity. Mr. Tate is less rigid than Mr. Winters in literary judgment; he does not expect perfection, nor criticize in terms of what *ought* to have been done (cf.

[5] For an excellent account of Mr. Tate's relationship to other modern critics, see R. W. Stallman's "The New Criticism and the Southern Critics," in *A Southern Vanguard*, ed. Tate (Prentice-Hall, 1947).

pp. 176–7). Mr. Winters is, of course, a moralist; and he regards action, conduct, as the goal; Mr. Tate exhibits on occasion an aristocratic contempt for the merely ethical. There is a strong Aristotelian element in Mr. Tate's whole philosophy: the highest good is the contemplation of absolute truth (for Mr. Tate, art), while practical ethics belongs to a lower realm (cf. the rejection of Babbitt's "war in the cave," *Reactionary Essays*, pp. 122–4); in aesthetic theory, *catharsis* and *mimesis* can be detected; and Mr. Tate's mind seems to work in terms of extremes vs. the mean (e.g., the two half religions vs. genuine religion; poetry of positive and negative Platonism vs. that of the center; poetry of extension and intension vs. that of tension; the innocent and social reader vs. the critical). In this emphasis on contemplation, not ethics, as the sphere of art, Mr. Tate is like Mr. Ransom, as also in the concept of poetry as knowledge. Mr. Ransom, however, is not so violently reacting against Positivism; his structure-texture formulation and many other aspects of his criticism are unlike Mr. Tate. Cleanth Brooks has tried to develop a critical theory similar to Mr. Tate's into a positive system; but it seems to me that one result of his excellent work has been to reveal certain contradictions more explicitly: for example, while maintaining the same kind of "historical fatality" in the relation of literature to society, he holds that contemporary literature is, without qualification, great, while the society is bad.

I do not wish to suggest that Mr. Tate's deficiencies in theory and logical inconsistencies (those I have pointed out; my interpretation cannot be entirely correct, and there may not be as many as I think) invalidate his criticism; many values, and those not the least important, are not dependent primarily on theory. In conclusion, I shall summarize what I take to be the chief permanent values of Mr. Tate's criticism. First, the essays aid one to understand Mr. Tate's own poetry: not only do they define the kind of poetry he is trying to write, but they state explicitly most of the ideas and attitudes found in the poems. And Mr. Tate's poetry is so fine that this use alone would justify the essays (though I doubt that Mr. Tate would entirely approve). Second, the prose exhibits the same gift of language that distinguishes the poetry—the same concentration, imaginative power, boldness combined with restraint. Mr. Tate can sum up a whole indictment, a whole philosophy, in a sardonic sentence or a vivid metaphor. Yet the style is refreshingly simple and unpretentious, for he holds the sensible view that "critical style ought to be as plain as the nose on one's face; that it ought not to compete in the detail of sensibility with the work which it is privileged to report on." (p. x) Third, in the realm of ideas, his conception of history—the contrast of the traditional religious imagination which sees the past as temporal and concrete with the modern historical method which sees it as abstract and detemporalized—is, with its corollaries and accompanying insights, his most important contribution. The bold simplification of reducing the enemy to Positivism, which is traced through its multiple metamorphoses, and the conception of poetry as the absolute, are (whatever the difficulties involved) effective and valuable formulations. Finally, Mr. Tate's greatest virtue is one I have had almost wholly to leave out of account in this review. His analyses of specific poems are masterly: their most remarkable feature is that they stress heavily the element of meter, rhythm, music, which most critics tend to neglect; Mr. Tate relates this element to the whole meaning and effect of the poem, and discusses it with an intelligence and sensitivity that are, as far as I know, unique. In reviewing contemporary poets Mr. Tate is free of the note of envy or malice which so often mars reviews of poets by poets; he does not reduce his critical apparatus to a formula, as even such excellent critics as Ransom, Brooks, and Winters tend, in varying degrees, to do. These reviews, generous yet just and penetrating, are perhaps the soundest judgments we have; their only defect is a tendency to blame the society for all the faults of the poetry, and that is a defect compounded of generosity and polemic intent.

The final impression this book leaves is one of admiration for Mr. Tate's independence and common sense and avoidance of cant; for his stubborn honesty and candor; his ideal of poise, integrity, and intelligence.

Allen Tate as Man of Letters

by ELISEO VIVAS

The man of letters," a phrase frequently employed by Allen Tate, gives us, I believe, the key to his criticism. The phrase seems obsolescent, but I take it that it has been commonly used in English in the past. Nor can any one claim for it a special force or expressiveness. Again, one might too easily dispose of Mr. Tate's fondness for it by reference to his evidently lively interest in things French, since it is in current use in France; but this fact, although true, does not account for the frequency with which we encounter it in his prose. In any case, its ordinary use in French or English is as a synonym for "writer" or "literary man" or "scholar." But for Mr. Tate the man of letters has a responsibility and a dignity that we do not ordinarily associate with the activities of the writer. And in spite of our critic's instinctive modesty and courtesy, it is not difficult to perceive that he thinks of himself as a man of letters. For this reason, the phrase serves as an index of the seriousness with which Mr. Tate takes his profession; and when we consider it in conjunction with the judgment he passes on the modern world, it also gives us the measure of the desperate courage that is required of a man who makes of the profession of letters the demands Mr. Tate does. This in turn gives us the measure of his stature and the means to define his place in contemporary literature.

What does the activity of the man of letters consist of? In the first essay of his last book, entitled "The Man of Letters in the Modern World," we are given the answer to our question. Our author suggests

EDITOR'S NOTE: Reprinted from *Creation and Discovery* by Eliseo Vivas (Chicago: Henry Regnery Co., 1966), pp. 267–81, by permission of the author and publisher. First appeared in *The Sewanee Review*, 62:131–43 (Winter 1954).

that we define the man of letters by what we need him to do. His immediate responsibility, "at our own critical moment," is for the vitality
of language. It is his task to distinguish the difference between mere
communication and the rediscovery of the human condition in the
living arts. This responsibility puts on the man of letters the burden
of inventing standards by which this difference may be known and a
sufficient minority of persons may be instructed. It ought to be clear
from this succinct statement alone that Allen Tate is going far beyond
what T. S. Eliot conceives to be the task of the poet. For Eliot would
have it that the duty of the poet is to preserve and develop the language. But both preservation and development are for Eliot controlled
by the need for expression, through the objective correlative, of feelings and emotions. Even when Mr. Tate conceives the immediate task
of the man of letters at our own critical moment, he is thinking of
that task in objective and not in subjective terms. Sentiments and emotions are no doubt important constituents of the world in which we
live, but they cannot give us the key to the whole.

The restricted "immediate responsibility" of the man of letters is
conceived by our critic in the context of a larger and more permanent
responsibility which is defined by him as follows: The man of letters
"must create for his age an image of man, and he must propagate standards by which other men may test that image, and distinguish the
false from the true." What Mr. Tate is saying is something that other
peoples at other times have known, but that we denizens of a positivistic world have chosen to forget—that the poet is the "seer." I ought
to warn the reader, however, that the word "seer" is mine and not the
author's. I am reasonably certain that he would not risk its use for
many reasons but chiefly, perhaps, because it carries with it all sorts
of absurd associations for the contemporary mind. A man of letters is
a "seer" but he is not one possessed, he is not an undisciplined mad-
man who allows the Muse or the Holy Spirit to speak through him.
But while disciplined, he is not "a specialist" in language, although
he is an expert in its use; he does not compete with Jespersen or Sapir;
he may know little of the mutations of English from Bede to Shakespeare, or of the difference between the structural devices of Chinook
and those of Papiamento; he may find Bloomfield and Sturtevant unre-
warding reading, and Mario Pei and H. L. Mencken only amusing.
One thing is fairly certain: he distrusts the relativistic attitude towards

grammar which seems to be the foundation of the so-called science of linguistics. And, what will be most astonishing to contemporary prejudice, his primary interest is not in language as a means of "communication"; he uses it primarily for the purposes of "communion"—a word which, no doubt, has an obscene connotation to the congenitally positivistic modern mind, but which Mr. Tate does not hesitate to employ. In the essay already referred to, he tells us that "literature has never communicated . . . it cannot *communicate*. . . . Our unexamined theory of literature as communication could not have appeared in an age in which communion was still possible for any appreciable majority of persons. The word communication presupposes the victory of the secularized society of means without ends. The poet, on the one hand, shouts to the public, on the other (some distance away), not the rediscovery of the common experience, but a certain pitch of sound to which the well-conditioned adrenals of humanity obligingly respond."

Because the man of letters seeks primarily to participate in "communion" he must take seriously the discipline of rhetoric. But here again the word is apt to be misleading; for as used by the writer, it is not intended to designate the activity of the rabble rouser or the man who has no argument and must therefore fall back on the naked appeal to passion and thoughtless prejudice, nor does it designate the activity of the mere lover of words. It refers to the activity which Professor Richard Weaver has recently defined in his important book, *The Ethics of Rhetoric*. In the essay entitled, "Is Literary Criticism Possible," we are told by Mr. Tate that rhetoric is "the study and the use of the figurative language of experience as the discipline by means of which men govern their relations with one another in the light of truth. Rhetoric presupposes the study of two prior disciplines, grammar and logic, neither of which is much pursued today, except by specialists." He goes on to assert that grammar is an essential instrument to the man who would employ language in order to participate in communion, since it makes possible the definition of the fundamentals of understanding. It does this because "all reading is translation, even in the native tongue; for translation may be described as the tact of mediation between universals and particulars in the complex of metaphor." This is an art no longer taught. For the scientific linguist language is as language does, and what it does is what men do with it and to it. In an equalitarian society, in respect to intelligence and culture all men are equal and no one can be more equal than another. Therefore the most illiterate and insensitive unskilled laborer, whose linguistic requirements are defined by the most elementary functions of social life, has as much of a right to do with and to language what he damn pleases as the next guy even if the next guy happens to be a Henry James, a T. S. Eliot or a D. H. Lawrence.

As to logic, teachers of philosophy will probably disagree with Mr. Tate. He tells us that neither grammar nor logic is any longer a prerequisite to the study of philosophy, and he seems to offer as evidence that an "Eastern university offers a grandiose course in Greek philosophical ideas to sophomores who will never know a syllogism from a handsaw." Professional philosophers will answer, and not without some specious force, that our critic seems to have generalized from an atypical instance. They may even call attention to a fact that I believe it would be difficult to deny: that the area of contemporary philosophy in which probably most creative energy is at the moment being spent and with most significant results, is logic. But Mr. Tate is nevertheless right. "Everybody knows," he tells us, "that modern philosophers, like their brother scientists, and not unlike their distant cousins the poets, are pursuing specialisms of various kinds." What goes by the name of logic today is not a discipline that can be used by the rhetor; it is an autotelic discipline cultivated by a small group of esoteric specialists who can no longer talk to one another in ordinary language, but who communicate among themselves in a script full of wiggles and waggles, with little relevance to the world of affairs.

If this is how Mr. Tate conceives the task of the man of letters I do not believe it would take much argument to demonstrate that what he is expected to do today, as things are for us, at our critical moment, is a desperately quixotic and probably anachronistic service.

But does not its anachronistic nature make it false? Let us hear the positivist's side. There might have been a time, the positivist will begin, when there was need for the poet's image of man; but there no longer is. We no more need poets today than we need medicine men. Surely Mr. Tate will not deny that whatever truth there may be in the images of man given us by the poets, their picture is ambiguous, incoherent and unverifiable, whereas the knowledge given us by the sciences is systematic, corrigible and universal? This is precisely what

our author denies. Whatever contribution the sciences may make
towards our knowledge of man, it is to the poet, Mr. Tate answers, that
we must go for *the complete* truth about man. The scientist may be
able to tell us what man does and what he can do, but he cannot
evaluate man's actions and elucidate the nature of his norms, and a
picture of man that leaves out this aspect of his nature is a sadly incomplete and relatively trivial picture. This issue is not one that can be
settled or even adequately defined in a review of a book on literary
criticism. But short of a complete discussion of it, there is an answer
that a man like Tate can give the positivist. It runs something like
this: Although positivists have not systematically developed their philosophy of history and some of them will even deny the validity of
such a discipline, in men like Dewey and Randall and even Reichen-
bach we find some of its basic assumptions fairly clearly delineated.
According to what is its most important tenet for our purposes, the
new age, whether we date it from Copernicus, Galileo, Darwin or
Freud-Ford, is distinguished from the pre-scientific past by the fact
that we have finally removed the practical and theoretical obstacles
that prevented the full and consistent application of the method of
science to the problems of men. Mr. Tate also believes that there is a
difference between the new age and the old. On the basis of this agreement he answers the positivist that the image the man of letters gives
us is not an objective image—if by "objective" be meant the value-free
statistical picture of man which it has been the ideal of the social sciences to obtain, and which still largely predominates. What the man
of letters can and ought to give us is a picture forged in his "conscience," in the French sense of this word: an image forged through
the joint action of knowledge and judgment. And he explains: "This
conscience has long known a severe tradition of propriety in discerning
the poet's particular kind of actuality. No crisis, however dire, should
be allowed to convince us that the relation of the poet to his permanent reality can ever change. And thus the poet is not responsible to
society for a version of what it thinks it is or what it wants. *For what
is the poet responsible?* He is responsible for the virtue proper to him
as poet, for his special *arête*: for the mastery of a disciplined language
which will not shun the full report of the reality conveyed to him by
his awareness: he must hold, in Yeats' great phrase, 'reality and justice
in a single thought.'"

Thus, in the final analysis, the heart of the quarrel between men like Tate and the positivists is as to the kind of world that ought to be created: our critic wants a world which will allow us in some measure at least to realize our human destiny; the positivists want the one which is already half born, the louring world of 1984 and beyond it (for the kind of hell we are in for cannot last forever) the worse hell of 632 A.F. In this brave new world of science and of pleasure humanity is not destroyed by forced labor in the frozen tundras of Siberia; it is destroyed by something worse: the social engineer painlessly performs a lobotomy on it and destroys its soul. Otherwise stated, the image of man that is created by the man of letters is not one that can be used by men who are bent on building a secularized society, the *fourmillante cité*—the secularism of the swarm. Such a society, taking God to be a silly and burdensome superstition, will substitute the image of Man for His image and under the illusion of humanism will worship naked power. This is the society that we have already begun to rear on both sides of the Iron Curtain. And if we have not seen in our day what we may expect from it, we can find it vividly sketched for us in Dostoevski and in Huxley.

Several reasons have made me emphasize the philosophical assumptions which control Mr. Tate's criticism. The least important of these is that he has been identified, of course correctly, with the so-called "new critics." And they are in turn assumed to be formalists, because they insist that the substance of a literary work is to be found by reference not to something outside itself but to something to be discovered in it. Yet there is a sense in which, in Mr. Tate's words, "the great formal works of literature are not wholly autonomous," and in which, therefore, the criticism which would make them available must be less autonomous than they. Adapting to our purposes of the moment a phrase of our author, he is a critic who is concerned with literary questions but who, in order to be effectively literary, must be more than literary.

There is a second reason for emphasizing the assumptions of Mr. Tate's criticism. I fear that unless we grasp them firmly and read him with them explicitly in mind we are apt to encounter certain incoherences and opacities in his writing that are extremely puzzling. These disappear when we read them in the light of his philosophical assumptions. Thus, one is puzzled by what seems to be a lack of consistency

in the writer's conception of the role of the man of letters. In the first
essay he recommends that the man of letters participate fully in the
action of society, and in the second, entitled "To Whom is the Poet
Responsible?" we are told that the poet has no business gadding about
"using the rumor of his verse to appear on platforms and view with
alarm." There is no contradiction if we see that Mr. Tate puts on the
man of letters a heavy social burden—that of giving us an image of
man—but that he also holds that this task cannot be accomplished
unless the poet undertakes it as poet and not as statesman or political
agitator. But there is a third and a most important reason for emphasizing the assumptions on which Mr. Tate's criticism is grounded:
unless we grasp these assumptions and perceive how they guide the
direction of his criticism and inform his actual discriminations, we
cannot appreciate correctly the uniqueness of Mr. Tate's position in
contemporary criticism.

Ours, it has been frequently observed, is an age of criticism. Our
critics are, one and all, endowed with considerable talent. And they
have added to this talent wondrous skills to achieve brilliant discriminations; they are endowed with subtle tools of analysis, they have at
their command the insights of the sciences and the pseudosciences of
today, and those who are put through the academic processing machinery—and most of them are in an age in which education is universal—
possess more than enough historical erudition for their purposes. But
it must also be observed that our critics are for the most part philosophically pauperized and are, hence, devoid of a coherent sense of
the place of man in society, the place of society in history, and the
relation of history to the universe. It is no wonder, therefore, that they
should have only the most trivial notions of the use of literature. One
school of critics, whose ponderous equipment of antiquated theory
rumbles over the literary landscape with the terrible noise of a thousand panzers, tells us, in all seriousness, that literature has as its end
pleasure produced through the play on the emotions. Another critic
tells us that the end of literature is not to give us truth, which is given
to us by science, but to give us "pure experience." How experience
without content is distinguished from the works produced by the emotional engineers of the Brave New World this critic forgets to inform
us. Another tells us that the end of literature is to organize our attitudes. And thus if our critics do not give us the stale vulgarities of

hedonism they give us the no less stale vulgarities of therapy. And so on down the dismal catalogue. None of these critics ask of themselves the simple question: How does it happen that art, that seems to be, and in a sense is, the most expendable of activities in human society, is one of the two most ineradicable, most indispensable modes of experience? Our critics cannot ask this question because, for the most part, they work in a philosophical vacuum. And they do because they lack a guiding body of convictions—of *prejudices*, in Edmund Burke's sense of the word—with reference to which the work of art is seen as an indispensable and unsubstitutable factor in the creation and maintenance of the human element in the animal, man.

It is ironic, but it is sadly true, that the only body of men in our day who have had a consistently serious sense of the importance of literature are the very men who in their hearts least of all care for it —the Marxists. Their materialism makes them as blind as the hedonists and the Freudians to the manner in which art actually functions in society; but at least they do not offer us the vulgarities of the hedonists or of the therapists. In contrast with the Marxists, and of course allowing for exceptions, neither conservative nor liberal critics seem to have a sense of the way in which art affects the lives of men. And the reason is simply that they do not base their criticism, whether new or old, whether historical or non-historical, whether sociological or psychoanalytic, on a tenable notion of the destiny of man. If you press them, all they can give you is a more or less dressed-up version of man as an animal essentially motivated by the pleasure principle. The conservative critic may add a sentence or two of pious and tenuous talk about "spiritual values." But what is intended by this notion at bottom is "the higher pleasure": whereas certain Indians of Eastern Bolivia entertain themselves shrinking heads, it is through music, poetry, the theatre that we entertain ourselves if we are civilized. Thus we can expect no more of the conservative than we can of the liberal critics; both are essentially committed to the same secular image of man, and on such a basis anything else than hedonism is absurd. The differences between them consist only in how much pleasure we should allow ourselves, and at what cost. For such men the role of art in human life cannot be central. Philosophically, ours is a bankrupt generation.

In contrast Mr. Tate is saying that art is important because human life is not capable of achieving what virtue or perfection it may achieve unless it is guided by an effective notion of the destiny of man. The poet makes his essential and indispensable contribution when he gives us "the image of man as he is in his time, which without the man of letters would not otherwise be known." Thus it is not an exaggeration to say that our author's fundamental concern as a man of letters is with the values men live by and the ends they serve. In his essay on Dante, what he explicitly proposes to do is "to look at a single image in the *Paradiso* [the image of light], and to glance at some of its configurations with other images." But when Mr. Tate is through with his analysis what he has given us is a contrast between the medieval imagination, which does not try to transcend the mediation of image and discourse, and "the angelic imagination" which "tries to disintegrate or to circumvent the image in the illusory pursuit of essence." What is suggested is a conception of man and, in sketch at least, a philosophy of history. Because the writer's own words can not be improved on, it is desirable to quote a long passage:

The symbolic imagination takes rise from a definite limitation of human rationality which was recognized in the West until the 17th Century; in this view the intellect cannot have direct knowledge of essences. The only created mind that has this knowledge is the angelic mind. If we do not believe in angels we shall have to invent them in order to explain by parable the remarkable appearance, in Europe, at about the end of the 16th Century, of a mentality which denied man's commitment to the physical world, and set itself up in quasi-divine independence. This mind has intellect and will without feeling; and it is through feeling alone that we witness the glory of our servitude to the natural world, to St. Thomas' accidents, or, if you will, to Locke's secondary qualities; it is our tie with the world of sense. The angelic mind suffers none of the limitations of sense; it has immediate knowledge of essences; and this knowledge moves through the perfect will to divine love, with which it is at one. Imagination in an angel is thus inconceivable, for the angelic mind transcends the mediation of both image and discourse. I call that human imagination angelic which tries to disintegrate or to circumvent the image in the illusory pursuit of essence. When human beings undertake this ambitious program, divine love becomes so rarified that it loses its human paradigm, and is dissolved in the worship of intellectual power, the surrogate of divinity that worships itself. It professes to know nature as essence at the same time that it has become alienated from nature in the rejection of its material forms.

This is also the theme of the two essays on Poe. In the first essay the writer demonstrates that Poe possessed the angelic imagination and used it without qualms and for this reason Poe is "the transition figure in modern literature," since he is the man who discovered our great subject, "the disintegration of personality, but kept it in a language that had developed in a tradition of unity and order." In the second essay, Mr. Tate makes clear why he is fascinated by this man of the nineteenth century. He writes, "in the history of the moral imagination in the nineteenth century Poe occupies a special place. No other writer in England or the United States, or, so far as I know, in France, went so far as Poe in his vision of dehumanized man."

One can disagree with Mr. Tate as regards details, and I shall do so presently. But I do not believe the reflective man can disagree with him as regards the substance of the issue. There are, in this quarrel, three possible positions. One can look forward to a totally secularized future, made glorious by science as it extends its sway; one can, with our author, look back on a past in which men, for all their sins, never seriously proposed a purely secular conception of human destiny; or one can deny these alternatives on the ground that the more things change the more they are the same. I take it that this denial of the alternatives is given the lie by the facts and that the disagreement between Mr. Tate and the positivists is as to the proper evaluation of the facts and what they seem to portend. Science has indeed made a difference: it has encouraged a swarm of false philosophies which claim its authority and whose business is to destroy the once solid metaphysics in the light of which we defined our destiny. It is not claimed, of course, that a single system of philosophy enjoyed uncontested supremacy in the history of the West. There has always been strife of systems, and this is a fortunate condition. But Dewey is right when he finds shared assumptions among warring systems in traditional philosophy, although we need not accept his own formulation of what these assumptions are. It becomes more and more clear that the positivist mind—whether in its logical empiricist variety, or its scientific humanist or its Marxist forms, whether represented by the vacuous rationality of a Carnap or an Ayer, or the vulgar hedonistic secularism of the Deweyans, or the threat-filled dialectic of the commissars—will do its termite work, and there is precious little that anyone can do to stop it from destroying our culture. I suspect that the muffled despair the reader discerns below the surface of Mr. Tate's essays springs from the fact that he knows that the things he loves are doomed. But Mr. Tate is no man to take the threat lying down. Informing his criticism and giving it remarkable consistency and force, is his protest against the meaning of the present and of the probable future.

I have to express disagreement with Mr. Tate, however, on a question of historical interpretation. Following Maritain, our critic traces to Descartes man's usurpation of the angelic imagination. It seems to me that this is to credit a philosopher with far more power than any one man, even a Descartes, could possibly have wielded. Descartes was not possible without conditions of an extremely complex nature which existed prior to his advent. In history we do not have parthenogenetic spontaneity. How far back we are going to go and to what factors we are going to trace the beginning of the difficulties which are Mr. Tate's basic theme, we need not decide here; but if we are to seek for them in the realms of intellectual history exclusively and not in the heterogeneous process of the whole of history, intellectual and material, it would be more exact to trace it, I suspect, to the Oxford Franciscans of the 13th Century than to Descartes. For it was these men who began the arduous preparation of the ground for the complex intellectual movements which according to Maritain, Descartes initiated. This movement was made possible by the work of men like Grosseteste, Thomas of York, Roger Bacon, and their followers and it leads to Descartes because it leads to the great age of science. To trace it to these men, be it noted, is not to allocate "blame." The men who in the 13th Century laid the ground for the scientific upsurge of the 16th and 17th Centuries were not "radicals" trying to destroy the world in which they lived. They were men honestly trying to expand the range of knowledge. Descartes was doing something more complex and more urgent: he was trying to harmonize two constellations of values that at the moment seemed to be in conflict and neither of which could be overlooked or denied. The Cartesian synthesis may not have been satisfactory to the reigning orthodoxy, but what the latter proposed was neither valid nor acceptable. It is in this respect that the great work of Descartes—with all its seeds for good *and* evil—must be appreciated in order not to confuse it with the work of positivists, who under the pretense of being pure knowers bore like termites at the foundations of our culture. If we blame Descartes because he made possible the usurpation of the angelic imagination, we suggest that the 17th Century could have provided for the development of science and yet maintained the values of the spirit in some other way than by the Cartesian synthesis. But what alternatives were there? A decadent scholasticism that had already lost all power over the creative minds of the century and a renascent materialism of which Hobbes was the most distinguished representative. But the Englishman was the positivist of his age—in the sense that he was a man endowed with a singularly powerful mind but who lacked almost completely an empirical and, for all his interest in literature and history, a genuinely humane grasp of the actual complex moral and religious problems of his age. If therefore the Cartesian dichotomy led to consequences from which we are suffering, suffer them we must, for there was nothing else that Descartes' contemporaries could have done but accept his views.

But my quarrel with Mr. Tate is after all a minor one—a question for erudites, as we say in Spanish. When Mr. Tate speaks of Descartes, I suspect that he is using names in the same manner I do, as convenient metaphors ready at hand that are (in language that Mr. Tate has as little use for as I have) "iconic" of the complex movements that they denote. For the disintegration of the modern personality was not the work of one man or of many, nor was it the work of philosophers or scientists or stupid statesmen—although all of them and all of us share in the responsibility for it. Helpful, therefore, and on certain occasions unavoidable, they are inexcusable when we take them as an adequate report of the historical reality. History is not the work of men but of Man, the creature whom we write with a capital "M"—the animal that stumbles through time from one stupidity into another, the angelic beast or the bestial angel, the inhabitant of the city of Man and not of the City of God, who in the pursuit of truth falls into error, in the search for virtue embraces sin, in the lust for happiness is led to misery, and in the search for God often runs into the Devil's arms. If there is one thing even more false than the belief in progress it is the belief in progress in reverse. Mr. Tate is philosophically too shrewd to make such a mistake. He is not a pure philosopher; he is a man endowed with a philosophic instinct (if I may so call it) that ought to be trusted more than the skill of the pure philosopher. The latter, the man who posits a factitious clarity as the exclusive end of his activity, is a fool who has not taken the first step on the road to wisdom and does not know that a man ought not to take his "ideas" too seriously. I take it therefore that when Tate speaks of "Descartes" he means "Descartes, the man and the icon," by which is in turn meant, "Descartes and those complex factors, whatever they happen to be, which made Descartes possible, and that are, therefore, back of the phenomena which, as literary critic, I am interested in." And I am not guessing that this is what the author means. In one of his most impressive pieces, the essay on "Ezra Pound and the Bollingen Prize," Mr. Tate reminds us that in "literature as in life nothing reaches us pure." And he continues, "the task of the civilized intelligence is one of perpetual salvage." This was the task that Descartes attempted, and if today Mr. Tate traces the usurpation of the angelic imagination to the Frenchman, we must read him in the light of the fact that he knows that in philosophy as in life nothing reaches us absolutely pure.

It would be interesting to look at each of the other essays that compose this volume and to show how each discloses its center of gravity, so to speak, when we appraise it in view of Mr. Tate's conception of man and of his philosophy of history. But to go through each of them picking out their virtues and summarizing their contents is to deprive the reader of the pleasure and profit he should have at first hand. Instead of attempting to deprive the reader of what ought to be his pleasure and profit, let me in closing pose the question that has intrigued me from the moment I unwrapped the book and looked at its title. Why *The Forlorn Demon?* The ambiguity is rich and it repays notice, I believe, for it throws some light on the complexity of Mr. Tate's central problem. Mr. Tate credits Poe with the phrase. But he does not tell us exactly why he chose the title. I am venturing a guess and it is altogether possible that my remarks will seem absurd and even impertinent. In one sense, I suggest, "the forlorn demon" is the modern man of letters, doomed to inhabit Baudelaire's *fourmillante cité*. He is a demon because he has aspired to become an angel, and by doing so plunged himself into hell. But the title suggests another interpretation, according to which the demon is now the Socratic

daimon, who is forlorn because we citizens of the swarming secularized
city of today disregarded his prohibition and attempted to do something we have no business attempting. The demon is forlorn because
in disregarding his prohibition we have betrayed ourselves and thus
betrayed him.

San Giovanni in Venere:
Allen Tate as Man of Letters

by R. P. BLACKMUR

Geoffrey Scott, at the end of his *Architecture of Humanism,* writes
of the church of San Giovanni in Venere—a very old church
indeed which still stands in the Abruzzi, deserted but a monument, "The Baptist lodged with Venus." In a footnote, Scott says that
"The structure is Romanesque, the name more ancient still; but not
until the Renaissance can its patrons have achieved their perfect recon-
ciliation, which now the browsing goats do not disturb." And in his
text he has this image: "Virgil attends on Dante, and St. John, in the
solitude of the Adriatic shrine he shares with Venus, may ponder if
ascetic energy is not best mated with classical repose. The architecture
of humanism has on its side the old world and the new; it has this
repose and this energy." The reader who cannot browse with the goats
of Fossacesia and is not content with the photographs in the Abruzzi

EDITOR'S NOTE: Reprinted from *The Sewanee Review,* 67:614–31 (Autumn 1959), copyright © 1959 by The University of the South, by permission of Joseph Frank and the
publisher.

volume of *Attraverso L'Italia,* will perhaps browse even better on the
longest slopes of his own mind. There is an image here for the human
reticulation of art, life, and religion. If one meditates one sees and is
sometimes able to say what literature is all about. As Scott observes,
"Every art that finds a penetrating pathway to the mind, and whose
foundations are profoundly set, must needs have precedent and parallel, ancestors and heirs." But my reason for setting this image of St.
John in the arms of Venus and making these quotations from Scott,
is that they make a good shadow and a good light in which to see the
occupation of the man of letters. We see under what impulse he admin-
isters and reflects the world of letters in relation to the other human
affairs of the mind, and in certain individual men of letters it seems
the intermittent best animation which redeems the waste of drudgery
and the worse waste of polemic which every man of letters finds fills
his life. Allen Tate seems to me such a case.

If Mr. Tate does not object to such an alignment I hope he will not
object, either, if I put him for the sake of my own sense of immediate
history also in the company where so to speak I found him pretty continuously, and where everybody must sometimes have found him, over
the past thirty years, the company of Ivor Richards and John Crowe
Ransom. It is the company I have myself kept and it is a pleasure to
think of still doing so. One would like to think that it is the company
that makes the members human and their speech understandable of
each other by the wonderful force and virtuosity of presence: it is in
the *presence* of another that one follows the contours of his thought,
as the *Phaedrus* taught us long ago. But I should begin to dine on
reminiscence if I did not proceed to the less tipsy thoughts that get
turned into vocabulary. All three of our men of letters were faced with
what had happened in English to French symbolist poetry and to its
connections with modern technical society in a world which seemed
to have become less and less human. Let us remember only a little of
the vocabulary of reaction—what is contained even in the titles *Practical Criticism* and *The World's Body* and *Reactionary Essays.* Our
vocabularies are among our desperate inventions. Ransom invented
structures and textures, architectures and qualifications, and he did
so along the lines of that school of poets and readers of poetry who
were raising the reputation of John Donne, but he did so with a wider
and more cantankerous taste. It is interesting to see that when he

tackles Shakespeare's *Sonnets* and Milton's "Lycidas," the sonnets largely disappear because he has not the means in *his* structure and texture to get at what Shakespeare's structure and texture were *of*, while on the other hand "Lycidas" comes out, after a vast amount of argument, rather well. "Lycidas," of old poems, has the characteristic vices of modern poetry, and like them may be taken as virtues. The structure and texture afford the chief access to the private world of that poem. The different temperament of Tate—more active, more engaged, more cavalier—responded by inventing tension, or in-tension —the relation of stress between the halves of irony and paradox—the stress by which structure is united with texture. Similarly he has also opposed the committed operation of imagination to the operation of the unseated will, the action of the lyric to the asserted action of the allegory (though I doubt he would use now just this vocabulary for just this purpose, and I notice he does not reprint the essays where he made the original opposition). That is, he slew allegory of the kind he thought to be mechanical manipulation of figures, and raised pastoral (as Empson was also to do and as, in effect, Ransom had done in treating "Lycidas") and the pastoral he raised was the ambiguous allegory of the pastoral that suited his needs, as we see in his poem about Aeneas in Washington; it was the way that to him knowledge could enter poetry: the struggling morals of felt life.

Richards was dealing according to his training (as charged by his temperament, so much more hopeful, so much more immediately evangelical than either Ransom or Tate) in psychology and linguistic metaphysic with much the same problems. Out of the *Meaning of Meaning* and the International Library of Psychology, Philosophy and Scientific Method (a noble experiment which should be repeated in a new tone of rational scepticism) he invented the supreme difficulty, fascination, and necessity of reading. That is, he put himself deliberately into the destructive quarrel of the vocabularies where with the fanaticism which substitutes for vital difference people refuse all common ground because the words are different. Richards is the supreme methodologist, in the good and the bad sense, of the situation of the loss of unconscious skills in the use of words which constitutes the new illiteracy. His counsel of desperation was the Basic English which would debase us all until we could rebuild our vocabularies. But to him, always, words were real things (both primed and stuffed with unconscious skills, with the *presence* of thought) and poetry the fullest form for reality. And so on.

What have these critics in common?—an ancestry in art for art, belief in the independence, or autotelism, or the absolute sovereignty of poetry, as these may be taken to agree as well as to conflict; with a distrust of rationality as the cumulus and discrimination of skills, and a tendency to make the analyzable features of the forms and techniques of poetry both the means of access to poetry and somehow the equivalent of its content. None of them would admit this as conviction or purpose and each of them would fight it; yet this is how they write when they write well, though each with a different addition, and each with a different flare for the fling of reality and the flash of the actual to hand and eye. One thinks of Goethe in their context. "One should explore the explorable and calmly worship the Inexplorable."

But there is more to say, and two little passages from the last pages of Richards's *Science and Poetry* may serve as texts for departure. "The necessity for independence [from beliefs] is increasing. This is not to say that traditional poetry, into which beliefs readily enter, is becoming obsolete; it is merely becoming more and more difficult to approach without confusion; it demands a greater imaginative effort, a greater purity in the reader." That is one passage; here is the other. "A poet today, whose integrity is equal to that of the greater poets of the past, is inevitably plagued by the problem of thought and feeling as poets have never been plagued before." These are relatively early statements (1926), and if Richards made them now it would not be in the same form and they would take a different emphasis. They were made from the curiously neutral position that "science" was able to take in those days: a neutrality in which conviction and belief, will and choice, were thought of as getting in the way of action and enjoyment, and required, for vitality, to be transformed into some other kind of knowledge, free of beliefs and impervious to the assaults of psychology: some other kind of knowledge which, for some, poetry stood ready to supply.

Richards, in 1926, followed Arnold explicitly, both in his epigraph which quotes one of Arnold's paragraphs about poetry replacing religion, and in his own last sentences. If psychology should win, he writes, "a mental chaos such as man has never experienced may be expected. We shall then be thrown back, as Matthew Arnold foresaw, upon poetry. It is capable of saving us; it is a perfectly possible means

of overcoming chaos. But whether he can loosen in time the entanglement with belief which now takes from poetry half its power and
would then take all, is another question, and too large for the scope
of this essay." Richards has largely occupied the rest of his life with
this problem of re-orientation, of the disentanglement of belief from
poetry. He has been chief public relations officer in the whole program
of saving man by poetry. Poetry to him is language, the highest form
of language, and language is the medium for communicating, expressing,
representing knowledge. This is an old idea; it is what individuals
have done with poetry when they loved it, and the worst poetry lovers
have done it most, but collectively it has not been done except for
entertainment or ritual or magic or hocus-pocus. Sir Winston Church-
ill, President Conant, and the Rockefeller Foundation for a long time
stood behind Richards, and it is not immediately clear that these institutions are likely to support anything we mean by poetry, or at any
rate poetry as such. I suspect that poetry was assigned a new content
in this program, which is much more likely than that poetry itself
should have changed as radically as the program made out. The program looked as if the mental chaos Richards was afraid of had arrived,
the chaos in which salvation seems possible by a trick of learning.

There are kinder things to be said; here all that is wanted is to
lodge Richards firmly in the long train of criticism that believes culture to be breaking up and that believes poetry has thereby acquired
new and difficult social tasks. For Richards these new tasks had to do
with knowledge in the sense that science is knowledge. Poetry is the
science of those knowledges not properly in the physical and social
sciences, including especially some knowledge improperly claimed
by the social sciences: to wit, our knowledge of our own experience.
Poetry, said Richards, is "a means of ordering, controlling, and con-
solidating the whole experience." Thus the *command* of words is the
command of life; or at any rate the command of all that kind of life
of which the experience is its justification.

This is quite an extraordinary claim. Richards, loving poetry, made
it in this way because he was a direct product of Cambridge at the end
of the First War: he was full of biology, anthropology, and psychology,
those great underminers of belief, those great analyzers of experience.
Richards accepted the relative destruction of belief—or did accept it;

but insisted on the power of poetry to reorganize, without belief, and as self-justified, the experience belief found precious.

Tate and Ransom also made claims that poetry is knowledge, and made them partly, as Richards did, as a result of the assaults of science on belief. They lived in the same world and suffered the same monstrous growth of the possibility of consciousness without conscience. Both of them, also, came heavily under the influence of Richards's ideas and methods, which indeed had by 1925 become a part of the haze in any literary atmosphere, and both made considerable use of Richards's critical vocabulary. But they responded very differently to the complex of Richards and the times. I suppose at bottom it may be from differences of personality which are insoluble, but it is more interesting to think from that sense of controversial possibility which keeps the mind alive. Tate responded by keeping up a running battle this quarter century, until, behind and around doctrine, each so to speak capitulated to the common ground between them. It was a feather bed they had been wrestling with. Tate's battle was against the Richards ideas, against any ideas not found directly in poetry itself, and in the particular poem itself, and against any positive or organized theory of literature. In short, he made the argument that poetry should be used only as poetry—not as *pure* poetry but as the poetry of experience. What poetry did to experience was the criticism of life it afforded, for there is a *practik*, to use a word Tate later coined out of Aristotle's *praxis*, a substance of action at the heart of poetry. Ransom responded by adapting and transforming Richards's ideas and vocabularies for the examination of poetry to correspond to his own purpose of both directly examining poetry and relating that examination to a theory of poetry allied to one or another branch of systematic philosophy. Neither Tate nor Ransom has ever taken serious stock in Richards's dominant preoccupation with language—with the general problem of expression and communication in which poetry gives only the highest instances. Let us run over a few stages in these matters.

Tate very kindly stated his deliberate position in the title of one of his volumes of essays (indeed each of his titles states a position): *On the Limits of Poetry*. His essays make a series of opinions, organized (or I should rather say *composed*, for to compose an opinion is better than to organize it) as near as possible on the unconscious skills of the mind, about what happens, what actually gets into, poetry, and how it was treated after it got there. It is to these skills that Tate refers, I think, when he uses the phrase historical imagination. Otherwise he makes a series of attacks on people who handle poetry in other ways and for other purposes. Here Richards regularly turns up as the friendly enemy.

"For poetry does not explain our experience. If we begin by thinking that it ought to 'explain' the human predicament, we shall quickly see that it does not, and we shall end up thinking that therefore it has no meaning at all. That is what Mr. I. A. Richards' early theory comes to at last, and it is the first assumption of criticism today. But poetry is at once more modest and, in the great poets, more profound. It is the art of apprehending and concentrating our experience in the mysterious limitations of form." This was in 1936, and in the next paragraph he says it again. "Poetry is one test of ideas; it is ideas tested by experience." And here he is in 1940, when he characterizes *The Principles of Literary Criticism* in these words: "Literature is not really nonsense, it is in a special way a kind of science . . . a kind of applied psychology." He goes on that "there is the significant hocus-pocus of impulses, stimuli, and responses; there are even the elaborate charts of nerves and nerve-systems that purport to show how the 'stimuli' of poems elicit 'responses' in such a way as to 'organize our impulses' towards action; there is, throughout, the pretense that the study of poetry is at last a laboratory science. How the innocent young men— myself among them—thought, in 1924, that laboratory jargon meant laboratory demonstration!"

All that Tate forgets here is that Richards, too, in 1924, was an innocent young man; but what he remembers is much more important, that these ideas of the innocent early Richards which he attacks are the dominant ideas of a whole school of criticism—the school which works through the techniques of psychology on one hand and the techniques of the logical theories of signs on the other hand; and Tate himself handsomely recognizes that it is Richards who has slain the dragon of psychology and the worse dragon of semasiology or semiotics in his *Philosophy of Rhetoric* and his book on Coleridge—that is, if they are slain. Only the mind which has been through the temptation of the gross application of an idea where it is meaningless can come to reject it with force and persuasion. Tate had hardly felt the temptation, which may mark his limitation. Just the same, it is at the end of

his handsome gesture to Richards across the dinner table that he makes
some of his own finest remarks about poetry and its criticism: "If
rational inquiry is the only mode of criticism, we must yet remember
that the way we employ that mode must always powerfully affect *our*
experience of the poem. I have been concerned in this commentary
with the compulsive, almost obsessed, application of an all-engrossing
principle of pragmatic reduction to a formed realm of our experience,
the distinction of which is its complete knowledge, the full body of
the experience that it offers us. However we may see the completeness
of poetry, it is a problem less to be solved than, in its full import, to
be preserved." This is pretty packed. These are the limits Tate finds
in poetry. They are pretty pure, pretty independent, pretty free of the
entanglements of belief; and aside from that they are free of theorizing.
Richards and Tate eat one bread.

For this is the singular virtue of Tate that both in his verse and his
criticism his mind operates upon insight and observation as if all necessary theory had been received into his bones and blood before birth.
That is why what is controversial in him is so often a matter either of
temperament or temper, and there is a strength to his language superior to any ideas that may be detached from it. From this one virtue
stem his two talents as a critic: one, to see through or around or
beyond the methods of other critics into an image or insight (for an
insight is seen like an image, that it gives light) of what those methods
left out; two, when he is practising direct criticism, his extraordinary
skill, surpassed only by Eliot, at illuminating quotation, especially
those made for the purpose of exemplifying what he calls the tension
between the different elements in a poem. Anybody who writes poetry
will understand what he is up to, even if disagreeing; anybody who
does not write poetry will feel as if he did. Tate is the man who is concerned with poetry as it always was. His taste is deep; hence the love at
the bottom of his contentiousness.

Ransom is a different mind. He makes no running fight on Richards
but (in *The New Criticism*) makes rather a hundred-page essay,
which is in itself too long, but which shows Ransom coming to terms
with himself, and how he came to substitute his own texture and structure for Richards's tenor and vehicle. Structure is how you get there
and texture is what you do with it or how you stay there. The remain-

der of *The New Criticism* deals with Empson, Eliot as Historical critic, Winters as Logical critic, and ends with a plea for an Ontological critic along the lines of close analysis supported by the new logic of signs as illustrated in the work of Charles Morris of Chicago. The volume represents and composes a part of Ransom's education, and we can share it (since none of us has ever found out what education is except by exposure to it in the minds of others); it exhibits continuously the processes of digestion, but nowhere, except indirectly, the processes of judgment or elucidation. Elucidation and judgment are there, but for us to put together. How this would be we can see by turning again to his essay on "Lycidas," which he calls "A Poem Nearly Anonymous." I assume this essay is familiar enough to need no quotation.

You will observe that there are no statements of importance in it as to what "Lycidas" is about; only statements about formal aspects of structure and texture and formal names—such as "wit"—for the values to be found in the texture. There is no sense at all of that side of Milton which made the poet a builder of cities and maker of men or which made a good book the precious life blood of a master spirit. Nor is there any sense of the yoking together of violently contrasting themes. There is only a mention of *The Waste Land* as a poem comparable in our time to "Lycidas." This seems to be highly characteristic of the kind of criticism Ransom stands for and of the kind of philosophy—19th and 20th century—which bends its attention so almost exclusively to the problem of knowledge. Epistemology and ontology are the media through which Ransom experiences the problem of the relation between thought and feeling. Here once again is the solipsist trying to find out how he knows the only thing he can trust in the world he creates—the formal aspects in which it appears; but trying also to find some formal means, through the relation of texture to structure, of discussing the actual burden of knowledge as also a set of formal relations. Ontology is being: being, one supposes, is not a relation at all, nor a form; and what Ransom is really after is what inhabits form and what suffers relations.

If Tate enjoys the power of received philosophy, Ransom enjoys the fascinated power of that mind which is concerned with manufacturing the mode of a philosophy that has not been received. He creates the scaffold of system after system for Tate to see through and beyond. This is why Tate instigates insight and why Ransom instigates practice, instigations which multiply each other's value.

Richards—not personally, but as a convenience—may be called responsible for the ways in which Tate and Ransom have shown their metal. I think he has done this largely by arguing and demonstrating the difficulties of reading poetry with the new self-consciousness and the greater difficulties of reading poetry in the absence of old skills. Together these became the enormous difficulty of reading at all and the almost certain futility of supposing that the reader ever reads what the poet wrote. This is the situation which compelled Tate to abandon a theory which prevented the purpose of the theory: to explain what went on. It is also this situation which compelled Ransom to insist on the genetic importance of logical structure in poetry with which Richards until lately has had nothing to do. If Tate and Ransom are right where then is Richards's value? He is a preparatory school for the greater part, quantitatively, of what literary criticism must consist in in a society like our own, and I think this is so even if we discount by about half every major statement of difficulty he has made. If this is so, it explains why those who make most objections to him are those who make most use of him. No schooling is ever adequate to the purposes of that schooling and each is even less adequate to the purposes of the pupil. Let us take as example of the schooling in difficulty offered by Richards in his *Practical Criticism*, published about thirty years ago, and still the most useful guide to normal failures to master what have become the difficulties in reading—let alone thinking or understanding or even arguing at a serious level where action is urgent.

Practical Criticism was the result of a controlled experiment where thirteen poems were given anonymously to a number of students at Cambridge over several years. The readers were interested, and were of as high a cultural level as may be found. The commentaries ("protocols" Richards called them) they turned in showed gross failures to understand, to appreciate, or to judge: that is, they had failed to *use* the poems at anywhere near the level the poems required or deserved. Yet the scrutiny they gave the poems was far greater than the scrutiny poetry gets from its regular readers. (I think it fair to say here that other experiments of Richards show that the readers of poetry are no worse than other users of language. Nobody seems to know with what angel Jacob wrestled.) These scrutinies Richards submitted to the rigorous and varied analyses of which he is the master when it comes to any question of the movement of thought into language or the shedding of thought upon language by words. What is most striking about all this is that it represents a decay in unconscious skills confronted by an inadequacy of conscious skills in reading. (Tate gives the example of the graduate scientist who could not use his wit on Dante because he lacked grammar; the student was unaware that, as Psellos remarked in the eleventh century, Rhetoric is necessary to raise man to general thought—but let us not parade rhetoric here.) The forms which excess of consciousness takes are—at least when analyzed —unsatisfactory for the purposes of consciousness. This is what Tate rejects as the secularization of the mind. Richards has two palliatives for the situation, both secular—one the deliberate creation of a thoroughly understood or mastered basic language, what he calls basic English, with vocabularies of different sizes for different levels of mastery. The idea there is the re-duction of our divided knowledge back to a universal vocabulary. It was his work in practical criticism that led him in this direction, and the history of our time only pushed him further. Our culture has always been carried, and especially for purposes of action, through words, and here was the use of words breaking down. This palliative Tate rejected, if I may apply words written in a different context, because it led to communication without prior or following communion, and was only another example of the demon of secularization in action.

For the élite, Richards had another palliative which comes near being a placebo, and that he proposed it suggests how straitened was the desperation in which he found himself. He went east to Confucius and came back with a "technique or ritual for heightening sincerity," which for Richards means the absence of self-deception and perhaps a freedom from entanglement in beliefs; but the ritual was to be applied only *after* every analytic effort had been made. I would suppose Tate would reject this palliative as also smacking of the secular.

I myself like better the more rational eloquence to which the study of Coleridge led him (towards the end of *Coleridge on Imagination*), and I like it better because it imposes a task with its own tests and checks on the sincerity of him who practices it; but I do not mean to discount the ritual method either. And in thinking of Richards I want

to keep them both in mind in order to remind us that the man who
has spent his life in applying the methodologies of the new consciousness to poetry and to language has done so with such a passion for life
and for poetry as can alone justify the new consciousness at all. It is a
combination of the method and the passion that makes his work a
good school for critics. And it is this that makes Ransom meet him in
the beginning, and this that makes Tate salute him in the end.

Tate's salute is from another territory, the territory which contains
in its soil and communicates to the air the expressiveness and the
oppressiveness of history—of what is time out of mind in the movement of the hand or the reservation of the eye—what is present in us
of the past and which, being present, we cannot ignore; but the history of the soul as well as the history of the land. Of all this Tate is
exceeding aware, with a kind of Mediterranean awareness; and it is
this awareness that has modified his peculiar role as man of letters.
Thus we find him saying: "What modern literature has taught us is
not merely that the man of letters has not participated fully in the
action of society; it has taught us that nobody else has either. It is a
fearful lesson." And at the other pole, where he is meditating the
Angelic Imagination in Poe (the imagination with direct access to
essences, and therefore divorced from perception): "Perhaps this dis-
crepancy of belief and feeling exists in all ages, and creates the inner
conflicts from which poetry comes. If this points to something in the
nature of the literary imagination, we are bound to say that it will
always lie a little beyond our understanding." And again, in writing
of Longinus: "In . . . D. H. Lawrence we get both extremes of pride:
the attack on the intellect in behalf of instinct, instinct itself hardening into a core of abstraction which operates as intellectual pride, as
thesis; not as realized form." And still again: "Our belief in the inferi-
ority of our own age to the past is due to the palsied irresponsibility
of the Ivory Tower. But this belief is the fundamental groundwork of
all poetry at all times. It is the instinctive counter-attack of the intelligence against the dogma of future perfection for persons and societies.
It is in this sense, perhaps, that poetry is most profoundly the criticism
of life." There is passage after passage of the same substance, and it is
the substance upon which he stands in a kind of violence of uncer-
tainty and conviction, deeply entangled in his beliefs and absurdly
outside them. One more will perhaps do for the whole host pressing

upon him. "The shadowy political philosophy of modern literature, from Proust to Faulkner, is, in its moral origins, Jansenist: we are disciples of Pascal, the merits of whose Redeemer were privately available but could not affect the operation of the power-state. While the politician, in his cynical innocence, uses society, the man of letters disdainfully, or perhaps even absentmindedly, withdraws from it: a withdrawal that few persons any longer observe, since withdrawal has become the social convention of the literary man, in which society, so far as it is aware of him, expects him to conduct himself."

If I may be permitted to exaggerate in the cause of contrast, I would say that this withdrawal is one Tate has never made; and the above sentences were written as a *cri d'esprit*, an acknowledgment of a horror yet to come. To think of Jansenism as the separation from and submission to the state is only a figure of that horror. Where Tate adopts this he makes an insight into a mood—an anti-Cartesian mode of the mind: the mood of fierce withdrawal with existential understanding of the cats and rats which made Pascal think his reason unhinged. It is characteristic of the human that he can not always be so; as the tiger burns sometimes brightly as a lamb, the human plays hyena. Pascal saw ordure in the hollow heart, and rejected humanity; thus he cut himself away from common things, except to see in them what he could not abide. Pascal is not a great man *manqué*; he is a great man, and also *manqué*. I think Tate only cries out with Pascal.

This he had reason to do. To those of old and perennial hopes it will seem that within the century government, which was balance, has become administration, which is manipulation, and this effects a dilution rather than a concentration of intelligence. Put another way, politics has become in general practice a machine—which gives enormous power to the persons who interrupt or alter where the machine goes. Yet the polity continues to exist in all the reality which goes with the contemplation of necessity: the area where chance and choice cross; and this polity is sometimes affected, and always guarded—if only in the enclave or the diaspora—by individuals, alone and in shifting groups, whose impersonal occupation is to bring out of contemplation, and engagement, force of mind. Force of mind, as it concentrates, is itself major human action, and attracts or compels other action. Words are a form of such action, and the man of letters has in his charge that form. He operates, in this aspect of his role, between the chance of history and the choice of vocabulary; and it is how we call our chances, and what we call them, that gives body to our conduct and articulation to our belief. It is this notion that is debased and disfigured when severe conflicts of interest are labelled or dismissed as problems of semantics, for semantics almost always makes wrong generalizations as to conduct and belief, since it omits consideration of the mystery in the element of choice and battens upon the confusion in the element of chance and is agreeable to the surrender of intelligence involved in doing so. The man of letters is he who is, or ought to be, unwilling to surrender his intelligence or his sense of the human condition as its chief regular informing agent. It is the intolerable task that makes life tolerable, it is, if you like, the drudgery of the soul and the soul of words.

Montaigne understood this very well, but people do not read that man of letters with much memory nowadays. "Je propose une vie basse et sans lustre, c'est tout un. On attache aussi bien toute la philosophie morale à une vie populaire et privée que à une vie de plus riche estoffe; chaque homme porte la forme entière de l'humaine condition." The man of letters will do as well with Emma Bovary or Hans Castorp as with the fall of Cromwell or the assassination of Lincoln, but he had better, so far as his intelligence is informed, attend the human condition in both. Montaigne found in Socrates his last overwhelming model, and when not Socrates, himself. Every life is "populaire et privée" when looked at by a man of letters, and so also are all human relations. It is this, and not Pascal's reasons, that keep us all outside and against the government, and why, too, we wish to run it with our earned prejudice. In his last essay, "On Experience," Montaigne reminds us that "He who remembers the evils he has undergone, and those that have threatened him, and the slight occasions that have caused a change in his lot, is thereby prepared for future mutations and for the understanding of his own condition. Caesar's life has no more examples for us than our own; and whether it be the life of an emperor or of a common man, it is still a life subject to all human accidents. Let us but give ear to it, and we tell ourselves everything of which we chiefly stand in need." I use Zeitlin's translation; in the last sentence the French is a tone stronger in the opening imperative: "Escoutons y seulement"; let us hear this only. It is precisely this the man of letters must hear first and always, whatever else he hears also

and besides, which will be everything he can that lifts him or strikes
him down. But he must do so, if he is to do so in a way worthy of
the inner action we call reading, in the tone of the last sentences of
the essay. "The fairest lives, in my opinion, are those which conform
to the common or human model, with order, but without miracle and
without extravagance. Now old age stands in need of being treated a
little more tenderly. Let us commend it to that god who is the protec-
tor of health and wisdom, but a gay and sociable wisdom." The god is
Apollo, who is also Lord of the Light's Edge, and Leader of the Muses.

It is in this spirit, because I think he deserves it of us, that I wish
to put into series certain of the notions concentrated in single words
and phrases in the essays of Allen Tate; and I still keep as my text,
to go with the words of Montaigne, the name of the old church in the
Abruzzi: San Giovanni in Venere.

For Tate, in his later essays, the curse of dissociated thought, and
unrelated meditation, has been given the name of Angelic thought or
imagination; which is thought freed from the senses, as if original, and
freed from *Common things*; and is thus the opposite of Dante who
saw Agape with Eros as a common thing in Beatrice's eyes—an *Incarnation* with which Tate has been increasingly concerned almost as if
it were a *Logic* of the life of the senses, as what he learned at school
gave to the mind a vital *Order*. These between them make available
to the grasping sensibility *Experience*. In all this he sees the need for
incubation and preparation by *Prejudice*, which is but the idiosyn-
cratic leaning one captures and inherits from the *Historical Imagination*, where fate and purpose are seen to mingle and impose their *Will*.
From these, taken all but the first in their order, he sees communication become *Communion*. Thus in the centre is Experience that in
the end may be understood by *Love*, for through the Love of God we
learn to love our mortal neighbors. This is the Discovery the man of
letters makes, when he thinks of San Giovanni in Venere.

This is Diplomacy on the high scale: how we learn to live with the
sons of bitches, which is the Human Condition so much at the bottom
of what we accept and damn and bless, in practical Wisdom—gay
and sociable, with Apollo presiding.

Crucial Questions

by EDWIN MUIR

The essays in this book[1] are inquiries into literature and through literature into life. The best criticism has always been of this kind, and it has been revived in the last thirty years or so. It aims at something more than the criticism of opinion and appreciation; it is also sometimes difficult to follow—an inquiry is never easy—but to the reader it is both rewarding and exciting.

This kind of criticism can lead us astray when it hardens into a method. Frequently it has done this both in America and here among the camp-followers of the New Criticism. There, if the method is employed without sensibility or imagination, the examination of a poem leads, after enormous labours, to an interpretation which is either quite banal, or quite false, or both. Mr. Tate is as intent on his subject as any New Critic could be, but he is a poet and he never detracts from the interest of his subject, but adds to it. And he has a style, at once exact and graceful, which is admirably suited to the difficult inquiries he undertakes.

The one fault I can find with him—and it turns out to be a virtue as well—is that he is unusually subject to "the fascination of what's difficult": perhaps it should be called now and then the fascination of what's impossible. For in the middle of a book of excellent criticism he raises the question, "Is Literary Criticism Possible?" The point here is that we do not know what literary criticism is, or what literature is: no definition of poetry, for example, that has ever been attempted, even by great poets, answers that question. Nevertheless we somehow

EDITOR'S NOTE: Reprinted from *The Observer*, 9 December 1956, p. 13, by permission of the publisher.

[1] *The Man of Letters in the Modern World, Selected Essays, 1928–1955.*

come to *know* literature and literary criticism, if they interest us at all, by simple experience and some kind of understanding which we do not understand: we come to know them very much as we come to know human beings. What they *are* is a different question, and seems to be beyond our answering. And it is not of essential importance. Yet this is the only essay in which Mr. Tate asks the impossible, and he asks it, I imagine, because he is so intensely concerned with the quandary of "the man of letters in the modern world."

To him the contemporary writer is in a desperate case, condemned to defend a whole series of positions, the first of which is language itself. The writer "has an immediate responsibility, to other men no less than to himself, for the vitality of language . . . He must discriminate and defend the difference between mass communication, for the control of men, and the knowledge of man which literature offers us for human participation."

The writer may fall through temptation or carelessness into the language of mass communication: "It is a tragedy of contemporary society that so much of democratic social theory reaches us in the language of 'drive,' 'stimulus' and 'response.' This is not the language of freemen, it is the language of slaves. The language of freemen substitutes for these words respectively, *end, choice* and *discrimination.*" "Drive," "stimulus" and "response" are used more frequently in America than here, but if one searched one would doubtless find words not quite the same which serve somewhat the same purpose. Mr. Tate brings out the point that by this language "for the control of men something may be said to have been transmitted, or 'communicated'; nothing has been shared in a new and illuminating intensity of awareness." The purpose of language has been corrupted.

From this point Mr. Tate goes on to "Literature as Knowledge," a very difficult question. What kind of knowledge does a work of imagination give us? I cannot follow him through his intricate argument, but here again he is dealing with language in one of its modes. Essays on "The Symbolic Imagination" and "The Angelic Imagination" (which is evil) follow, for symbol is also a mode of language. These and the book itself, should be read by everyone who practises the art of writing, as well as by every serious reader. There are essays on Donne, Keats, Poe, Emily Dickinson, Yeats and Hart Crane, all of which throw new light on their subjects.

The book raises a reflection. Mr. Tate is a man of faith and a traditionalist. If he had been a pragmatist living in a given world, could he have asked these questions at all, would they even have occurred to him? Could he have felt "the fascination of what's difficult"? Yet they are the questions that must always be asked.

A Metaphysical Athlete: Allen Tate as Critic

by GEORGE CORE

When one is diffident, or more diffident than usual, he had better go ahead and admit it: and on this occasion I do so at the outset, being confronted with the fact of Mr. Tate's criticism of the past forty-odd years and with the curious lack of understanding (not attention) which it has received. By now it should be clear to nearly everyone what Tate is about in his critical pieces—what he believes literature of the first order involves and how it should be approached by intelligent readers. Yet the clichés which are often attached, mechanically, like so many ring-pins to the face of the mountain which is called the New Criticism, simply will not bring the unwary climber to the summit; and that is where much of the difficulty lies. Beyond that one can only say that Tate's best criticism, like that of Johnson, Coleridge, Arnold, and Eliot, is in itself literature of great moment and must be taken accordingly.

EDITOR'S NOTE: Reprinted from *The Southern Literary Journal*, 2:138–47 (Autumn 1969), copyright © 1969 by *The Southern Literary Journal*, by permission of the publisher.

Allen Tate is that rare phenomenon—the man of letters in the modern world, and nobody is more aware of the anomaly of the position during the twentieth century than he. That he has consistently upheld and personified the profession of letters goes without saying: Andrew Lytle remarked it upon meeting Tate in the twenties and many others have before and since, including Herbert Read, John Hall Wheelock, and Eliseo Vivas. It is a rôle, a way of life, not often seen in any time; and in this country it begins with Poe and then reappears in varying ways in James, Pound, Eliot, and Ransom. (Other contemporary names could doubtless be added to this list.) During the course of Tate's career the man who best represents the rôle, even more than Eliot or Read or Ransom, is an Englishman who spent much of his last years in the United States—Ford Madox Ford.

In 1936 Ford praised Allen Tate for having "a sort of lapidary sureness and hardness" as a poet, and he might have well said the same thing of Tate's criticism which has a diamond-like brilliance and density. It is cut and polished almost flawlessly, and therefore the reader must find it difficult to see within and to get at the essential nature of that brilliance. Tate is not a systematic critic, although he says he writes "programmatic" essays (programmatic for his purpose as poet); he is not a new critic in the strict sense of the term (as he has insisted all along); he is not by any means a literary historian. He is, quite simply, what the occasion demands, and is at the same time always himself.

For the most part Mr. Tate has (by his own account) been able to limit his criticism to subjects which are of genuine interest to him, and usually he has written on poets whom he could use, at the same time justifying, however consciously or unconsciously, his own poetic procedures. This is also true in similar ways with the other subjects he has wrestled with. Tate has accordingly been able to bring a special concentration to bear upon the work at hand, a special urgency and authority. Moreover, he has the enormous advantage of a classical education, a far-ranging mind, and an incisive wit. (I often get the uncomfortable feeling when reading Tate that he sprang into the world, like Athena from the head of Zeus, with a fully-formed intelligence and style. Skeptics should read "Emily Dickinson" which he wrote in part at the old age of twenty-nine.) Tate also "enjoys the power of received philosophy," as R. P. Blackmur puts it; and he is possessed of an imagination which is both literal and historical. So much for the preliminaries.

Herbert Read calls Tate a "metaphysical athlete" who cleanly uses the tools of his trade: "The action is graceful, nervously rhythmic, but long sustained." It is a classical poise and balance which has the quality of Yeats's Major Robert Gregory, the natural ease—"all that he did done perfectly." Indeed one can become so beguiled by watching Mr. Tate's acrobatics as to forget the sleight of hand which he often performs. One aspect of his typical address to the audience is facetious self-mockery: "The Angelic Imagination" begins, "With some embarrassment I assume the part of amateur theologian and turn to a little-known figure, Edgar Allan Poe, another theologian only less ignorant than myself." Another complementary manner is a certain sense of futility which will be overcome, slyly but firmly, in the course of an essay: when Tate announces at the end of the same piece that "Poe as God sits silent in the darkness," we assent to the argument—and to the idea that Poe is a forlorn demon looking at his own image and nothing else.

Mr. Tate would have us follow the way of the symbolic imagination as represented triumphantly by Dante, not the angelic as seen in Poe; for as he says, "The reach of our imaginative enlargement is perhaps no longer than the ladder of analogy, at the top of which we may see all, if we still wish to *see* anything, that we have brought up with us from the bottom, where lies the sensible world." Therefore the imagination has first got to be *literal* before it can conduct "an action through analogy, of the human to the divine, of the natural to the supernatural, of the low to the high, of time to eternity." It must begin with something so simple as the hovering of a fly or the turning of a lathe, and the critic who will discover the paradigmatic essence of a great literary work starts and ends with the concrete examples of the artist's generative themes. Thus Tate quotes James approvingly: "No theory is kind to us that cheats us of seeing." We begin by looking at the actual world as the artistic imagination dramatically embodies it for us, and through the pressure of analogy the actual world and literature become one and "achieve a dynamic and precarious unity of experience," redeemed by knowledge. Analogy brings the life-giving dimension to form by making the technical abstraction concrete in the rendered experience, in characteristic and believable human behav-

ior. Through analogy the artist not only relates one experience to
another, one character to another, and one theme to another, but he
controls and shapes the materials of his art and brings order. Hence,
as Tate says, poetry "is the art of apprehending and concentrating our
experience in the mysterious limitations of form."

Allen Tate's subjects are varied, but there are obvious recurrent interests, and I note them here, giving a representative essay for each: the
South and southern literature ("A Southern Mode of the Imagination"),
metaphysical and modern poetry ("The Point of Dying: Donne's 'Virtuous Men'"), the importance of poetry and criticism—or the poet and
the critic—in the modern world ("To Whom is the Poet Responsible?"), critics past and present ("Longinus and the New Criticism").
It is significant, I find, that the subject Tate nearly wrote a book on
(for William Sloane's new American Men of Letters series)—and to
which he has devoted three essays—Poe, is a southern writer, and that,
furthermore, the subject he has treated most fully is the southern literary tradition. The reason is natural enough and need not detain us for
long, although Tate has from time to time disavowed his intense interest in the South, even as he has said he is not a new critic while at once
defending the New Criticism. The fact is that Allen Tate, no less than
Ransom or Davidson or Lytle or Warren, has always thoroughly identified himself with the South—and that much of his finest writing has
sprung directly from that unflinching personal and regional awareness
of time, place, and selfhood. It is a matter of some importance that
Tate has turned to autobiography and is now writing his memoirs,
after having begun his career with biography. This is true of other
Fugitives and Agrarians, and it derives ultimately, one suspects, from
a continuing interest in the way history connects past and present.
There is also the larger and more complicated matter of myth.

There are three myths which Tate has used metaphorically to define
the South. The first is the obvious one—that the Old South was a
medieval society patterned after the feudal autocracies of the Middle
Ages; the second pattern of likeness he remarked (some thirty years
after writing "Religion and the Old South") in "A Southern Mode of
Imagination" is the parallel with Sparta—and, more clearly, Republi-
can Rome; the third, mentioned casually in the obituary on Faulkner
in 1962, is still farther back in history—the Greco-Trojan myth. This
last parallel takes us a good deal further than the first two, at least to

the extent that we have often encountered the others. Tate develops
the analogy in "Sanctuary and the Southern Myth," a major statement
about Faulkner and southern letters, even though it repeats things the
author has said elsewhere. Tate sees Faulkner's principal subject—and
that of his contemporaries—as the Greco-Trojan myth. "The 'older'
culture of Troy-South was wiped out by the 'upstart' culture of Greece-
North. *Sunt lacrimae rerum*; and the Yankees were therefore to blame
for everything— until, as I have pointed out, the time of the first World
War. This myth, inadequate as it may appear to the non-Southern
reader, has permitted a generation of Southern novelists to understand
and to dramatize (that is, depict in action) much of the Southern historical reality." Needless to say *The Fathers* is, among other things, one
of the most powerful fictive embodiments of this myth so transformed.

This view of the South provides the foundation for Tate's many
trenchant observations on its literature. As Hugh Holman has
remarked, "almost every idea which has proved fruitful for the serious
critic [of southern literature] is at least adumbrated" in the *Collected
Essays* of 1959. Tate has said that "myth should be in conviction immediate, direct, overwhelming" and that it is "a dramatic projection of
heroic action . . . upon the reality of the common life of a society."
The society which embodies such a mythology is regional and religious,
traditional and unified, primitive or highly refined, "extroverted" and
unselfconscious. The last traditional society in this country was largely
extinguished by the Civil War, and in entering the modern world and
becoming a part of the United States after the First World War, it
became aware of its peculiarly historical predicament in a way that had
escaped it previously; and the agency of self-consciousness was accomplished through the determined work of many brilliant writers, of
whom Allen Tate is of course one.

In seeking to define the strange brilliance of the southern renascence
Tate is at once probing his own artistic conscience with the intense
historical, aesthetic, and moral judgment which is typical of him. Since
the Old South provides Tate with the concrete model for a traditional
Christian society, it is only natural that he fully understands the fictive
works which have sprung from the consciousness of writers who like
himself have painfully recognized that society's passing. Tate is perfectly aware of the failings of the Old South, yet it remains his chief
model for his whole life—and one much closer in time and more pal-

pable than, say, Yeats's Byzantium, which is largely a historical and mythopoeic reconstruction by one man. Hence Tate's connections with the South—by inheritance, kinship, custom, and manner—have furnished him with what Blackmur has deemed a central allegiance. Out of the tension between Tate's personal allegiance and his awareness of what he has called "a deep illness of the modern mind" has come the enkindling subject of his work as a whole: Andrew Lytle has said that it is "simply what is left of Christendom."

Again and again one encounters this historic and mythic perspective in Tate's criticism. As Blackmur noted in 1934, Tate writes as though we are not living in a largely post-Christian age; and he has said: "We are a Christian civilization or we are nothing." The felt presence of that view is such as to give his criticism a special weight and force. This belief as it informs Tate's prose has something in common with Eliot's religious position, but it is not so pressing and doctrinaire. Essays so dogmatic as Eliot's "Thoughts after Lambeth" have been excluded from Tate's collections. In so doing he has steered towards literature as a form of expression more complete than that offered by any other discipline or mode of discourse. In arguing this position he has, however, too often involved himself in elaborate operations against the enemies of art—positivism, social science, semantics, and the other myopias which have slowly eroded classical education and have at once caused, or been caused by, education of the modern dispensation. He has smitten these enemies of culture and civilization, much as Arnold and Eliot did in their separate ways. But he has not been so involved in these preoccupations as his friend Eliot who once complained that Arnold couldn't find time for literature because he was too busy cleaning up the country.

In addressing the question too long evaded, let me say that what Tate characteristically does as critic is to select a passage in the work under consideration and show us, by and through it, the elements of that fiction which are typically overlooked (or avoided) by other critics, regardless of their persuasions. The trick here is to find the precise passage—one that illuminates the text as a whole but does not blind the reader with its dazzling virtues. For *Madame Bovary* he chooses the scene in which Emma contemplates suicide but is thwarted by the coincidence of the hour; for poetry of the highest order—of the "creative spirit"—he selects quotations from Shakespeare, Donne, and

Dante; for the same kind of poetry, poetry exhibiting an equipoise of tensions, he chooses these poets and adds others, notably Yeats and Eliot. This is Tate's forte—not long and detailed exegesis of whole poems or short stories or novels (although some of his commentaries are indeed brilliant—the readings of "Ode to a Nightingale" and "Ode on a Grecian Urn" and his analyses in *The House of Fiction*). What he had done in part is improve upon Eliot's practice of quotation (which he, in turn, got from Arnold and Pound). But there is more involved, and Tate generally has a sharper historical perspective and is less inclined to pursue abstractions. He also has not been so strenuous in attacking poets he disliked and could not use for his own purposes —and in defending those he liked and could use.

The issue between form and value, or technique and substance, is joined by Mr. Tate in his criticism by his constant practice of examining the subject not only against the standard of his own taste and judgment but against the standards of others—and, equally important, in terms of its time. Tate always knows a technical convention when he sees one, just as he knows a departure from, or a modification of, that convention. Ultimately the technical convention springs from the author's attitude towards his age, and the age's way of looking at the world—the social convention: hence we get the metaphysical conceit, a subtle poetic equivalent of the Euphuistic sentence which derived from an elaborate pattern of courtly behavior. The conceit was also forced into being by the fragmentation of the Elizabethan world picture, as Tate has shrewdly observed. The guarded style and the verbal shock of modern poetry similarly arose in this century out of the failure of such conventions, both social and artistic. Allen Tate constantly discovers the informing conventions of the artist and therefore enlarges the light of our seeing beyond the page in front of us.

In his prefaces Mr. Tate says that he "should like to think that criticism has been written, and may be again, from a mere point of view" which is essentially mysterious, both to the critic and his readers. He has also remarked that he is "on record as a casual essayist of whom little consistency can be expected" and that, moreover, he is "writing, in the end, opinion, and neither aesthetics nor poetry in prose." In reading these observations I am reminded of Ransom's subtleties of self-deflation, which like Tate's can often catch the reader unaware; for the mere point of view and the mere opinion are everything, and the style, although it meets Tate's standard of being as plain as the nose on one's face, is often poetic in its tone and cadences, in the rightness of its language and nuance.

In his criticism Allen Tate over and again meets the exacting test of R. P. Blackmur: "To combine conceptual honesty and the act of vision is the constant athletic feat of the artist. . . . The test of success is enduring interest; and there, in enduring interest, lies the writer's whole authority and his sole moral strength." In short, Mr. Tate's athletic ability as critic has only improved as time has gone on, although it must be said that his finest criticism was written in the early fifties. He continues to walk over the yawning abyss that has sundered the modern world along a tightrope which grows increasingly perilous and which, unlike the road Bunyan's pilgrim travelled, seems to have no end. Those who follow may be sure in their guide, but unfortunately they will find the way is more demanding than Tate's apparently effortless performance indicates. Few will safely cross, and many will be lost, even as I probably have been in the course of my own acrobatics. (As E. B. White has said, "A writer, like an acrobat, must occasionally try a stunt that is too much for him.") But this in no way affects Allen Tate's certain progress as he seeks a more civilized world.

A Note on Allen Tate's Essays

by RICHARD HOWARD

I shall not patronize Allen Tate by pretending to be impartial: it is precisely because he is more than a man of parts, because he is a whole, that I am partial to him; I shall take him, merely, at his word, the only place to take a poet, even in his prose. And in his prose Tate's word is the same as in his poems—why, forty years ago he admonished us: "all the books of a poet should ultimately be regarded as one book—it was to this end he worked." And the word I take him at is that *he has never been able to concentrate on what could not be useful to him.*

Tate's essays, then, will be a concentration on what could—when they are not a dilatation, as in one or two after-dinner instances, on what could not—be useful, and they substantiate that famous remark of his, whose arrogance is exceeded, as arrogance always is, only by its humility: "if our duties are not specific they do not exist." Specific duties; the nisus here, the function of Tate's criticism, is to search out, to comb and card from text (Emily Dickinson) and character (Hart Crane), from history ("Religion and the Old South") and theory ("Longinus and the New Criticism"), *what may serve Tate's poems.* And the effect, when the books of this poet *are* ultimately regarded as one book, is of life pressing round a dedicated victim decked with all the gauds of immolation—dedicated, that victim, to the grand-mannerist acknowledgment of the Natural Order, which is the Repudiation of Eschatology.

EDITOR'S NOTE: Reprinted from *Poetry*, 116:43–45 (April 1970), copyright © 1970 by the Modern Poetry Association, by permission of the author and the editor of *Poetry*. The original title, "Tate's Essays," has been changed by the author.

His criticism is a part, as I have said, the contralto part, a middle voice taken and sustained within what Blackmur has called Allen Tate's *virtuosity of presence*: one utterance among many voices—verse, fiction, biography, essay, history, gossip, invective—though the voices speak but one language to articulate but one subject. So immense is the urgency of the voices toward that subject, so militant their conviction of its truth, that I cannot afford here, in a mere and marvelling note, to engross Allen Tate's objects: the South as a way of life, certain literary figures in their representative achievements (though we may remark that Dante and Dr. Johnson are particularly prized: the autocrats of order, of Superior Form), the theory of literature, the theory of the imagination. Instead of entering upon these things which have been useful to Tate, I would try to set forth, with some sway of citation, what they have been useful *for*, and my response is to be searched, of course, as much from the demonology of *Stonewall Jackson the Good Soldier* as from the angelism of the more impenetrable poems ("I cannot believe I have illuminated the difficulties some readers have found in the style," Tate remarks, "but then I cannot, have never been able to, see any difficulties of that order"), from the essays everywhere as in the emblematic heft of the figure as a whole, the-man-of-letters-in-the-modern-world resumed for my generation. The clarion enunciation of Tate's subject—so passionately entertained as to have become his subjection—occurs in his splendid novel *The Fathers* (1938); the passage contains, exemplifies *en abyme*, as the heraldist would say, by the very unreleasing momentum of the phrasing, his utter effort, his innermost persuasion:

The moment had come that all waiting had been for, but the moment was lost in each new movement, each new step. . . . There was of course no one moment that it was all leading up to, and that piece of knowledge about life has permitted me to survive the disasters which overwhelmed other and better men, and to tell their story. Not even death was an instant; it too became part of the ceaseless flow, instructing me to beware of fixing any hope, or some terrible lack of it, upon birth or death, or upon love, or the giving in marriage. None of these could draw to itself all the life around it or even all the life in one person; not one of them but fell short of its occasion, warning us all to fear not death or love, or any ecstasy or calamity, but rather to fear our own expectancy of it, or our own lack of preparation for these final things.

Nothing ends without having to be broken off, for everything—the poet tells us, in his poems—everything is endless. That is why the South, in these essays, is regarded as a *style of life* representative of the continuities of blood, and so of ritual and tradition. That is the source of Tate's enormous repudiations, for he is truly, as he says, "talking most of the time about what poetry cannot be expected to do to save mankind from the disasters in which poetry itself must be involved." Again and again, the critic rehearses what the poet calls "the deep coherence of hell," reiterates "a commitment to the order of nature, without which the higher knowledge is not possible to man." He wants one thing to lead to another, wants it so hard that his thirst becomes aphoristic:

An absolutely independent judgment would be an absolutely ignorant judgment.

The future is no proper subject for criticism: we shall not derive our standards of human nature and of the good society from an unexperienced future.

Taste is the discipline of feeling according to the laws of the natural order, a discipline of submission to a permanent limitation of man.

We must judge the past and keep it alive by being alive ourselves. Thus he rejects Basic English (the secularization of the mind) as he rejects the Protestant, scientific North (the secularization of the body politic) because it leads to communication without prior or following communion. "Poe," he says in one of his great dismissals, "Poe circumvented the natural world. Since he refused to see nature he was doomed to see nothing. He overleaped and cheated the condition of man." Essentially Catholic, then, Tate's imagination (and he would say, all imagination) rejects an heretical Apocalypse, rejects that compulsion to cast out nature, to uproot whatever seems external to redemption, whatever might intervene between the self and God. "The task of the civilized intelligence," Tate insists, "is one of perpetual salvage." His is the tact, as he says of Dante somewhere, "the tact of mediation between universals and particulars in the complex of metaphor."

Patience, then, in the full sense of the word, the sense that shares, with passion, *suffering*—patience, salvage, and death ("the general symbol of nature is Death") are this poet's articles of faith, and they work to his concentration in the criticism. "The singular passion / abides its object" one poem says, and that is the attainment of his prose.

III. THE NOVELIST

The Fathers

by ARTHUR MIZENER

T he *Fathers* was published in 1938. It sold respectably in both
the United States and England, perhaps because people
expected it to be another *Gone With the Wind*: it is in fact
the novel *Gone With the Wind* ought to have been. Since its publication it has received very little attention, considering that it is one of
the most remarkable novels of our time. Its occasion is a public one,
the achievement and the destruction of Virginia's antebellum civilization. Within that occasion it discovers a conflict between two fundamental and irreconcilable modes of existence, a conflict that has
haunted American experience, but exists in some form at all times.
The Fathers moves between the public and the private aspects of this
conflict with an ease very unusual in American novels, and this ease
is the most obvious illustration of the novel's remarkable unity of idea
and form, for it is itself a manifestation of the novel's central idea, that
"the belief widely held today, that men may live apart from the
political order, that indeed the only humane and honorable satisfactions must be gained in spite of the public order," is a fantasy.

The formal ordering of *The Fathers* which makes this unity possible
is quite deliberate. "I wished," Mr. Tate has written, ". . . to make
the whole structure symbolic in terms of realistic detail, so that you
could subtract the symbolism, or remain unaware of it, without losing
the literal level of meaning . . . but if you subtract the literal or
realistic detail, the symbolic structure disappears." The main device

EDITOR'S NOTE: Reprinted from *The Sewanee Review*, 67:604–13 (Autumn 1959), by
permission of the author and publisher. This essay is also the introduction to *The
Fathers* (Chicago: Swallow Press, 1960; London: Eyre and Spottiswoode, 1960). It first
appeared in *Accent*, 7:101–9 (Winter 1947), in a slightly different form.

for achieving this end is the book's narrator. Lacy Buchan is an old man who, as a boy, had participated in the events he is describing. As a character, he allows Mr. Tate to move back and forth between the mature but removed judgment of the old man and the partial understanding but direct sensuous reflection of the boy whom the old man remembers. "In my feelings of that time," as Lacy says, "there is a new element—my feelings now about that time . . . the emotions have ordered themselves in memory, and that memory is not what happened in the year 1860 but rather a few symbols, a voice, a tree, a gun shining on the wall. . . ." It is thus that every event of the novel is made at once psychologically probable and symbolically significant. So complete is this process that even the young Lacy Buchan is, in the narrator's memory, a realization of the novel's theme: the life of the Buchan family at Pleasant Hill had half completed the slow process of civilizing young Lacy, but "I shared," as the narrator says, "George Posey's impatience with the world as it was, as indeed every child must whose discipline is incomplete."

This narrator also allows the events of the narrative to be presented out of chronological order without loss of probability whenever their meaning requires it. Thus, the novel opens on the day of Mrs. Buchan's funeral at Pleasant Hill in April 1860. After we have seen Lacy's brother-in-law, George Posey, refuse to attend the funeral, Lacy's mind jumps, quite naturally, back to a point two years earlier, when George was wooing Susan Buchan. This recollection then fills in for us the whole two years between that time and the day of Mrs. Buchan's funeral, though it is in its turn thrice interrupted, again quite naturally, by incidents that occur on the day of the funeral, in order that these events may be communicated to us in juxtaposition with events of the time two years before with which they are significantly related. During the whole of this double narration we are aware that Mrs. Buchan's funeral occurred fifty years ago and that what we are hearing is not a contemporary account of it but an old man's memories of it. Complex as this method may sound in this description, it is only the familiar narrative procedure of the epic done realistically. Its purpose is to provide the opportunities for non-temporal patterning that the novel's meaning requires without destroying our sense that we are observing actual events occurring in actual time. By its means the novel's meaning is made to take on the probability of the novel's events and becomes, not so much the author's, as life's.

The central tension of *The Fathers*, like that of its design, is a tension between the public and the private life, between the order of civilization, always artificial, imposed by discipline, and at the mercy of its own imperfections, and the disorder of the private life, always sincere, imposed upon by circumstances, and at the mercy of its own impulses. We see, on the one hand, the static condition a society reaches when, by slow degrees, it has disciplined all personal feeling to custom so that the individual no longer exists apart from the ritual of society and the ritual of society expresses all the feelings the individual knows. We see, on the other hand, the forces that exist—because time does not stand still—both within and without the people who constitute a society, that will destroy the discipline of its civilization and leave the individual naked and alone. "People living in formal societies," says the narrator, "lacking the historical imagination, can imagine for themselves only a timeless existence." So it is with Major Buchan. But George Posey, for all his great personal gifts—his generosity, his kindness, his charm—must receive "the shock of the world at the end of his nerves" because, living in no society, he is wholly unprotected. He is a man who, having nothing to tell him how to act or where to go, is always in violent motion; without understanding quite why, young Lacy sees him as "a horseman riding over a precipice." "Excessively refined persons," he thinks as an old man, remembering the difference between the Posey family and his own, "have a communion with the abyss; but is not civilization the agreement, slowly arrived at, to let the abyss alone?"

The richness of life with which *The Fathers* realizes this theme is remarkable; it makes one suspect that, if *The Fathers* is ever read with attention, Mr. Tate may become very unpopular in The South, for he knows he is not Major Buchan and never can be, knows that he is as completely excluded from the world of Pleasant Hill as George Posey was, and therefore shares George's sense of its radical absurdity. But he also understands that world and sees that, though time has—inevitably, perhaps even rightly—destroyed it, it was civilized in a way our life is not. This attitude is very like that of the speaker in the "Ode to the Confederate Dead"; it takes account of an astonishing range of feelings, even on the smallest occasion. When, for example, Major

Buchan leads his family, single file, into a hotel and says to the clerk, "We need rain, sir!" we are at once charmed by the perfection of his manners, astonished by the innocent confidence with which he performs them, and amused—not very creditably—by his simplicity—for it is this same simplicity that makes him leave his place in his wife's funeral procession to "take the brown hand [of his wife's maid] to lead her into the line and make her take her place ahead of us just behind the body of her mistress." Major Buchan's manners are like Cousin Custis' literary effusions, of which Major Buchan says, "Custis is a most accomplished gentleman. A very fine artist, sir! In the heroic style. And an elegant speaker." They are like the prayer of Dr. Cartwright over Mrs. Buchan's grave, "just a voice, in the *ore rotundo* of impersonality, no feeling but in the words themselves."

This same complication of feelings flows out from the details of the novel into the pattern of its incidents—and, ultimately, into its whole structure. Consider, for example, what we are made to feel when the drunken John Langton challenges George Posey after the tournament. As Major Buchan is an embodiment of the best possibilities of his civilization, so John Langton is an embodiment of its worst, "a bold and insolent man who deemed himself an aristocrat beyond any consideration for other people." When he and George meet on the field of honor, George first makes a magnificent practice shot and then, suddenly, throws his pistol away and knocks Langton down. "I never did like Langton, from the time we were boys," says Jim Mason, his second, "But that ain't the point. . . . Mr. Posey agreed to come here and there was only one thing to come for. Not for this." He is right. As always, George cannot objectify his feelings in terms of the world he must live in, because he is not a part of it. For all his personal splendor, "the heightened vitality possessed by a man who knows no bounds," he has failed to realize himself; his defeat is far worse than John Langton's, for all Langton's personal vileness.

The implications of this scene are further complicated by the fact that we watch it with Lacy Buchan, from under the pavilion. There Lacy has found a contemporary, Wink Broadacre. " 'God damn,' he said. 'Son of a bitch. Bastard. Say, Buchan, cain't you cuss? Jesus Christ.' He lay on his elbow gazing at me with a smirk. 'You want some of it?' " And he points to "a half-grown mulatto girl with kinky red hair and muddy green eyes in a pretty, Caucasian face" who is lying on her back a short distance away. This episode is a prologue to the duel; its sexual and social evil, like Langton's malicious arrogance, is a part of civilization, and we have to face that fact squarely. Yet there is something almost humorous, almost Tom-Sawyerish, about Wink Broadacre ("Say, Buchan, cain't you cuss?"). Like Langton's, this is the unintended and limited evil of an otherwise ordered world; before we condemn that world because it contains such evil, we must contemplate the equally unintended but unbounded evil produced by the wholly personal sincerity of George Posey's love for Susan Buchan that involved him in the duel. "There is no doubt," as the narrator says, "that [George] loved Susan too much; by that I mean he was too personal, and with his exacerbated nerves he was constantly receiving impressions out of the chasm that yawns beneath lovers; therefore he must have had a secret brutality for her when they were alone." In the end he drives Susan mad.

The first part of *The Fathers* is an ordered sequence of scenes that show us the contrast between the old and still dominant way of life and the new. There is a sense in which, because of the date of the action, these scenes constitute an explanation of the concealed change that had already defeated the Virginia way of life before the War, just as there is a sense in which every realistic fiction is, and intends quite seriously to be, history. As such, however, these scenes are also a demonstration of how time, working within a civilization and its members, destroys it. This contrast between old and new comes to a climax in the scene where George does not ask for Susan's hand but says, "Major Buchan, I intend to marry your daughter." At the scene's beginning, Major Buchan has put George in his place as firmly as he knows how to; he has failed to ask after George's family, "the first thing he always did when he met anybody, black or white," and he has told George that "I don't know that we are entitled to your kindness—no sir, I don't know that we are." But George is not put in his place; "he was incredibly at ease, the way a man is at ease when he is alone." Confronted by this imperviousness, Major Buchan is helpless and can only "look as if someone entitled to know all about it had denied the heliocentric theory or argued that there were no Abolitionists in Boston." This is high comedy, comedy filled with tragic implications. "Our lives," Lacy thinks, "were eternally balanced upon a pedestal below which lay an abyss I could not name. Within that invisible ten-

sion my father knew the moves of an intricate game that he expected
everybody else to play. That, I think, was because everything he was
and felt was in the game." His helplessness before George Posey's
refusal to play reminds Lacy of "the only time I had ever seen my
father blush; somebody had tried to tell him his private affairs, beginning, 'If you will allow me to be personal,' and papa had blushed
because he could never allow anybody to be personal." In the same
way, Major Buchan's inability to conceive of a competitive society
makes him helpless before the financial conception of property.

But money, though he hates it as such, gives George Posey a sense
of reality. He even thinks of Yellow Jim, his half-brother and slave, as
"liquid capital" and sells him, an attitude toward slavery that shocks
the Buchans, who cannot understand the wholly personal attitude of
a man who will give ten dollars to a beggar woman, and embarrass
himself in the process, but will not pay his "free labor enough to buy
bacon and meal." George's contribution to the Confederate cause is
smuggled goods, shrewdly purchased in the North, and—satchel full
of money in hand after one of these sales—he says to Cousin John,
"Mr. Semmes, your people are about to fight a war. They remind me
of a passel of young 'uns playing prisoners' base." Yet the man who
ignores the rules of Major Buchan's game, or some such game, as
George Posey does, is left to the mercy of random impulse. George
Posey is unprotected from what is outside him, and, what is worse,
from what is inside him.

Lacy once recalls for us how his mother dealt with a child's question
about why a bull had been brought to Pleasant Hill. " 'He's here on
business,' my mother said, and looking back at that remark I know
that she was a person for whom her small world held life in its entirety,
and who, through that knowledge, knew all that was necessary of the
world at large." But when George Posey, walking with Major Buchan,
comes on a young bull that has been turned into a herd of cows—"I
looked at George Posey. He was blushing to the roots of his hair. He
looked helpless and betrayed. I saw papa give him a sharp and critical
glance, and then he said, 'Mr. Posey, excuse me, I have some business
with Mr. Higgins. I will ask Lacy here to take you back to the house.'
Papa's eyes were on the ground while George Posey mastered himself."
"The Poseys," as the narrator remarks elsewhere, "were more refined
than the Buchans, but less civilized."

There is the same contrast between the Buchans and George Posey in the face of death. Major Buchan "was crushed [by his wife's death] but in his sorrow he knew what everybody else was feeling, and in his high innocence he required that they know too and be as polite as he." So great is his pride in his own dignity and honor that he is even polite to George when George, after refusing to attend the funeral, turns up again. It teaches the young Lacy a great lesson. "It seemed plain [at my age] that a great many people had to be treated, not as you felt about yourself, but as they deserved. How could you decide what people deserved? That was the trouble. You couldn't decide. So you came to believe in honor and dignity for their own sakes since all proper men knew what honor was and could recognize dignity; but nobody knew what human nature was or could presume to mete out justice to others."

But George flees the funeral because he "needed intensely . . . to escape from the forms of death which were, to us, only the completion of life, and in which there could be nothing personal." When George returns, he greets Semmes Buchan, who is a medical student, with agonized brutality: "I reckon you'll be cutting up your cadavers again this time next week"; and he says to Lacy: " 'By God they'll all starve to death, that's what they'll do. They do nothing but die and marry and think about the honor of Virginia.' He rammed his hands into his pockets and shouted: 'I want to be thrown to the hogs, I tell you I want to be thrown to the hogs!' " (At the end of *The Fathers* only the devoted propriety of Mr. Higgins saves the body of Major Buchan from the hogs.) "As to all unprotected persons," Lacy understands later, "death was horrible to him; therefore he faced it in its aspect of greatest horror—the corrupted body." When his uncle says to George at his own mother's death, "Nephew, it pains me to greet you in these melancholy circumstances. Your mother—" George, "looking at him as if he were a child," interrupts him: "She's dead, ain't she?" "When death could be like this," Lacy thinks, "nobody was living. If [the Poseys] had not been of their Church, they would have thrown one another at death into the river." And, indeed, George does throw his half-brother, Yellow Jim, into the river after Semmes has shot him. This is the consequence of having grown up in "a world in which the social acts became privacies."

Because George Posey cannot live in the objective world of custom and ceremony that exists, he must always try to invent, on the spur of the moment, some world he can live in, some gesture that will realize what he is. He has no resources except his impulses and can realize himself only in improvised and violent action. "He is alone," as grandfather Buchan says, "like a tornado," possessing nothing with which to face experience except his terrifying personal sincerity. He cannot face death at all; he makes a tragic mess of his passion for Susan; and, having shot Semmes Buchan on an impulse that astonishes him, he tries to explain to Major Buchan why he did it. "Brother George," Lacy thinks, "had been sincere . . . had been appallingly too sincere."

Between George Posey and Major Buchan stands the figure of Susan, George's wife and the Major's daughter. "She could not have known [before her marriage] that George was outside life, or had a secret of life that no one had heard of at Pleasant Hill. To Susan the life around her in childhood had been final." But after she has lived with George and his family—each of them isolated in his room and the shell of himself, hardly knowing, as George's uncle does not, whether it is day or night—she learns that these are not just peculiar old people; they are not really old at all; they are people who have dropped out of life and forgotten how to get back through the looking glass except by smashing it, like the Alice of Mr. Tate's poem. This discovery makes Susan determined to prevent her brother's marrying Jane Posey; and she does, by allowing—indeed almost making—George's colored half-brother to attack that sister. As a result Semmes, like a good Buchan, shoots Yellow Jim; George, like himself, shoots Semmes; and Susan goes mad.

"Why," the narrator wonders, "cannot life change without tangling the lives of innocent persons? Why do innocent persons cease their innocence and become violent and evil in themselves that such great changes may take place?" For they had all been innocent and they had all, in different ways, become more or less evil. Thus, either because of changes in themselves that made the world unbearable to them, as with George, or because of changes in the world about them such that "unnatural vices are fathered by our heroism," as with Major Buchan, or because of both, as with Susan, time and change manifest themselves concretely in the action of the novel.

Such, then, is *The Fathers,* a novel with an action of a certain magnitude that satisfies the demands of probability and is, at the same time, a sustained, particularized, and unified symbol. Because it is, its meaning is not merely a lyric and personal response to experience but takes on the full, public life that only a probable action can give, as George Posey's self could not, as Major Buchan's did. The motive of *The Fathers'* action is a meaning, and the life of that meaning is an action. It is an imitation of life.

The End of the Old Dominion

by *JANET ADAM SMITH*

A tournament is about to begin. At the back of the pavilion a flag flies from a tall pole. In front sit the ladies from whom will be chosen the Queen of Love and Beauty. A bugle blows; the riders line up, then at a prancing walk pass the pavilion in the Parade of Chivalry, each carrying a slender lance and wearing his colours on his sleeve. The rider on the big bay mare wears a black and orange mask. In turn they ride at the ring. Two lift it off on their lance every time; but on points of skill, the judgment goes to the knight in orange and black . . . You might think it was Scott describing the days of chivalry in *Ivanhoe*; or Disraeli describing the revived medievalism of the Eglinton Tournament in *Endymion*. But the flag over the pavilion is that of Virginia, the runners who bring the rings back to the riders are Negroes; and the scene is from a novel by Allen Tate first published in 1938 and now reissued with a most illuminating preface by Arthur Mizener.

It is not only the tournament that brings Scott to mind in *The*

EDITOR'S NOTE: Reprinted from *The New Statesman*, 59:718–19 (14 May 1960), by permission of the publisher.

Fathers; the novel, however, with which it has affinities is not *Ivan-hoe*, but *Waverley*. The span between the action of *The Fathers* (1860–61) and the writing of it is comparable to the span between 1745 and the writing of *Waverley*. Both novelists write of events out-side their own memories, but within that of people they have known. Both write of the last days of an order—the clan system in the High-lands, the half-feudal order of antebellum Virginia; both are realists. As there was no room in the Scotland of David Hume and the agri-cultural improvers for the chieftain Fergus MacIvor and his 500 claymores, so in the America of the Pennsylvania steel-mills and the spreading railroads there was no room for Major Buchan supporting, on his conservatively cultivated estate of Pleasant Hill, the ever-increas-ing families of his Negro servants. Yet the old orders had a style, a set of values—rating honour above personal advancement, hospitality above wealth—to which their commercially minded successors looked back with nostalgia. It is to the doomed men that both novelists give the finest passages—Fergus MacIvor's speech before his execution at Carlisle, meeting his death with a line from Virgil; Major Buchan's answer to the Yankee officer who gives him half an hour to leave his home before it is burnt—"There is *nothing* that you can give to me, Sir"—before he goes in to hang himself.

Scott's statement of his aim in *Waverley*—"to awaken the imagina-tion, and benefit the understanding"—would not, I think, be disowned by Mr. Tate, but their means could hardly be more different. Scott, charging along in the dawn of the historical novel, told his tale with artless gusto, stuffing it with information to prove his serious intention. Tate, writing after this particular currency has been debased—but after the scope of the novel as a whole has been so extended—con-structs his story with the most conscious art and skill. It is told by Lacy Buchan in his old age, remembering the private and public events of 1860–61, when he was a boy of fifteen, and what they did to himself, to his father, his brothers, his sister Susan and her husband George Posey. He remembers them because he can still not fully understand: "Is it not something to tell, when a score of people I knew and loved, people beyond whose lives I could imagine no other life, either out of violence in themselves or the times, or out of some misery or shame, scattered into the new life of the modern age where they cannot even find themselves? Why cannot life change without tan-

gling the lives of innocent persons? Why do innocent persons cease
their innocence and become violent and evil in themselves that such
great changes may take place?" The resonance between his clear memory of the events and his lifetime's brooding over their significance is
one of the finest things in the book.

We come back to the tournament. The knight in orange and black
is George Posey: the girl whom he chooses as Queen of Love and
Beauty is Susan, daughter of Major Lewis Buchan of Pleasant Hill.
George Posey is the outsider in this assembly of Virginian gentry: he
has won, because of the excellence of his bay mare Queen Susie; he
was able to buy her because he had sold a Negro for fifteen hundred
dollars, telling the man—"You're liquid capital, I've got to have
money." The Buchans find this horrifying: "He rode away on the back
of a bay Negro" says one, bitterly. Money is disrupting a traditional
society. But it is not a case of North v. South. George Posey is as much
a Southerner as the rest of them; and Lacy Buchan in old age, musing
on the differences between Buchans and Poseys, is trying to make out
why George should have become the agent of destruction.

The Buchan household at Pleasant Hill seems to contain all the
goodness of the old order. It is a society where, "in order to make their
livelihood, men do not have to put aside their moral natures." To
Major Buchan, Negroes can never be "liquid capital": they are old
Coriolanus who sits by him in his study, or old Lucy whom, at his
wife's funeral, he leads by the hand to head the procession behind the
coffin of her mistress. He speaks of his neighbours by the names of
their estates—Carters of Ravensworth, Careys of Vaucluse—but he
never calculates what they are worth, for houses are places to be
enjoyed by a man and his heirs, not commodities which might be sold.
The front gallery of Pleasant Hill sags on its posts, the paint on the
weatherboarding is cracked, but he punctiliously entertains his neighbours and kinsmen. Life is lived with decorum and personal emotion
does not intrude. At his wife's funeral, "the old gentleman was crushed
but in his sorrow he knew what everybody else was feeling, and in his
high innocence he required that they know it too and be as polite
as he."

The Poseys used to have an estate in Maryland; but they left it to
settle in Georgetown, where they are too grand to merge into the rising
middle-class. They have ceased to have any function in society, and

have trailed off into private lives of fantasy and obsession. George's mother sits in her room labelling cardboard boxes filled with the beads and gloves and knick-knacks of her youth; in the attic is his uncle Mr. Jarman, who only comes down once a year. Surrounded by slop-pails, eggshells and dirty quill pens, he contemplates a Gibbonian history of civilisation, traces romantic genealogies, and converses in Ciceronian periods. It is a dead house, and there has been no family life for George to grow into, no channel of custom for his fierce energies. He is a man without people or place; unprotected by a code, he "receives the shock of the world at the end of his nerves." He has to make his own life, work out its own forms; he goes after money, for money is personal power. He wins the tournament and the hand of Susan Buchan, but he cannot find a place in the ordered Buchan world; their decorum and ceremony are to him as meaningless as the Gibbonian fantasies of Mr. Jarman. When all the connection has assembled at Pleasant Hill for Mrs. Buchan's funeral, George shocks them by mounting the bay mare and riding away: " 'I can't even remember their names. I meet them but I don't know who they are. And by God they'll all starve to death, that's what they'll do. They do nothing but die and marry and think about the honour of Virginia.' He rammed his hands into his pockets and shouted: 'I want to be thrown to the hogs. I tell you I want to be thrown to the hogs.' "

But the clash is not only between Buchans and Poseys—between settled tradition and violent individualism. As the story opens out, we begin to see the forces already sapping the civilised facade of Pleasant Hill from inside. Semmes Buchan, the brother who has brought George Posey into the family, casts an accounting eye over the unproductive estate—"Twenty Negroes are too many for this place"—and fixes with George Posey for some Negroes whom his father thinks he has freed, to be sold to a slave-dealer and reduce Major Buchan's debt at the bank. The decorum which Major Buchan cultivates so scrupulously is no defence when his assured world begins to crumble. It fits him to disinherit his secessionist son "reluctantly and without passion," but not to understand why his son is a secessionist. He reads *The Vanity of Human Wishes* and admires the poetic drama of G. W. P. Custis, *Cincinnatus Americannus: or the Triumphs of General G. Washington* ("Custis is a most accomplished gentleman. A very fine artist, sir! In the heroic style. And an elegant speaker") but when it comes to the passions and perplexities of his own children he is more helpless than old Coriolanus. The *ore rotundo* can school a man to meet the foreseen blows of death and bereavement with dignity; it can't cope with madness, or obsessive jealousy, or the extremes of passion, or unnatural death. Lacy sums it up: "Our lives were eternally balanced upon a pedestal below which lay an abyss that I could not name. Within that invisible tension my father knew the moves of an intricate game that he expected everybody else to play." Elsewhere he reflects, "Is not civilisation the agreement, slowly arrived at, to let the abyss alone?"

Rooted in his Virginian loyalty, Major Buchan has no conception of the rest of the South, of the tensions on the cotton plantations of Alabama and Georgia. He lives by the historic myth that Virginian civilisation is the heir to the civilisation of Greece and Rome (and, indeed, to the code of medieval chivalry, as filtered through *Ivanhoe*). This myth has given dignity and style to life but it can no longer teach men how to live, either politically or personally. The culture is too thin, the disruptive forces too strong. Before the war begins, it is cracked beyond repair.

So, for his only novel, Mr. Tate has taken a great subject. But it is a subject that he has never been far from during his forty years of writing: the nature of American—particularly Southern American—civilisation. Often, in the narrator's reflections, *The Fathers* echoes those essays of Mr. Tate that consider the nature of tradition and its limitations: the relation of the individual to society; the illusion that the good personal life can be found entirely apart from the political order. Often the beautifully worked symbolism of the novel—the sagging gallery-post, the bay mare, the rifle on the wall—recalls the poet of "Emblems," "Aeneas at Washington," "To the Lacedemonians" and "Ode to the Confederate Dead." But in *The Fathers* Mr. Tate does what essay and poem cannot do: he works out these questions of men and society in terms of people, not abstractly, but with passion. We see the fine values of Virginian society lived out in Major Buchan, and in George Posey the destructive impulses of the man of heightened vitality and no direction. And in the whole story—clear in its outline but worked out with great subtlety, a masterpiece of formal beauty— we see people we can believe in, impelled by their roots, their upbringing, their ideals, to act at a certain moment of history in certain ways.

The old man brooding over the events of fifty years ago keeps wondering if . . . if . . . might it not then have happened otherwise? But at the end of his tale—the house burnt, his father hanged, his brother killed, his sister mad—he cannot disentangle "the domestic trials and the public crisis." This portrayal of men in society, with all the interplay of the private on the public, the public on the private, is something only the novel can do; very rarely has it been done as powerfully as here. *The Fathers* completes and complements Allen Tate's other work; and it deserves to be recognised as one of the outstanding novels of our time.

Southern Style

by a *TIMES LITERARY*
SUPPLEMENT REVIEWER

There are two generalizations which are often made about major American fiction. One is that in Hawthorne or Melville or even in the Mark Twain of *Huckleberry Finn* the novel is both something less and something more than, say, the greater English novels of the Victorian age. It is less in that it does not give us the sense of a weight and thickness of social pressure around the characters; they are more alone and more free, live more in their thoughts and less in their "world" than the characters, say, of George Eliot. On the other hand, such classic American novels often seem to have a meaning in depth, a poetic quality, an underlying pattern of moral fable or covert allegory, which is, on the whole, lacking in major

EDITOR'S NOTE: Reprinted from *The London Times Literary Supplement*, 59:496 (5 August 1960), by permission of the publisher.

Victorian fiction. The other generalization sometimes made is that owing to the hopefulness, the largeness, the newness of the American scene American fiction tends to lack the tragic sense of life. The American hero handles and controls circumstances, rather than feeling hemmed in by them.

In 1938 a distinguished Southern poet and critic, Mr. Allen Tate, produced his only novel, *The Fathers*. It has just been republished in a slightly revised version. To it the first generalization only half applies. It is a book remarkable for the way in which it re-creates a sense of the weight and thickness of social pressure in the Old South, just before and just at the beginning of the Civil War. But, though it can be read straight through as a realistic fiction, it does have an underlying pattern which much enriches it. It is partly a kind of fable or allegory about the relation of the individual to society. And it does display, movingly, a tragic sense of life. It is not a poet's novel in the sense in which Mr. Lawrence Durrell's Alexandrian books are a poet's novel. The prose, the imagined narrative of an old man looking back on his youth, is deliberately bare and plain. Mr. Tate, in fact, gets some of his finest effects by writing a dramatic situation down, not by writing it up. It is a poet's novel, however, in the unusual depth of its conception and in the way in which it manages to give scenes and episodes, which might seem slight or ordinary in themselves, an air of ominous implicit meaning.

The Fathers is a tragic novel both in the medieval and the classical sense of the word. It exhibits the turnings of fortune's wheel; Major Buchan, the father of the narrator, is a generous, dignified, courteous man, presiding, when the story opens, with a properly impersonal grief and a proper consideration for his domestic slaves and his remote relations, at his wife's funeral ceremonies; ceremonies which are the occasion for a gathering of the "connexion" and for what we would call in England a garden party. Major Buchan is a model of what a Southern gentleman should be; if he has a moral fault it is that he is proud (but his pride never makes him violent or unjust); if he has an intellectual flaw it is that he is a little stupid; but the story in the end exhibits stupidity as almost a desirable quality, a safeguard against the abyss.

By the end of the story Major Buchan's Unionist politics have isolated him from his friends and estranged him from his sons, his son-in-law has shot his son, the son-in-law's wife is mad, Federal troops have burnt his house down, and he has hanged himself. He has lived by "custom and ceremony," in Yeats's phrase, an example to his fellows, and has suffered the common fate of upholders of "custom and ceremony" in a changing world. Major Buchan is hardly a person; it is his dignity, it is his representative aristocratic quality, that all his reactions to life are impersonally representative. He enacts his given role. His is the medieval tragedy, like the tragedy of the Duke of Buckingham in Sackville. The classical tragedy in *The Fathers* is that of the Major's son-in-law, George Posey.

Posey is a man rather nobler than the rest of us, who brings progressive destruction upon everybody he cares for, because he does not care for the habits that they care for; he has become excessively personal; his responses are unpredictable, even to himself. Posey is, in a way, the modern man in a traditional society. He brings personal passion and free intelligence to bear on a network of traditions at once so complex and so fragile that they cannot bear that pressure. He is nothing so simple or so obviously dangerous as the radical or the rebel. He is merely the man who takes the public life as the inert background to the personal life. He is above, or outside, not opposed to, the tribe; he seeks to help the tribe, often, in his individualistic ways. He is fully an individual human being in a sense in which, in a traditional society, it is not safe to be. He seeks private or personal satisfactions outside the public order. That public order is, in any case, like Major Buchan, doomed; but, within the circle on which he makes his immediate impact, George Posey notably hastens and in a sense "personalizes" the impact of the doom.

Mr. Tate is best known as a poet and critic, as one of the founder members of the group of young Southern writers who first forgathered, around 1922, in Nashville, Tennessee. Nashville is not known to everyone. For those who have never been there Mr. John M. Bradbury's book on the Fugitive group gives the impression that in some ways it is like an English Midland provincial town: many factories, many Rotarians, a great strength of Methodism; it has, too, an old-fashioned tradition of Southern oratory. The group of the Fugitives were looked at a little askance when they started, until they began to make a reputation. Mr. Tate began to write good poems when he came to New York. It was from the perspective of New York that he began to see the South passionately, took his stand, wrote his biographies of Stonewall Jackson and Jefferson Davis. He has made the Old South, in his criticism and in his poetry, bear the weight of a lust for tradition that is partly pastoral but is partly Yeats's dream of "unity of being," Mr. Eliot's belief that there was some period or place in history where a "certain dissociation of sensibility" had not set in.

The South is a tragic region, which is why Mr. Tate is able to write a tragic novel, and why Mr. Faulkner's novels have their violent truth. It is a region which has suffered European experiences; defeat in war; something like occupation; an effort of industrial reconstruction that bought moral independence at the expense, almost, of traditional identity. That traditional identity was never that of a high, literary, artistic, or philosophical culture in the European sense. The Old South, as Mr. Tate notes in his collected essays, had no place in its social life for a man of purely literary genius (and of dim family connexions) like Edgar Allan Poe. The men of the Old South loved words, but they saw law and politics as the proper outlet for a rhetorical gift; poetry, as a full-time preoccupation, was not quite a man's job. The old Southern idea of civilization was based partly on custom and tradition, on social ritual, and partly also on self-respect. They preferred, Mr. Tate notes somewhere in his essays, rhetoric to dialectic; they loved, as most Americans love, the anecdote as a conversational instrument, the simple fable carrying a moral. Neither metaphysics nor poetry carried a high prestige with them, and therefore, when the argument jammed, when there was no communicating image, when self-respect was severely offended, they often shot one another. It was a mannerly but leisurely and sometimes almost slovenly civilization.

The hero of Henry James's early novel *The Bostonians* is a typical Southerner. Stranded in Boston, he longs for a rocking chair, a hot evening, a long glass of mint julep. He is at first amused and astonished, in the end bored and exasperated, by the restless urge for vague self-improvement of the New England mind. James sees him half ironically, half romantically. He rescues the heroine from her dreadful wilful-intellectual, unconsciously Lesbian monitress; but still for the heroine, James hints sadly, he is not great catch. Henry Adams was at Harvard with the son of Robert E. Lee, Rooney Lee. He says of him: "Tall, largely built, handsome, genial, with liberal Virginian openness towards all he liked, he had also the Virginian habit of command

. . . . For a year at least . . . [he] was the most popular and prominent man in his class, but then seemed to drop slowly into the background. The habit of command was not enough, and the Virginian
had little else. He was simple beyond analysis; so simple that even the
simple New England student could not realise him." There was the
same splendid simplicity in his father who during the Civil War used
to refer to the enemy as "those people over there."

Nobody could call Mr. Tate "simple beyond analysis." He would
perhaps be an even better critic than he is (he is a very good critic
indeed) if he had not such an absorbing curiosity about, and such a
gift for expounding, commenting on, qualifying and placing other
men's ideas. Often in this collection of his main critical essays one
could wish that so much effort was not spent on courtesies and reservations about the ideas of Mr. Eliot or Dr. I. A. Richards, for instance,
or on noble shadowboxing with the ideas of the progressive, positivist,
scientific mind, and more effort on pure criticism, pure appreciation,
pure placing, for which in, for instance, his essays on Poe, on Hart
Crane, on Emily Dickinson, on John Peale Bishop, Mr. Tate shows
an exceptional gift.

He often cannot get to the core of what he has to say till after a few
paragraphs of Southern oratory in the relaxed and informal mode,
paragraphs which are in a way an apology for doing something so
personal, and untraditional, as putting sharply a complexly definite
point of view. But possibly the simplicity under the sometimes
laboured and cumbrous expository procedure is the great moral quality. There is a fine short late essay on Hart Crane, which does not
dodge the subject of Crane's homosexuality; what expiates that, for Mr.
Tate, is that Crane was unwillingly homosexual; had passionate attach-
ments to women, not middle-aged women, but women of his own age;
died in the middle of a normal love-affair; had such appalling parents
that his homosexuality is explicable, and, as Mr. Tate notes, it is a
Christian commonplace that God takes account of conditions.

The same fine simplicity comes into two essays on Mr. Pound, an
early one on the *Cantos,* a late one on the controversy about the Bollingen Award (for which Mr. Tate voted). The *Cantos* for Mr. Tate
are conversation, conversation about nothing—or nothing continuous
or important—but conversation made poetry. About the Bollingen
Award he makes it clear that he thinks Mr. Pound's ideas crude and

incoherent to the last degree, that he has no personal bias towards him (Mr. Pound having always treated his own poetry with the utmost contempt), that Mr. Pound's anti-Semitism shames him (like most Gentiles he has felt himself, and been ashamed of, impulses of anti-Semitism) but that, in honour bound, as a man devoted to poetry, he must pay his tribute to a gift for revivifying language; a gift which he does not associate with any central wisdom in Mr. Pound.

And the simplicity, and the admiration for simplicity, come out even more in *The Fathers*: it seems, as one reads it again after twenty years, possibly one of the great novels of our time. It is as short, and as free of any material extraneous to the narrative line and the thematic pattern, as a novel by Turgenev. It is about a kind of Turgenev society, or a society like that depicted by Somerville and Ross, under the surface, in the *Irish R. M.* books; a patriarchal or cavalier society, in unconscious fatal decay. The decay is there in the richness of the funeral gathering at the beginning, a richness which George Posey, too refined to be civilized, cannot bear. He cannot bear the formalities, the introductions to remote connexions whose names and faces he forgets as soon as he has met them, the making of death, or of its marking, a kind of heavy celebration. He is always thinking, planning, using his intelligence; and therefore, in a traditional society, many people admire George, but nobody quite trusts him.

They are right not to trust George. After all, by the end of the tale, without meaning to, when he takes a positive step without quite knowing why he does it, George has shot two men dead, one his brother-in-law, driven his wife mad, broken the hearts of his father-in-law and of his younger brother-in-law, Lacy, who tells the story. George rides away unscathed; Lacy is left alone, to try to prop the ruins of a tradition.

It is a large argument for simplicity, for the impersonal authority of a code. But the book is a tragedy because George is a hero, not a villain; Mr. Tate knows all the dangers of personal impulse and unbridled intelligence; but his celebration of Major Buchan's slow, impersonal, social rectitude is also a criticism of the vulnerability of the unexamined social life. As a fine poet of strain and tension, as a critic who notes how strain and tension are held together sometimes, and transcended, in good poems, Mr. Tate knows that intelligence can be murderous; he also knows we cannot do without it.

Old Orders Changing
(Tate and Lampedusa)

by FRANK KERMODE

I t is an ancient and productive literary habit to compare things as
they are with things as they used to be. "We are scarce our fathers'
shadows cast at noon." Decisive historical events, types of the aboriginal catastrophe, acquire the character of images upon which too
much cannot be said, since they sum up our separation from joy or
civility. So, in Imperial Rome, men looked back to the Republic; so
to this day they look back past the Reformation or the Renaissance
or the Civil War, the points at which our characteristic disorders
began. The practice has its dangers; the prelapsarian can become
merely a moral and intellectual deep shelter, and there is some difficulty in drawing the line between the good old days of the vulgar
myth and the intellectual's nostalgia for some "organic society." The
lost paradise lies archetypally behind much worthless historical fiction,
and agreeable though it may seem that the community as a whole
appears to share the view that the second Temple is not like the first,
the fact is that the first can be reconstructed on the South Shore, or on
a Hollywood set, far more comfortably than in a work of imagination.
The first requirement for such a work, on such a theme, is dry intelligence working on real information. To be obsessed by the chosen
historical moment, as a theologian might meditate the Incarnation, so

EDITOR'S NOTE: Reprinted from *Puzzles and Epiphanies* by Frank Kermode (New
York: Chilmark Press, 1962; London: Routledge, 1962), pp. 131–39, by permission of
the publishers. This essay first appeared, in a slightly different form, in *Encounter*,
15:72–76 (August 1969).

that one shares it with everybody yet avoids all contamination from less worthy and less austere intelligences—that is the basic qualification. Put another way, it is a power of self-criticism perhaps found only in an aristocratic, but not barbarian, sensibility. A few modern historical novelists have this quality. The authors of these two books[1] have it to an extraordinary degree, especially Mr. Tate, whose theme, the break-up of the Old South, is known to be unusually productive of gushing nonsense.

If, as we are told, many Americans have a confused and erroneous idea of the Old South, it is not very likely that we, founding ours on *Uncle Tom's Cabin* and *Gone with the Wind*, can avoid mistakes. Mr. Tate, of course, is thoroughly informed, but it is not his business to impart information. His novel is Virginia-colour, steeped in the province, but if he mentions, say, Helper—a book studied by his principal character and locked away from other members of the household—he will not add that this book was called *The Impending Crisis in the South* (1857), or explain its importance. And this necessary reticence extends to matters more subtle: to the landscape and the climate, still to the European and the Yankee surprising, exotic; to the Jeffersonian politics of the old Southern aristocrat; to the archaic manners of the South and particularly to its views on personal honour, which make credible the violence of Mr. Tate's climax. In fact, as presented, this climax is hardly violent at all; Mr. Tate's strategy requires the maintenance of a very even tone and the preservation of the reader's distance from the events described. All the meanings are qualified by this calmness and this distance, and at certain crucial moments, narrative and symbolic, one senses the huge invisible effort the feat required. Explanation, discrimination between fact and myth, would have falsified all this, but their absence makes the work a delicate undertaking for English readers; for the tension between fact and myth is essential to the novel.

The myth of a valuable and archaic southern civilization is not without basis. Crèvecoeur could call Charleston the most brilliant of American cities. The antebellum South thought of itself as in a great tradition, the heir of Greece and Rome; and if its account of its aristocratic provenance was largely spurious, it was for all that essentially

---

[1] *The Fathers.* By Allen Tate. *The Leopard.* By Giuseppe di Lampedusa.

aristocratic in its structure. Yet it was a perversely democratic aristocracy, if only because of the slaves, whose very existence made it impossible to set difficult barriers between different classes of whites. In any
case, the population was bound together by blood, by a network of
cousinships that took no account of status and even included slaves.
The Negro was not feared or hated in the antebellum South, and he
was not—effectively at any rate—exploited (all parties, including Mr.
Tate's Agrarians, seem to be agreed that the slave system was extremely,
perhaps disastrously, wasteful). Any civilization is built on paradoxes, but few so curiously as this one. These backward-looking, fine-
mannered men had the activity of pioneers and hunters, and their natural violence was fostered by the alternately languid and vehement
climate. Civic and personal pride coexisted with a central hedonism,
a passion for gaming, drinking, love-making, talking. It was a world
no outsider could improve, and one could represent the Yankee attack
on slavery as directed not only against one's way of life, but against
civility itself, even against God. The emphasis on personal honour is
a feature of societies which feel themselves highly privileged; and the
South had its duelling, and was strong on the honour of women—the
"fragile membrane" as Faulkner calls it, that needs so much male blood
to protect it. At the climax of Mr. Tate's novel a Negro enters a girl's
room and attacks her; the consequences are death, madness, sterility.
But what seems a myth—the revival of some incredible tabu—is a matter of fact. Such tabus are protection from what Mr. Tate calls the
abyss, essential though atavistic elements of civility.

An image of civility so distinctive, and so decisively destroyed by
war, can stand quite as well as that of England before its Civil War
for the vanquished homogeneous culture that preceded some great dissociation, the effects of which we now suffer. It had all the gifts save
art; and that, as Henry James said, is a symptom of the unhappy society. What the English Civil War meant to Mr. Eliot the American
means to Mr. Tate; the moment when the modern chaos began, though
it cast its shadow before. His book is about the antebellum South under
that shadow.

The war, so considered, is also a myth with correlative facts. It is
commonplace that one thing more than any other sets the Southerner
apart from other Americans: he is the only American who has ever
known defeat, been beaten, occupied and reconstructed, seen his

society wrecked and had no power to rebuild it on the old lines. Hence, as Cash said in *The Mind of the South*, a division developed in the "Southern psyche"—the old hedonism warred with a new puritanism, old loyalties with new destinations. A tolerant society became bigoted. The Klan attacked not only the now-hated Negroes but Jews, atheists, fornicators. And Yankee culture moved in. The link with the past, the "traditional men," was gone. In Mr. Tate's poem the Confederate graveyard stands, in his own words, for "the cut-off-ness of the modern 'intellectual man' from the world." Could anything be saved? Mr. Tate and his friends in the 'twenties proposed and developed an Agrarian solution for the South, and were accused of sentimental organicism, of naïvely hoping to revive the virtues of the antique world by restoring its economic forms. What they really wanted was a new society uncontaminated by the industrial capitalism of the North, a society living close to life in a manner made impossible by the great dissociation. "I never thought of Agrarianism as a *restoration* of anything in the Old South," Mr. Tate says explicitly, "I saw it as something to be created . . . not only in the South . . . but . . . in the moral and religious outlook of Western man." He sought a way of life having the kind of order that is now found only in art; an order available to all, and not only to the estranged artist. Mr. Tate also proposed a theory of "tension" in poetry (an extensive literal statement qualifies and is qualified by intensive figurative significances) which is a translation to aesthetics of this view of life. And his meditations on the South, or the image of it he has made, include these complementary literal and figurative aspects. Finally, in 1938, in this novel, he presents the image itself at its most complex, containing the maximum tension between letter and spirit, fact and myth.

Thus the calm of the book is not merely a matter of Southern dignity (though that has its place in the effect) but of intellectual control, the tightened bow. The South is matter of fact; but it is also

> a pleasant land
> Where even death could please
> Us with an ancient pun—
> All dying for the hand
> Of the mother of silences.

The "place" of the Buchans is called "Pleasant Hill,"[2] in recognition

---

[2] Mr. Tate tells me his own family home was called "Pleasant Hill."

of the basic myth; but it is not Paradise, it is merely a place where the radical human values are recognized, where the community and not the individual owns the myths which fence off the abyss. The time is just before the War. The narrator is Lacy Buchan, now old, speaking of the pleasant land as he saw it in boyhood. Memory works on a series of images: the death of Lacy's mother and the mourning of the "connexion"; a chivalric tournament; the beginning of the fighting; a Faulknerian family disaster; the burning of Pleasant Hill by Union troops. It would be difficult to exaggerate the skill and integrity of the presentation, the slow unfolding of figurative significance. The principal characters are Major Buchan and his sons and daughter; George Posey, caught between the Old and the New South, who becomes Buchan's son-in-law; Yellow Jim, a Negro half-brother of Posey's. The basic fable is virtually Greek; rarely outside Greek drama is there to be found this blend of civilization and primitive ritual, the gentleman who is *euphues* but at home in actual life, and with his roots in immemorial custom.

Major Buchan's mistake—his *hamartia*—is the honourable one of backing the wrong version of history; he finds himself giving his daughter to Posey, whom he cannot understand, and adhering to the Union when his family yields to the overwhelming emotional attraction of Confederacy. All depends, in the book, upon the successful rendering of his dignity and authority, the order of his house. But the detail that shows his life and his house to be in some ways less than great— archaistic revivals of a dead past, like the splendours of the jousting—is also important. Woven into the myopically rendered texture of the book are the qualifying facts: Mr. Broadacre forgetting to spit out his tobacco before making a formal oration on Southern chivalry, unsurpassed in the world; Lacy's mother conducting a household task as a little ritual "not very old to be sure but to my mother immemorial"; the revived custom of duelling. These are the newly created traditions that Posey, the new man, dishonours. He is stronger than his opponent in the duel but will not fight it; he cannot be disarmed by the only weapon Major Buchan uses against him, a subtle withdrawal of courtesy. But his disregard for the absurd forms of his society is a symptom of his estrangement. He fears the dead, is embarrassed by the sight of a bull mounting a cow. The nature of the Buchan commitment to life he does not understand. "They'll all starve to death," he says. "They do nothing but die and marry and think about the honour of Virginia." He sells Yellow Jim, his half-brother, treating him as "liquid capital," and so precipitates the domestic crisis of the attack on his sister. Even then Posey is half-hearted about the obligation to kill Jim, and the job is done by Semmes Buchan, Lacy's elder brother, whom Posey kills instead. He also kills his enemy Langton, a man as representative of the Old South in his corrupt activity as Semmes is in his archaic sense of honour. Posey's position in the War is ambiguous; he smuggles arms, carrying the carpet-bag which a few years later was the hated emblem of Yankee exploitation. Posey destroys the Buchans as surely as the War, and he does it out of a modern confusion, doing evil "because he has not the will to do good." The Old South is the Major, disowning his son for choosing Confederacy, but surrendering his house and his life rather than tell a Yankee officer that he himself is not "seecesh." As Lacy and Posey leave his grave, Lacy to return to the fighting, Posey to disappear on his own occasions, we learn of the last Buchan victim: Lacy. We know what to make of Posey, but there is always more to be made; as when Lacy, in his last sentence, declares his allegiance in the remarkable sentence, as rich a sentence as ever ended a novel: "If I am killed it will be because I love him more than I love any man." This is the reward of Mr. Tate's method: his images, though always sufficient, accrete significance as the narration develops, so that the whole book grows steadily in the mind.

The dignity and power of this book depend upon the power of a central image presented with concreteness and profundity, and not upon one's acceptance of Mr. Tate's history. But without his integrity of intellect and imagination the image would have been false and imperfect in ways that might have exposed it to such disagreements. By a bold device, the intervention of a ghost, Mr. Tate hands on this image to us through three generations of Buchans; it is as if ratified by a time-defeating community of sentiment, and the life in it is good and transmissible as well as tragic. If we could rescue the word "civilized" from the smart and fashionable, we could apply it, in deep admiration, to this book.

The Leopard is also a deeply meditated book, extremely original and possessing an archaic harshness of feeling, more alien and more ancient than the civilized calm of *The Fathers*. It is, however, a less consistently well made work; there are one or two sermons, points where the exposition of ideas gets the better of the total figuration of the image; there is also an episode (Father Pirrone's intervention in a peasant marriage dispute) which makes a relevant point but which adheres much more loosely to the main body of the novel than anything Tate would permit. It is also, of course, an aristocratic novel, but with a very different heritage from that of *The Fathers*. If it has the brilliant intelligence of Stendhal it has also something of his superior carelessness. But only a little; it is a work entirely worthy of that master (whose admiration for Ariosto Lampedusa evidently shared) and it is also in many ways a work of this century. The coincidence of theme with Tate's is remarkable. A Southern world is changed by soldiers from the North; but now the South is Sicily and the soldiers Garibaldi's. The time (1860) is the same. The theme—the break-up of a civilization—is the same, though what is lost here is, for all its power, a world of death. And at a level not far below the surface the theme of *The Leopard* is death, the conditions under which men as well as societies long for it.

The novel opens with a wonderful scene; the Prince of Salina at his devotions, surrounded by his family. The women rise and expose the wall-paintings, the mythological gods of a religion that dominated Sicily before Christianity and still lends it life. The Prince, physically vast, sensual, irresponsible, walks with his dog Bendicò in a garden full of the nauseating rich scents of a Sicilian summer, the European flowers tormented by the heat into giving Eastern odours. He scratches some lichen off a decaying Flora, and remembers the smell of a soldier's corpse found rotting in the garden. He thinks of his king, of a monarchy with death in its face. After dinner, at which the family retreat into silence from the mere threat of his irritability, he takes himself off to Palermo (forcing his Jesuit chaplain to accompany him) in order to obtain from Mariannina the satisfactions not to be had from his pious wife. But he lives for his astronomical studies, associated in his mind with the calm, as women are associated with the pleasure, of death. He is the old order, arbitrary, cruel, careless, yet in sympathy with the country and its peasants; above all in love with death.

The rise of the class which threatens the supremacy of Salina's is represented by such men as Calogero, who arrives at the Prince's dinner-party in tails, when the Prince has, out of consideration for him, not dressed. Tancredi, the Prince's nephew, is the Posey of the book, a penniless, charming, trimming aristocrat, who fights with Garibaldi—herald of the new order in which Calogero is the equal of Salina—but does so only in order to save what can be saved of the old ways. For the same reason, though also for love, he marries Angelica, Calogero's daughter. It is Tancredi's way to get the girl and the money and the Prince's favourite peaches into the bargain. But the old order does change. The Prince betrays the past. (He has wine-glasses with the initials F.D. engraved on them, gifts of the King; but when he drinks Tancredi's health in a single gulp, "the initials, which stood out clearly on the golden colour of the full glass, were no longer visible.") He changes his manners to fit the needs of survival in the new world. But as he watches a shot rabbit die in landscape that had not changed since the Phœnicians laboured across it, observing the paws uselessly mimicking the contractions of flight, he knows that it is hopeless; the Southern wish for death is near fulfilment. He is the last of the Leopards. In a remarkable appendix we hear of his barren daughters surrounded by bogus religious relics and throwing away the stuffed body of Bendicò, the last relic of the Prince. His death—another extraordinary passage—is like the death of a world. The corpse of the soldier sends its sweet, rotten smell through the book.

The languor and the violence of this more desperate South is beautifully conveyed; the book is held in the grip of its opening sentence—*Nunc et in hora mortis nostrae*—throughout. Always associated with this knowledge of death are the Prince's love of the undisturbed stars, and a pervasive sensuality made civil by easy autocratic wit. The wit of Lampedusa is equal to the demands of a crucial dinner-party; and in describing the sensuality of Tancredi's wooing in the great house at Donnafugata—a new-style courtship stained with the dead dust of centuries—he achieves something absolutely original, a kind of erotic fugue. Lampedusa's talent was clearly enormous; Mr. Colquhoun's translation has immense resource; and the book is, as it stands in English, worthy of all the admiration that it has received. The civilization that ends with Salina is greater and darker than Major Buchan's; and Lampedusa has got its presence into his book, which therefore is a bigger book than Tate's. There is nothing that a Major Buchan can do which has the sheer historical weight of significance that Salina's dealings with the Jesuit, in part submissive, in part insulting—as when he makes the priest help to dry his magnificent and recently sinning body—have as a natural right. Yet of the two books Mr. Tate's is the more perfect. It cannot be more than once or twice in a lifetime that a critic might have on his table, at the same time, two new novels of such rare quality.

IV. THE POET

Allen Tate's Poetry

by CLEANTH BROOKS

llen Tate's poetry illustrates a structure of violent synthesis. He constantly throws his words and images into active contrast. Almost every adjective in his poetry challenges the reader's imagination to follow it off at a tangent. For instance, in the "Ode to the Confederate Dead," November becomes not "drear" November, "sober" November, but "*Ambitious* November with the humors of the year" [italics mine]. The "curiosity of an angel's stare" is not "idle" or "quiet" or "probing" or any other predictable adjective, but "brute" curiosity. This is the primary difficulty that Tate's poetry presents to the reader who is unacquainted with his dominant themes: the surface of the poem, in its apparently violent disorder, may carry him off at tangents.

There is some justification, therefore, for approaching Tate's poetry through an account of his basic themes—all the more since these themes are closely related to the poetic method itself. We may conveniently begin by examining a very important passage in his essay on "Humanism and Naturalism." In discussing attitudes toward history, he describes two ways of viewing the past. The first is that which gives what may be called the scientist's past, in which events form a logical series; the second is that which gives what Tate himself calls the "temporal past."

EDITOR'S NOTE: Reprinted from *Modern Poetry and The Tradition* by Cleanth Brooks (Chapel Hill: University of North Carolina Press, 1939; New York: Oxford University Press, 1965), pp. 95–109, by permission of the University of North Carolina Press.

151

". . . the logical series is quantitative, the abstraction of space. The temporal series is, on the other hand, space concrete. Concrete, temporal experience implies the existence of a temporal past, and it is the foundation of the religious imagination; that is to say, the only way to think of the past independently of . . . naturalism is to think religiously; and conversely, the only way to think religiously is to think in time. Naturalistic science is timeless. A doctrine based upon it, whether explicitly or not, can have no past, no idea of tradition, no fixed center of life. The 'typically human' is a term that cannot exist apart from some other term; it is not an absolute; it is fluid and unfixed.

"To de-temporize the past is to reduce it to an abstract lump. To take from the present its concrete fullness is to refuse to let standards work from the inside. It follows that 'decorum' must be 'imposed' from above. Thus there are never specific moral problems (the subject matter of the arts) but only fixed general doctrines without subject matter—that is to say, without 'nature.'"

In other words, the artist today finds that his specific subject matter tends to be dissolved in abstractions of various sorts. His proper subjects—specific moral problems—are not to be found in an abstract, logical series, for in such a series there are no standards of any sort—and nothing specific, nothing concrete.

Tate's preoccupation with history and time in his poetry is thus closely related to John Crowe Ransom's characteristic problem: that of man living under the dispensation of science—modern man suffering from a dissociation of sensibility.

Tate goes on to say in the same essay: "The 'historical method' has always been the anti-historical method. Its aim is to contemporize the past. Its real effect is to detemporize it. The past becomes a causal series, and timeless . . ." Tate's concern here is with the neohumanists, but the generalization may be applied to the arts without distorting it too violently. Carl Sandburg, for example, will supply an example pat to our purpose. Consider his "Four Preludes on Playthings of the Wind."

After the first Prelude with its "What of it? Let the dead be dead," and after the second Prelude which describes an ancient city (Baby-

lon?) with its cedar doors and golden dancing girls and its ultimate
destruction, Prelude Three begins:

> It has happened before.
> Strong men put up a city and got
>   a nation together,
> And paid singers to sing and women
>   to warble: We are the greatest city,
>   the greatest nation,
>   nothing like us ever was.

But, as the poem goes on to point out, the ultimate dancers are the
rats, and the ultimate singers, the crows. The poet's intention, presum-
ably, is to contemporize the past. The real effect is to detemporize it.
Babylon or Nineveh becomes interchangeable with Chicago. Chicago
receives a certain access of dignity from the association; Babylon, a certain humanity and reality; and the poet is allowed to imply, with a
plausible finality, that human nature fundamentally doesn't change.

Sandburg's primary impulse seems to be a revulsion from the "literary" past—the people of the past, too, hired singers, ran night-clubs,
and joined booster societies. But Sandburg's contemporizing of the
past springs also—probably unconsciously—from the fact that he is
immersed in a scientific civilization.

Tate not only cannot accept Sandburg's detemporized past; he must
strive actively to ascertain what meaning the past can have for modern
man who has so many inducements to consider it merely as a logical
series. This, I take it, is the primary theme of "The Mediterreanean,"
"Aeneas at Washington," and even—in a varied form—of the "Ode to
the Confederate Dead." Aeneas possessed a concrete past—moved from
a particular Troy to found a particular Rome. We, on the other hand,
who have "cracked the hemispheres with careless hand," in abolishing
space have also abolished time. The poem is not a lament, nor is it a
"sighing for vanished glories." It is a recognition and an exploration
of our dilemma. Modern man, like the Aeneas of Tate's poem, is
obsessed with the naturalistic view of history—history as an abstract
series. He sees

> . . . all things apart, the towers that men
> Contrive I too contrived long, long ago.

But Aeneas has been acquainted with another conception of history.

> Now I demand little. The singular passion
> Abides its object and consumes desire
> In the circling shadow of its appetite.

(We may gloss the last quoted lines as follows: In his "Religion and the Old South," Tate argues that the naturalistic view of history is intent on utility; but in the case of concrete history, the "images are only to be contemplated, and perhaps the act of contemplation after long exercise initiates a habit of restraint, and the setting up of absolute standards which are less formulas for action than an interior discipline of the mind.")

Modern man with his tremendous historical consciousness is thus confronted with a dilemma when asked for the meaning of his actions:

> . . . Stuck in the wet mire
> Four thousand leagues from the ninth buried city
> I thought of Troy, what we had built her for.

The problem of history receives a somewhat similar treatment in the fine "Message from Abroad." The form into which the problem is cast is peculiarly that of the American confronted with the lack of "history" of his own land and thrown up against the immense "history" of Europe. Stated in somewhat altered form, it is the problem of man, who requires a history in which he can participate personally, lost in the vast museum galleries of western civilization.

> Provençe,
> The Renascence, the age of Pericles, each
> A broad, rich-carpeted stair to pride
> . . . they're easy to follow
> For the ways taken are all notorious,
> Lettered, sculptured and rhymed. . . .

But "those others," the ways taken by his ancestors, are

> . . . incuriously complete, lost,
> Not by poetry and statues timed,
> Shattered by sunlight and the impartial sleet.

He can find, to mark those ways,

> Now only
> The bent eaves and the windows cracked,

> The thin grass picked by the wind,
> Heaved by the mole. . . .

The tall "red-faced" man cannot survive the voyage back to Europe:

> With dawn came the gull to the crest,
> Stared at the spray, fell asleep
> Over the picked bones, the white face
> Of the leaning man drowned deep. . . .

And the poet is finally forced to admit that he cannot see the ancestors, and can merely conjecture

> What did you say mornings?
> Evenings, what?
> The bent eaves
> On the cracked house,
> That ghost of a hound . . .
> The man red-faced and tall
> Will cast no shadow
> From the province of the drowned.

Obviously Tate's poetry is not occupied exclusively with the meaning of history. But his criticism of merely statistical accounts of reality serves as an introduction to the special problems of his poetry in much the same way that Ransom's comments on the relation of science to the myth serve as an approach to his.

Attention to his criticism will illuminate, for example, the positive position from which he comments on our present disintegration:

> The essential wreckage of your age is different,
> The accident the same; the Annabella
> Of proper incest, no longer incestuous:
> In an age of abstract experience, fornication
> Is self-expression, adjunct to Christian euphoria. . . .
>   ("Causerie")

Or, to make the application to the subject of poetry itself, one may quote from the same poem:

> We have learned to require
> In the infirm concessions of memory
> The privilege never to hear too much.

> What is this conversation, now secular,
> A speech not mine yet speaking for me in
> The heaving jelly of my tribal air?
> It rises in the throat, it climbs the tongue,
> It perches there for secret tutelage
> And gets it, of inscrutable instruction. . . .

The situation described is peculiarly that of the modern poet. His speech is a mass of clichés—of terms which with their past associations seem too grandiloquent and gaudy, or, with their past content emptied, now seem meaningless. "Vocabulary / Becomes confusion," and without vocabulary man is lost.

> Heredity
> Proposes love, love exacts language, and we lack
> Language. When shall we speak again? When shall
> The sparrow dusting the gutter sing? When shall
> This drift with silence meet the sun? When shall
> I wake?

We may state the situation in still other terms: Man's religion, his myths, are now merely private fictions. And as Tate has remarked in one of his essays, ". . . a myth should be in conviction immediate, direct, overwhelming, and I take it that the appreciation of this kind of imagery is an art lost to the modern mind." The lover in Tate's "Retroduction to American History," has lost his appreciation of such imagery. He "cannot hear. . . . His very eyeballs fixed in disarticulation . . . . his metaphors are dead."

Tate's metaphors are very much alive; it is through the production of energetic metaphor, of live "myths" that the poet attempts to break through the pattern of "abstract experience" and give man a picture of himself as man. Hence his preoccupation with time and mortality and "specific moral problems." But as a matter of integrity, he cannot take the short cut which Tennyson tends to take to these subjects. One cannot find a living relation between the present and the past without being honest to the present—and that involves taking into account the anti-historical character of our present.

In his "Retroduction to American History," the poet asks why "in such serenity of equal fates"—that is, why, if life is merely a causal sequence, merely abstract experience—has Narcissus "urged the brook with questions?" In a naturalistic world, the brook, like Mr. Ransom's cataract, is only so much water; and we have the absurdity which the poet proceeds to point out:

> Merged with the element
> Speculation suffuses the meadow with drops to tickle
> The cow's gullet; grasshoppers drink the rain.

Self-scrutiny, introspection, in a purely mechanistic universe, is merely a romantic gesture—"Narcissism." In the "Ode to the Confederate Dead," Narcissism figures again, though without a specific symbol.

As Tate has written: "The poem is 'about' solipsism or Narcissism, or any other *ism* that denotes the failure of the human personality to function properly in nature and society. Society (and 'nature' as modern society constructs it) appears to offer limited fields for the exercise of the whole man, who wastes his energy piecemeal over separate functions that ought to come under a unity of being. . . . Without unity we get *the remarkable self-consciousness* of our age [italics mine]."

In the "Ode," the Narcissism of the present forms one term of the contrast; the "total" world in which the dead soldiers fulfilled themselves, the other. But the poet refuses to take the easy romantic attitude toward the contrast. The world which the dead soldiers possessed is not available to the speaker of the poem, for that kind of world is the function of a society, not something which can be wrought out by the private will. Moreover, the poet is honest: the leaves, for him, *are* merely leaves.

The irony expressed in the poem, then, is not the romantic irony of the passage quoted from Tate's criticism in Chapter III. It is a more complex irony, and almost inevitably, a self-inclusive irony. Such an irony is found also in "Last Days of Alice," "The Sonnets at Christmas," "The Meaning of Life," and "The Meaning of Death."

Before considering these poems, however, it is well to note a further criticism of naturalism in Tate's prose. The naturalistic view of experience (history as an abstract series) suggests an "omnipotent human rationality." It can only predict success. The poet (who, by virtue of being a poet, is committed to the concrete and particular) is thus continually thrown into the role of Tiresias.

A number of Tate's poems are ironical treatments of rationality, "The Eagle," for example. It is not the heart which fears death, but the mind, "the white eagle." And in the "Epistle to Edmund Wilson,"

"The mind's a sick eagle taking flight. . . ." The theme is most powerfully stated in the last of the "Sonnets of the Blood." The brother is
cautioned to

> Be zealous that your numbers are all prime,
> Lest false division with sly mathematic
> Plunder the inner mansion of the blood. . . .
> . . . the prime secret whose simplicity
> Your towering engine hammers to reduce,
> Though driven, holds that bulwark of the sea
> Which breached will turn unspeaking fury loose
> To drown out him who swears to rectify
> Infinity. . . .

If the blood is a symbol of the nonrational, concrete stuff of man
which resists abstract classification, by the same token it symbolizes
man's capacity to be more than an abstract integer, and therefore
signifies man's capacity for sin. In an age of abstract experience sin
is meaningless.

In "Last Days of Alice," the logical, self-consistent but inhuman
world of *Through the Looking-Glass* becomes an ironical symbol of the
modern world. The poet maintains most precisely the analogy between
Alice gazing "learnedly down her airy nose" into the abstract world
of the mirror, and modern man who has also turned his world into
abstraction. The subsidiary metaphors—"Alice grown . . . mammoth
but not fat," symbolizing the megalomania of the modern; Alice
"turned absent-minded by infinity" who "cannot move unless her
double move," symbolizing the hypostasis of the modern—grow naturally out of the major symbolism. The poem is witty in the seventeenth-century sense; the reference to the Cheshire cat with his abstract
grin, a witty comparison. But the wit, the sense of precision and complexity, is functional. It contributes the special quality of irony necessary to allow the poet to end his poem with the positive outcry:

> O God of our flesh, return us to Your Wrath,
> Let us be evil could we enter in
> Your grace, and falter on the stony path!

Man's capacity for error, his essential unpredictability, is referred
to in a number of Tate's poems. It is the basis of the beautiful "Ode
to Fear."

My eldest companion present in solitude,
Watch-dog of Thebes when the blind hero strove:
'Twas your omniscience at the cross-road stood
When Laius, the slain dotard, drenched the grove.

Now to the fading, harried eyes immune
Of prophecy, you stalk us in the street
From the recesses of the August noon,
Alert world over, crouched on the air's feet.

You are the surety to immortal life,
God's hatred of the universal stain. . . .

There is an especially rich development of this theme in the twin poems, "The Meaning of Life," and "The Meaning of Death." The first opens with a dry statement of the point as if in a sort of apologetic monotone:

Think about it at will; there is that
Which is the commentary; there's that other,
Which may be called the immaculate
Conception of its essence in itself.

But the essence must not be turned into mere abstraction by the commentary, even though the commentary is so necessary that the essence is speechless without it. The poet goes on to apologize for the tone of tedious explication:

I was saying this more briefly the other day
But one must be explicit as well as brief.
When I was a small boy I lived at home
For nine years in that part of old Kentucky
Where the mountains fringe the Blue Grass,
The old men shot at one another for luck;
It made me think I was like none of them.
At twelve I was determined to shoot only
For honor; at twenty not to shoot at all;
I know at thirty-three that one must shoot
As often as one gets the rare chance—*
In killing there is more than commentary.

---

* I shall expect some one to wrench this statement into a symptom of the poet's "Fascism." A prominent critic, in order to make such a point, has already twisted out of its context Tate's statement that the Southerner can only take hold of his tradition "by violence." In the context in which it occurs, it obviously means "by politics" as opposed to "by religion."

Our predicament is that the opportunity for any meaningful action rarely offers itself at all.

With the last lines the poet shifts the tone again, modulating from the half-whimsical, personal illustration into a brilliant summarizing figure:

> But there's a kind of lust feeds on itself
> Unspoken to, unspeaking; subterranean
> As a black river full of eyeless fish
> Heavy with spawn; with a passion for time
> Longer than the arteries of a cave.

The symbol of the concrete, irrational essence of life, the blood, receives an amazing amplification by its association with the cave. The two symbols are united on the basis of their possession of "arteries." The blood is associated with "lust," is "subterranean" (buried within the body), is the source of "passion." But the added metaphor of the cave extends the associations from those appropriate to an individual body to something general and eternal. The reference to the fish may be also a fertility symbol. But the fish are "eyeless" though "heavy with spawn." The basic stuff of life lacks eyes—cannot see even itself; and filled with infinite potentialities, runs its dark, involved, subterranean course. The metaphor is powerful and rich, but it gives no sense of having been spatchcocked on to the poem. The blood symbol is worked out only in terms of the cave symbol; the two cannot be broken apart. Moreover, it has been prepared for in the casual personal allusion which precedes it. It too is a part of "old Kentucky / Where the mountains fringe the Blue Grass."

"The Meaning of Death" also begins quietly, as "An After-Dinner Speech." The speech is addressed to us, the moderns, who have committed ourselves to commentary—complete, lucid, and full. We have no passion for time—have abolished time.

> Time, fall no more.
> Let that be life—time falls no more. The threat
> Of time we in our own courage have foresworn.
> Let light fall, there shall be eternal light
> And all the light shall on our heads be worn
>
> Although at evening clouds infest the sky
> Broken at base from which the lemon sun
> Pours acid of winter on a useful view. . . .

The concession announced by "although" is important in developing the tone. Incorrigible optimists that we are, we say hopefully that there shall be eternal light although one must admit that the evening light does not suggest the warmth of life but freezes the landscape with cold, pours acid upon it, turns it into something which is a vanity and meaningless. (The psychological basis for the symbolism here is interesting. The "lemon sun" indicates primarily the color of the evening sun, but "lemon" carries on over into a suggestion of something acid and astringent.)

But, the poet observes, our uneasiness is really groundless. Tomorrow surely will bring "jocund day" and the colors of spring. If one in boyhood connected fear with the coming on of the dark at evening, that was merely because one was a small boy. We, at least, have given up that past with its irrationalities and superstitions:

> Gentlemen! let's
> Forget the past, its related errors, coarseness
> Of parents, laxities, unrealities of principle.
>
> Think of tomorrow. Make a firm postulate
> Of simplicity in desire and act
> Founded on the best hypotheses;
> Desire to eat secretly, alone, lest
> Ritual corrupt our charity . . .

Ritual implies a respect for the thing as thing; it implies more than an abstract series—implies a breach in our strict naturalism. That naturalism must be maintained

> Lest darkness fall and time fall
> In a long night . . .

and thus spoil our plans for the conquest of time—spoil our plans for the reduction of everything to abstraction where, we hope,

> . . . learned arteries
> Mounting the ice and sum of barbarous time
> Shall yield, without essence, perfect accident.

The past phrase suggests the final metaphor of "The Meaning of Life," and with the final line of this poem, the speaker drops his ironical pretense of agreement with the "gentlemen" and shifts into another quality of irony, a deeper irony, returning to the cave metaphor: "We are the eyelids of defeated caves." We are the generation that has broken with history, the generation that has closed the mouth of the cave. The word "eyelids" indicates the manner of the closing: the suggestion is that the motion is one of languor and weariness as one might close his eyelids in sleep. The vitality is gone.

A similar theme is to be found in "The Oath" though the setting and the treatment of the theme in this poem are very different. The two friends are sitting by the fire in the gathering twilight.

> It was near evening, the room was cold,
> Half-dark; Uncle Ben's brass bullet-mould
> And powder-horn and Major Bogan's face
> Above the fire in the half-light plainly said:
> There's naught to kill but the animated dead.
> Horn nor mould nor major follows the chase.

Then one of the friends proposes the question, "Who are the dead?"

> And nothing more was said. . . .
> So I leaving Lytle to that dream
> Decided what it is in time that gnaws
> The aging fury of a mountain stream
> When suddenly, as an ignorant mind will do,
> I thought I heard the dark pounding its head
> On a rock, crying: *Who are the dead?*
> Then Lytle turned with an oath—By God it's true!

The thing that is true is obvious that *we* are the dead. The dead are those who have given in to abstraction, even though they may move about and carry on their business and be—to use the earlier phrase in the poem—the "animated dead." A mountain stream ceases to be a mountain stream when its bed has become worn level. It might even be termed a "defeated" mountain stream when it has lost the activity which gave its career meaning.

The Courage of Irony:
The Poetry of Allen Tate

by KATHERINE GARRISON CHAPIN

Allen Tate is essentially a man of letters in the broadest meaning of the phrase. As a poet, critic and prose writer his influence on his contemporaries has been great for more than three decades. His early biographies of Stonewall Jackson and Jefferson Davis, and a psychologically penetrating novel, *The Fathers*, set in Virginia during the Civil War, link him to a South which he knows never quite existed except in his nostalgic memory. The novel, using a symbolic mode, where action and physical environment are transmitted through consciousness—memories of the past intruding on the present—with its shrewd naturalism, was a reaction against the sentimentality gathering about the war and the changes it effected. Published in 1938 and reissued here and in England in 1960, *The Fathers* bridges the gap between Virginia Woolf's stream-of-consciousness and the current era of morbid naturalism.

Tate's essays, belonging to and supplementing his poetry have been collected (in 1959) in one volume. His criticism has always been exact, authoritative and subtle, unencumbered with the self-consciousness so often found in the modern Freudian approach. For a brief time his reputation as an outstanding critical authority tended to overshadow his poetry. But poetry is Tate's chief concern, and it is about his

EDITOR'S NOTE: Reprinted from *The New Republic*, 153:4–5, 22–24 (24 July 1965), copyright © 1965 by Harrison-Blaine of New Jersey, Inc., by permission of *The New Republic*.

poetry that I want to speak now. Published in single volumes from 1930 on *The Collected Poems* (1960) is his definitive selection.

There has been little enlightened discussion of Tate's poetry, though occasional comment and criticism of individual poems by Robert Fitzgerald, Howard Nemerov, Delmore Schwartz, and Cleanth Brooks; and a booklet (1964), *Allen Tate*, by George Hemphill in the University of Minnesota pamphlet series on American writers, and in 1963 R. K. Meiners's excellent study, *The Last Alternatives*, to which I am indebted for helpful and valuable suggestions.

Tate's conception that "poetry was the unification of experience through the dynamics of form" carried him beyond his own early influences—Coleridge, the French symbolists, Baudelaire, Eliot's analyses—into Yeats' powerful lyrical irony. Tate's classic idiom—what has been attacked as his "Latinity"—springs from an absorption in Latin and Greek poetry and mythology, rooted in his early education. This diction, however, has no relationship to ponderous Victorian "classicism." Under the spell of Vergil and Homer he never drops into the English of translation. Images are re-created or combined to suit his needs. "The peaked margin of antiquity's delay," in "The Mediterranean," links time and space. Not the words, but the quality is Vergilian. His love of Dante preceded his religious conversion to Catholicism, and much of Dante's thought and image became a part of Tate's poetry. Such influences do not account for the vehement emotion which underlies so much of his writing, and is reflected in the intensity of his style. Meiners calls this the "tragic element." It springs from Tate's spiritual concern with man, which is never fully resolved.

A basic element that has nourished Tate's poetic response is his relationship to his land and his view of its history—the Southern civilization both in its flowering and its decadence. He is the only modern American poet so deeply involved. One thinks of John Crowe Ransom and Robert Penn Warren, but Tate is less romantic, less tolerant, and, though less limited in his approach, is more passionate. His "angry love" of the South, as an English critic has said, has made him criticize but never abandon the image of what that life once was. In his memory, land and people together express the beauty, intelligence, and wit of a classic age. His memory of actual events has supported his poetic vision. The tragedy of defeat adds to its heroism.

His agrarian theories, which he shares with other Southern writers

—once centered in the Fugitive group at Vanderbilt University—sprang from a belief in the essential relationship between the land and the living. Tate would keep the values of the South, with its noble past, though now a poor section of the earth, against the sterile and anonymous environment of vast urban conditioning. He does not think of agrarianism alone as restoring the old South—something new must be created in the moral and religious outlook of Western man. That the Southern way of living inevitably took for granted the existence of a class society has not troubled Tate, though it has disturbed some of his liberal admirers.

Tate has been called "a border man," an expression which in his time and country has a genuine meaning, and draws on the twin inheritance of Virginian aristocracy and the sturdy substance of men in Kentucky valleys and Tennessee riverland. His form of religion became another "border," between his maternal grandfather's Roman Catholicism of his Maryland boyhood and his father's Scotch-English Protestantism. He has always been able to live in the two worlds of the theology of *The Divine Comedy* and the modern guilt complex of Freud. They are both found in his poem "Seasons of the Soul."

When he began to look back with an appraising eye he realized that he did not altogether belong in any nostalgic past, even as a myth to sustain his poetry. He may have remembered what Valéry once said, that history of the past makes little sense except for the man who finds in himself a passion for the future. Tate is a part of both present and future, though he finds it impossible to accept the changes wrought by World War II to his universe. He does not completely reject the modern world, but deplores the cultural and spiritual decay toward which he believes we are moving. Unlike many contemporary poets he is not a defeatist. But he finds the vexed question difficult to answer.

He understands the spiritual needs that move men, the hunger for a meaning in life, the unrewarded search for unity, the need for a God who has disappeared. These are the realities that reaffirm man's dignity. As a man of letters he has defined poetry in terms not of "communication" but of "communion." Communication deals with abstract man, communion presupposes participation between concrete men. Love, which demands the surrender of one kind of integrity in the service of another, he contrasts with lust, which is life in its subterranean, groping aspects. He even accepts the blessedness of being returned to the "wrath of God, in order to enter into His grace" ("Last Days of Alice"). His sense of tragedy springs from the frustration that comes from the ever unresolved conflict between the ideal and the actual.

Tate expresses this frustration in a poetry that cannot be read or understood "inadvisedly or lightly." His meaning is not often on the surface. His style is elliptical and powerful. There are qualities like the poetry of the 17th Century, particularly Donne, in the baroque wit, the play on words, the metaphysical slant, and the religious circle of emotion.

The intellectual vision is so emphatic in Tate that emotion is seldom loosened or set free at once. Rather it is embedded in the image and must be forced out to reach the reader. Violence is never the primary motivation of a poem; the pulse, the feeling comes first and the explosive expressions, far from being elaborately induced for effect, are held back in a tight leash. What has been called the violence of his style is found in the startling union of opposites: "the bleak sunshine shrieks its chipped music," or "the idiot greens the meadows with his eyes." And these opposites can also create a sensuous melodic tempo:

> . . . all the sweet afternoon,
> The reaching sun, swift as the
>   cottonmouth,
> Strikes at the black crucifix on her
>   breast.
> . . . the thickening blue grass
> All lying rich forever in the green
>   sun.

Sometimes there is a lack of tenderness or warmth in his poems, a shining bleakness; more often a deeper sense of horror than any sense of hope. One does not expect to find consolation, and there is little spontaneous joy. But there is stimulation of honesty and challenge of courage in what one might call his "stance" to meet calamity head on; he summons defenses in which irony is a weapon, not an escape, though it may act as a shield. The wound can still bleed behind the shield, but the spear is lifted and the voice speaks: There is a moment of respite in the midst of an encounter with life at a dark hour. The courage of irony is Tate's unique contribution, and the originality and power of his language are poetry of "a mind imperishable if time is."

An example is the poem, so often quoted and discussed, "Ode to the Confederate Dead." The word "ode" suggests a public commemoration. Instead the poem is made of thought uttered to himself by a lonely man at a graveyard where nature stirs the memory:

> The singular screech-owl's tight
> Invisible lyric seeds the mind
> With the furious murmur of their
> chivalry.

Tate has been able to speak ironically of the war that was still so close to him. The past, present and future have become one. In "To the Lacedemonians" and "Aeneas at Washington" he has merged Antietam and Troy.

The style of vers libre has never tempted Tate. His form, so essentially a part of his thought—"the language of the poem is the poem" —fits into two general modes, a meditative blend of rhymed verse which introduces a theme and then discusses it; or in what he calls "the immaculate conception of its essence in itself." To me Tate's most successful poems are his condensed lyrical perceptions. Tate is not a man of action, he is a man of thought, of books, of language. But his scholarship is never dry.

"The Cross" (1928) is an excellent example of his concentrated style. The poem, placed in our time and dealing with man's vision of his spiritual predicament, is short, but its range is broad and vital. In an essay on Emily Dickinson, Tate remarked that "she never reasons, she sees." Here Tate "sees." To "see" is one of his favorite verbs with many levels of meaning.

> There is a place that some men
> know,
> I cannot see the whole of it
> Nor how I came there. Long ago
> Flame burst out a secret pit
> Crushing the world with such a light
> The day-sky fell to moonless black,
> The kingly sun to hateful night
> For those, once seeing, turning back.

The poem presents the Christian image, which we can no longer "see," the realization that love, death and salvation stand before the world destroying pit, facing the last alternatives of life. We have become blind to the natural world of living, and yet have no access to the other world.

> For love so hates mortality,
> Which is the providence of life
> She will not let it blessed be
> But curses it with mortal strife,
> Until beside the blinding rood
> Within that world-destroying pit
> —Like young wolves who have
>   tasted blood,
> Of death, men taste no more of it.

In "The Mediterranean," rhythm and meaning are in complete harmony, and Tate's concern with modernity, vis-à-vis the legendary past, is given lyrical expression. Within a rich texture of rhyme, using assonance and dissonance, the poem moves forward, as a narrow boat with its long, black hull glides on the waters. Beginning in the present, a day of Mediterranean sea and sun, passing across the borders of time, the lines summon another expedition.

> Where we went in the boat was a
>   long bay
> A slingshot wide, walled in by
>   towering stone—

At once the high cliffs of the *calanque* have become "the peaked margin of antiquity's delay." Tate's casual summer outing takes on a new quality—"we went there out of time's monotone." The ocean "where our live forefathers sleep"; the thunder-tossed green coast of Africa; all the surroundings bring memories of Aeneas and his companions returning after Troy, bearing the prophecy of the eaten plates and the possibility that they may never reach the land they sought. A sense of the famous age, "eternal here yet hidden from our eyes," overwhelms the voyagers. Where shall they go? "We've cracked the hemispheres with careless hand!" They ask the question Venus asked of Jupiter in *The Aeneid*: "What limit do you set to their labors, Great King?" the epigraph of Tate's poem (in Latin). The voyagers must go "westward, westward till the barbarous brine / whelms us to the tired land where tasseling corn . . . fat beans rot on the vine." And here a voice of the frustrated modern being within the poet speaks: "In that land were we born." A land of richness, of power, of opportunity—but never a land of heroic greatness.

"Seasons of the Soul" moves beyond nostalgia, into the center of a new "dark wood" where death and violence threaten to overwhelm the values of a whole society. Written during World War II, and dedicated to his friend, the poet, John Peale Bishop (1892–1944), this is a work of such depth and richness that it rightfully belongs with such source poems of our generation as *The Waste Land*, Aiken's *The Coming Forth by Day of Osiris Jones* and Pound's Cantos. When it was first published in *The Kenyon Review* in 1944, Tate was deep in religious and psychological thought. From legend and history, actuality and dream, images press together in a sharpened form. There is no easy approach. Divided into four parts—"Summer," "Autumn," "Winter," and "Spring"—these seasons of the soul do not represent divisions in time, or move with the life of man. The substance of the poem is in its whole—circular, without beginning or ending. There is no time passing, only a sense of its recurrence and futility.

An epigraph from the *Inferno* (Canto XIII) carries Dante's symbol of death by suicide—a human soul imprisoned in a tree—and suggests the tone of man's violence against himself by his own deeds, his own choices, his own decisions. Each season shows the soul of man in different incarnations; as a political figure (summer), an abandoned sufferer (autumn), a sexual being disillusioned by love (winter), a man desperately appealing before death for spiritual insight (spring).

"Summer," in short and rhymed stanzas, uses a pattern which few modern poets would attempt:

> Summer, this is our flesh,
> The body you let mature;
> If now while the body is fresh
> You take it, shall we give
> The heart, lest heart endure
> The mind's tattering
> Blow of greedy claws?
> Shall mind itself still live
> If like a hunting king
> It falls to the lion's jaws?

"Summer" celebrates the present, which has grown out of the past. When the body gives itself up to violence (war) must the mind and heart follow its destruction, and "fall to the lion's jaws?"

Tate moves from allegory to reality:

> It was a gentle sun
> When, at the June solstice
> Green France was overrun
> With caterpillar feet,

. . . and the consequences of war's confusion; "no head knows where its rest is," "the summer had no reason."

"Autumn" creates the dream picture of a personal hell, a narrow dreadful descent, ending in a familiar house, where he meets faces of the past, who do not recognize him—

> My father, in a grey shawl,
> Gave me an unseeing glint
> And entered another room!
>
> .   .   .   .
>
> I saw my downcast mother
> Clad in her street clothes,
> Her blue eyes long and small.

This description of loss of identity which leads to madness, stands apart from the rest of the long poem, in its personal story—no apostrophe, no invocation, no suggestion of a voice to be answered—simply the defeated man again talking to himself.

"Winter" brings a realization of the violence man can do to his own creative impulses. He turns to ancient gods, as a last resort. The lewd goddess Venus brings only the *livid* wound of love, as against the *living* wound which he craves. All her insignia are death-dealing—a shark for a dove, hollow rind of the winter sea, and

> Beyond the undertow
> The gray sea-foliage
>
> .   .   .   .
>
> The rigid madrepore
> Resists the winter's flow.

In "Spring," an "irritable" season, infusing warmth, burning but not lighting the way, there is an appeal to the "Mother of Silences." This arresting figure is identified variously as a mediaeval saint, the Virgin, or a symbol of spiritual love. Her "silences" suggest that there is no adequate answer. Nevertheless the poem ends with a passionate invocation to her, no longer ironic, needing no evasion—not even of courage.

> Speak, that we may hear;
> Listen, while we confess
> That we conceal our fear;
> Regard us, while the eye
> Discerns by sight or guess
> Whether, as sheep forgather
> Upon their crooked knees,
> We have begun to die.

Once in a symposium on religion Tate said that all his poems were about the suffering that comes from disbelief. Civilizations as well as men rise and fall as they hold fast to or lose an active faith. We need mediation between the carnal and the spiritual, between *eros* and *agape*. When man is debased into violence all human actions become evil, even love.

Allen Tate's Use of Classical Literature

by LILLIAN FEDER

onsciousness of History cannot be fully awake, except where there is other history than the history of the poet's own people: we need this in order to see our own place in history." In his essay "What Is a Classic?" T. S. Eliot discusses this consciousness of history as one of the requirements of the mature poet, and he suggests Vergil as an example of the poet who exhibits this awareness of his relation not only to the past of his own nation but to the past of a civilization before his. Vergil himself has provided for Allen Tate a means of extending his view of history, and, as the "story of Aeneas" was for Vergil "a statement of relatedness between two great cultures," so it became for Tate a symbol of both the "relatedness" and the tragic separation between the past and the present.

Critics have written much on Tate's use of historical material, but they have, for the most part, concentrated on one tradition—that of the old South. The influence of that "other history," the *publica materies,* the myths and literature of the ancient classical world, which helped to form Tate as a poet, has hardly been explored. Yet, to understand the poetry of Tate, it is necessary to study his "classicism," which manifests itself in his basic ideas and themes, his adaptation of ancient myths and history to poetic symbols, and his language and imagery.

In any discussion of classicism in contemporary literature, it is

EDITOR'S NOTE: Reprinted, with some minor changes, from *The Centennial Review,* 4:89–114 (Winter 1960), by permission of the author and publisher.

impossible to ignore the work of T. E. Hulme, whose ideas on the subject, though often inconsistent, were none the less extremely influential and have caused much confusion about the nature of classicism in modern poetry. Though Tate has declared himself a follower of Hulme, it can be shown that the direct influence of classical literature was far more important in Tate's development as a poet than were the ideas of Hulme, and that a sounder view of certain qualities of modern classicism can be derived from the observation of Tate's use of ancient literature than from Hulme's speculations on the classical point of view.

Defining classicism in his essay "Romanticism and Classicism," Hulme is concerned with three main subjects: man, society, and poetry. According to Hulme, classicism presupposes limitation: the limitations of man's capacities, the limitations society must impose upon man, and the limitations style must impose upon a poet's conception. "Man," he says, "is an extraordinarily fixed and limited animal whose nature is absolutely constant. It is only by tradition and organization that anything decent can be got out of him." Classicism in poetry results from such an attitude toward man and society, and this attitude is revealed by what Hulme calls "the dry hardness which you get in the classics."

Hulme's definition seems to be derived from his own prejudices about man rather than from the experience of classical literature. Only a very "limited" view of Homer, Aeschylus, Sophocles, or Vergil could suggest that their conception of man is so narrow. True, "limitation" has come to be one of the favorite cliches substituted for a definition in handbooks on the subject, and there is some justification for its use. The word undefined or incorrectly interpreted, however, is merely misleading.

The ancient poets and dramatists do deal both explicitly and indirectly with man's limitations, but in their work this theme is not oversimplified; it is almost always combined with two other themes which are equally important in any consideration of classicism. According to the classical view, it is not because his nature is constant that man is limited; on the contrary, Homer, Aeschylus, Sophocles, and other ancient poets and dramatists offer much evidence of the way in which man can and does change. Man is limited because, tragically, he cannot realize in fact the magnitude and quality of his visions. Moreover, he is warned about his limitations so that he may keep a sense of perspective. In war he must be mindful of the larger world of which war is only a part, as the engravings on the shield of Achilles remind us; at his heights he must be aware of possible defeats. But no other literature has ever depicted man so exalted in defeat, so capable of exceeding through the extent of his vision and his enlightenment the fact of his limitations.

Thus, limitation in classical literature is tragic, a view which invariably produces eloquence rather than "dry hardness." The conciseness and orderliness of the form of an ode or of a *kommos* in Greek tragedy is often in apparent contrast with the violent disorder of the feelings thus expressed, but is this contrast not a means of revealing the essential conflict in man's nature which the ancient classics elucidate? The acceptance of limitation in classical poetry and drama implies no petty bargain with destiny: we are aware that Achilles and Aeneas perform the *virtutis opus*, accepting the inevitable condition that theirs is a limited means of finding fulfillment; for Oedipus, wisdom and finally glorification as a sacred figure accompany the acceptance of limitation.

All this should be perfectly clear to anyone who knows classical literature, but unfortunately Hulme and his disciples seem to ignore the evidence of classical or even much of neo-classical literature when they use the adjective critically. As Kathleen Nott points out in *The Emperor's Clothes*: "Both Classicism and Romanticism, as applied by the neo-scholastics to poetry, are false and arbitrary abstractions."

Yet an authentic classical influence is apparent in contemporary literature. The real spirit of classicism is to be found in contemporary poetry rather than in criticism, which sometimes seems to negate the practice of the very poets who write it. With more insight into this subject than Hulme, Wallace Fowlie says: "Modern poetry will one day be described as the vindication of the profoundest principle of classicism where the most universal problems of life are transcribed in a style of language that has reached a high degree of enchantment" (*Mid-Century French Poets*). The classical influence reflected in the work of many contemporary poets manifests itself in (1) a tendency to relate a specific problem of their age to the general metaphysical problems of man's relation to time, history, and the universe; (2) a "tragic sense of life," the acceptance of the double nature of enlightenment—at once the price and the reward of man's struggles with his limitations; (3) a dramatic rather than a decorative use of myth and of allusions to legendary and historical figures of the ancient world; (4) conciseness and exactness of language, conveying a tension between the order of strict form and the violence of the emotions expressed. It is these qualities of Tate's poetry which mainly concern us here: his treatment of contemporary problems against the background of universal ones, and the power of his language, which at once recalls and revitalizes ancient myths, symbols, and images.

II

In both "The Mediterranean" and "Aeneas at Washington" Tate deals with the problem of modern man's loss of a tradition, and in both poems the Vergilian world provides an ideal against which Tate measures the present. The ancient world is not simply a means of showing up the shortcomings of the present, however; it is also an image of the potential if unrealized nobility inherent in modern man, who denies his own heritage and thus his own power.

The epigraph to "The Mediterranean," *Quem das finem, rex magne, dolorum?* in which Tate substitutes the word *dolor* for Vergil's word *labor* (*Aeneid* I, 241), suggests both Tate's ironic method and the theme of the poem. When Aeneas prays for an end to his *laborum*, he is asking for respite from the suffering involved in completing the heroic task of founding the Roman nation, which exacts a price of pain but offers the reward of self-fulfillment. Modern man, however, deprived of a heroic goal, a *virtutis opus*, can only cry out for an end to his *dolorum*, his grief or mental anguish. The difference, of course, lies not only in the quality of ancient and modern men, but in the societies in which they live.

Tate uses the classical past in his poetry to represent a unified society in which man's behavior is directed by a heroic code of conduct. Aeneas in "The Mediterranean" and "Aeneas at Washington" is Tate's conception of the traditional man, inspired by his attachment to his nation and his people; he can live by a heroic code of conduct and perform a heroic task because he is able to forego personal satisfaction for the larger pursuit of a national goal.

In "The Mediterranean" we, modern men, sail on a pilgrimage through the very seas on which Aeneas struggled to achieve his heroic mission. Tate's language here echoes Vergil's: "long bay" is a literal translation of *secessu longo* and "towering stone" calls to mind *vastae rupes* (I, 159–62). The phrases help to recall Aeneas' journey, but more important, they imply that modern man attempts to relive Aeneas' experience.

The first three stanzas begin with the words, "Where we went," and the next two with the word "Where." In this way Tate suggests the compulsive repetition of our quest. Like Aeneas and his men, we wander and search. As the travellers reach shore, the real meaning of the quest becomes clear. The desperation of their need is contained in the most important image of the poem, the image of feasting. Tate evokes the ancient ritual to suggest modern despair and frustration. For Aeneas the eating of the "mensas," the cakes that served as "tables," was a casual act symbolic of the great deeds to be performed; for us it is a desperate, secret need.

We, "hastening to drink all night / Eat dish and bowl to take that sweet land in!" We try through imitation of an ancient ritual to re-create the world in which it was possible to live heroically. The dramatic urgency of these lines conveys the need of modern man for a noble goal, but at the same time the futility of his quest is implied by Tate's adaptation of the myth to image. Aeneas did not attain the destined land because he ate the tables; this act was merely a sign of his accomplishment. We seek the magic of the sign, of the ceremony, of the legends the past has left us, for we have no goal of our own beyond that of personal gratification. Therefore, we devour dish and bowl only to ask: "What prophecy of eaten plates could landless / Wanderers fulfill by the ancient sea?" We merely "taste the famous age," but we cannot participate in its spirit, and so we cannot fulfill ourselves.

"Aeneas at Washington" contains the same theme. Here Aeneas is both the legendary figure of the ancient past and modern man yearning for the heroic destiny which this heritage seemed to promise him. The first four lines of the poem, taken from Aeneas' account of the Trojan disaster, are a literal translation of *Aeneid* II, 499–502. Tate apparently feels that these lines contain the essence of the tragedy of Troy, Priam's fate representing the destruction of the majesty and power of Troy; Neoptolemus, the savagery of the destroyer. The passage describes the suffering which Aeneas has witnessed and endured, and presents Aeneas as Vergil depicted him at a crucial point in his life.

Tate then goes on to give his own view of what followed these events. His interpretation of Aeneas' conduct and his description of Aeneas as part of a modern American scene suggest what happens to the heroic figure alive today, the heroic nature of man in today's world, and the heroic heritage of modern man in modern society.

Tate's interpretation of Aeneas' conduct and deeds begins at line 5:

> In that extremity I bore me well,
> A true gentleman, valorous in arms,
> Disinterested and honorable.

Much of what Tate says in these lines sums up the traditional view of Aeneas. The word "disinterested," however, offers a new view of his conduct, and I think is significant for what it tells us not only about Aeneas but about Tate's conception of heroism. Aeneas, as Vergil depicts him, is "disinterested" because he is concerned with the task at hand, not with his personal safety. He can act "objectively" in that "extremity"; he sees what must be done, and even in retreat he acts nobly. In other words, Aeneas is not hampered by inability "to function objectively in nature and society." He is not the victim of what Tate calls "solipsism," a theme he discusses in "Narcissus as Narcissus" and develops fully in the "Ode to the Confederate Dead," but which cannot be ignored in this poem.

In "Narcissus as Narcissus" Tate says that "solipsism" is "a philosophical doctrine which says that we create the world in the act of perceiving it." It "denotes the failure of the human personality to function objectively in nature and society. Society (and 'nature' as modern society constructs it) appears to offer limited fields for the exercise of the whole man, who wastes his energy piecemeal over separate functions that ought to come under a unity of being."

Aeneas can be "valorous" and "disinterested" and thus a "true gentleman" because he is a member of a society which lives by a heroic code. Even at the moment when he witnesses the destruction of that society, he is able to function as a "whole man," that is, to set forth to found a new land.

The four lines of the second section of the poem create a brilliant transition, for they describe both aspects of Aeneas: the hero of the

Aeneid and the man he has become, now "at Washington," faced with the problems of modern man.

> (To the reduction of uncitied littorals
> We brought chiefly the vigor of prophecy,
> Our hunger breeding calculation
> And fixed triumphs)

Both the founders of Rome and of America brought to the "reduction" or conquest of the land "the vigor of prophecy." Tate's use of the Latinism "littorals" recalls, of course, the landing of Aeneas on the *litora* or shore of Italy, but it also suggests that to the settlers of America the country was not merely a shore on which to land but one which contained all the promise of the *litora Italiae*. It implies that they came with a sense of dedication which their tradition, their knowledge of and belief in the ancients, had taught them. But for both the Romans and the Americans, "hunger [,] breeding calculation," limited their "triumphs" to materialistic ones. "Hunger," the very image which Tate forms out of the Vergilian myth of eating the tables, to symbolize the desire for a prophetic vision, is used here ironically to imply the need for material fulfillment.

Thus Tate prepares us for the third section in which Aeneas, mindful of his own history, is shocked by the contrast between the promise of the past and the actuality of the present. Now, he "see[s] all things apart" because, no longer a member of a "traditional society," a society "that permitted [men] to develop a human character that functioned in every level of life" ("What Is a Traditional Society?"), his personal desires have little to do with his nation's needs.

> The singular passion
> Abides its object and consumes desire
> In the circling shadow of its appetite.

A modern man, he has been affected by "solipsism." He "wastes his energy piecemeal over separate functions that ought to come under a unity of being." The advantage of Aeneas as a symbol here is that Aeneas' career represents history as man once saw history; he symbolizes our tradition and the resources of man as a heroic figure. Aeneas, looking back nostalgically to his own glorious past and questioning the meaning of Troy, symbolizes the tragic nostalgia and conflict of modern man. Our tragedy is not that of a day or a period; it is given

significance by its place in history, in time, as Tate sees it, for the past
is present in our very defeats, and awareness of it gives us perspective.
The remembrance intensifies the shame of our present weakness, but
it also indicates our inherent strength. It warns us against self-destruction; its very living presence is proof that our lives need not be so
narrow as we choose to make them. The memory of Troy and "what
we had built her for," words which contain both tragic insight into
the quality of the past and at the same time a plaintive question as to
its meaning in the present, imply that we built Troy not only literally but figuratively or poetically out of our need for a heroic destiny
and a meaningful way of life. After all, Troy even to the Romans was
essentially a myth, and it can, Tate seems to say, serve us as it served
them. It is the myth of our own past.

The "Ode to the Confederate Dead," Tate says, is about "solipsism."
(All the critical comments quoted in connection with the "Ode to the
Confederate Dead" are from Tate's essay "Narcissus as Narcissus.")
In the "Ode" Tate suggests, as he does in "The Mediterranean" and
"Aeneas at Washington," that the solipsism of modern man results
from the fact that contemporary society denies him his traditional
right to fulfillment through a heroic goal. This is the positive quality
of the "Ode." The dual themes of solipsism and the need for the virtutis opus, which are, of course, really one, are developed more fully
and more deeply in the "Ode" than they are in the two poems discussed above, and again they are expressed through the imagery of
the ancient world.

Tate remarks on the general form of the poem: it is an ode ". . .
even further removed from Pindar than Abraham Cowley. I suppose
in so calling it I intended an irony: the scene of the poem is not a
public celebration, it is a lone man by a gate." Though Tate does not
say so, he implies that the contrast between the personal quality of
his ode and the public nature of the Pindaric expresses the solipsism
of modern man. The man at the gate has the "secret need" of the wanderers on the Mediterranean, and like them he makes a lonely journey
into the past. Obviously, Tate expects his readers to be aware of the
nature of the traditional odes, the Pindarics, not of the specific details
of their contents, but their tone, which always implies that the poet
speaks to and for a society united in triumph. The Pindarics are not
simply victory odes; they are poems in which a particular hero is

regarded as the worthy bearer of a great tradition. Tate's adaptation of the ode form implies that if modern man is trapped by his personal conception of the world, so is the very character of the ode transformed by this view. The lone man speaks for himself, and, if what he says represents the thoughts of others, it is their defeat which he expresses, for they, like him, are cut off from the heroic past and the actual present.

This defeat is symbolized most intensely in the leaf image, which Tate uses not only in the refrain but in the first and last strophes. The image is an extremely interesting and important one. In the first strophe Tate says of the leaves: "They sough the rumors of mortality." The leaves, "of nature the casual sacrament / To the seasonal eternity of death," remind man of his own mortality. "Autumn and the leaves are death," says Tate in "Narcissus as Narcissus." The leaf image replies with finality to the cry for an "active faith," which constitutes the second theme of the poem.

There is a striking similarity between Tate's and Homer's use of the leaf image. Homer's passage containing this image is perhaps one of the best known in the *Iliad*. Diomede and Glaucus meet on the battle-field, and Diomede asks Glaucus who he is. Glaucus replies: "Great-souled son of Tydeus, why do you ask about my lineage? Just as the generation of leaves, so is that also of men. The wind scatters the leaves upon the earth, but the forest as it flourishes, puts forth others when spring comes. So one generation of men springs up while another passes away. However, if you want to, you may know my lineage. There are many who do know it" (VI, 145–51). In this passage the contrast between man's struggle to live heroically, between his justified pride in his past and present achievements and his tragic destiny is clearly set forth. Man is like a leaf but he is also man. The agony of his tragic end is all the more terrible because, unlike a leaf, he struggles to per-form heroic deeds, yet like a leaf he passes away to extinction. The very points at which the simile is inadequate contain its greatest emo-tional force.

In Homer the leaf image provides a commentary on the constant feats of heroism which his heroes demand of themselves and which it is assumed they owe their society. "Be a man," says one warrior to another. In other words, act nobly; perform the heroic deeds which offer man his one chance of redemption, his chance to snatch from

life a glory which defines it. That the very act which may destroy a
man is what offers him a measure of release from his doom is the
tragedy of human life.

Tate's repeated references to the leaves in the "Ode to the Confederate Dead" recall the leaf image in the *Iliad*. In the "Ode" the image
of the leaves provides the answering strain to the quest for heroism
in history, in man himself, and vainly, in society. Like the *Iliad*, the
"Ode" is "a certain section of history made into experience." Tate
uses history both literally and symbolically, fusing with ease the recent
American past with antiquity. Before discussing the leaf image in the
"Ode," it is necessary to observe how Tate develops "the theme of heroism," which he himself says is the second theme of the poem.

III

Tate says that the strophe beginning "You know who have waited
by the wall" contains "the other terms of the conflict. It is the theme
of heroism, not merely moral heroism but heroism in the grand style,
elevating even death from mere physical dissolution into a formal
ritual: this heroism is a formal ebullience of the human spirit in an
entire society, not private, romantic illusion—something better than
moral heroism, great as that may be, for moral heroism, being personal
and individual, may be achieved by certain men in all ages, even ages
of decadence." He goes on to quote Hart Crane's definition. "the
theme of chivalry . . . active faith." He describes an ideal way of life
based upon conduct, and the heroic code of conduct he speaks of is
that clearly defined in the *Iliad* and the *Aeneid*, the code which could
make Aeneas "disinterested," which makes Glaucus, even after he has
expressed the tragic irony of man's doom, go on to tell his enemy of
his ancestors, prepared to fight as bravely as they did and as nobly as
the code of his society demands that he fight and live. Both his desire
to fight Diomede and his subsequent acceptance of his friendship are
motivated not by personal whim but by the code of his society.

Tate tells us that the passage in the "Ode" beginning "You know
who have waited by the wall" is "meant to convey a plenary vision,
the actual presence of, the exemplars of an active faith." This plenary
vision appears in two main symbols: the warrior and the ancient philosophers, Zeno and Parmenides. The warrior is the traditional symbol of heroism. Though Tate concretizes his warrior through his list

of names connected with the Civil War, he does not limit him to this particular time, for he is the warrior whose heroism results from a view of the world represented by the philosophical system of Parmenides and Zeno. His warrior is once again the man who lives by a heroic code of conduct. "Muted Zeno and Parmenides" represent the world view which makes such a code possible.

Of those who have the heroic vision, Tate says:

> You know the rage,
> The cold pool left by the mounting flood,
> Of muted Zeno and Parmenides.

Parmenides and his disciple, Zeno, were the first to separate existence into being and becoming. Theirs is a philosophical system which makes a distinction between the objective and unchanging world of being and the subjective world of becoming. Parmenides (in Frag. VI) warns against the "way of seeming" (the state of solipsism, Tate would say). He warns against the subjective blindness of mere dependence on the senses for knowledge of the world. Thus, Parmenides and Zeno represent for Tate an objective, "whole" view of life. Moreover, Zeno, not only in his thought but also in his conduct, exemplifies the heroic way of life. According to tradition, when captured by the tyrant he was opposing, he bit off his tongue rather than give the information demanded by his enemy. "Muted Zeno," therefore, has a double meaning: Zeno made mute by his own act of heroism and Zeno, the heir and exponent of a philosophical system which regards the universe as whole and knowledge as objective, muted in what Tate calls the "fragmentary cosmos of today."

The heroic vision, as Tate presents it poetically, is composed of heroic action based on a view of the world which is objective, whole, and unchanging. Moreover, it is a vision created out of the ancient past combined with the recent one. It is a vision which suggests a continuity in human thought, conduct, and feeling, broken only in the world of today.

"In contemplating the heroic theme," says Tate, "the man at the gate never commits himself to the illusion of its availability to him. The most that he can allow himself is the fancy that the blowing leaves are charging soldiers, but he rigorously returns to the refrain: 'Only the wind'—or the 'leaves flying.'" The wind-leaf refrain provides the answering strain. The lone man, striving to be one with those who waited by the wall, tries even to transform the leaves into fighting men. But, as in Homer, we are struck by the dissimilarity. In the *Iliad* the simple quality of the leaf is contrasted with the complex and tragic nature of man, doomed to the same end. In Tate's poem man's inability to transform the leaf into a symbol of heroism suggests that the certainty of man's tragic fate overpowers any thought of his potential heroism. The man at the gate cannot identify himself with the leaves "as Keats and Shelley too easily and too beautifully did with nightingales and west winds." The leaf is a symbol of his mortality and his aloneness.

In both Homer and Tate, the leaf image, with its implications of death, is combined and contrasted with a scene of heroism in warfare. In Homer, Glaucus, even as he sees these implications, suggests by his very conduct that through heroism man can redeem himself if only partially and tragically. Tate, looking back on the history of his own nation with the traditionally epic view, finds that in the present there is not even the possibility of tragic redemption. Thus, his departure from Homer is as important as his echo of him, for the very contrast between the two poets' use of the leaf image suggests the theme of Tate's poem.

Tate's last use of a classical allusion in the "Ode" is an entirely ironical one. The jaguar, he tells us, is substituted for Narcissus. Of course, Narcissus by his very absence is immensely important. Replaced by the jaguar, the destructive and self-devouring elements of the Narcissus figure are made explicit. As the "jaguar leaps" we see the lovely boy Narcissus for what he really is. In giving solipsism this concrete form, Tate reveals its ugliness and brutality, and he adds a dimension to the myth he adapts.

"Ode to the Confederate Dead" cannot be understood without the framework of the classical world. Here, as in "The Mediterranean" and "Aeneas at Washington," Tate speaks of the present only in relation to the past, and his view of the past is the epic view, heroic, exalted, the poet's past rather than the historian's.

IV

Though Tate is not always as dependent on the classical past as he is in the three poems just discussed, he none the less uses references to classical literature consistently to point up through a heroic or tragic association the significance of a contemporary event or problem. A striking example is his incorporation of the well-known epitaph by Simonides into the monologue of an old soldier reminiscing on the Civil War. In calling his poem "To the Lacedemonians," Tate suggests at once that the old soldier belongs to the heroic tradition; the past he recalls is part of the epic past of ancient history and legend. Moreover, the old soldier addresses not us but the Lacedemonians. We overhear the remarks. He excludes us not out of snobbery but out of his sad realization that the only ones who can understand him are those who lived by a heroic code. The title implies his loneliness and isolation, and our inadequacy as an audience. However, the poem, though addressed to the Lacedemonians, is of course written for us; to the extent that we comprehend the remarks we overhear we participate in the spirit of those who understood the language of heroes.

The old soldier's visit to the past is another secret pilgrimage: "I am here with a secret in the night," he says. Comparing the "elegance" of the past with the "luxury" of the present, he wonders why the men of the present generation are without tradition or imagination. "Where have they come from?" he asks. Then, he goes on to echo Simonides' epitaph for the heroes of Thermopylae:

> Go you tell them
> That we their servants, well-trained, gray-coated
> And haired (both foot and horse) or in
> The grave, them obey . . . obey them,
> What commands?

The old man's adaptation of the epitaph implies that he lived and fought by the heroic code of the Spartans. But that is only one of its meanings. He regards himself not only as the "servant" of a literal leader, but also as the "servant" of a tradition. Not only he but the dead ("or in/ the grave") serve that tradition. The words "them obey . . . obey them" seem to express the faltering thoughts of an old man, and, since the Greek word order is τοῖς κείνων ῥήμασι πειθόμενοι (of them the words obeying), his faltering seems to imply his struggle to remember the original words and thus their original meaning, for he goes on to ask tragically, "What commands?" He is questioning himself, the experiences of his youth, and finally the ancient past, which clarifies the meaning of his own history.

Imagery drawn from classical literature almost always provides the answering strain in Tate's poetry to a modern oversimplification of a problem, to vulgarity and triviality. "Antiquity breached mortality with myths," he says in "Retroduction to American History." In that poem he exposes the vulgar misuse of the classical past in modern America:

> Narcissus is vocabulary. Hermes decorates
> A cornice on the Third National Bank. Vocabulary
> Becomes confusion, decoration a blight; the Parthenon
> In Tennessee stucco, art for the sake of death.

Such vulgarization of the classical past is a way of avoiding its meaning. It is the "practical" man's means of dismissing the intricacy and tragedy of experience recorded in ancient myth, while retaining a cheap version of it to satisfy his vanity. It is myth used decoratively rather than emotionally or dramatically.

In several poems Tate evokes the vitality of ancient myth to argue against materialism and the naturalistic view of life. In his very use of myth as image lies his whole argument. "False Nightmare" is an attack on Whitmanism, on Whitman's naturalism and individualism in his approach to man and his land. Whitmanism to Tate is arrogance:

> My five and ten cent shelf
> The continent is: my targe
> Bigger than Greece.

Tate's reply is contained in the image of Europa and the bull:

> In bulled Europa's morn
> We love our land because
> All night we raped her torn . . .

The paradox of man's love for his land and his violence toward it, his identification with it, his self-realization in relation to it, his manhood achieved in terms of it; all the complexity of Tate's approach to his land as contrasted with the self-conscious primitivism of Whitman's attitude is expressed in this image. In using the image Tate seems to insist on the vitality of the past. The myths of the past which Whitman repudiates provide the answer to his argument.

"Unnatural Love" deals again with the problem of naturalism, and again Tate's answer is expressed through a classical image. He ad-

dresses the poem to Landor, the last of the neo-classicists. His tone at
the beginning of the poem is faintly ironic, the tone of a man made
wise by experience in a disordered world addressing an innocent, a
neo-classicist who is unaware that he lives in a society in which naturalism has already separated art and nature. Both art and nature "served"
Landor "sweetly"; however,

> From us I see them part
> After they served, so sweetly, you—
> Yet nature has no heart:
> Brother and sister are estranged
> By his ambitious lies
> For he his sister Helen much deranged—
> Outraged her, and put coppers on her eyes.

The image of Helen, though it appears at the end, dominates the
whole poem. Through this image Tate creates a dramatic shift in
tone; furthermore, it contains his theme. From rather light sarcasm in
his address to Landor, Tate shifts to bitter, even tragic irony. And it
is the image of Helen with all its ancient associations, outraged by
nature, or really the naturalistic view of life ("'nature' as modern
society constructs it"), which creates this tone. For such a view of life
denies the "heart," the feelings; its exponents are preoccupied only
with their arrogant attempts to account for the complexity and mystery
of human life through their "ambitious lies." Helen is not simply a
static representation of art: her name evokes her history, her power,
but more important, the power of the poet who created her and of all
the poets who kept her alive. Now nature, having killed her, puts
"coppers on her eyes" to make certain that the eyes of beauty, potent
so long, may not though dead assert their power.

"The Eye," which is concerned with the same theme, deals with the
effect of naturalism on man rather than on art. The poem begins with
an epigraph from Callimachus: λαιδρὴ κορώνη, κῶς τὸ χεῖλος οὐκ ἀλγεῖς·
It is taken from the *Iambi* (1.278), one episode of which tells the story
of the quarrel between the laurel and the olive, each of which is trying
to prove her superiority. The olive concludes her recitation of her own
virtues by repeating the flattering remarks of the birds, for these provide more evidence of her superiority. She then interrupts her report
and addresses the birds in two parenthetical lines. In the first, she
speaks to all the birds, calling them "unwearied chatterers." Though

she enjoys their flattery, she feels obliged to scold them for their exces-
sive praise. In the second line, she turns to the crow, and asks, apparently with self-conscious modesty, "shameless crow, how is it that your
lip does not hurt you?" which is the line Tate quotes.

The poem is a complicated one. With a series of adjectives generally
associated with physical matter, Tate describes the "eye" of "mineral
man." His way of looking at the world and his conception of life are
determined by the limitations of his view, for his eye is "agate," "nuclear," "carbolic." Finally, there is "nothing in the eye." For this
"natural man" the sky is "sphereless." He is a man who takes the
"fatherless dark" to bed and the "acid sky to the brain-pan"; having
excluded the mystery of the past and the realm of the imagination from
his life, he "calls the crows to peck his head." Obviously, the last line
of the poem is related to the epigraph. Modern man, the victim of his
own scientific naturalism, calls the flatterers to offer him the only
vision he can now seek—the vision of his own self-importance. The
rather naive remark of Callimachus' olive is thus given a new meaning
through the shift in point of view: as the original protagonist's commentary it is a disarming remark; as the poet's recollection in a new
context it assumes bitterness. The word "peck" reveals the true meaning of this flattery, its compulsive and destructive nature.

An important theme in Tate's prose and poetry is that the naturalistic or pragmatic approach to life reflects modern man's unwillingness
to face the problem of evil in the world. In VIII of "Sonnets of the
Blood," Tate, in demanding that modern man accept the presence of
evil and the necessity of dealing with it, revokes the Oedipus of Sophocles' play, who is both defeated and triumphant. Oedipus' recognition
of his terrible deeds and his enlightenment are both the price and the
reward of his tragic stature. Oedipus has been willing to pay the enormous cost in suffering for self-knowledge, but his victory over inner-
blindness is as much a triumph as his physical blindness is a sign of
defeat. Oedipus' experience has taught him more than the moral lesson
the chorus recites; he has solved the riddle of himself.

Tate's use of Oedipus as a poetic symbol suggests this complicated
and tragic figure. In VIII of "Sonnets of the Blood" Tate considers
the question of what will "keep us whole in our dissevering air," the
foul atmosphere which permeates a society of dissociated experience.
And his answer is expressed through ancient myth:

> Call it the house of Atreus where we live—
> Which one of us the Greek perplexed with crime
> Questions the future: bring that lucid sieve
> To strain the appointed particles of time!
> Whether by Corinth or by Thebes we go
> The way is brief, but the fixed doom, not so.

Again the Greeks provide an example of fitting conduct. Tate begins with "the house of Atreus," which represents the overpowering evil of our society, corrupting all who come in contact with it. Then he shifts to the myth of Oedipus, who left Corinth to escape his destiny only to meet it at Thebes.

Since crime or evil exists, Tate asks, which one of us dares to face it with the courage of Oedipus? To overcome our confusion and apathy, we need the "lucid sieve" with which the ancient Greek could "strain the appointed particles of time." With ethical and intellectual courage he analyzed his "appointed" or fated experience. In the face of a "fixed" destiny, he exercised control over even irrational evil, for he dared to probe its meaning with reason and insight, and thus he imposed order through knowledge. Which one of us dares to question the future in terms of the past, as Oedipus did, and to pay the price of self-knowledge?

Clearly, the world of the classical past provides for Tate one essential means of expression and for the reader one important key to his basic themes and methods as a poet. One does not need to label Tate a neo-classicist because he imitates the Horatian epode or the eclogue form or because he constantly employs imagery taken from ancient myth; yet it is a mistake to ignore or to underestimate the importance of the classical tradition in his poetry.

V

Critics have discussed this strain in Tate's poetry but have failed to deal adequately with it. In "The Poetry of Allen Tate," Vivienne Koch has attempted to show "that Tate is a poet of romantic sensibility who has tried with varying success to compress his talents into a chastely classical form and that, in inverse degrees to his willingness to do so, his best poetry has been written." She regards Tate's translation of the *Pervigilium Veneris* as his "valedictory, from a safe distance, to the Fugitives, to the South, to the 'classical' tradition, to his masters. The quickest way to get over the goodbyes is to say them in a strange language." One may ask, what strange language? The language of Tate's translation of the *Pervigilium* is more "classical" than that of the original poem. It is cryptic and economical, as elegantly colloquial as Horace's, and full of incredibly graceful Latinisms. It is well known that the *Pervigilium Veneris* has many Romantic elements. However, that Tate chose to translate this poem proves nothing about his attitude toward classical literature except that his interest in it is broad and varied. It is illogical to assume, as Miss Koch does, that Tate's translation of a late Latin poem which is outside the strictly classical type is a sign that he has lost his feeling for and response to classical literature as a source and an influence. Moreover, the facts are against such a point of view.

Miss Koch says that "in Tate's recent poetry the traditional influences (whether of structure, idea, or both) operate as qualities not as models." This judgment is no doubt correct if one recognizes the importance of such "qualities" in Tate's poetry. In her analysis of "Seasons of the Soul," which in some respects is excellent, Miss Koch seems to underestimate or to ignore certain qualities which depend upon classical literature and which express some of Tate's most subtle and most significant ideas.

She remarks that Tate's phrase the "living wound of love" seems to have been suggested by Lucretius *aeterno volnere amoris* and says· "I take the implication to be that Love, growing from a 'livid' wound into the 'living' wound is the only possible power which can rescue man from his otherwise maimed existence. The passionate and suppliant address to Venus makes clear that she is the complex erotic symbol around which cluster the poet's hopes for various kinds of regeneration." She then goes on to show the relationship between Venus and the Mother of Silences, who is "a particular mother (St. Monica), the Virgin, the Mystery, and through Augustine's unmentioned wound she is identified further with the principle of Love. Love, then, is the luminous agency common to all the referents of the symbol. Yet, in the end, one feels that the hope of regeneration through Love is reluctantly abandoned and death is sought as the only certain 'kindness' to which men can aspire."

This reading is a fine one, but Miss Koch seems to ignore the relationship between Tate's imagistic use of Venus and other references to classical literature in the poem. The first occurs in the second stanza, in which Tate says that the soul must "seize or deny its day." This is not merely a variation and extension of the phrase *carpe diem*, but a significant application of its meaning and associations in a new context. The soul, says Tate, must have vitality and courage despite man's mortality. All the associations of the *carpe diem* theme repeated and developed in poetry from Alcaeus to Marvell are evoked through Tate's use of the phrase. It suggests the intensity and tragedy of man's struggle not only in our time but throughout time to wrest from life satisfaction and meaning. Tate's unique adaptation of it reveals the plight of man's soul in our time: it must struggle for and seize the place that has been denied it or give up entirely.

The ancients, Tate says in the fifth stanza, lived in an eternal summer, a world of "timeless day," a period when to "seize the day" implied an easy pleasure as compared with the anguish of the soul struggling to live in a world without belief. We have lost this peace, but it is a part of our past. We recall its spirit as part of our history, our own childhood.

The invocation to Venus is a cry to the spirit of creation and love which we recall and inherit from the past. The image of Venus is contrasted with two images of futility and death which are taken from two ancient symbols: Plato's cave and Sisyphus' eternal frustration. Tate combines the two brilliantly:

> It burns us each alone
> Whose burning arrogance
> Burns up the rolling stone
> This earth—Platonic cave
> Of vertiginous chance!
> Come, tired Sisyphus,
> Cover the cave's egress
> Where light reveals the slave,
> Who rests when sleeps with us
> The mother of silences.

The earth is both the stone Sisyphus rolls without purpose and the cave in which the entrance of light reveals only human blindness and limitation. Death, for Tate, is not merely literal extinction, but life without goal or purpose. If man is to accept the role of Sisyphus, let him then complete his daily act of frustration by accepting death.

Though it is true that "Seasons of the Soul" is a tragic poem, it is not therefore a morbid one. Both Vivienne Koch and Richmond C. Beatty, in "Allen Tate as Man of Letters," whose interpretation of the poem is similar to hers, emphasize the mood of despair. Yet "Seasons of the Soul," while it deals with suffering and loss of faith, also portrays the heroic contest man has always fought against the despair which has seemed overpowering. He has even descended into hell to find knowledge of love, the source of life:

> Wilfully as I stood
> Within the thickest grove
> I seized a branch, which broke;
> I heard the speaking blood
> (From the livid wound of love)
> Drip down upon my toe:
> "We are the men who died
> Of self-inflicted woe,
> Lovers whose stratagem
> Led to their suicide."

Often in Tate's poetry his bitterest condemnations of man's conduct spring from his recognition of the contrast between man's heroic potentialities, his creative energies, and what Tate calls his "tragic fault," his misuse of these qualities. The ancient symbols of Venus and Sisyphus represent the two ways man may take. Tate implies at the end of the poem that man may accept death, but his invocation to Venus is a moving and powerful affirmation of the potentialities of life.

According to Miss Koch, classicism was an inhibiting influence on Tate. On the contrary, Tate is never held back by his sources and models, but instead uses them freely for his own purposes and transforms them to his own conception. He is not a neo-classicist in the sense that he decorates with a classical flourish or repeats the old formulas, such as nothing too much or the simple life is best. He knows the classics too well. His classicism exists not in external, imitative manners, but in his way of thought and of feeling in poetry. His nostalgia is associated with the Homeric longing for heroism; in expressing his distress at contemporary values he gains both proportion and depth through a Vergilian image. Like the poets of classical antiquity, Tate employs traditional material to suggest the universality and continuity of his themes.

Regarding man's limitations, as did the ancient classicists, from the tragic point of view, Tate often emphasizes the tragic contest, out of which man can emerge with "knowledge carried to the heart," a reward of the very struggle which may reveal his inevitable limitations. This knowledge is expressed in Tate's poetry to a large extent through classical myth transformed into symbol. He often employs an ancient story—that of Aeneas or Oedipus—as a dramatic and concrete representation of traditional values or perennial conflict. The mythical story is sometimes told cryptically, implied more than stated, for Tate's language is classical in its precision, suggesting the tension produced by controlled feeling. In adapting the ancient myth of eating the tables to a modern metaphor, "Eat dish and bowl to take that sweet land in," Tate reveals our overwhelming need of a heritage to guide us, by suggesting hunger and violent consumption in a hopeless attempt to appease it; yet the concreteness and simplicity of his image control the intense feelings and give them form. The result is not "dry hardness," but emotion eloquent through restraint. The leaf as a symbol of mortality in the "Ode to the Confederate Dead" is not romanticized or sentimentalized, but, through the Homeric associations it evokes, suggests tragic experience in the past and the present. Classical literature served Tate by broadening his view; if it imposed limits on him, they were only those resulting from the creative process of emulation, a discipline through which the "individual talent" can often flourish.

Origins and Beginnings

by M. E. BRADFORD

John Orley Allen Tate has been, in each of his now familiar roles—as poet, critic, historian, novelist, and diagnostician of cultural decline—always very much the same person his friends were to know and respect soon after he came down from the Bluegrass to take a degree at Vanderbilt. Or, at least, he has moved steadily toward being that very exceptional person: completing, not altering, the fledgling original. His precocity as an undergraduate is to this day proverbial. At twenty he knew literature to be his proper business and was on his way through the standard classics of poetry in English; at twenty-one he had confronted and mastered many of the French, English, and expatriate American innovators of the era; and, finally, upon graduation and after an apprenticeship with *The Fugitive*, the first distinctive Southern magazine of verse, he commenced immediately to challenge his own resolve and to test his poetic and critical ability and preparation. This past, like that of the other members of the Fugitive and Agrarian circles, was prologue. It foreshadowed all that was to come from talent well employed. For, at the end of his seventh decade, Tate continues to set a mark for his peers and juniors in the literary fraternity while playing his chosen, public role: continues to hold an advantage in soundness of judgment and in the easy authority with which he endows that faculty's responsible exercise while writing and judging of writing.

But if the consistency of Tate's achievement is noteworthy, even

EDITOR'S NOTE: Reprinted, with some minor changes, from *Rumors of Mortality: An Introduction to Allen Tate* (Dallas: Argus Academic Press, 1969), pp. 3–17, by permission of the publisher.

more so has been its aforementioned variety. The one description does not belie the other; rather, it confirms. In the consciously sculptured poetry the critic is revealed; the poet is obviously present in the range and emphasis of the criticism. Both poet and critic are revealed in the single major venture into fiction, *The Fathers*, as well as in the socio-political documents. Without a doubt, the total performance has been one of the remarkable achievements of this specialized, compartmental age: a greater wonder because it appeared and flourished in the company of many kindred marvels. As his critics have noted, Mr. Tate, like most of the original Nashville fellowship, is an example of that now rare species—the man of letters in the antique European sense. Of their number (and perhaps among all of his American contemporaries), he is the most complete example. Hence, it is unwise to take apart, by a kind of chronology, his overall career. With John Crowe Ransom, Robert Penn Warren, Andrew Nelson Lytle, or Donald Davidson, distortion inevitably follows upon such controversial procedure. The result with Tate would be even worse; and for reasons thus detailed, he is here considered in all of his capabilities at once. The logical ground for their exposition is biography. Admittedly, such a design is not adopted for the sake of its rhetorical merit. The resistance of Tate, the man of letters, to all familiar formulations will allow for no less difficult approach. And even this tactic is ultimately inadequate. Of a piece though his work may be, it is an irrefrangibly complicated study. Fortunately, there are instruments, thematic and aesthetic, which make possible at least a beginning.

> Maryland Virginia Caroline
> Pent images in sleep
> Clay valleys rocky hills old fields of pine
> Unspeakable and deep
>
> Out of that source of time my farthest blood
> Runs strangely to this day
> Unkempt the fathers waste in solitude
> Under the hills of clay
>
> Far from their woe fled to its thither side
> To a river in Tennessee
> In an alien house I will stay
> Yet find their breath to be
> All that my stars betide—
>   ("Emblems," 1–13)

Almost everything that can be argued of Tate is attributable to the place and time of his birth, Clark County, Kentucky, 1899; and to the kind of family into which he came, a combination of the basic Southern strains, upcountry and tidewater. Something very similar might be said of most Southern writers of his generation, certainly of his immediate literary connections. It halfway follows with all those who contributed to that most Southern of modern books, *I'll Take My Stand.* But it cannot be asserted on these grounds alone; for that volume drew together intransigent individualists who have since its publication (1930) demonstrated their variety; even as regards the South. Yet any who would dispute the generalization should read Tate's own essays—for example, "The Profession of Letters in the South" or "A Southern Mode of the Imagination." And then let those who doubt consider what it once meant to be a Southerner, insofar as a world view was implied by the title. There are, despite much dispute, a hundred useful authorities on the subject (the best is Richard Weaver). But for my purpose in this essay, a brief personal summary and syncretism will have to do: a summary intended to illuminate the design and the burden of what Mr. Tate has written.

First of all, a Southerner has (or had) a certain piety toward Being and the disposition of its components as he encounters them. The effects of history, nature, and the fruits of personal choice enjoy in his eyes a prescriptive status: they are either the imposed will of an inscrutable Providence or the operations of a natural law set up by that Providence to accommodate human free agency to Its purposes. Man himself is among these constants, his moral and mental constitution (and therefore his potential for mischief and improvement) itself one of the "givens," *one* of the imposed features of a less than malleable frame of things. Next, the Southerner is a little disposed to exalt envy or Promethean overreaching into spiritual principles—and therefore is ordinarily immune to the characteristic viruses of the modern dispensation. But because modernity has always surrounded the Southerner and because he has never been allowed to forget that it is there, his typical mood is one of alarm: in brief, it is apocalyptic. Hence, he is a baleful supernaturalist, rationally distrustful of unaided private reason, teleological, and not in any way (save as he regards death and wickedness), equalitarian. Natural law having been everywhere violated by presumptuous assaults on Being, by arrogant attempts to rearrange or improve on the exactions of divine will, future history is bound to register God's displeasure. All of which is to say that he is very much out of step with the temper of the abstract "nation" within whose boundaries he must act his part, very far removed from the Adamic New England mentality that defines itself (and the United States with it) over against Europe—and against history in the largest sense. He has no feeling of special innocence or special guilt, no millennialist or fatalist eschatology, and no desire to impose his viewpoint on others or to display his soul to the public view. The Southerner, without being cramped or confined in the process, is what he is by definition, a traditional man. He does not evolve and is not converted, except perhaps from sin or simplicity. He does not work at being Southern or think about it; and he is happy to be free of the necessity of discovering the world for himself.

Now it is certain that Allen Tate does not subscribe to all these propositions all of the time or with equal conviction. But then, in the South, they are not ideas in the strict sense of the word. Rather, they are ingredients in what we usually mean by "sensibility." Until the time of World War I they remained axioms, commonplaces too well accepted even to be discussed. For Tate or any other Southern writer they were the inevitable point of departure, the referent of which they became conscious only when alternative assumptions became familiar to them. They can, with difficulty, be rejected or revised. But ignored, never! Certain details or facets of Tate's work are, of course, available to other explanation. And I must specify, before continuing, that by "South" or "Southern" I mean in this connection (as Tate did from the first and even in the midst of the Agrarian effort of 1927–1937) the entire framework of civility and proportion, the general accordance of status and function as conditioned by manners, usually signified by "Christendom" or "The West." It is a provincialism in space which precludes the now characteristic provincialism in time, an ontological and epistemological posture more than a political position: a view of Being and of ways in which it may be known. The dynamic of American and European history plus climate, the Negro, and a certain collective stubbornness permitted its implausible survival below Mason and Dixon's line. To repeat, only an American Southerner with his memory intact and his eyes open to the world around him could, in the second and third quarters of this century, have produced Tate's commentary, his verse, or his fiction.

The second important biographical factor is the circumstance of fortuitous associations. Mr. Tate grew up in Kentucky (with occasional visits to relations in Virginia) and there received the fragments of a preparatory schooling, rounded with a year at an academy affiliated with Georgetown University. What befell Allen Tate in his early years was largely what could be expected in the old Kentucky world of farms and small towns: a world still suffused with the recollection of injuries long past and with the consequences of those misfortunes. That their effect would be confirmed and made indelible by the choice of a university could by no means have been foreseen. Nor was it possible to predict that other young future writers would at approximately the same time make the same selection. Nonetheless, the difference that this choice and these associations made is well recorded in Louise Cowan's *The Fugitive Group* and in Virginia Rock's forthcoming study of the Agrarian movement. No more mutually auspicious conjunction of talent has occurred in the region's literary history. Assuredly it did nothing to dilute Tate's Southernness. When we add the significance of Tate's first marriage (1924—two years after finishing Vanderbilt) to the novelist Caroline Gordon (another Kentuckian), the background is finished. What thereafter occurred in his life that is of importance to this essay is literary biography—which brings me back to Tate's poetry

Though I have thus far stressed the traditional background of Tate's formative years, it was not with the intent to suggest that he came into his majority unaware of the developments in the great world outside of his homeland. Far more than most of his Nashville friends, young Tate knew that the "center will not hold" when "things fall apart." As he was the first of their company to master modernist poetry, the first to read and appreciate T. S. Eliot, so was he the earliest to recognize that his culture, though still worthy of defense and useful as a measure, was no longer intact. Furthermore, in combination with his grasp of the implications of scientism, urbanization, economic determinism, and depersonalized power politics, Tate came swiftly to understand why the South could not remain successfully "at bay." Very early he perceived, in philosophical terms, what inherent weaknesses foredoomed it to "absorption" into all that now passes for national and international "unity." And, knowing modernity and the sources of its

power for what they are, this poet determined, in his early twenties—
almost as soon as he began to write verse—what strategies could serve
his purpose in addressing the audience he intended. That tactic was,
as I have already mentioned, highly conscious, dramatic, and impersonal—a procedure calculated (after Eliot, the French Symbolists, and
Yeats) to circumvent the modern reader's resistance to poetry in general
and to traditionalist poetry in particular. Contrivance and austerity
are the usual complaints made against Tate's work, complaints which
ignore the fury shaped and rendered by that conscious craft. Said simply, the assumption embodied in much of Tate's first two decades of
poetry is that *persona means purchase*: that the modern reader can be
influenced by dramatic presentation of a mind in motion to participate
in attitudes or emotions he would not ordinarily tolerate if they were
thrust upon him with direct assertion. It is true that Tate has produced
a little more or less straightforward, meditative work throughout his
career. Moreover, the self-disguise in some of his poems is often so
transparent as to have the effect of parody, not drama. In addition,
there is indication in *The Winter Sea* (1944) and thereafter in "The
Maimed Man," "The Swimmers," and "The Buried Lake" of Tate's
will to write in a less guarded, less oblique style: a desire to be the
"symbolic" anagogical poet, after his new master, Dante (see his essay
on that writer, "The Symbolic Imagination"). Yet, despite a chasten-
ing of tone, a muting of the habitual metaphoric and prosodic violence
and exaggeration, the original irony and indirection are still present
in Tate's post-conversion, "Catholic" work. Even when he speaks *in
propria persona* or in obvious sarcasm, dramatic properties remain in
his voice, some inference that it is the Promethean positivist or his
latter-day disoriented heir who is before us, who is sailing the cold sea
and judging himself as he goes. It is the recollection of all surviv-
ing members of the Fugitive circle that Tate's fiery indirections in
verse were the occasion of his most serious participation in their
debates. That his poetry follows from the aesthetics and general assess-
ment of poetic possibilities made in his twenties is the argument I
shall next pursue.

Three or four of Mr. Tate's earliest poems will serve as a partial
documentation of my previous generalizations on the indirect and dramatic property of his work: "Horation Epode to the Duchess of Malfi,"

"Death of Little Boys," "Homily," and "The Subway." These clearly reveal the poet in the making. After them I shall turn to an inceptional statement of his purpose in (or view of) poetry, "Mr. Pope."

The "Horation Epode" appeared in *The Fugitive* for October 1922. The little tribute to John Webster's high-spirited widow (epodes are diminished odes—vehicles for something less than full-throated salute, for sentiments more casual or vulgar) is not, at first glance, dramatic— not a rendering of tension observed nor a searching mirror of disorder (compare "Tension in Poetry"). With Tate, as with T. S. Eliot and many others of their generation, there is a temptation to identify the speaker in the work with its maker. And, again as with Eliot, regardless of the reinforcement given such temptation by title, design, or even content, the poem disappears into pseudo-sophistical verbal posturing unless its reader realizes that Tate speaks through a mask, adopts a character (i.e., persona) so as to make that created, summary self available to the reader's independent judgment. A vapid and world-weary species of subjective lyric association (what Tate in "The Angelic Imagination: Poe as God" calls "angelism") or an equally artificial and even more limited "pure" (i.e., thought-free, value-free) imagism were the poetic modes in vogue when Tate began his career. Both are consequences of the aesthetic impasse toward which the entire craft had been moving since the Renaissance—since the abnegation of its ancient responsibilities forced upon poetry by the authority of positivistic science (see his 1965 *Southern Review* essay, "The Unliteral Imagination; Or I, Too, Dislike It"). And, as Tate and his Fugitive friends recognized from the first, no poet serious about his calling could employ either. Yet these very modes did (and still do) define the expectations of any audience he could anticipate, condition the intellectual equipment brought to the reading or hearing of verse by even the most literate contemporary. There was only one way out of this trap, a procedure followed by some of the best poets since the Seventeenth Century and doubled in modern fiction by the artistry of Henry James and his heirs. The tactic is what Robert Langbaum has defined as "the poetry of experience" (*The Poetry of Experience* [New York, 1957]); it is a method for registering and figuring forth the recalcitrant particularity of "the world's body" without either claiming the now-denied authority of the muse or refusing to exercise that authority. In refracting through telling language what is observed of that external complex of contingencies, the "submissive imagination" operates. "Horation Epode" belongs to this poetic order.

The epigraph to this poem, as in so many others by Tate, is a clear indication of its meaning. The purpose of the speaker, as I said above, is to give voice to his admiration of the Duchess. She has lifted him into life, disturbed his naturalistic equanimity: has made him doubt the scientific myth (alluded to in references to "infusorian" and "eohippus") which replaced the old "divinities." From comfortable atheist, he has turned agnostic, a doubter of all "authorities" and thus a complete modern, in response to the "strict gesture" of her death which "Split the straight lines of pessimism / Into two infinites." Webster's heroine, the subject of lines very much admired in the Twenties ("Cover her face; mine eyes dazzle; she died young") as exemplary poetry, recalls the classical analogy (a requirement of the epode as a stage in tribute) of a Greek girl who died for love. But the impression that can be made by even her pure "pride" in the heart's truth cannot draw this skeptic beyond his vision of "Probability"; nor can it compel him to deny that man is but a "salvatory of green mummy," a "box of worm-seed." The kathartic passion occurs only in a fully human audience. And soon enough the familiar ethos of "the street cars" that are "still running" cancels the heterodox impulse engendered by the play's reading. The effect rendered is not so much about the poem's announced theme or intent as it is about the voice it embodies. This modern, like the masks of his successors, is judged by himself—and his kind with him.

In "Death of Little Boys" Tate approaches the reader from a slightly different stance. But his topic and objective are unchanged. Here the poet stands just outside the mind of a representative contemporary. Yet, playing the epistemological poet once more, that mind is what he presents. And the impression we get is of consciousness rendered in motion and found wanting in the process.

The poem reads as follows:

> When little boys grown patient at last, weary
> Surrender their eyes immeasurably to the night,
> The event will rage terrific as the sea;
> Their bodies fill a crumbling room with light.
>
> Then you will touch the bedside, torn in two,
> Gold curls now deftly intricate with gray

As the windowpane extends a fear to you
From one peeled aster drenched with the wind all day.

And over his chest the covers in the ultimate dream
Will mount to the teeth, ascend the eyes, press back
The locks—while round his sturdy belly gleam
Suspended breaths, white spars above the wreck:

Till all the guests, come in to look, turn down
Their palms, and delirium assails the cliff
Of Norway where you ponder, and your little town
Reels like a sailor drunk in a rotten skiff.

The bleak sunshine shrieks its chipped music then
Out to the milkweed amid the fields of wheat.
There is a calm for you where men and women
Unroll the chill precision of moving feet.

Once more, death is the occasion—death, the chief of checks on mortal pride and traditionalist educator *par excellence*. More than other "rumors of mortality" (the phrase itself well describes the body of Tate's verse), the passing of children scandalizes the positivist's expectation of a secular beatitude, challenges his sense of total power over his condition. Hence, "the event will rage terrific as the sea" while bodies fill a crumbling room with light." For as contemplation of youthful remains indicts the delusion all men at times entertain—that we, in our "new wisdom," are become gods and masters of our own respective fates—the beholder of those remains is bound to see in the "peeled aster" beyond the "windowpane" a memorial of his own corpse in "gray" upon the selfsame catafalque. Then for all the deathbed guests, the assembled townsfolk, there is only the maelstrom of "delirium," a steady drifting into the great suck of despair. In time-honored rituals alone, in the collective formalities of bereavement which contain (by implication) some affirmation of death itself, is there surcease from the pain of disillusion, from the "immeasurable surrender." And even that, once the substance is gone out of the forms, is cold relief.

"Homily" contains advice for folk such as those troubled by "little boys grown patient at last"—advice within advice.

The poem is a short one:

If thine eye offend thee, pluck it out

If your tired unspeaking head
Rivet the dark with linear sight,

Crazed by a warlock with his curse
Dreamed up in some loquacious bed,
And if the stage-dark head rehearse
The fifth act of the closing night,

Why, cut it off, piece after piece,
And throw the tough cortex away,
And when you've marvelled on the wars
That wove their interior smoke its way,
Tear out the close vermiculate crease
Where death crawled angrily at bay.

The title refers to the epigraph, from Matthew 18:9. But here the offending member is the head, which "rivets the dark with linear sight." Its sleepless unease, however, is to its credit; and the eagerness of its possessor, in his waking hours, to be rid of the "warlock" of his dreams (a rationalist's equation of *momento mori* and superstition) is the folly by indirection considered. The effect of Tate's counsel to the unwillingly disturbed keeper of the new pieties is acid and merciless. If the modern would be immune to the truth of his mortality, then he must cut down through the skull—through the seat of reason into the primitive fundament of his consciousness, "the close vermiculate crease," ere he can isolate and remove the thought that troubles his subconscious. The suggestion here is plain: the cortex, full of the evidences of internal "wars," as the seat of vain notions, rules by day; and it would deny "the fifth act of the closing night." But the primordial components resist such nonsense, and in the "loquacious bed" the truth of man's destiny and origin "rehearse," *sub specie mortis.*

Another violent confrontation with the spirit of the times occurs in "The Subway." This much admired sonnet is the "cold revery" of a character half persona and half person observed—something in between the presence in the two poems examined above. Its matter is infernal, and the hell it explores nothing but manmade and contemporary—the fruitage of wars in the cortex, the self-destructive impetus of rationalism. The subway's rushing underground descent metaphorically and perhaps even mythically informs and hardens the entire poem. Once more, as in "Death of Little Boys," madness is the consequence of an experience that is seen well into but not quite comprehended, a madness that has, after harsh disabusement, its only alternatives—that is, for a man who has had his faith in science—in the offhanded fashionable casualness of the voice in "Horatian Epode" or the self-destruction mockingly recommended in "Homily." This speaker, however, is aware of the satanism in the rush of his fellows in their "business of humility" down "into the iron forestries of hell." No street cars can call him back nor any "chill precision" remove his memory of "angry worship." Therefore he comes again under the sky to find himself an "idiot," no longer capable of contemplating the universe under any aspect save those of geometry and associated subway-creating abstractions. He is like the Alice of Tate's later poem—or, rather, as she would have been had she been able to get back through the looking glass: "broken," but not reformed—dazed, while the "wordless (i.e. pointless) heavens bulge and reel" above him.

"The Subway" is a good place for the turning of this discussion toward Tate's maturity. With such poems he found what was to be his characteristic manner in *Poems: 1928–1931* (1932); *The Mediterranean and Other Poems* (1936); and *Selected Poems* (1937). There is no wry irony here, no play. His fashion has become neo-metaphysical, even before 1930. And that is the tenor of much verse from his middle years. The comic and parodic, inflative and deflative mock-heroics which Tate admired in the English Augustans (and emulated) keeps its place in the work of the Thirties and late Twenties. But these ingredients are absorbed into something more serious and sober and, furthermore, are dignified in the process, transformed into what they were not, as a line of meditation introduced by them takes its final startling shape. Moreover, with this shift the spirit in his work appears to be more and more public, less and less restrictively lyric, indirect, and narrowly dramatic. Though the searching of the fragmented sensibility continues, it is not ended *in vacuo*. A network of specific times, events, and circumstances is included. And the result is assuredly an additional poise and authority. Said another way, Allen Tate emerges with these changes as one of the characteristic poetic voices of his time —and as a Southern poet. The narrowly epistemological and ontological emphases of his earlier work are supplemented and defined by the addition of a frame of history perceived as a reflection of meaning: *his* teleology. The poetics with which Tate entered into this period and the degree of control and purposiveness which he hoped to bring to their application are specified in a poem which he wrote just before it began.

"Mr. Pope" may be set alongside Eliot's *Homage to John Dryden* and certain items by the Sitwells (Edith and Sacheverell), Roy Campbell, and T. E. Hulme as an early and curiously metaphysical acknowledgment from modern poetry of its debt to neo-classicism. In his poem Tate honors those qualities in Pope that he would have in himself.

> When Alexander Pope strolled in the city
> Strict was the glint of pearl and gold sedans.
> Ladies leaned out more out of fear than pity
> For Pope's tight back was rather a goat's than man's.

To begin, Pope addressed himself to and commanded the respect of the world where he was born—both the "human condition" in general and "the total complex of sensibility and thought, belief and experience" which was Eighteenth Century England (see the essay, "To Whom Is the Poet Responsible?").

But there is another issue raised in the first quatrain, that of the private Alexander Pope—the deformed hunchback of less than five feet—and his connection with Pope the poet. Stanzas two and three deal with this question and turn it around to prepare for the peroration / eulogism of the last two lines:

> Often one thinks the urn should have more bones
> Than skeletons provide for speedy dust,
> The urn gets hollow, cobwebs brittle as stones
> Weave to the funeral shell a frivolous rust.

> And he who dribbled couplets like a snake
> Coiled to a lithe precision in the sun
> Is missing. The jar is empty; you may break
> It only to find that Mr. Pope is gone.

> What requisitions of a verity
> Prompted the wit and rage between his teeth
> One cannot say. Around a crooked tree
> A moral climbs whose name would be a wreath.

All is quiet, restrained, conversational though forceful and well calculated. The person who is *Mr.* Alexander Pope (the formal address is no mere Southernism) is unavailable—"missing." The urn can contain far more than the flesh provides. No answer to the question of why the poet flailed the Dunces and "bit" (Pope liked the word and hence Tate's snake imagery) whatever enraged him can be extracted from "speedy dust." Put otherwise (as for instance in Tate's essay "Narcissus as Narcissus"; also in his "Miss Emily and the Bibliographer" and in the aforementioned "The Unliteral Imagination"), earlier Romantic and more recent psychological criticism of the work of traditional poets is beside the point. All that Tate will say of his subject is that he *did* draw drafts, as with a bank, on a truth; *did* refract in the language of which he was a faithful steward the shape and feel of what he found before him. And the consequence of his character *qua* poet was a "strictness" (an enactment of "fear") in that polity. Such, Tate has argued in essay after essay, is the duty of the poet: to create communion, not communication; self-contained wholes or "incarnations" for contemplation, not marching orders or testimonials ("Poetry as Knowledge," "Tension in Poetry," and "To Whom Is the Poet Responsible"). He does not deny that the motives behind a man's creations are rooted in "personality" (hence the organic figure, the tree; and its peculiarity, crookedness). But he insists that, if the artist is to be loyal to his craft, it is the handiwork that should interest us, the thing made and not the subliminal causes of its fashioning. Therefore, upon a crooked tree (the Pope *with us*: the work, not the urn) gathers a moral (i.e., aesthetic) that deserves a poem.

All that Allen Tate, as poet, critic, and novelist, became in future years is foreshadowed in his origin, his birthplace, his education, early friendships, and his early verse. The purely "dramatic" beginnings of the poems I have examined here (and the aesthetic behind them) are subsumed in the performance of Tate's maturity, in his markedly Southern works and his later, more explicitly "religious," compositions. He has been one man (and one poet) all the time.

The Serpent in the Mulberry Bush

by LOUIS D. RUBIN, JR.

T hat poem is 'about' solipsism, a philosophical doctrine which says that we create the world in the act of perceiving it; or about Narcissism, or any other *ism* that denotes the failure of the human personality to function objectively in nature and society."

That poem, as Tate goes on to say about the "Ode to the Confederate Dead," is also about "a man stopping at the gate of a Confederate graveyard on a late autumn afternoon." Thus the man at the cemetery and the graves in the cemetery become the symbol of the solipsism and the Narcissism:

> Autumn is desolation in the plot
> Of a thousand acres where these memories grow
> From the inexhaustible bodies that are not
> Dead, but feed the grass row after rich row.
> Think of the autumns that have come and gone!

A symbol is something that stands for something else. What I want to do is to point out some of the relationships between the "something" and the "something else."

Richard Weaver has written of the Nashville Agrarians that they "underwent a different kind of apprenticeship for their future labors. They served the muse of poetry." In a certain sense that is true, but the word "apprenticeship" is misleading in Tate's instance. Allen Tate did not become a poet merely in order to learn how to be an

EDITOR'S NOTE: Reprinted from *Southern Renascence: The Literature of the Modern South*, ed. Louis D. Rubin, Jr. (Baltimore: The Johns Hopkins Press, 1953), pp. 352–57, copyright © 1953 by The Johns Hopkins Press, by permission of the publisher.

Agrarian. He was a poet while he was an Agrarian; he continued to be a poet after his specific interest in Agrarianism diminished, and now he has become an active communicant of the Roman Catholic Church and he is still a poet. One must insist that for Allen Tate poetry has never been the apprenticeship for anything except poetry.

"Figure to yourself a man stopping at the gate of a Confederate cemetery . . . ," Tate writes in his essay "Narcissus as Narcissus." He continues: ". . . he pauses for a baroque meditation on the ravages of time, concluding with the figure of the 'blind crab.' This creature has mobility but no direction, energy but from the human point of view, no purposeful world to use it in. . . . The crab is the first intimation of the nature of the moral conflict upon which the drama of the poem develops: the cut-off-ness of the modern 'intellectual man' from the world."

> The brute curiosity of an angel's stare
> Turns you, like them, to stone,
> Transforms the heaving air
> Till plunged into a heavier world below
> You shift your sea-space blindly
> Heaving, turning like the blind crab.

If the Confederate Ode is based upon a moral conflict involving "the cut-off-ness of the modern 'intellectual man' from the world," why did Tate choose as his symbol the Confederate graveyard? The answer lies in the history of the region in which Allen Tate and his fellow Fugitives and Agrarians grew up. Tate was born and reared in the Upper South, and he attended college in Nashville, Tennessee, and there was a symbolism in the South of his day ready for the asking. It was the contrast, and conflict, between what the South was and traditionally had been, and what it was tending toward. "With the war of 1914–1918 the South re-entered the world," Tate has written, "—but gave a backward glance as it stepped over the border: that backward glance gave us the Southern renascence, a literature conscious of the past in the present."

What kind of country was the South upon which Tate and his contemporaries of the early 1920s looked back at as well as observed around them? It was first of all a country with considerable historical consciousness, with rather more feeling for tradition and manners than existed elsewhere in the nation. There had been a civil war just a little over a half-century before, and the South had been badly beaten. Afterwards Southern leaders decided to emulate the ways of the conqueror, and called for a New South of cities and factories. Such Southern intellectuals as there were went along with the scheme. Men of letters like Walter Hines Page and John Spencer Bassett preached that once the provincialism of the Southern author was thrown off, and the Southern man of letters was willing to forget Appomattox Court House and Chickamauga, then Southern literature would come into its own.

When it came to forecasting a literary renascence in the South, Bassett and his friends were absolutely right, but they could not have been more mistaken about the form that it would take. What brought about the renascence—what there was in the time and place that made possible an Allen Tate and a William Faulkner and a Donald Davidson and a John Ransom and a Robert Penn Warren and an Andrew Lytle and three dozen other Southern writers—was not the eager willingness to ape the ways of the Industrial East, but rather the revulsion against the necessity of having to do so in order to live among their fellow Southerners. By 1920 and thereafter the South was changing, so that Tate's modern Southerner standing at the gate of a Confederate military cemetery was forced to compare what John Spencer Bassett had once termed "the worn out ideas of a forgotten system" with what had replaced that system.

And what had taken its place was what Tate and his fellow Agrarians have been crying out against ever since: the industrial, commercially-minded modern civilization, in which religion and ritual and tradition and order were rapidly being superseded by the worship of getting and spending.

Thus the Confederate graveyard as the occasion for solipsism, and the failure of the human personality to function objectively in nature and society, because for Tate there could be no question about where the young Southern writer should stand in the matter. The agrarian community that had been the Southern way of life was with all its faults vastly preferable to what was taking place now. As he wrote in 1936, "the Southern man of letters cannot permit himself to look upon the old system from a purely social point of view, or from the economic view; to him it must seem better than the system that destroyed it, better, too, than any system with which the modern planners, Marxian or any color, wish to replace the present order." Surveying the heroic past and the empty present, the young Southerner could

only feel himself in isolation from what were now his region's ways.
In the words of the Confederate Ode,

> What shall we say who count our days and bow
> Our heads with a commemorial woe
> In the ribboned coats of grim felicity,
> What shall we say to the bones, unclean,
> Whose verdurous anonymity will grow?
> The ragged arms, the ragged heads and eyes
> Lost in these acres of the insane green?
> The gray lean spiders come, they come and go;
> In a tangle of willows without light
> The singular screech-owl's tight
> Invisible lyric seeds the mind
> With the furious murmur of their chivalry.

> We shall say only the leaves
> Flying, plunge and expire

> We shall say only the leaves whispering
> In the improbable mist of nightfall
> That flies on multiple wing. . . .

We are, that is, inadequate, cut off, isolated; we cannot even imagine
how it was. All we can see is the leaves blowing about the gravestones.
So Mr. Tate's modern Southerner felt.

The "Ode to the Confederate Dead" dates from about 1926, and that
was the year, Tate recalls, that he and John Crowe Ransom began
toying with the idea of "doing something" about the Southern situation, a project which soon led to plans for the book entitled *I'll Take
My Stand*, in which Tate, Ransom, and ten other Southerners set
forth Agrarian counsels for what they felt was an increasingly industrialized, increasingly misled South. The central argument was stated
in the first paragraph of the introduction, which Ransom composed
and to which all the participants gave assent: "All the articles bear in
the same sense upon the book's title-subject: all tend to support a
Southern way of life as against what may be called the American or
prevailing way; and all as much as agree that the best terms in which
to represent the distinction are contained in the phrase, Agrarian
versus Industrial."

The problem that the twelve Agrarians felt confronted the modern
South was the same problem, then, as that which Mr. Tate's modern
man at the graveyard gate faced. And in a very definite sense, *I'll Take*

My Stand represented their recommendations for a solution, in a particular time and place, of the central moral problem of the "Ode to the Confederate Dead."

The Agrarians declared in their symposium that industrialism was predatory, in that it was based on a concept of nature as something to be used. In so doing, industrialism threw man out of his proper relationship to nature, and to God whose creation it was. The Agrarian quarrel, they declared, was with applied science, which in the form of industrial capitalism had as its object the enslavement of human energies. Since all activity was measured by the yardstick of financial gain, the industrial spirit neglected the aesthetic life. It had the effect of brutalizing labor, removing from it any possibility of enjoyment.

It must be remembered that most of the Agrarians were speaking not as economists or sociologists or regional planners or even as professional philosophers; they were speaking as men of letters. They believed that an Agrarian civilization was the way of life which permitted the arts to be an integral and valuable social activity, and not, as Ransom put it, "intercalary and non-participating experiences." Donald Davidson wrote of the Agrarians that "they sought to force, not so much a theory of economics as a philosophy of life, in which both economics and art would find their natural places and not be disassociated into abstract means and abstract ends, as the pseudo-culture of the world-city would disassociate them."

In an Agrarian community aesthetic activity would not be subordinate to economics. The artist would be a working member of society, not a person somehow set apart from the everyday existence of his neighbors. Nature, religion and art would be honored activities of daily life, and not something superfluous and outmoded, to be indulged when business permitted. Knowledge—letters, learning, taste, the integrated and rich fullness of emotion and intellect—would be "carried to the heart," as Tate said in the Confederate Ode, and not an unassimilated, discordant conglomerate of fragments. In the words of the poem,

> What shall we say who have knowledge
> Carried to the heart? Shall we take the act
> To the grave? Shall we, more hopeful, set up the grave
> In the house? The ravenous grave?

Shall we, he is asking, who still possess this full knowledge and who live in a world from which we are increasingly cut off by its insularity and isolation, in which we have mobility but no direction, energy but no outlet—shall we wait for death, or better still, court it?

In one sense, the program put forward in *I'll Take My Stand* constituted an answer to that question. But for all the book's effectiveness (and 23 years later it is receiving more attention from young Southerners than ever before in its history), it would be a mistake to believe that the Agrarian program was the only, or even the most important, statement of the problems of modern man as Tate and his colleagues saw them. One must always remember that Tate, Ransom, Davidson and Warren were poets primarily, not social scientists. The place to look for Allen Tate's ultimate statement of views is in his poetry.

Cleanth Brooks has pointed out the relevance of Tate's poetry to this central moral problem. Not only is this so in regard to subject matter, however; we find it implicit in the poetics as well. What is the most obvious characteristic of the poetry of Tate and his colleagues? I think we find it stated, and recognized, from the very outset, in the first reviews of the anthology, *Fugitives*, published in 1928. "Fugitive poetry makes one distinctly feel that one of the serious and fundamental defects of nineteenth century poetry was that it was too easy," one critic wrote. "Mr. Ransom, Mr. Tate and Miss [Laura] Riding are not for those who read and run," another reviewer asserted. The poet John Gould Fletcher, himself soon to join the Agrarians in the symposium, declared in a review that the Fugitive poets had become the main impulse in America in the leadership of "a school of intellectual poetry replacing the free verse experiments of the elder school."

The kind of poetry that Allen Tate was writing, then, represented a disciplined, intellectual, difficult poetry, requiring of the reader, in Tate's own words, "the fullest co-operation of all his intellectual resources, all his knowledge of the world, and all the persistence and alertness that he now thinks of giving to scientific studies." It was therefore a direct challenge to the attitude that aesthetic concerns were a subordinate, harmless activity "for those who read and run." It claimed for art as important and as demanding a role in human affairs as that played by science and business. As Ransom wrote, art "is a career, precisely as science is a career. It is as serious, it has an attitude

as official, it is as studied and consecutive, it is by all means as difficult,
it is no less important."

Another characteristic of Tate's poetry is its concentrated use of
image and metaphor, as in the concluding lines of the Confederate
Ode:

> Leave now
> The shut gate and the decomposing wall:
> The gentle serpent, green in the mulberry bush,
> Riots with his tongue through the hush—
> Sentinel of the grave who counts us all!

Of those lines Tate says that "the closing image, that of the serpent,
is the ancient symbol of time, and I tried to give it the credibility of
the commonplace by placing it in a mulberry bush—with the faint
hope that the silkworm would somehow be explicit. But time is also
death. If that is so, then space, or the Becoming, is life; and I believe
there is not a single spacial symbol in the poem. . . ."

Why, though, if that is all that Tate "meant," did he not write
something like the following:

> Let us leave the graveyard now.
> Time runs riot there
> And time brings death to bear
> And wears it on its brow.

The answer is that those lines are simply the abstract statement of
what Tate was saying—and not even that, because Tate was not
simply declaring that one should not remain in a graveyard because
it reminds one of time and time brings death. Such a statement represents merely the "message" of the lines. Its purpose would be to give
instruction concerning the course of action to be followed at a cemetery gate. One may decide that it is "true," which is another way of
saying that the idea expressed is in accord with the findings of science;
or that it is "false," in which case the advice is non-scientific and not
an advantageous basis for action. If the former, the poet is not saying
anything startling, and certainly a clinical psychologist could present
much more convincing proof of the validity of the action than the
poet would be doing. And if one decides that the advice is not scientifically plausible, then what else remains? The lines contain nothing

but the advice; the "meaning" represents the lines' sole reason for being.

Tate's lines, however, do not simply give "advice"; they do not base their appeal on their adaptability to counsel. They are not dependent upon any scientific "proof" of their correctitude. Both alone and in the context of the Ode they *create their own validity*. They do not pretend to be representative of scientific knowledge and proof; they *are* their own knowledge and proof. They are about serpents and mulberry bushes and shut gates and decomposing walls, and not advice to grave-yard visitors. Tate's poem isn't a mere pseudo-scientific statement, and it doesn't depend upon a paraphrase of a scientific statement, and its validity is neither confirmable nor refutable by scientists. It may or may not contain a statement of scientific truth, but that would at most be a portion, only one of a number of parts, involved in the whole creation of the poem. The poem, therefore, does not depend upon science; science plays only a relatively minor role. The relationship is obvious to the Agrarian belief in the equality of the aesthetic pursuits with the scientific.

Tate and his colleagues have insisted in their poetry and criticism that the image possesses a priority over the abstract idea. They have taken over the pioneering work done by the Imagists and gone further. They have been instrumental in reviving contemporary interest in the Metaphysical poets of the seventeenth century, constructed as that poetry is with complex imagery and metaphor. An idea, Ransom has written, "is derivative and tamed," whereas an image is in the wild state: "we think we can lay hold of image and take it captive, but the docile captive is not the real image but only the idea, which is the image with its character beaten out of it." The image, Ransom declared, is "a manifold of properties, like a field or a mine, something to be explored for the properties." The scientist can use the manifold only by singling out the one property with which he is concerned: "It is not by refutation but by abstraction that science destroys the image. It means to get its 'value' out of the image, and we may be sure that it has no use for the image in its original state of freedom."

A poetry of abstract ideas, Tate and Ransom held, is a poetry of science, and as such it neglects the manifold properties of life and nature. Just as an economist used only the special interests of eco-nomics to interpret human activity, so the poetry of ideas was concerned with only one part of the whole. This led to specialization and isolation, fragmenting the balance and completeness of man and nature into a multitude of special interests, cutting off men from the whole of life, destroying the unity of human existence.

And here we come again to Tate's main theme in the Confederate Ode, "the failure of the human personality to function objectively in nature and society," "the cut-off-ness of the modern 'intellectual man' from the world." It is a constant refrain in Tate's work. In 1928, for instance, we find these two sentences in a review by Tate of Gorham Munson's *Destinations*, in the *New Republic*: "Evasions of intellectual responsibility take various forms; all forms seem to be general in our time; what they mean is the breakdown of culture; and there is no new order in sight which promises to replace it. The widespread cults, esoteric societies, amateur religions, all provide easy escapes from discipline, easy revolts from the traditional forms of culture." And 25 years later he is still saying just that, as in his recent Phi Beta Kappa address at the University of Minnesota: "the man of letters must not be committed to the illiberal specializations that the nineteenth century has proliferated into the modern world: specializations in which means are divorced from ends, action from sensibility, matter from mind, society from the individual, religion from moral agency, love from lust, poetry from thought, communion from experience, and mankind in the community from men in the crowd. There is literally no end to this list of dissociations because there is no end, yet in sight, to the fragmenting of the western mind."

Modern man of the dissociated sensibility, isolated from his fellows, caught up in a life of fragmented parts and confused impulses; thus Allen Tate's Southerner waiting at the gate of the Confederate cemetery contemplates the high glory of Stonewall Jackson and the inscrutable foot-cavalry of a day when ancestors of that Southerner knew what they fought for, and could die willingly for knowing it:

> You know who have waited by the wall
> The twilight certainty of an animal,
> Those midnight restitutions of the blood
> You know—the immitigable pines, the smoky frieze
> Of the sky, the sudden call: you know the rage,
> The cold pool left by the mounting flood,
> Of muted Zeno and Parmenides.

> You who have waited for the angry resolution
> Of those desires that should be yours tomorrow,
> You know the unimportant shrift of death
> And praise the vision
> And praise the arrogant circumstance
> Of those who fall
> Rank upon rank, hurried beyond decision—
> Here by the sagging gate, stopped by the wall.

Times are not what they were, Tate's Southerner at the gate realizes; it has become almost impossible even to imagine such days:

> You hear the shout, the crazy hemlocks point
> With troubled fingers to the silence which
> Smothers you, a mummy, in time.

Even the title of the poem stems from the irony of the then and now; "Not only are the meter and rhyme without fixed pattern," Tate wrote, "but in another feature the poem is even further removed from Pindar than Abraham Cowley was: a purely subjective meditation would not even in Cowley's age have been called an ode. I suppose in so calling it I intended an irony: the scene of the poem is not a public celebration, it is a lone man by a gate."

If in the Confederate Ode there is regret and irony over "the failure of the human personality to function objectively in nature and society," then in Tate's poem "Seasons of the Soul" the malady has attained the proportions of desperation. The poem is Tate's equation of the present-day dissociation of sensibility with the medieval Hell. It begins with a quotation in Italian from Canto XIII of the *Inferno*, and the English equivalent is to this effect:

> Then I reached out my hand before me
> And severed a twig from a thorn bush;
> And the trunk shrieked, 'Why do you tear me?'

The passage is that in which the poet is conducted to a wood in which the souls of lovers who died by committing suicide have become trees, and which are eternally rended by Harpies which feed on the branches. "Seasons of the Soul" is in four parts, and in the course of the poem the pestilences of modern man are set forth, each in its anguish. War—

No head knows where its rest is
Or may lie down with reason
When war's usurping claws
Shall take the heart escheat—
Green field in burning season
To stain the weevil's jaws.

Rootlessness, a world peopled by ghosts—

My father in a gray shawl
Gave me an unseeing glint
And entered another room!
I stood in the empty hall
And watched them come and go
From one room to another,
Old men, old women—slow,
Familiar; girls, boys;
I saw my downcast mother
Clad in her street-clothes,
Her blue eyes long and small,
Who had no look or voice
For him whose vision froze
Him in the empty hall.

Godlessness—

For the drying God above,
Hanged in his windy steeple,
No longer bears for us
The living wound of love.

Bestiality—

The pacing animal
Surveys the jungle cove
And slicks his slithering wiles
To turn the venereal awl
In the livid wound of love.

In the last section of the poem, "Spring," the poet recalls his childhood:

Back in my native prime
I saw the orient corn
All space but no time,
Reaching for the sun
Of the land where I was born:

> It was a pleasant land
> Where even death could please
> Us with an ancient pun—
> All dying for the hand
> Of the mother of silences.

As Vivienne Koch has pointed out, "the mother of silences" appears to be a figure symbolizing both the Virgin and death. In time of pestilence, the poet says, who knows what is to come, death or salvation? "In time of bloody war / Who will know the time?" he asks; "Its light is at the flood, / Mother of silences!"

With certain reservations one can say that "Seasons of the Soul" is Tate's own telling of the Waste Land. The poem is renewed evidence of the accessibility to a common tradition shared by Tate and the Southerners on the one hand, and Eliot and his followers on the other. The Southerners, Fugitives and Agrarians both, in many ways have said for their time and place what Eliot has been saying for the same time but another less particularized place. The theme of "Seasons of the Soul" could hardly be better explicated than in recent remarks by Eliot in his *Notes Toward A Definition of Culture:*

We can assert with some confidence that our own period is one of decline; that the standards of culture are lower than they were fifty years ago; and that the evidences of this decline are visible in every department of human activity. I see no reason why the decay of culture should not proceed much further, and why we may not even anticipate a period of some duration in which it is possible to say that it will have *no* culture. Then culture will have to grow again from the soil; and when I say it must grow again from the soil, I do not mean that it will be brought into existence by any activity of political demagogues. . . . Culture is the one thing that we cannot deliberately aim at. It is the product of a variety of more or less harmonious activities, each pursued for its own sake.

Eliot's proposed course of action for modern man is well known: it is the deliberate and disciplined cultivation of spiritual values, through religion. That he feels that his advice will not be followed, and that disaster will result, in no way diminishes his belief that only through God can civilization survive. For the Southerners, Agrarianism was one way of saying this, too. Though *I'll Take My Stand* did not base its recommendations upon a religious revival, the role of religion in the agrarian life was insisted upon. Significantly, too, Tate's essay was on the Southern religion, calling for the spiritual values of wholeness and unity through religion.

Recently Tate has remarked, in discussing the impact of *I'll Take My Stand*, that "I never thought of Agrarianism as a *restoration* of anything in the Old South; I saw it as something to be created, as I think it will in the long run be created as the result of a profound change, not only in the South, but elsewhere, in the moral and religious outlook of western man. The South is still a region where an important phase of that change may take place; but the change will not, as I see it, be uniquely Southern; it will be greater than the South. What I had in mind twenty years ago, not too distinctly, I think I see more clearly now; that is, the possibility of the humane life presupposes, with us, a moral order, the order of a unified Christendom. . . ."

Again we find the philosophy mirrored in the poetics. The demand for a conscious quest for the order and unity of a spiritual existence runs throughout his poetry and his criticism of poetry. His famous definition of tension in poetry, for instance, is in direct relationship to this concept: "the meaning of poetry is its 'tension,' the full organized body of all the extension and intension that we can find in it. The remotest figurative significance that we can derive does not invalidate the extensions of the literal statement. Or we may begin with the literal statement and by stages develop the complications of the metaphor: at every stage we may pause to state the meaning so far apprehended, and at every stage the meaning will be coherent." The definition is a demand that poetry embody and reflect a unity. Together with the belief in a poetry of rich imagery, it constitutes a pronouncement against the poetical equivalent of "easy revolts from the traditional forms of culture," "illiberal specialization," and the dissociation of sensibility. Tate insists that the poem constitute a whole, full and rich and multi-faceted, with no insular scientific abstraction from the whole for the sake of facility or "usability"; and he demands that the whole be unified, disciplined, and coherent all along the way, rather than formless and fragmentary. It is his desire for all forms of our overly-disjointed modern life, especially the theological: "If there is a useful program that we might undertake in the South," he has recently declared, "would it not be towards the greater unity of the

varieties of Southern Protestantism, with the ultimate aim the full
unity of all Christians?"

Tate's newest poem has been appearing by installments in various
magazines, and one awaits with eagerness its publication in full. The
poem has a strong and obvious narrative level, which in the two por-
tions thus far in print concerns the poet's childhood. The first section,
"The Maimed Man," published in the *Partisan Review*, tells of a boy
who is confronted with the corpse of a man with the head severed
from the body. Another, entitled "The Swimmers" and published in
Hudson Review, describes five youths out swimming in a creek:

> Bill Eaton, Charlie Watson, "Nigger" Layne
> The doctor's son, Harry Dueslér who played
> The flute; Tate, with the water on his brain.

But the narrative style is deceptively easy; and one looks with expectation for clues to something else—because that "something that stands
for something else" is always present in a Tate poem, too. So that one
notices in "The Swimmers" that the five youths encounter a posse
searching for a lynched Negro, and that twelve men are in the posse,
but only eleven men ride back:

> eleven same
> Jesus Christers unmembered and unmade,
> Whose corpse had died again in dirty shame.

And as the youths watch the sheriff, the leader of the posse, with the
corpse,

> A single horseman came at a fast lope
> And pulled up at the hanged man's horny feet;
> The sheriff noosed the feet, the other end
> The stranger tied to his pommel in a neat
> Slip-knot. I saw the Negro's body bend
> And straighten, as a fish-line cast transverse
> Yields to the current that it must subtend.
> The sheriff's God-damn was a facile curse
> Not for the dead but for the blinding dust
> That boxed the cortege in a cloudy hearse
> And dragged it towards our town.

Then one remembers the story of the Crucifixion, in *John*, and of the
burial of Christ's body by Joseph and Nicodemus, and it suddenly

becomes clear that Tate is not just telling about five Southern boys who see a lynched Negro; the Passion is being reenacted. One recalls the lines in the first section, "The Maimed Man," which serve to preface the poem:

> Teach me to fast
> And pray, that I may know the motes that tease
> Skittering sunbeams are dead shells at last.
> Then, timeless muse, reverse my time; unfreeze
> All that I was in your congenial heat . . .

It would seem, then, that Tate is prepared in his new poem to look at his childhood again, and perhaps all his life, through the eye of his adult religious faith, and that what we shall get is a poem in which each day the Passion is reenacted for the modern man, in everything he does, all around him. One realizes, too, that the rhyme scheme of Tate's poem is that of the *Divine Comedy*. The poet seems to be reliving his past—the South, his boyhood there—against the perspective of the eternal, and equating his childhood reactions to evil, in all the innocence of boyhood, with his mature attitudes:

> O fountain, bosom source undying-dead
> Replenish me the spring of love and fear
> And give me back the eye that looked and fled
> When a thrush idling in the tulip tree
> Unwound the cold dream of the copperhead.

The serpent again—the passage of time, evil, the lynching—is awakened from its sleep by an act of beauty; the child sees and flees, recognizing evil without pretense, rationalization, or callousness to it. The poet asks that now, with the strength and purposiveness given him by his belief in God, he be permitted to see things whole again, not with the untried innocence of childhood but in the experience of the adult who has been living in time.

Twenty-three years ago Allen Tate called for the South to "reestablish a private, self-contained, and essentially spiritual life." For longer than that he has been advocating a spiritual outlook which will provide a unity against chaos, a discipline of religious values against the nihilist threat of new dark ages. "As I look back upon my own verse, written over more than twenty-five years," he declared recently, "I see plainly that its main theme is man suffering from unbelief; and I cannot for a moment suppose that this man is some other than myself." During this time he has widened his scope and interests to include his nation and his civilization, without for a moment ceasing to speak to and for his native region. His poetry, his criticism, and his other writings have all mirrored his times. That he now addresses the whole of Christendom hardly makes what he has to say any less relevant for the South. For it was the South that taught him how to say these things in prose, and in his poems embody them.

On "The Cross"

by R. K. MEINERS

In the preface to *The Last Alternatives*, from which book the following discussion of "The Cross" is taken, I committed myself to the judgment that Allen Tate was among the "three or four most important" writers from that generation of American writers who came to maturity in the late 1920's. In the intervening years I have changed my mind about many things, and were I to write a book on Allen Tate today I would, naturally, go about things at least somewhat differently, for one must think that he has grown not only older but at least a little wiser. Among other things, I would probably take out the "three or four most important" phrase: not because I have changed my mind, but because it is typical of that sort of useless judg-

EDITOR'S NOTE: Reprinted, with some minor changes, from *The Last Alternatives: A Study of the Works of Allen Tate* (Chicago: Swallow Press, 1962), pp. 145–52, by permission of the publisher. Permission to quote from *The Letters of Hart Crane*, ed. Brom Weber (New York: Horace Liveright, 1952), has been granted by Mr. Weber.

ment, offering more precision than it can demonstrate, which will convince no one of anything, and can appeal only to those already inclined to agree. I would say, instead, that for me Allen Tate was, and has remained, one of the indispensable writers. I would say, moreover, that insofar as I understand the development of modern literature in this country, Tate has played a role which has been central, and in some ways unique.[1]

Other writers in this collection will speak of Allen Tate as a critic, a poet, a man of letters. The following piece on "The Cross"[2] was written out of the belief that it was in many ways Tate's best short poem, and therefore worthy of careful examination; and that although the poem might seem at first acquaintance complex and forbidding, the complexity was justified by the difficult subject, and was beautifully controlled. I would add to those comments the further one that the fusion of concept and image in this poem is accomplished in a manner which is completely Tate's own, and that no one has ever *successfully* imitated it, though many have tried.

In a recent essay ("Poetry Modern and Unmodern," in *Essays of Four Decades*), Tate has spoken of his attempts to develop a poetry of "sub-lyrical satire," and those comments should tell a reader a good deal about the mode in which Tate's poetry often operates. "The Cross" is perhaps not so good an example of the mode as some of his other poems, unless we broaden our understanding of both "lyric" and "satire" beyond the bounds of our usual understanding. It would be pointless for me to invent another genre, such as the "intellectual lyric," for use in describing "The Cross": with the advent of Mr. Frye and his disciples we now already have more genres than we know what to do with. Let it suffice to say that "The Cross," with its extraordinary realization of conceptual and emotional experience in primarily visual imagery, is probably the best example I know of what most critics have usually thought they were describing when they spoke of *metaphysical* poetry, and that it is one of relatively few

---

[1] I amplify these points to some degree in my recent *Everything to be Endured: An Essay on Robert Lowell and Modern Poetry* (Columbia: University of Missouri Press, 1970).

[2] Originally it was entitled "The Pit"; the change to "The Cross" is one more indication of some of the far-reaching polarities in the poem that I have attempted to suggest in my reading of it. The discussion of the poem in *The Last Alternatives* has been slightly revised here.

twentieth-century poems which will bear genuine comparison to the methods of the poems of John Donne. By "comparison" I do not mean to suggest a facile identifying of the work of a seventeenth-century poet and a twentieth-century poet; we have, surely, learned better than that, and like any modern poem "The Cross" can be compared only analogously with the poetry of the past. For if it is anything, "The Cross" is a twentieth-century poem. It exists in an area which is very close to the heart of some of the most, shall I say, *crucial* dilemmas which we have faced in this time.

"The Cross" is a very early poem if one excepts the early things published in *The Fugitive* and *The Double Dealer*. It is a very tight and difficult poem, and not many critics have tackled it. Perhaps they have felt, and perhaps many readers still feel, as Hart Crane did when he wrote to Tate: " 'The Cross' keeps me guessing a little too strenuously. I can't help thinking it perhaps too condensed, and . . . a not entirely fused melange of ecclesiastical and highly personalized imagery. In which case you sin no more than Eliot in the recent 'Ash-Wednesday.' "[3]

Now, Crane was quite wrong. The poem *is* "highly condensed," but it is not "too highly condensed." The demands it places upon the reader are no more than those made by many other great short poems. The meanings of the "ecclesiastical" imagery are available: more available even now, for example, than the symbolism of, say, Blake or Yeats. As for the "highly-personalized" imagery, there is no doubt that Tate's imagery is in many ways peculiar to him, but this is true of all important poets, and the problem can be met by some education in the traditions of modern thought and a study of Tate's other poetry and his prose.[4]

"The Cross" was written in 1928, long before Tate's prose demonstrated much concern with Christianity, and well before the more overtly religious viewpoint of his later writing had emerged. Yet "The Cross" is a religious poem; or, rather, it is a religious poem *about* history, and it almost perfectly manifests a fundamental quality in Tate's work. Though he is a writer preoccupied with history, that preoccu-

[3] Brom Weber, ed., *The Letters of Hart Crane* (New York, 1952), p. 355.
[4] In *The Last Alternatives*, of course, I attempted to supply some of this context in other chapters.

pation has been what may be fairly called a religious concern from the beginning of his career.

But the poem is not, of course, an illustration of a theme, or a cartoon of some pattern of belief; and one should study it with the conviction that any poem must carry its own justification.

> There is a place that some men know,
> I cannot see the whole of it
> Nor how I came there. Long ago
> Flame burst out of a secret pit
> Crushing the world with such a light   5
> The day-sky fell to moonless black,
> The kingly sun to hateful night
> For those, once seeing, turning back:
> For love so hates mortality
> Which is the providence of life   10
> She will not let it blessèd be
> But curses it with mortal strife,
> Until beside the blinding rood
> Within that world-destroying pit
> —Like young wolves that have tasted blood 15
> Of death, men taste no more of it.
> So blind, in so severe a place
> (All life before in the black grave)
> The last alternatives they face
> Of life, without the life to save,   20
> Being from all salvation weaned—
> A stag charged both at heel and head:
> Who would come back is turned a fiend
> Instructed by the fiery dead.

Though the poem is short, its controlling idea is as large and vital as any in our experience; the handling of it is very fine. It is apparent, I believe, that although the poem is in a sense explicitly religious, its meaning expands until it includes the large historical and cultural concerns which inform all Tate's work. That the poem should do so much in such a short length and still remain under control, with no unspecified or dissembling images, is astonishing. That the poem accomplishes so much in the short length is one measure of its greatness.

The poem is concerned with man's religious predicament and the historical consequences of it: once a man or a culture has obtained a knowledge of Christianity, that knowledge cannot be ignored except

at great peril. And since this is the subject of the poem, it is not surprising that Tate should use religious, even theological, terms in it.
The meanings of these terms are not esoteric; it is not as if Tate were
demanding knowledge of a minor Buddhist sect of the ninth century.
Hart Crane found it too ecclesiastical and difficult. If the same comment holds true for other readers, that fact might be a vindication of
the poem's theme: the culture has placed itself in danger by forgetting,
even destroying, the forces that have made it.

It is typical of Tate's concern for "unity" and "full experience" that
he phrases a problem of religious faith and epistemology in visual
terms. It is a mode of writing which is typical of all Tate's poetry, but
here the practice is much sharpened and refined. In his early essay on
Emily Dickinson, Tate remarked that she never reasons; she *sees*. The
same observation might be made, perhaps more accurately, of "The
Cross." There is no theological reasoning in it; it is all *seeing*.
The theme is quite absorbed into its images. The first two and one-
half lines are extraordinarily laconic. One is merely *there*; where that
is, one cannot at first say. The "place" of the first line is completely
unspecified, and only gradually becomes visible. And what "I" see
there is quite terrifying. This "place," which has at first no content,
must be understood in Christian terms: this becomes apparent in the
first few lines. This initial impression is reinforced immediately by
the juxtaposition of "know" and "see." Both words, despite their surface simplicity, have tremendous implications. "Know" is used in the
New Testament sense: knowledge unto salvation. "See" also has theological overtones, for since the "place"—the cross—is not seen completely, the efficacy which it once had cannot be obtained. If the protagonist of the poem is blind, it is a spiritual blindness.

And yet, it is also a physical blindness. The religious concern
merges with a more purely aesthetic concern. We may assume that
men once *saw* the cross. I am not speaking in what is usually called
a figurative manner; there was a time when the sign of the cross would
call into mind a fairly organized body of conceptions. But this is no
longer so. We can no longer see the cross; we can no longer "see" traditional Christianity. Our vision is generally flawed, and nothing is seen
whole and flawless. Whether it ever *was* seen whole and flawless is
another question, one we cannot entertain here; but for modern man
it may fairly be said that his powers of sight have been thoroughly

confounded with his introspection, his meditations and scruples. The implications of the word "see" are always important for Tate; it is one of the most loaded words in his vocabulary.

The speaker of the poem is placed in such a position that his awareness is challenged by the central fact of Christianity. Yet, he does not know how he came to be in such a position; it has just happened. Christianity is, we assume, a part of his culture which had not much interest for him before its awful significance burst upon him. For that is how we must read the passage beginning with the last words of line three.

The third through the eighth lines carry the significance beyond the individual to the entire Western tradition. The bursting flame is a fairly stereotyped expression for the revelation of Christ's glory. On the other hand, "secret pit" causes trouble if we read in this fashion, for it carries inevitable overtones of the Christian hell. I do not believe there has been any religion which has developed an identical notion of eternal punishment (though there are of course analogies which could be made with other religions). Furthermore, the gospel tradition directly links Christ and hell; he descended into hell before he assumed his position of majesty. So the ambiguity: the revelation of Christ's glory is at the same time the revelation of terrible potentialities. Those who are accustomed to thinking of Christ as the bearer of peace and love, and in the pastoral imagery of the lamb of God, will have some difficulty with this reading. For if one thinks exclusively in that fashion, it may be difficult to see that Christ was in a very real sense a destroyer. Theologically and psychologically, he destroyed both a view of nature and a view of human experience: for man, after Christ, could never feel *quite* at home in the world, or that the state of nature was beneficent. In the Christian scheme of salvation, the state of natural man after the Fall is a state of sin. This is a hard doctrine, and that side of Christ represented by such sayings as "I bring not peace, but a sword," is equally hard. The protagonist of the poem seems to be struggling with such aspects of Christian revelation.

This revelation, in one sense, *crushed* the world (line five). The emotional force of the word is plain, I think. But it might be well to observe in passing that this kind of imagery is very typical of Tate. Kinetic and visual images are joined; the concept which hovers in the images is never stated, but rather appears somewhere in the juxtaposition between the two sensory orders. Most modern readers take imagery of this sort for granted; but it may be useful to remember that the rationale for such imagery is probably best understood by those who have studied Baudelaire and his followers. For when "The Cross" was written, it had not been long before that Tate had translated the famous sonnet "Correspondences." In this passage there is a successful example of what Baudelaire (and others) called "correspondence": the transposition of an image from one order of experience to another. "The Cross," we may notice, is considerably more conservative in this respect than some of Tate's other poems, and it is probably the better for it. Though "The Cross" has less of the remarkable wit which distinguishes many of Tate's other poems, it also avoids the failures of this mode of imagery, the *préciosité* which is so often Tate's major vice.

The assertions of lines six through eight cause no particular difficulty if we have grasped what goes before. The sun, which once ruled human destiny, either as a personified deity or as the chief phenomenon of nature, can no longer have its old significance for those who have encountered the awful force of the new religion. The specifically Christian imagery of the earlier lines is here replaced by Pagan images, which are in turn dismissed. Perhaps this, after all, was the meaning of the darkness after the crucifixion: "the day-sky fell to moonless black."

The next lines revolve primarily around a subtle juxtaposition of love and hate. It takes a nice bit of theological dexterity to get around the seeming negations of lines nine through thirteen. The love is the love of God revealed in Christ. Mortality is just that: the condition of being mortal, with all its implications of finiteness and naturalness. But Christ's role, as we have seen, is in some ways most ambiguous; and Christ's *love* is similarly ambiguous. Consider this: "a new commandment I give you, that you love one another." But genuine love cannot be *commanded* to exist. And here in Tate's poem we have another version of the ambiguities involved in the notion of "love" within the Christian tradition. Christ is the manifestation of God's love, yet he may destroy. The relationships of this mortality-providence-blessed-mortal strife sequence furnish almost limitless ambivalences. The terms act as prisms in which the significance of each succeeding term is refracted, modified, and transformed in a *progression d'effet.* Mortality is the providence of life in the sense that all men are mortal; death is part of the human experience, that which is provided or foreseen. But providence also implies the doctrine of Christian providence—the care of God for his creatures. The providence of God is a blessing; but it may reverse upon the recipient and become a curse. The love of God, in this poem, has a strange way of turning, for those who apprehend it but fail to acquire it, into something which has an effect very unlike love.

I have mentioned ambiguity and ambivalence, but it is neither the structure of the poem which is ambiguous, nor the imagery. The ambiguity lies in the condition the poem examines, the meaning of the Christian tradition in the present time. The images grow logically out of this concern and are organic with the conception; they never deteriorate to mere decoration or illustration. And since the images here are so organic to the conception, the assertions that the cross is blinding and that one can stand, at the same time, *beside* the cross and *in* a world-destroying pit (lines thirteen and fourteen) are explained by the fundamental irony that knowledge may indeed damn. It damns here not only an individual but also, in a sense, a culture.

The image of the "young wolves that have tasted blood" which begins in line fifteen and qualifies the succeeding lines is among the very finest in Tate's verse, and it absolutely must be grasped. The preceding lines have made the cross both a preserver and a destroyer. It destroys the old life of the "world"; i.e., it has changed the situation of nature: it makes a purely natural form of salvation impossible. On the other hand, it offers a supernatural salvation but does not guarantee it. The word "blood" looks in two directions. Imagistically, it functions as a symbol of the historical and metaphysical tensions in which modern man finds himself. He cannot return to the world of natural religion once he has glimpsed the significance of the supernatural any more than wolves that have tasted blood can return to some pre-carnivorous diet (I have heard this called a cliché; it does not seem one to me, and if it were, it seems none the less true). "Blood" also has obvious connotations with the blood of Christ. The problem here is: in what form can we find salvation? The answer is, if we may call it an answer, that the difficulties facing this task are nearly insuperable. Modern man—the "dull critter of enormous head" of the "Sonnets at Christmas"—is caught between two salvations, the natural

and the supernatural. His intellect rebels at the thought of supernaturalism, but once he has become aware of its significance and been
deeply touched by it, he can certainly not return to the joys of a pre-
Christian paganism, nor can he easily acquiesce in a naturalistic
perspective.

The last eight lines are among the finest in Tate's poetry, though
the remark seems irrelevant when applied to a uniformly fine poem.
There is the very great beauty of precise, austere phrasing in line
seventeen, a line which is overtly one of the least pretentious of the
poem: "So blind, in so severe a place." There is little to say except
"exactly." We can notice the repetition, the very slightly inverted and
formal syntax, if we wish: but it is still the force of the conception
which carries the strength. We, as the heirs of the Christian tradition,
have become "blind" to the "world"—it no longer nourishes us. The
line and the one immediately following ("All life before in the black
grave") carry an ironic twist on the Christian symbolism of baptism.
We have in a sense been "buried with Christ," in the words of the
formula, but we have been buried to a form of living death, not to
the "new life" which baptism was meant to symbolize.

Whether we agree or disagree with the doctrine which generated
the notion, we give assent to an ordered world of imagination. The
situation is such that sight—in the sense of the first lines—is desperately needed, yet men are desperately blind. And thus blindly, without real life, a race of men who have forsaken both the older love of
the world and the supernatural love they cannot believe in, seek to
discover issues as mysterious as the meaning of life. The result is: a
hatred for the world in which they supposedly live; a hatred for themselves and the way they live; and a hatred for God if he exists, or a
hatred toward something for failing to exist. It is like a skeleton that
hates its own bones, seeking some substitute for flesh to pull over
them. In the words of a later Tate poem, "Winter Mask," we cannot
tell

> Why it is man hates
> His own salvation
> Prefers the way to hell,
> And finds his last safety
> In the self-made curse that bore
> Him toward damnation:

> The drowned undrowned by the sea,
> The sea worth living for.

In such a condition the last alternatives of life are faced (lines nineteen and twenty). The alternatives are, of course, the questions of life and death in a supernatural sense. But still, "without the life to save": the meaning of "life" has shifted from the previous line. The usage of a single word with double meanings is typical of Tate. Here, the life which cannot be saved is life in *this* world. This is one more insistence on the impossibility of returning to a pre-supernatural life. Such a return might be comforting, but it is historically and psychologically impossible.

The last lines do not resolve the tension; they aggravate it. If we prefer useful maxims, this will irritate us; but it is likely that the problem is insoluble (unless it is simply ignored, and one must have a certain kind of mind to do that). In the line "Being from all salvation weaned" the word "being" is most naturally read as a participle that continues the meaning of the preceding line. The dilemma remains: there is a paradoxical doubt of supernatural salvation, even though we have been weaned from the world. We cannot return to simple naturalism any more than a child can return to the breast of the mother. Though it runs the danger of quibbling, I am also tempted to see a further extension in "being" and read it as a noun: being itself, the *quidditas* of life, has gone bad.

The stag image works beautifully. It develops conceptually and imagistically out of the earlier material. These lines work; they function as images should. Their most striking quality is the perfectly planned supra-conceptual implication in the progression of images. The stag image is prepared for by the image of the wolves tasting blood. We consent immediately on a purely imagistic level to the legitimacy of the stag charged at heel and head before we have debated the intellectual proprieties. And then the conceptual level becomes plain: modern man is caught in the middle, between two salvations, with no hope of retreating to the level of natural piety and little hope of attaining the supernatural vision.

If we try to repudiate the supernaturalism which we have once known, our will is perverted; it is dominated and made impotent. The consequences are grave. It is not possible to escape that world-destroying pit, nor to think one's way out of it. Once there the inhabitants—

those, I imagine, who have earlier faced "the last alternatives" and have failed to deal with them—make certain of our loyalties by making our forms identical with theirs.

If one grants the artist his *donnée*, as Henry James said we must, I can think of no way to make the poem more powerful. It seems to me that there is nothing which should be taken out, nothing added. There have been those—including Yvor Winters—who have thought they have seen incoherencies or redundancies in it. But, re-reading "The Cross" carefully now after some years, I cannot agree: it seems to me a nearly perfectly achieved poem of its kind.

The kind of detailed examination presented in this reading is really only propaedeutic to criticism in its larger dimensions. But with Tate's work it is perhaps even more true than with most poets that we must be very careful not to merely skate over the upper surfaces of the language before leaping off into the seductive greater significances. With a poem like "The Cross," as with Tate's other poetry, we must be sure that we have read carefully and accurately before seeking the larger dimensions of "criticism." I trust that this essay may have accomplished at least that limited purpose.

The Meaning of War:
A Note on Allen Tate's
"To the Lacedemonians"

by DONALD DAVIDSON

T he centennial of the great American war of the eighteen-sixties
—variously known as the Civil War, the War between the
States, the Confederate War, the War for Southern Independence, and in certain official records of the Federal government, as
the War of the Rebellion—has at last gone by. There have been some
patently half-hearted "celebrations" and rather stilted "re-enactments"
of the battles and incidents of the War. Of actual commemoration in
a truly solemn and deeply felt sense there has been little. Now and
then some minutes or quarter-hours of expensive television time; the
photographs, serialized "histories," and specialized supplements put
forth by newspapers; the more pretentious booklets and brochures of
state commissions, often "touristic" in slant; and the publication of
many useful biographies and military studies (some really notable,
like Mr. Clifford Dowdey's *Lee's Last Campaign* and his *Seven Days*)
—all this has hardly broken for more than a few moments the formidable ennui of the American people. They have merely continued to
step in and out of automobiles, jet planes, ocean liners, cabin cruisers,
trucks, tractors, and elevators in their mesmerized clutching for the
welfare state's carrot or their uneasy flinching from its stick.

Especially noticeable—to anyone who bothered to notice—has been

EDITOR'S NOTE: Reprinted from *The Southern Review*, n.s., 1:720–30 (Summer 1965),
by permission of Mrs. Donald Davidson.

the general silence of the poets during these four years of the Centennial. And they have been absent from the supposedly celebrative public occasions. *Poetae tacent*! It is not a good omen. No such silence, no such absence would have been possible in former times. True, in those former times the tradition that brought a poet (or poetaster) to the rostrum brought with it much undistinguished or execrable verse. Yet the role of the poet was recognized. Not to have a poet for some great memorial occasion would have been thought improper—almost like Holy Communion without the priest! If the poet be a poor performer, so too, often enough, may the cleric be something much less than an Ambrose or Augustine. But the cleric has the liturgical form to follow, and that cannot fail, no matter how fumbling he may be.

What form has the poet to follow? The answer is—for ceremonial occasions—none; at least none that the modern poet and the modern audience alike recognize as appropriate. Between Henry Timrod and his Charleston audience of nearly a century ago there was still some sense of what was appropriate for a memorial occasion. The Horatian tradition, modified a little by eighteenth century neo-classicism and the romanticism that succeeded it, served Timrod well in his "Ode" ("Sleep sweetly in your humble graves") that was sung—not read— during the memorial exercises at Magnolia Cemetery, Charleston, on June 16, 1866. Sidney Lanier, invited to compose a poem (really a kind of libretto) to be set to music by Dudley Buck for the Philadelphia Centennial Exposition of 1876, was less fortunate than Timrod. Today such terms as "Ode" and "Elegy" belong to textbooks and to a relatively narrow circle of scholars and literati. If to his surprise a poet is invited to offer a poem for some public occasion, he has all the freedom he wants to choose or improvise the form. He may find this a dubious privilege when he reflects that not ten people out of a thousand will know or care what form he uses, even though his audience be jam-packed with college graduates and mortar-boarded Ph.D.'s that make a point of wearing the garments of academic tradition.

It is instructive, for poets at least—and may be a little reassuring for many others—to consider how Allen Tate, a traditionalist by firm principle yet no less firmly a modern poet, met this difficulty for a celebration of more than three decades ago.

"To the Lacedemonians" was first published on the front page of the Richmond (Virginia) *Times-Dispatch* for June 21, 1932. The

occasion was the forty-second annual reunion of the Confederate veterans. Some fifteen hundred of the old Confederate soldiers were
expected, according to the *Times-Dispatch*. Most of these—nearly all,
surely—would have been in their 'teens in 1861. Allen Tate's poem,
set in a two-column box beneath a photograph of the capture of Fort
Stedman, is just about the most prominent item on this front page
that also reports the arrival of General Alfred De Saussure, commander-
in-chief of the veterans, and tells how he was welcomed with a 17-gun
salute and an escort of a company of the Richmond Blues. A little
later, just prior to an address by Governor Pollard of Virginia—"While
the band of the Little Rock, Ark., High School played 'Dixie,' the
Stars and Bars were hoisted upon the Capitol by Miss Jessica Randolph
Smith, daughter of the designer, while Major-General William McK.
Evans of Richmond, who had stood in Capitol Square in 1861 when
Virginia's secession was announced, looked on."

Parenthetically, by way of providing a full context, I should note
that this was a presidential election year—in fact, the Roosevelt vs.
Hoover year, and everywhere the Great Depression was notable evidence of one of the long-range results of Appomattox. On this same
front page a Civic Employment Committee announced final returns
for its "job-hunting campaign." Senator William E. Borah, the mav-
erick from Idaho, declared in the Senate chamber that he would not
support President Herbert Hoover for re-election. New Federal taxes
were to go into effect on this very June 21, and a raise in postal rates
would occur on July 6. Nine bottles of "home-brew" blew up with a
bang in Richmond's police court, wounding a city policeman in the
leg (the Federal prohibition amendment was still in effect as the
generally disregarded "law of the land"). And the *Times-Dispatch*
announced that it would carry a blow-by-blow description of the
heavy-weight championship bout between Max Schmeling, German
champion, and Jack Sharkey, American challenger, in a special extra
edition to be issued immediately after the fight. The weather? Warm,
with temperature in the middle seventies and thundershowers likely.

But our concern is with the poem itself. The speaker in Allen Tate's
poems—when a speaker appears—is usually "I"—a "first person" who
is not necessarily Allen Tate the individual, though with full traditional right he may be the author in his capacity as poet. Or else "I"
may be a much more generalized "first person," an unidentified Some-

body speaking in a high dramatic sense, yet surely not just Any Man or Everyman. Pronouns are a matter to be noted in various poems. In "Ode to the Confederate Dead," for example, the unidentified man who is meditating at the gate of the cemetery says "we" at some points, "you" at others, nowhere "I."

"To the Lacedemonians" is an exception to Mr. Tate's general practice. The speaker is identified, though not by name, as a Confederate veteran about to attend a reunion. He becomes a spokesman for his Confederate comrades, alive or dead, and, no doubt more broadly, for the generations of Southerners who experienced the War itself or its ruinous aftermath and its persistently enduring results on down to the poet's own time. Yet since the poem is by no means as partisan as the situation seems to imply, much of what this old Confederate says could also be said by a veteran on the opposing side—for example, by a member of the Grand Army of the Republic like Joshua Chamberlain of the Twentieth Maine, the chief character of Louis Coxe's play *Decoration Day*. "The backstairs creeping to power; the infighting where power has its source," is what this old Federal officer says at one point.[1]

This more general aspect of what the old Confederate says is emphasized by changes that Allen Tate makes in the explanatory sub-title (or "stage direction") of the poem in its successive appearances. In the *Times-Dispatch* the complete heading is as follows:

TO THE LACEDEMONIANS . . .

The Old Confederate on the Night Before the
Reunion Speaks Partly to Himself, Partly to
Imaginary Comrades:

In *Selected Poems* (1937) the heading is slightly altered: "*A Confederate on the night before the veterans' reunion talks partly to himself, partly to imaginary comrades.*"

In *Poems: 1922–1947* (published in 1948) the word "Confederate" is dropped, and the explanatory sentence takes the form it has subsequently kept: *An old soldier on the night before the veterans' reunion. . . .*

Comparison of the three texts of the poem will reveal how skilfully and thoroughly Tate revised his original version before publishing it in *Selected Poems*, 1937. The poem undergoes a general tightening

---

[1] *Quill: Bowdoin College Literary Magazine*, LXXX (Winter, 1965), p. 61.

up, weak lines are cancelled, and thirteen new lines in Tate's finest vein are added. These changes, like the changes in the explanatory subtitle, tend to shift the poem somewhat away from *the* war of the Sixties to war as such, though the names of battles, the oft-quoted "All are born Yankees of the race of men," and one of the new lines "Kinsmen and friends from Texas to the Tide" remain to identify the conflict historically. In *Selected Poems*, 1937, "To the Lacedemonians" stands in third place in Part I, being preceded only by "The Mediterranean" and "Aeneas at Washington." For *Poems, 1922–1947* Tate makes only minor revisions, but places "To the Lacedemonians" and "Ode to the Confederate Dead" as the two last poems in Part I. Thus "To the Lacedemonians" becomes a companion piece and in many ways a counterpart to the "Ode." One can hardly take this arrangement to be merely casual, despite the poet's prefatory statement in his 1948 volume that he is not sure whether he could explain why he thinks "certain poems go with others." If Part I were to be given a title (as it well might be), "Fathers and Sons" would be fairly appropriate; but "Fathers" should be taken to go as far back as Aeneas and the Aeneadae, or even farther, and "Sons" would include both the firm-minded soldier of "To the Lacedemonians" and the man of infirm mind in the "Ode" who cannot quite successfully link himself with "the immoderate past" and the "inscrutable infantry" that rise like "Demons out of the earth."

For all who have the zeal and moral fibre to learn, Allen Tate's revisions offer a remarkably fine lesson in the practice of the art of poetry. Scholars and critics will eventually examine them for reasons of their own. I shall here refer to only a few of them. I return to the question: what form can the modern poet use for an important anniversary or other ceremonial occasion if he should have the rare chance of writing a few lines for it? Or, as Allen Tate said, simply and sharply, in the preface to his first collection of critical essays: "The poet's special question is: How shall the work be done?"

The work in this instance had to be done for the printed page, first of a newspaper, later of a book. It could not have the assistance of music or even of the speaking voice to mark its rhythmic pattern and heighten its immediate carrying power. It had to accept the limitations of the printed page, which seems to condemn the poem to a silent reading (if any) by a public invisible to the poet and pretty much

unknown to him. On the other hand it could exploit the opportunities
that a printed page affords. Such opportunities arise through the liberty that printing allows the poet—in this instance the liberty to make
a very complex and subtle use of metaphor. If this liberty is wisely
used, the poem becomes, in the end, highly symbolic; but paradoxically it must also operate dramatically at the level of the "realism"
now enforced by the skepticism of our times—that makes history and
science arrogantly hostile to poetry—and by the particular human
situation in which the poet finds his theme. This poetry does not
imitate the broad and obvious rhetoric of the oration. It does not need
to do so. It is not something to be *said* and therefore *heard* for a
matter of ten or twelve minutes. It is for the new kind of "reading"
that began as far back as the sixteenth century. It can be pondered
long, for it is always there waiting to be pondered. It is inexhaustible.
It is the poetry that Allen Tate defines in "Tension in Poetry" the
poetry in which "the remotest figurative significance that we can
derive does not invalidate the extensions of the literal statement."

The governing trope of "To the Lacedemonians" inheres in the
title, which comes straight from the epitaph composed by Simonides
for the Spartans who died in defense of the pass at Thermopylae during the second Persian attack on Greece in 480 B.C. Halfway through
the poem, when the painfully disconcerting contrast between past and
present has been fully established, the old soldier recites the ancient
epitaph, a little haltingly, and furthermore extends the elegiac distich
of Simonides to fit his modern case:

> Go you tell them
> That we their servants, well-trained, gray-coated
> And haired (both foot and horse) or in
> The grave, them obey . . . obey them,
> What commands?[2]

Does the *in*tension of this powerful metaphor—the Confederate
veteran (or other veteran?) in the character of a Greek hoplite, one of
Leonidas' famous Three Hundred—in any way invalidate the *exten*-
sions of the literal statement? I think not. Rather the contrary. The
metaphor boldly validates as poetry what otherwise might be straight

[2] Literally translated, the epitaph of Simonides says: "O stranger, carry the message (Gr. *aggellein*) to the Lacedemonians that here we lie, their commands obeying." See Herodotus, VII, 228, 8–9.

realism, merely circumstantial, merely reportorial. Allen Tate has appropriated for his poem the "stream-of-consciousness" device developed for modern realistic fiction in order to render the subjectively real experience—the realism of the interior. The veteran's meditation is a "talk" only in that sense. It could be carried over into prose fiction —as indeed much of Tate's "Records I: A Dream" is carried over into a scene in *The Fathers*.[3] The form that Allen Tate uses is, then, not the "dramatic monologue" that Robert Browning in some short poems developed to perfection but more often spoiled by sheer loquaciousness and his penchant for historical bric-a-brac. The "talk" of Tate's old soldier is actually nearer to the idiom of Greek drama: for example, to one of the longer speeches of Oedipus in *Oedipus at Colonus*, in which the pain of memory comes forth as "literal statement" yet is never mere realism.

But the stream-of-consciousness device does provide the element of "statement" in its extended form. We readily assume that the old soldier has been met at the railroad station by a welcoming committee and has been taken by automobile to his hotel room. Thus he has seen in actuality the people already lining the streets—

> The people—people of my kind, my own
> People but strange with a white light
> In the face: the streets hard with motion
> And the hard eyes that look one way.

So Allen Tate wrote for the Richmond newspaper—except that in line 2 he at first had "*Homefolks* but strange with a *new* light." He changed the two words italicized to "people" and "white," and then added three new lines:

> Listen! the high whining tone
> Of the motors, I hear the dull commotion:
> I am come, a child in an old play.

The image of harsh, purposeless, mechanical motion, which gradually becomes a metaphor, develops in a kind of counterpoint set over against the purposeful valor of the soldier, Spartan-or-Confederate, and the memory of his youth (lines 29–32). We soon mark aimless

---

[3] Cf. the text of "Records I," *Poems, 1928–1931*, p. 24, with *The Fathers*, 1938, pp. 266–69.

motion that arrives nowhere as something that the old soldier instinc-
tively—and prophetically—fears as hostile and, worse than that, as
degenerative. The "white light" that makes strange the faces of the
people "of my kind" is the pallor of death-in-life. The citizens "not
born in my father's / House, nor in their fathers'" are "By motion
sired, not born; by rest dismayed." Then, in two lines added to the
earlier version, the soldier asks a formidable question:

> The tempest will unwind—the hurricane
> Consider, knowing its end, the headlong pace?

As Anne Clark Hunter has pointed out in her recent close study, we
find in these and various other lines of the poem a forecast "of the
un-traditional modern man" that Allen Tate develops in George Posey
of *The Fathers.*[4]

For a moment the soldier drops into an old Southern (or American)
colloquialism: "It warn't in my time. . . ." Then in two of the new
lines which—somewhat as in the "leaves" refrain of the "Ode to the
Confederate Dead"—"time" the poem, allow the reader "occasions of
assimilation, and . . . thus [ease] the concentration of imagery,"[5] the
veteran reproaches himself for his own feebleness:

> Yet I, hollow head, do see but little;
> Old man: no memory; aimless distractions.

But then immediately comes the beautiful contrasting passage in
which he *does* remember his boyhood, and regrets that now men "Put
the contraption before the accomplishment" and thus attain luxury,
but not elegance. "Where have they come from?"

At this point he begins to recite the epitaph for the Three Hundred.
But all the time, in the high metaphorical sense, he has been saying,
"Go, stranger, carry a message to the Lacedemonians." Remembering
this, we can begin to understand a difficult passage that I have passed
over:

> I am here with a secret in the night;
> Because I am here the dead wear gray.

[4] "Attitudes Toward Tradition in Allen Tate's The Fathers." M.A. Thesis, University of North Carolina, 1964, pp. 32–33 and *passim.*
[5] "Narcissus as Narcissus," in Tate's *Reason in Madness,* 1941, p. 143.

> It is a privilege to be dead; for you
> Cannot know what absence is nor seize
> The odor of pure distance. . . .[6]

I take "you" to refer to the people of his own kind, now become strange, who lead a life of sensation only and therefore are unable to "see" the gray-clad soldiers as anything but "dead." To people that are a mere breed "by motion sired," anything belonging to the past is "dead." That is the secret upon which he has come in the night—a night both literal and metaphorical. It is a secret that perhaps he tells to his "imaginary comrades" when he says, "Gentlemen, my secret is damnation." What the people of his own kind no longer understand is the view set forth in John Ruskin's old-fashioned essay that the soldier's part is not just to kill, but it is to die, to be willing to die. "There is no civilization without death," says the soldier of this poem. That is the meaning of war. And, amending Lee's famous words at the battle of Fredericksburg, he further says, "Well may war be / Terrible to those who have nothing to gain / For the illumination of the sense." These are the materialists. But in the "unshadowing restriction of our day"—when society still retained an accepted principle of order and therefore of "manners, virtue, freedom, power" (if not precisely what Wordsworth attributed to the society of Milton's day)—young men could go to war "to win the precincts of the light."

Now, remembering the "hard eyes" that looked "one way" at the beginning of his meditation, the soldier asks his imaginary comrades to consider the young men of the new day (if indeed it is "day") who watch from the curbs. The "seventy years of night" under which they are to be regarded, taken literally, must refer to the seventy years since 1862—the year of the true beginning of the Civil War. Seventy years prior to June 21, 1932, the date of the assemblage for reunion, would place the beginning of "night" at the time when Robert E. Lee, having taken over command of the Army of Northern Virginia from Joseph E. Johnston, was about to attack and if possible to destroy the much larger army of George B. McClellan which was almost within artillery range of Richmond and in position to capture it. Lee defeated McClellan in the Seven Days battles, but did not destroy his army. If we accept the well-supported view of Mr. Clifford Dowdey, this result

---

[6] In the editions of 1948, 1960, and 1961, *odor* is unfortunately misprinted.

meant the end of any possibility of a "negotiated peace" between the
warring North and South. For McClellan's intention was to end the
war quickly by use of overwhelming force and then effect a settlement
that would "preserve the Union without destroying the Nation." But
his views were intolerable to his political opponents at Washington,
and their hostility was an important element in his defeat.

Taken metaphorically, "seventy years of night" may also mean lack
of true vision which ultimately may lead a people to take the wrong
path. The old soldier earlier has spoken against "luxury." Considered
in terms of the dominant figure, this is the ancient Greek charge of
"Medism" brought against those Greeks who adopted the luxurious
manners and dress of the Persians or even went over to the Persians in
a political and military sense. It is no wonder that the final words of
the soldier express a tragic melancholy:

> Soldiers, march! we shall not fight again . . .
> All are born Yankees of the race of men
> And this, too, now the country of the damned.

The "hard eyes" of the young men belong to—

> Poor bodies crowding round us! The white face
> Eyeless with eyesight only, the modern power—

They have the defect of vision complained against by the man in Allen
Tate's poem, "The Eye"—the man who tries to see "*in* the agate eye
. . . the nuclear eye . . . the carbolic eye" and who in desperation
pulls down "the sphereless sky for cover," takes "the fatherless dark to
bed," and beseeches the crows to peck the head that has served him so
inadequately, so wrongly, so traitorously.

The soldier's vision is of the true kind, for he sees through, not with,
the eye. And it is also the vision of Allen Tate in one of the noblest
and most prophetic poems of our time.

The Current of the Frozen Stream

by HOWARD NEMEROV

My occasion is the publication of Mr. Tate's collection, *Poems 1922–1947* (Scribner's, 1948), my purpose the elucidation of a major duality in his poetry, which I would regard as in some sense its generating or operative principle. In some sense . . . those beautiful precautionary and beforehand words which serve the critic so well through all life's appointments and will make him a satisfactory epitaph; but used here with particular intent to deny that the results of this (or any such) study are conceived as historically applicable, as suggesting the origin of the poetry. I am concerned to show the design that exists in the poetry; this does not extend to saying that the design has "caused" the poetry, though it may extend, if the distinction is permissible, to showing that the design could have caused the poetry to be what it is, that the design is a sufficient reason of the poetry though not its specific occasion, and may therefore be taken as really a "generating" principle. The design is a formal, though not a proximate, cause.

It will be objected by some, I think, that any method which commits itself to the discovery of a "major duality" in any body of work offends against right practice by reducing the text to that point of abstraction at which, as the design becomes clear, the poetry vanishes. I do not see that this need be so, not more so at least than is general with analytic criticism. All will depend, naturally, on the success of demonstration

EDITOR'S NOTE: Reprinted from *Poetry and Fiction: Essays* by Howard Nemerov (New Brunswick: Rutgers University Press, 1963), pp. 101–11, by permission of the author and publisher. This essay first appeared in *Furioso*, 3:50–61 (February 1948).

from the text, on the right election of essences, on showing that the
figuration of the poet's thought in a pair of abstract terms may legiti-
mately be drawn from particular antagonisms or juxtapositions in the
poetry—the distinction of light from darkness does not exclude any
shadings of civil, solar or sidereal twilight, and the local weather will
also have much to do with the color of the sky.

Now there is, I conceive, one duality that underlies a great deal of
poetry, especially the kind of poetry that is called (aptly, as I think)
"metaphysical": it is, in largest terms, the duality of the One and
the Many. Metaphysical poetry is a poetry of the dilemma, and the
dilemma which paradoxes and antitheses continually seek to display
is the famous one at which all philosophies falter, the relation of the
One with the Many, the leap by which infinity becomes finite, essence
becomes existence; the commingling of the spirit with matter, the
working of God in the world. This is not precisely my theme, and I
cannot give space here to supporting it (but it is a fairly well-known
position and the objections to it are also sufficiently current), yet it
seemed proper to notice it at the beginning, since my considerations
will indirectly refer back to it.

The central concern of Allen Tate's poems is with time and history,
their major theme man's attachment to the past, the allegiance of his
blood, the queer liaisons of his mind. But to put this statement in a
right relation with Tate's text it is necessary to add that it does not
mean the entertainment known as "world-history" in which scholars
seek to demonstrate the ultimate likeness of the world to an Automat.
The past for Tate is seen as always, in times not necessarily less confused or angry than the present, first-rate poets have seen it—as the
composition of the human will with the unknown and implacable
justice or injustice. History, in Tate's poems, is history in the same
kind as *Judges, Samuel, Chronicles, Kings*, where the existence of idea
and theme is known through the violence of individuals, and especially
in the same kind as *The Divine Comedy*, where people named Ulysses
and Boniface and Frederick have exactly the importance of people
named Lano and Jacomo da Sant' Andrea and Pier delle Vigne; and
in the same kind as the histories of Shakespeare whose heroes and
antagonists are demonstrated actually to have fought for what, the
sociologist tells us, would have "inevitably" happened anyhow. For
Tate history is primarily a matter of generation and choice, that is of

myth, not of pattern and system; the situations of history are family
or at least local situations, not paradigms composed of least common
denominators called wars, truces, migrations and laws. As Yeats wrote,
"A father, mother, child (a daughter or a son), / That's how all natural or supernatural stories run." And the following passage from Paul
Valéry (with whose thought Tate's is at many points in accord) gives
the matter the clarity of definition: "Le caractère réel de l'histoire est
de prendre part à l'histoire même. L'idée du passé ne prend un sens et
ne constitue une valeur que pour l'homme qui se trouve en soi-même
une passion de l'avenir. L'avenir, par définition, n'a point d'image.
L'histoire lui donne les moyens d'être pensé. Elle forme pour l'imagination une table de situations et de catastrophes, une galerie d'ancêtres,
un formulaire d'actes, d'expressions, d'attitudes, de décisions offerts
à notre instabilité et à notre incertitude, pour nous aider *à devenir* . . .
L'histoire alimente l'histoire" (*Regards Sur le Monde Actuel*).

   This sort of history will perhaps always be a scandal and an offense
to those pragmatical positivists who are reassured to see the creation
programmatically "working itself out" in terms of "trends," "forces,"
"cycles" and "designs"; because these terms in excluding the will exclude also man's responsibility, and because the mind that is satisfied
with such terms finds it unlikely that the local, the named, the limited,
should assume mythic and universal importance, since after all (they
might protest) the world is so full of a number of things. To this view
it is unfriendly of the Word to put on flesh, and tends to give a particular a depth of meaning disproportionate to its statistical value.
But it is the theme of Tate's poetry, and the theme of tragedy, that
man chooses the accident of his fate and by his choice creates necessity,
which is his sole dignity. Against this choice the poet places our society,
which with its abstract and statistical regard for the past provides a
context in which choices are said not to matter, in which we are violent
without idea and condemned to self-violence, suicide, "self-inflicted
woe." The only possible prayer is not for goodness but for a situation
in which good and evil have some reference:

> O God of our flesh, return us to Your wrath,
> Let us be evil could we enter in
> Your grace, and falter on the stony path.
>   ("Last Days of Alice")

Mr. Tate has said in a note to *Poems 1928–1931* (I regret that I have not his exact words available) that all the books of a poet should ultimately be regarded as one book; at any rate that it was to this end that he worked. This statement, though it evidently does not license us to disregard the individuality of particular poems, suggests the poet's responsibility towards his themes, attitudes, evaluations, and implies our permission to use on one poem what we have found more fully or more clearly elucidated in another, to expect throughout the work certain recurrent elements not only of theme but of manner and imagery as well. Having just now discussed theme as much as possible in isolation and abstractedly, I wish at this point to begin afresh by considering more particular matters and to be led back to the theme by way of illustration and example.

The composition of the poems may be divided into two general sorts, roughly correspondent to a fundamental distinction of the thought. "there is that / Which is the commentary; there's that other, / Which may be called the immaculate / Conception of its essence in itself." The first sort is reflective, meditative, rhetorical in manner, executed often in a considerably distorted blank verse and given over to the explicit discussion of theme: such poems as "Causerie," "Fragment of a Meditation" and "Retroduction to American History" are of this kind. The other manner is characterized by brevity, concision, great formality of rime and meter and (for the reader) those difficulties which must go with subtle thought of which the connections are allowed to remain implicit by a kind of lyrical absolutism: "Ode to Fear," "The Traveler," "The Paradigm," "The Cross."

The two modes are not always to be found in isolation; often both hold place in a single poem, as in "To the Lacedemonians," for example, which begins as public speech and ends with a lyric of six quatrains; or less obviously in "The Meaning of Life," whose explicit discussion of its material issues at last in a splendid and inexhaustibly allusive figure; or in the "Ode to the Confederate Dead," where the rhetoric is controlled by rime and by the dramatic situation.

In these two modes of composition, as I have suggested, we may see the attenuated and *formal* replica of a duality, a basic division—mentioned above as Essence and Commentary—which is central to Tate's poetry and creates his myth, giving rise to the kind of recurrent figure which is this poet's "representative anecdote" about the world. The crucial antithesis is most clearly and explicitly presented in two coupled poems, "The Meaning of Life" and "The Meaning of Death," the first "a monologue," the second "an after-dinner speech." The first begins:

> Think about it at will: there is that
> Which is the commentary; there's that other,
> Which may be called the immaculate
> Conception of its essence in itself.
> It is necessary to distinguish the weights
> Of the two methods lest the first smother
> The second, the second be speechless (without the first).

And immediately afterward the poet shows his awareness of the two modes of composition, and of their implications ("I was saying this more briefly the other day / But one must be explicit as well as brief.")

It is the speechless conception which is life, which bears its "meaning" in itself or (no matter) has no meaning, and needs none. This is demonstrated by anecdote: as a boy the speaker wished not to be like the old men in Kentucky who "shot at one another for luck"; at twelve he decided he would shoot only for honor, at twenty he thought he would not shoot at all; but at thirty-three, that age of crucifixion, "one must shoot / As often as one gets the rare chance— / In killing there is more than commentary."

There is a history here, in brief, of rationale, or the explication of motive, of commentary: the old men who shoot at one another for luck live in a universe of possibly placable demons whose will is unknown; they are offensive to secular codes of behavior (honor) and the rational principles of ethical religion (there is no God but if there had been He would have wished us not to shoot at all), but their behavior is not superficially distinguishable from a mystical insistence on mortal and all-committing action.

Before dealing with the concluding figure of "The Meaning of Life" I will consider the antithetical poem. In "an after-dinner speech" the meaning of death is ironically presented as the meaning of life:

> Time, fall no more.
> Let that be life—time falls no more. The threat
> Of time we in our own courage have forsworn.
> Let light fall, there shall be eternal light
> And all the light shall on our heads be worn . . .

It is, is it not, the earthly paradise currently called the World of Tomorrow? It is to depend on the denial of time, the legislation of

eternal light and on "our own courage," on that modern combination
of virtues and vices which Dostoevsky called "enlightened greed" and
"titanic pride." A program for further action is outlined towards the
end of the poem:

> Gentlemen, let's
> Forget the past, its related errors, coarseness
> Of parents, laxities, unrealities of principle.
> Think of tomorrow. Make a firm postulate
> Of simplicity in desire and act
> Founded on the best hypotheses;
> Desire to eat secretly, alone, lest
> Ritual corrupt our charity . . .

The antithesis between the two poems is wonderfully clear at this
point simply as a matter of argument and exposition; the speaker in
the second poem, taking the attitude of protestant scientism, rejects the
past because "what happens is therefore imperfect," rejects ritual because ritual rejoices in the repetition of the past and stresses "useless"
elements in "useful" charity: he proposes an action based on "the best
hypotheses." This attitude, then, would rid itself of the world; it is the
attitude of the successful revolutionary who cannot bear, in his triumph, that common things should be called by their ancient names
and so invents a new calendar.

But in their combining imagery the two poems ironically develop
the opposition by metaphors that have the same scene. "The Meaning
of Life":

> One's sense of the proper decoration alters
> But there's a kind of lust feeds on itself
> Unspoken to, unspeaking; subterranean
> As a black river full of eyeless fish
> Heavy with spawn; with a passion for time
> Longer than the arteries of a cave.

And "The Meaning of Death":

> Lest darkness fall and time fall
> In a long night when learned arteries
> Mounting the ice and sum of barbarous time
> Shall yield, without essence, perfect accident.

> We are the eyelids of defeated caves.

Life exists speechlessly but essentially in the fish heavy with spawn, who are not blind, not defective, but simply "eyeless," sight being not an "essential" quality (compare, in "To the Lacedemonians," "The white face / Eyeless with eyesight only, the modern power—"). In the revulsion from time and all continuance, in the election of science, which leads to "perfect accident," is death, and the after-dinner speaker by a superb turn of irony and drama is permitted to know it and to say it, to realize where his program is taking him. The fish are eyeless, but the speaker and his audience in the cold sleep of science close the eyes of the world.

Mr. Cleanth Brooks, in his admirable analysis of these two poems (*Modern Poetry and the Tradition*), has this to say of the closing figure of the first: "The symbol of the concrete, irrational essence of life, the blood, receives an amazing amplification by its association with the cave. The two symbols are united on the basis of their possession of 'arteries.' The blood is associated with 'lust,' is 'subterranean' (buried within the body), is the source of 'passion.' But the added metaphor of the cave extends the associations from those appropriate to an individual body to something general and eternal."

Precisely. And I think this insight may be carried further, and that the division it offers is, in various guises, at work throughout Tate's poetry, of which it is the radical judgment and generative principle. I will try to demonstrate this.

The blood, and the cave: liquid and solid, the hot and the cold, that which is fluid and that which is rigid. The combination occurs over and over in the poems, though it need not take the form invariably of blood and cave; it is the relation which is so insistent. It is used to characterize the relation of becoming to become, of life to death, of process to result; in its more general form it suggests the common metaphor whereby forms "harden" or "freeze" into lifeless conventions, and means that civilization is achieved by "hardening of the arteries," that all effort produces monuments. In "Aeneas at Washington" the hero stands by the Potomac and confesses in these terms, "The city my blood had built I knew no more." In "To the Lacedemonians" the old soldier says, "I was a boy, I never knew cessation / Of the bright course of blood along the vein." And later, "Life grown sullen and immense / Lusts after immunity to pain." And the abstract statement completes the figure: "There is no civilization without death." Likewise the

"Romantic Traditionists" are accused of neglecting the essence for the commentary: "Immaculate race! to yield / Us final knowledge set / In a cold frieze, a field / Of war with no blood let."

Sometimes the symbol for generation is water instead of blood, and it is set against "ice," as in the beautiful line from the "Ode to Fear" which I have used as the title of this paper, where Fear is addressed: "You are the current of the frozen stream, / Shadow invisible, ambushed and vigilant flame." (Often flame is equated with generative force, as in "Sonnets of the Blood" II and VI). And again in "Winter Mask" where the poisoned rat, "driven to cold water, / Dies of the water of life"; by this inversion the figure is seen also as Cocytus, the lowest hell where the traitor is "damned in eternal ice." There is more than a hint of the metaphor in "The Oath" when the speaker decides "what it is in time that gnaws / The ageing fury of a mountain stream" (where "gnaws" carries over to suggest the action of the stream on its bed, which confines it) and thinks he hears "the dark pounding its head / On a rock, crying: *Who are the dead?*" And in the ninth of "Sonnets of the Blood" the sestet employs the relation. The octave has warned the "captains of industry" against their "aimless power" which will lead to the plundering of "the inner mansion of the blood":

> Yet the prime secret whose simplicity
> Your towering engine hammers to reduce,
> Though driven holds that bulwark of the sea
> Which breached will turn unspeaking fury loose
> To drown out him who swears to rectify
> Infinity, that has nor ear nor eye.

The prime secret (he has already mentioned prime numbers) is the secret of that which is indivisible and thus closed to analysis and commentary; were this not so, and could the towering engine reduce the bulwark, which is regarded as, generally, form, structure, the continence of life, the sea (which is in the terms of the sonnets the blood) would "turn unspeaking fury loose," life would turn destructive once its form had been violated, and would stain the earth, as in Yeats' poem, "The Gyres," with "irrational streams of blood."

As the blood may be conceived as water, as ocean or stream or pond, so the other term, the cave, has thematic extensions, as a well ("Seasons of the Soul"), as the depth of the Inferno, the "vast concluding

shell," as womb and tomb (Christ's tomb especially) and Plato's cave;
all of these seem to work into one fine passage:

> It [light] burns us each alone
> Whose burning arrogance
> Burns up the rolling stone,
> This earth—Platonic cave
> Of vertiginous chance!
> Come, tired Sisyphus,
> Cover the cave's egress
> Where light reveals the slave,
> Who rests when sleeps with us
> The mother of silence.
>
> ("Seasons of the Soul," IV)

This relation, some form of which seems to pervade the work, is in
my opinion the central irony of Tate's poetry and fully involves his
judgment of the world and of the human situation. In "The Meaning
of Life" essence and commentary were described as antithetical elements, both of which in composition form the life of man: the problem
is of a certain proportion that must be maintained, and in modern
society is not maintained (see "The Meaning of Death" and the ninth
"Sonnet of the Blood"). The Freudians employ a somewhat similar
trope in their division of the ego and the id; life is of the id, dark, irrational (what Blake called Energy?) and the ego draws on this stuff for
the creation of order, but if the ego rejects, out of pride, its rude and
raw basis, it rejects its roots and must wither (John Crowe Ransom
has a poem, "A Painted Head," which deals with this division). But
again I find in Valéry a lucid and beautiful description. In a piece called
"Man and the Shell," translated by Lionel Abel and printed in the
second number of *The Tiger's Eye*, a periodical, he says:

I note first of all that "living nature" is unable to fashion solid bodies
directly. In this state, stone and metal are useless to it. Suppose the
problem is to produce a lasting object of invariant shape—a prop, a
lever, a rod, a buckler; to produce a tree-trunk, a femur, a tooth or a
shield, a skull or a shell, nature always makes the same detour: it uses
the liquid or fluid state of which every living substance is constituted,
and strains off the solid elements of its construction. All that lives or
lived results from the properties and changes of certain liquids. Besides,
every solid has passed through a liquid phase, melted or in solution.
But "living nature" does not take to the high temperatures which

enable us to work "pure bodies," and give to glass, bronze or iron in liquid or plastic states the forms desired, and which cooling will make permanent. Life, to model its solid organs, is limited to the use of solutions, suspensions or emulsions.

Certain kinds of perfection, then, do not belong to life but to death. In various thematic combinations this distinction of the poet's thought is developed, applied, enriched. The blood and the cave are extreme terms for extreme kinds of life, of man, of society. Characteristically, in the War between the States, the South is regarded as the way of life most representative of essence, of blood and so of ritual and tradition, while the North is conceived as protestant, scientific and without history; speaking of the present, the old soldier in "To the Lacedemonians" says, "All are born Yankees of the race of men / And this, too, now the country of the damned." Again,

> And in that Blue renown
> The Gray went down,
> Down like a rat,
> And even the rats cheered.

The tragedy, for Tate, is the loss of the possibility of value through the suggestions of positivism, "social science" and all modes of merely statistical consideration, that man is without sin, is ultimately and progressively perfectible, is through with the past. This is the philosophy of the cave, of the commentary. Against this there is the myth of the blood, the "unspeaking fury," the "lust" that feeds on itself, which insists that the past is undeniable, insists on the necessity of finding and seizing one's tradition with (and not despite) all the many imperfections that are the simple result of existence, and on the impossibility of a life cut off from its roots in the personal and deeply familiar earth of time.

I hope I have not too much simplified this matter; probably I have, but necessarily when one is exercising oneself to make the theme clear there will be other matters to which one is not (not verbally, anyhow) attending. It seemed an important subject, to consider as closely as possible what is the myth of this poetry, the assumption by which it operates and about which its meanings are organized. The matter of the duality seemed especially worth noticing in some detail, if only because of what reviewers are still likely to call the "obscurity" of these poems. The poems are, I think, hard, but the complaint about obscurity does not seem just, and may deserve some suspicion of being a rather easy disguise for a very hard moral complaint: some may find it more comforting not to know what the poet is doing than to be forced into a coherent attitude towards his work, and in this sense Mr. Tate's poems still suffer at the hands of critics whose idea of what a poem is has not the splendid certainty to be found in their idea of what Mr. Tate ought to be. Thus, recently, a professor of English: "It is no longer possible to dismiss Mr. Tate's poetry with such adjectives as cultivated, fastidious and morose." Ah, would it were still possible, meanwhile remarks his tone, those were the halcyon days—something we would perhaps not be entitled to say had we not found later in his review what we expected to find: . . . "It is much easier to discover what Tate is against than what he is for." And, at last, a poet like Tate is "recusant to the wholeness of humanity and it is unlikely that he will attain a higher status than that of poets' poet."

Strong words, and on the whole remarkably without meaning: if one does not know what the poet is "for" one does not know that he is "recusant to the wholeness of humanity," whatever all that may mean. And the question, what a poet is for, with its delicately swaddled ambiguity (what does he like? how can we use him?) may not be, after all, the right kind of question to ask. What, after all, is Shakespeare for? Or what is Yeats for? the poet whose themes Tate's perhaps most closely resemble, and who wrote

> Even the wisest man grows tense
> With some sort of violence
> Before he can accomplish fate . . .

But the antitheses are present always, the ranges in which value roams: what happens and history; violence and idea; accident and necessity. You have, the tragic poets say, your choice.

The Poetry of Allen Tate

by VIVIENNE KOCH

I should like to propose two revisions of the customary valuation put upon the poetry of Allen Tate. First, it has become increasingly evident with each new work that Mr. Tate is a fugitive from the Fugitives. The Fugitives were that talented group of Southern writers who, finding the Northern poetic climate of the early twenties too exacerbatingly modern, reaffirmed their allegiances with "tradition," a term they took some care to define. While we commonly think of the Southerners as a group, and while in a loose personal sense this may be so, it is my belief that in a veiled but not altogether deceptive fashion Mr. Tate has been seeking to free himself from the claims of group loyalty, claims which at one time had threatened the temper of his own sensibility.

Curiously enough, Tate's first symptomatic departure from his "tradition" came in what would seem, on the surface, to be the apotheosis of his conformance to it. It came in his translation of *Pervigilium Veneris* (1943), that neglected little classic never happily Englished, upon which he chose to exercise his powers, not so much as a Latinist, but as a poet of classical affiliations. Yet I think his choice of this delicately tinted but uninnocently erotic poem was perhaps motivated by the fact that, as Professor Mackail points out, it represents "the first clear note of the new romanticism which transformed classical into mediaeval literature. . . . Nothing could be less like either a folk-song or an official ode. It touches the last refinement of simplicity. In the delicately running, softly swaying verses, that ring and glitter and

EDITOR'S NOTE: Reprinted from *The Kenyon Critics*, ed. John Crowe Ransom (Port Washington, N.Y.: Kennikat Press, 1951), pp. 169–81, by permission of the publisher.

253

return on themselves in interlacing patterns, there is germinally the essence and inner spirit of the whole romantic movement. All the motives of the old classical poetry survive, yet all have undergone a new birth." The *Pervigilium Veneris* is Allen Tate's valedictory, from a safe distance, to the Fugitives, to the South, to the "classical" tradition, to his masters. The quickest way to get over the goodbyes is to say them in a strange language.

My second proposal flows from the historic process I have just described and is, at the same time and paradoxically, anterior to the whole development. I believe that Tate is a poet of romantic sensibility who has tried with varying success to compress his talents into a chastely classical form and that, in inverse degrees to his willingness or ability to do so, his best poetry has been written. Where his romanticism gets the better of him, or, to shift the metaphor, finds the classicist nodding, there we get the most enduring, vital and original poetry Tate is capable of writing. The *Pervigilium* was playing romanticism with the rules; with the publication of *The Winter Sea* it became clear that Tate was playing his own way.

In short, we have been assessing Tate too long in terms of his origins (the genetic fallacy) and his prose judgment (the doctrinal fallacy). It is time we began to follow the lead of the poems.

2

In Tate's *Selected Poems* (1937) it is possible to group together the work of the early twenties on several grounds. "Obituary," "Death of Little Boys," "Horation Epode to the Duchess of Malfi," "The Subway," "Ditty," "Retroduction to American History," and "Mr. Pope" all bear the imprint of the Eliot of "Prufrock" in the characteristic quatrain (or aggregation of joined quatrains) with the typically anticlimactic, sometimes parenthetical usage of the fourth line. Similarly, the vocabulary is often derived from Eliot: "You have no more chance than an infusorian / Lodged in a hollow molar of an eohippus. / Come, now, no prattle of remergence with the *ontos on*." All, without a single exception, whether the subject be Webster, Pope, the death of little boys, or their sleeping, reveal a bitter, angry and passionate rejection of the present, of contemporaneity where "you, so crazy and inviolate" are "hurled religiously / Upon your business of humility / Into the iron forestries of hell; / . . . Dazed, while the worldless heavens bulge and reel / In the cold revery of an idiot."

It is a present in which even "little boys grown patient at last, weary / Surrender their eyes immeasurably to the night," and other "Little boys no longer sight the plover / Streaked in the sky," while "men, who fail . . . will plunge, mile after mile of men, to crush this lucent madness of the face, / Go home and put their heads upon the pillow. Turn whatever shift the darkness cleaves, / Tuck in their eyes, and cover / The flying dark with sleep like falling leaves." I hope it is excusable to resort to the kind of mosaic I have just composed in order to point a paradox: Allen Tate, at the start of his career in the early twenties, was affirming his allegiances with the classical past in the unsigned editorials of *The Fugitive* and, at the same time, betraying in every poem he was writing a frankly nihilistic temper which, in its alternating violence and absolution, was a romanticism of a somewhat more fiery brand than his criticism might have endorsed.

Perhaps the gauge of Tate's youthful romanticism may be best explored in his much-admired "Death of Little Boys" published in the *Nation* in 1925 when he was twenty-six years old:

> When little boys grown patient at last, weary,
> Surrender their eyes immeasurably to the night,
> The event will rage terrific as the sea;
> Their bodies fill a crumbling room with light.
>
> Then you will touch at the bedside, torn in two,
> Gold curls now intricate with gray
> As the windowpane extends a fear to you
> From one peeled aster drenched with the wind all day.
>
> And over his chest the covers in an ultimate dream
> Will mount to the teeth, ascend the eyes, press back
> The locks—while round his sturdy belly gleam
> The suspended breaths, white spars above the wreck:
>
> Till all the guests, come in to look, turn down
> Their palms, and delirium assails the cliff
> Of Norway where you ponder, and your little town
> Reels like a sailor in his rotten skiff.
>
> The bleak sunshine shrieks its chipped music then
> Out to the milkweed amid the fields of wheat.
> There is a calm for you where men and women
> Unroll the chill precision of moving feet.

The only "classical" element in this adventuresome poem is the plural in the title and the first line. The generalizing character of "boys" extends or is intended to extend an individual experience of death to a universal statement of it. But apart from this gesture (a successful one) there is no concession anywhere in the poem (unless it be in the rather diversified quatrains) to any poem I am familiar with in the "tradition" of English literature up to 1925. The poem is a consideration of the problem of identity or, more philosophically, the problem of permanence and change. The "you" of the second paragraph is not merely rhetorical address which seeks to involve the reader with the death of little boys, but it achieves exactly that. The bedside is "torn in two" by the "event" of death, which, let us note, does not destroy the little boys but rather the room which crumbles with light. (The room, of course, may be everything which is contained in it.) The "gold curls" are "now deftly intricate with gray" because of the blinding vision of death in which "you" (the onlooker, father, or little boy grown up) must participate because you too feel the fear extended by the windowpane (night or death to which the little boys have in Stanza One surrendered their eyes). The emotional effects throughout are persistently ascribed to the landscape.

In Stanza Three the death is individualized in the singular pronouns (abandoning the universal), in the magnificently concrete, yet symbolic detail of the "sturdy belly" round which "gleam the suspended breaths" of the dead boy, or rather boy-in-man, and "you" (like another Hamlet, a questioning, dubious intellect) pondering on your cliff feel delirium (death, shifting identity) assailing it (just as, in a similar transfer of affects, it was the *room* and not the body which crumbled in Stanza One), and your little town (something built, *made*, the ego, perhaps) "reels like a sailor in his rotten skiff." Here the image of the dead boy as a wreck and the little town (the ego) about-to-be-wrecked converge in the sea symbolism. It is at this point (the crisis of the poem) that the fusion of meanings is consummated and the question of permanence (identity) arises like a lonely phoenix from the wreck of little boys (your wreck, of course). The last stanza is an anticlimax, and is so intended. The "bleak sunshine," the discordant shriek of its "chipped music," reaches out to the level of external quotidian existence (milkweed, etc.) where there are no more "events terrific as the sea" but only an ironic calm whose inevitable "precision of moving feet" implies an ultimately similar dissolution of the almost-wrecked ego.

Perhaps this explication will have seemed forced. In that event, I suggest returning to the sea metaphor introduced in Stanza One, picked up and developed in Three and consummated in the harsh despair of "reels," "drunk," and "rotten," to say nothing of the flimsy, useless phonetic fluff of "skiff." By that route, it seems to me, almost the same reading may be developed as the one I have got by the long way. Little boys die in men before men die. Man is torn in two by his past (his little boyhood) and his present. The agency of childhood is mysterious and terrifying in the personality of the man (the aster is man "peeled"—revealed—by his youth). The certainty of identity (integration of personality) is seriously threatened in Stanza Four. In Five there is a sick rebound: the world and its dull, mechanic inevitability must be met again. The let-down in diction, the clarity of the last stanza as opposed to the complexity of the others, is Tate's cold and disdainful bow to the outer world, to the nowness he *will* not recognize. This, then, is the kind of poetry Tate was writing when he was raging with youthful hauteur against the *nouveaux-arrivés* "experimentalists." To recapitulate: "Death of Little Boys" is a very good poem; it is revelatory of Tate's "original" temperamental bent (if learning had not already disguised the interior man); it is certainly as "experimental" as any poem I know of written at that time, including the "romantic" experimentalism of Tate's friend, Hart Crane.

The following five years, 1925–30, are crucial to the direction of Tate's growth. Some residence in England and France during that time leave superficial traces in his work. If Tate ever thought of himself as an exile (and at least one poem, "Message from Abroad," bears witness that he did) it was certainly not the kind of willed exile represented by Joyce's categorical imperatives for the artist, "Silence, exile and cunning," nor by Henry James's ambassadorial *rapprochements*, nor by Eliot's British repatriation. Europe merely reinforces for Tate the feeling he started out with in Kentucky. He is exiled not from a place, but from a condition. The present (and Europe is just as contemporaneous as the South) exiles him from the past. He is cut off *through no fault of his own* from a more meaningful condition of living. He will begin to try in these years to find, focus, and define the character of that past and so, perhaps, to possess it. . . .

Perhaps the most ambitious poem of this period, and one which summarizes Tate's intellectual situation in the early thirties, is "Causerie" (1925–31). The tone is again forensic but the vigor of the indictment is sustained throughout. Unlike his practice in "Meditation" Tate here depends on a rugged, irregular blank verse manipulated with great flexibility in terms of caesura to effect a swelling and urgent rhetoric. The poet is the prosecutor; yet he is himself among the accused:

> I've done no rape, arson, incest, no murder,
> Yet cannot sleep . . .

Through another means he asks the question of "Message from Abroad": "Where is your house, in which room stands your bed?" In ironic answer comes a swift, Elizabethan-in-texture arraignment of the fate suffered by the South:

> Have you a daughter,
> Daughters are the seed of occupations . . .
> Let her not read history lest knowledge
> Of her fathers instruct her to be a noted bawd.

The argument proceeds by a kind of rhetorical causality (note the force of "For" in the passage connecting with the above):

> For miracles are faint
> And resurrection is our weakest point of religion.

Later, the moral confusion of modern life is attributed to a loss of absolutes:

> In an age of abstract experience, fornication
> Is self-expression, adjunct to Christian euphoria,
> And whores become delinquents; delinquents, patients;
> Patients, wards of society. Whores, by that rule,
> Are precious.

The result is "a race of politic pimps" without "The antique courtesy of your myths." What Tate regrets is the loss of the principle of evil, a loss of which Wallace Stevens was to say fifteen years later: "the death of Satan was a tragedy / for the imagination. . . ." But, and I think this is a distinction which illuminates Tate's special quality as a moralist, he does not, like Stevens, relate this loss to its effect on art, but rather to its effect on conduct. This is a didactic poetry of such high order that the didacticism is (as in Blake) through the purest rhetorical fusion indistinguishable from the poetry. The control is sure and adult. The entirety of the loss is acknowledged; there is no longer an effort to reclaim the lost from "the province of the drowned." The poet is operating on a higher level of social "reality," but there is no acceptance—yet.

3

We can measure the range of Tate's later progress by a study of *The Winter Sea* (1944). Although containing less than a dozen poems, it yet projects an almost complete break with Tate's earlier work in the forthright abandoning of the tendency to allow "philosophic metaphors" about tradition to determine the structure and content of the poems. It is possible that his fine historical novel of the antebellum South, *The Fathers* (1938), had served Tate as a sieve for draining off this long-nourished interest into the more flexible formal unit of experience of the story. *The Fathers*, like "The Ode," is about those who were destroyed through what Hart Crane in a letter to Tate calls "an excess of chivalry." The only echo of the past to be found in the diverse emphasis of the poems in *The Winter Sea* is the concern with childhood guilt noted in "Sonnets at Christmas." This theme now advances into a more elevated symbolic use in "More Sonnets at Christmas" and in "Seasons of the Soul."

It would not be over-emphasizing the personal situation revealed by this volume to say that it releases in Tate the full force of the romantic strain which had seemed successfully inhibited during the preceding years. Still, the didactic impulse and conscious moral aim is too habitual to suffer serious diminution and courses along, a parallel stream of intention, with the revitalized romanticism. Tate's own critical prescription for this mode of moral inquiry is certainly met by his achievement in "Jubilo," in "Ode to Our Young Proconsuls of the Air," and in "Eclogue of the Liberal and the Poet." "The moral intelligence," he had written in 1940, "gets into poetry . . . not as moral abstractions, but as form, coherence of image, and metaphor, control of tone and rhythm, the union of these features." Tate's essays in the satire are vigorous, witty and, as in classical satire, full of honest prejudices. A prejudice, let it be noted in passing, is different from a *willed* belief. "Jubilo," using as refrain a phrase from a Negro popular song, is a tongue-in-cheek celebration of boys who "caress the machines they ride." The mock-heroic epic, while not at all a model, makes itself felt in "Ode to Our Young Proconsuls" in the deliberately heightened mock-allegorical language which raises the invective to dramatic irony.

"False Nightmare," a telling although not altogether just indictment of Whitmanism, is sure to be quoted by Tate's enemies as evidence of his "reactionary" views. It is a bitter poem but, carefully read, as reactionary as Jeremiah.

We become aware, then, that in Tate's recent poetry the traditional influences (whether of structure, idea, or both) operate only as qualities, not as models. Thus, one is barely conscious of the Dante influence in the impressive "Seasons of the Soul," but it is there in the deeply religio-ethical purpose of the poem as well as in the implied descent of the poet into his own hell. In the same poem the influence of the *Pervigilium Veneris* is felt in the erotic elements as well as in the subtle use of refrain. "Seasons of the Soul" can, I think, be thought of as the summation of Tate's present position. It is an instructive guide to his technical practice; it is a map to his present values, even though it merely poses a problem. But it is by the way in which a problem is framed that the nature of its solution is implied. Let us examine the frame.

The scheme of the poem is simple: the four seasons correspond to the four elements of the ancients. Thus the chronicle is of the four ages of man in relation to the four aspects of the universe he inhabits. More specifically, however, it is modern man whose spiritual biography Mr. Tate records. Summer is the first season; the background is now:

> It was a gentle sun
> When, at the June solstice,
> Green France was overrun
> With caterpillar feet.
> No head knows where its rest is
> Or may lie down with reason
> When war's usurping claws
> Shall take the heart escheat—

This suggests another summer (the summer of childhood which is identified with the summer of classical antiquity in its clarity and innocence) when "The summer had no reason; / Then, like a primal cause / It had its timeless day."

In Autumn, technically the most interesting section, the surrealist device of a dream is employed to enable the poet to prophesy, as it were, a vision of his own old age which is revealed to him as a trap. He is caught in a deep well, an empty house (the house of the past) peopled only by ghosts, his ancestors, who refuse to recognize him. The house of the past is not real, "The door was false—no key / Or lock . . . yet I could see / I had been born to it / For miles of running brought / Me back where I began." The failure of parents to recognize a son is another way of stating the problem of identity. We have seen how in his earliest writing this question engaged Tate. Now the dilemma is extended to the profoundest sort of personal epistemology: If your progenitors do not know you, if you are cut off from communication with your contemporaries ("I was down a well"), if, in short, there is no objective recognition of your identity, who are you? Along with this return to a study of his past, Tate also reverts to the more sensuous and concrete imagery of the early "romantic" poems, an imagery determined by inner, emotional connections and not by logical ones. I think especially of the father-mother imagery of Section II and the sea imagery of Section III.

From the frustration of this cyclical returning upon himself, the poet in "Winter," a strikingly beautiful section, pleads with Venus to return to her element. Christianity ("the drying God above / Hanged in his windy steeple") is dead and "No longer bears for us / The living wound of love." There is every reason to suppose that we must take this as Tate's mature view of the religious problem, a problem which he could not resolve with such brutal finality in the middle years. In "More Sonnets at Christmas," composed a little before "Seasons of the Soul," he had implied the dismissal:

> Ten years is time enough to be dismayed
> By mummy Christ, head crammed between his knees.

The violence of this image, its quasi-obscenity, even, is the measure of the distance Tate traveled in the ten dismaying years from the time when the question of anti-miraculism disturbed him. It is clear enough now that, as Tate once flippantly remarked, the question of Mr. Eliot's submission to the Thirty-nine Articles was never to be a live option in his own poetry.

But the pagan values are dead, too ("All the sea-gods are dead"). There is sex: The pacing animal who turns "The venereal awl / In the livid wound of love." Again, a strange surrealist image connects the general with the poet's particular plight: In a grove under the sea the poet seizes the branch of a madrepore from which drips a "speaking blood / From the livid wound of love":

> We are the men who died
> Of self-inflicted woe,
> Lovers whose stratagem
> Led to their suicide
> I touched my sanguine hair
> And felt it drip above
> Their brother who, like them,
> Was maimed and did not bear
> The living wound of love.

The "living wound" of love would seem to be suggested by the famous Proem to *De Rerum Naturae* in which Lucretius, looking on a war-torn Italy, calls upon Venus (as a fertility-principle) to inflict upon Mars the eternal wound of love (*aeterno volnere amoris*) and thus win peace and increase for the Romans. For Tate the "eternal wound" becomes the "living wound" and I take the implication to be that Love, growing from a "livid" wound into the "living" wound is the only possible power which can rescue man from his otherwise maimed existence. The passionate and suppliant address to Venus makes clear that she is the complex erotic symbol around which cluster the poet's hopes for various kinds of regeneration:

> All the sea-gods are dead
> You, Venus, come home
> To your salt maidenhead.

This reading, I think, is confirmed by the next section "Spring," a liturgical chant (still within the frame of the ten-line iambic trimeter stanza) to the Mother of Silences, a figure who simultaneously suggests the principle of the Virgin (the Mother, Life) and the principle of Death (the Mystery); the figure, significantly, never speaks. The symbol has a certain obscurity not altogether relieved by the following passage:

> Come, mother, and lean
> At the window with your son
> And gaze through its light frame
> These fifteen centuries
> Upon the shirking scene
> Where men, blind, go lame:

Now the mother appears to be Saint Monica as she appears in Book IX of St. Augustine's *Confessions*. Mother and son stand alone "leaning in a certain window, from which the garden of the house we occupied at Ostia could be seen"; cataloguing a set of earthly conditions, which, could they be "silenced," would enable them to arrive at an apprehension of the "hereafter." Soon after, Monica dies and leaves Augustine with a living wound "from having that most sweet and dear habit of living together suddenly broken off." Thus the Mother of Silences is a particular mother (St. Monica), the Virgin, the Mystery, and through Augustine's unmentioned wound she is identified further with the principle of Love. Love, then, is the luminous agency common to all the referents of the symbol. Yet, in the end, one feels that the hope of regeneration through Love is reluctantly abandoned and death is sought as the only certain "kindness" to which men can aspire.

"Seasons of the Soul" will stand as a major event in Tate's career as a poet. It is lyrical, sensuous and tragic. It is, for whatever meaning that chameleon term may still carry, romantic. In "Tension in Poetry," an interesting essay written some years ago, Tate distinguishes the metaphysical from the romantic poet in the following way: "The metaphysical poet as a rationalist begins at or near the extensive or denotative end of the line. The romantic or Symbolist poet at the other, intensive end; and each by a straining feat of the imagination tries to push his meaning as far as he can toward the opposite end, so as to occupy the entire scale. . . ." But there is to be recommended a "poetry of the center," that is, "poetry of tension in which the strategy is diffused into the unitary effect." I am not sure after several rereadings how this strategy is implemented. Indeed, the concept of "tension" has been used by some critics, although not by Mr. Tate, to get around critical problems more taxing to unravel than to designate as illustrative of "tension."

However, if there is a poetry of tension and if there is a living practitioner of this awesome and marvelous feat of poetic balance between

the classic and the romantic, the metaphysical and the Symbolist
among us, surely it is Tate himself. But it has become increasingly
evident that the idea of the poet as the daring young man on the flying trapeze is giving way to a less perilous but more fruitful enter-
prise: the paradoxical roles of suppliant and teacher have lost their
separate identities in a profound and humble appreciation of what de
Unamuno calls "the tragic sense of life." In "Winter Mask to the
Memory of W. B. Yeats" (1943) Tate writes:

> I asked the master Yeats
> Whose great style could not tell
> Why it is man hates
> His own salvation,
> Prefers the way to hell,
> And finds his last safety
> In the self-made curse that bore
> Him towards damnation:
> The drowned undrowned by the sea,
> The sea worth living for.

Allen Tate's Inferno

by SISTER MARY BERNETTA, O.S.F.

> Gentlemen, my secret is
> Damnation. ("To the Lacedemonians")

Certain critics have called the verse of Allen Tate Augustan, pointing out in particular his affinity to Pope; others have labeled it metaphysical, after the poetry of Donne's age; still others, in the tradition of the Greco-Roman classics. Yet his basic concern, especially as revealed in *Poems: 1922–1947*, is medieval. In the Middle Ages there was one drama which took precedence over all other conflict: the struggle of Everyman to win beatitude and to escape eternal reprobation. Tate recognizes the issue as a subject most significant for literature. With the old veteran of "To the Lacedemonians" he announces: "Gentlemen, my secret is / Damnation." One way to penetrate the meanings of his work, the difficulty of which is largely due to the complexity of his ideas rather than to verbal experimentation, is to trace the implications of this secret throughout his lyrics.

Damnation, of course, has its prelude. Without guilt, such a concept would be meaningless. Tate acknowledges the two kinds of guilt peculiar to the Christian dispensation: original and personal. Frederick Morgan comments in *The Hudson Review* on the first aspect as it appears in the latest collection: "What these poems are built of, then, is a sense of Original Sin, grasped in all of its unpleasantness with an uncompromising honesty. Tate is a good antidote in a time when sin

EDITOR'S NOTE: Reprinted from *Renascence*, 3:113–19 (Spring 1971), by permission of the author and publisher.

is creeping home through the back door, by way of Kafka and Auden, half-recognized, but with the emphasis on the pathos of the suffering individual, and leaving plenty of room for the well-intentioned meliorism of social reformers. If there is Original Sin, it is in the blood (and see what Tate does with blood imagery); it too is our inheritance." To a civilization with no roots, as today's America appears to be, the transmission of primordial guilt, of a "universal stain," is nonsense; to an individual ever aware of the links going backward immemorially from the latest to the earliest of the race ("Emblems," "The Ancestors") it is a logical enough doctrine. The 1932 version of the eighth "Sonnet of the Blood" concretizes this belief that descendants must suffer for the crimes of those who have preceded them. Tate's whole moral philosophy, moreover, as expressed in his essays is antipathetic to the evasions of responsibility predicated by heredity-environment social thought; the verse, not discontinuous with his other interests, reflects this unflinching readiness to accept the consequences of impaired human faculties and of free will. He has no patience with the substitution of abstractions for concrete instances of evil—no tolerance for the kind of mentality which formulates a faulty enthymeme wherein whores become precious wards of society. If evil is removed, life itself disappears, as in "To the Romantic Traditionists." Morgan goes on to say: "These poems, then, dramatize fallen man in a divided society; the measure of their success is that they make the reader participate in the general predicament and know it for himself."

Tate not only recognizes the effects of original sin but also the necessity of answering for one's own moral actions. The second of the "Sonnets at Christmas" is really an examination of conscience, at the conclusion of which he meditates before the December fire, "Punished by crimes of which I would be quit." One crime emerges specifically from the past, a lie told when he was twelve which caused the whipping of a black boy; eight years later, in "More Sonnets at Christmas," he is still brooding over his fault, magnified by retrospection—an illustration of his thought epigrammatically put in "Causerie": "Manhood like a lawyer with his formulas / Sesames his youth for innocent acquittal."

"Mother and Son" emphasizes the isolation to which guilt (as well

as the emotional danger Tate himself has called attention to) condemns the man who:

> . . . lies upon the bed of sin
> Where greed, avarice, anger writhed and slept
> Till to their silence they were gathered in.

". . . Think not much on mortal sin," the brother, in the adaptation
from Catullus, ironically advises the corpse he has come over land
and waters to honor; one feels in the background the poet's stricture
of a materialistic society, impervious to truths which ought to be meditated on, and beyond this that stern view of individual culpability
which is enunciated in "Sonnets of the Blood": "Dignity's the stain /
Of mortal sin that knows humility." "Causerie" is a monologue at
midnight by a modern for whom sleep has been murdered, though he
is innocent of rape, arson, incest, homicide; a nameless oppression at
the absence of grace suffocates him. Tate can discern that lack in his
contemporaries (Wilson, Warren, Ransom), thirsty beside the living
waters; he suspects it to be his own case ("The Cross"); he is sometimes overwhelmed with implications of the situation, such as he
depicts in the account of his dream when nine years old: the child he
then was, the man he was to become, and his great-grandfather were
walking along the Ox Road until they came to a country store run
by the devil, at whose appearance and speech

> The pines thundered, the sky blacked away,
> The man in breeches, all knowledge in his stare,
> A moment shuddered as the world fell.
>   ("Records")

Invariably he rejects attempts to dispense with grace, to reach salvation by secular means alone—a prime fallacy of the present era.

Whatever the outcome of the human predicament, Tate in his verse
does not blame God. It is man who has defaced Nature in "The Eagle,"
even though the last line refers to the result of this vandalism as "God's
hideous face." Damnation, if it comes, will be self-inflicted. Incredible
as it seems to the young, it is possible for man to prefer hell to heaven.
Such a horrifying paradox troubles the poet, who goes to his most
famous contemporary for enlightenment:

> I asked the master Yeats
> Whose great style could not tell

> Why it is man hates
> And finds his last safety
> In the self-made curse that bore
> Him toward damnation:
> His own salvation,
> Prefers the way to hell,
> The drowned undrowned by the sea,
> The sea worth living for.
>   ("Winter Mask")

In "Jubilo" the patient sucks his own blood; then his arteries, blood-less, are filled with salt serum: "Till his lost being dries, and cries / For that unspeakable salt land / Beyond the Day of Jubilo." Note how this lyric particularizes Judgement under the title of the Day of Jubilo, taken from the refrain of an old Negro song; the second of the sonnets named "Inside and Outside" further sets the scene by contributing the Biblical angelic annunciation: "When Gabriel's trumpet ends all life's delay, / Will crash the beams of firmamental woe . . ." The latter image is rephrased in one of the "Sonnets at Christmas" in a manner reminiscent of Donne: "Let the round trumpets blow." The poem goes on to proclaim the identity of the Judge; on the last day (the Dies Irae is twice referred to specifically in Tate's verse) the souls will be under "The ancient crackle of the Christ's deep gaze." The sentence will be an irrevocable one: "Whether by Corinth or by Thebes we go / The way is brief, but the fixed doom not so." (It is interesting to notice that in *Poems: 1922–1931* the doom was not *fixed* but *just*.)

Since Tate believes that abstraction is the death of everything, reli-gion included, it is natural for his treatment of the infernal regions to be a concrete one, even as Dante's was. The entrance to hell is a secret passageway ("Inside and Outside"), the portal locked with a privy lock ("False Nightmare"), with "nether bolts" ("The Traveller"). Whereas the conventional allusions to perpetual bliss stress the idea of rest, quiet, peace, the soul on its way to and in hell is busy ("Elegy," "Inside and Outside"); in "Procession" the poet says that "Hell's ener-gies march . . ." The devil is more than a cosmic force of evil: he is Belial, the taskmaster of Jefferson Davis; he is described in "Records" thus:

> . . . a tall fat man with stringy hair
> And a manner that was innocent of sin,
> His galluses greasy, his eyes coldly gray,
> Appeared, and with a gravely learned air
> Spoke from the deep coherence of hell . . .

In fact, he is real enough to have a human parody in Edmund Wilson, even to the nice selection of the adjectives *sly* and *unwearied*. In "Epistle," a lyric not included in the most recent grouping, he may possibly be "the idiot king of a savage court" for whom Wilson is said to toil.

The fiery dead and archfiends who have been the *materia* of the poet's nocturnal cogitations inhabit this inferno, where the punishments of Dante's epic reappear. In that Jarrell-like dialogue, "The Robber Bridegroom," wherein no threat but that of mutilation can wring a scream of terror from the courageous bride, there are echoes of the Second Circle: "The house is whirling night, the guests / Grains of dust from the northwest." This section of Dante has been brilliantly glossed by Tate in "Tension in Modern Poetry," in which through the use of river imagery he identified Francesca with her sin of incontinency. The Ugolino episode is resurrected in "Winter Mask":

> Both damned in eternal ice,
> The traitor become the boor
> Who had led his friend to slaughter,
> Now bites his head—not nice,
> The food that he lives for.

In "To the Lacedemonians" the Seventh Circle penalties are employed: "Damned souls, running the way of sand / into the destination of the wind." "The Twelve" brings out even more realistically this idea of the lost driven by a burning wind as in a heavenly storm. The forest of bleeding boughs is another concept taken over from the *Divine Comedy*. Perhaps the most concrete version of Hell which Tate has written is Part II of "Seasons of the Soul." The speaker of the elegy finds himself in a place identifiable by its autumnal smell—the smell of death. As in Canto XIV of Dante's *Inferno* ("So was the falling of the eternal heat, / By which, like tinder under steel, the sand's / Keen scorch with an intenser torment beat") the air is filled with sand, but the atmosphere is cold, not burning. People, familiar and strange, pass him in the horribly unreal manner of Kafka's *The Trial*. Indeed, reviewing the total references, one sees that the picture of hell as contained in those of his poems selected in 1947 as most worth preserving is not that of the "dim and doubtful" region of "Credo in Intellectum Videntem," which appeared in an edition of twenty years back.

Tate's vision of hell, like that of so many writers in the twentieth century (e.g., Eliot, Crane), is a double one: post- and pre-death. Cleanth Brooks in *Poetry* says: "*The Winter Sea*, for all that it is a tissue of Dante references, does not pretend to give Dante's vision. It could not and keep its full integrity. Dante's doctrine is not available to him except as reference. Moreover, he is not like Dante, the detached observer of the damned." Along with Hart Crane, he perceives the spiritless life surging under New York as a terrestrial inferno, the diabolic symbol of which is the subway, hurled like a shell "Into the iron forestries of hell." Again there is the "busyness" characteristic of those dead for whom there is no rest; even the shell is credited with the "business of humility," the last word in the phrase an instance of the poet's ability to get at the fresh springs of meaning in earlier uses of language. "Last Days of Alice," a grim, nightmarish reversal of the Grecian-urn theme, shows us a twilight world where everything is hopelessly resistant to melioration. Even this earthly hell is eternal, since man has abolished time as well as space. Just as after the eruption of a volcano (the title is obviously patterned after *Last Days of Pompeii*), all will be forever the same, but the reality preserved is "a lost and twilight age." The recurrence of twilight imagery in Tate's verse is even more marked than that of blood or beast figures: "twilight of my audacity," "eddying twilight," "blank twilight," "the cave / Of twilight," "the low twilight," "the air / Waits twilit for their echo," "twilight certainty of an animal," "Broken, our twilight visions fail," "a twilight / Amid stuttering houses," "old twilights," "The twilight is long fingers and black hair," etc. Sometimes a whole lyric is devoted to the strange emotions aroused by the hour of falling night ("The Ancestors"), when we are more than usually aware of mortality, through instinct rather than through the senses. Clarity was once a property of the world, but that world is now shrouded in the dusk that Joyce describes so well in *Finnegans Wake*. "Darkness falls"; there are only "emblems of twilight"; America is "the country of the damned."

Although Tate admires Yeats most among modern poets, his own solution of the human predicament is far removed from that of his master, a chasm caused partly by the difference between his and the

Irish writer's attitudes toward personal responsibility, partly by his refusal to follow Yeats in the romantic path of softening unpleasantness by magical fancies and fantasies, pseudo-folklore, synthetic mysticism. In "Winter Mask," an elegy for Yeats as fine as Auden's, he invites the reader to:

> Just look into damned eyes
> And give the returning glare;
> For the damned like it, the more
> Damnation is exempt
> From what would save its heir
> With a thing worth living for.

"The Cross" is another poem of damnation while still alive. The scene described in the first lines may be the crucifixion; it may date even further back to the creation of hell. At any rate, Tate is one of the "some men." Untangling the antecedents, one sees that love struggles until at the foot of the cross, in the pit of death, men paradoxically taste no more of mortality. All previous existence is buried in the black grave, where the last alternatives of life are faced. But then comes that agonized cry of the graceless moderns "without the life to save, / Being from all salvation weaned." These souls are assaulted by fear of death and of life simultaneously, as a stag is charged both at head and heels by young wolves. Those who realize their dilemma and then try to lead a life as before are damned while the heart yet beats. The fiery dead themselves have instructed such men.

The consciousness of this truth came to Tate and his friend Andrew Lytle as they sat together at dusk in a Southern country house. In "The Ancestors" the poet tells us about those dead who are also living; in "The Oath," record of this twilight conversation with Lytle, he tells us of those living who are also dead. Lytle is stirred to an oath by the revelation, coming out of a meditation made among the relics of former inhabitants of the room. Brooks in *Modern Poetry and the Tradition* speaks of this moment of awareness: the thing that is true is obvious, that *we* are the dead. The dead are those who have given in to abstraction, even though they may move about and carry on their business and be—to use the earlier phrase in the poem—the "animated dead." Other poems take up the same idea. The "Eclogue of the Liberal and the Poet" announces that in Europe "all men are dead." The second of the "Sonnets of the Blood" speaks of the secret fire

that consumes both the poet and his brother, concluding: "Our property in fire is death in life / Flawing the rocky fundament with strife,"
two lines revised to point up the living-in-hell motif. Finally there is
that beautiful tribute to John Peale Bishop, introduced by a tercet
from the *Divine Comedy*. Of this Vivienne Koch writes in the *Kenyon
Review* for Summer, 1949: "Thus, one is barely conscious of the Dante
influence in the impressive 'Seasons of the Soul,' but it is there in the
deeply religio-ethical purpose of the poem as well as in the implied
descent of the poet into his own hell." The last stanza of the Summer
section gives a description of that hell in the form of a human bestiary
such as "Winter Mask" mentions:

> Two men of our summer world
> Descended winding hell
> And when their shadows curled
> They fearfully confounded
> The vast concluding shell:
> Stopping, they saw in the narrow
> Light a centaur pause
> And gaze, then his astounded
> Beard, with a notched arrow,
> Part back upon his jaws.

Incidentally, a study of Tate's animal symbolism is illuminating;
besides the traditional centaur in the passage quoted above, his symbols include the cat (history), stag (modern man), lamb (Christ),
eagle (mind), cuttlefish (memory), wolf (death), and a host of others,
a device further connecting him with the medieval period.

An examination of the theme of damnation as it informs the twenty-
five years of Tate's poetry brought together in this latest collection
leaves one with the impression that, though he has been told "Purusha
sits no more in our eyes," he is not convinced. He accepts the fact of
the grave but continues to turn over and over in his mind aspects of
immortality. The crucial matter of salvation, the destiny of the soul
in terms of Christian eschatology, remains for him as for Dante and
other writers of the Middle Ages, a subject pre-eminently worthy of the
poet's art.

Culture and Technique in Tate

by FRANCESCO MEI

translated by Brewster Ghiselin

In Europe the usual tendency in thinking of an American writer is
to regard him as a genial barbarian, talented but without critical
conscience or intellectual maturity. To be very highly thought of,
an American writer should at least have worked in a restaurant or fac-
tory, gone to sea as a cabin boy, devoted some time to the profession
of selling neckties, perhaps have hunted whales in the Pacific or killed
lions in Kenya. It does not matter in the least if he has read Shakespeare or educated himself in the Greek classics.

In reality the idea that the American writers lack university education and know little or nothing of European thought, history and
literature is simply a myth. To cite only a few examples among the
more notable and recent, it will suffice to point out that Dos Passos
was educated at Harvard and was one of a group of exquisites and
esthetes, that Thornton Wilder was educated in the Greek and Latin
classics, that Hemingway himself, despite all his posing as a primitive,
is a profound connoisseur of Elizabethan literature and a student of
Flaubert. If this is true of the fiction writers, it is all the more true of
the poets. Most American poets today are also critics, often university
professors. Far from being immediate and spontaneous, theirs is among
the most difficult forms of poetry ever produced, the most dense with
erudition and with thought, the most disciplined technically. Our
own hermetic poets, by comparison, represent a prodigy of simplicity.
It is enough to open at random a page of Eliot or Pound, to find before

EDITOR'S NOTE: Reprinted from *Il Quotidiano*, July 1954, by permission of the author.

273

one texts loaded with infinite allusions, historic, philological, and literary, which range from obscure quotations from the Chinese and Indian to close-packed references to works of the whole western tradition. Among the others, the case of Allen Tate is one of the more significant. Here we have a poet who, besides writing verse that displays a consummate technical perfection of rhythm and meter, confronts in his critical prose the most difficult esthetic problems, ranges from the political and historical sphere to the social and religious, and treats the most complex questions of philosophy and of culture.

Born in Winchester, Kentucky, in 1899, Tate belongs to that group of American intellectuals and artists deriving from the agrarian aristocracy of the South, such as John Crowe Ransom, Robert Penn Warren, and Cleanth Brooks, who under the name of *Fugitives* reacted against the culture of the industrialized and pragmatic North, reaffirming the value of tradition, of form, and of artistic discipline. Shaping itself afresh through recourse to the classics, this movement affirmed the importance of literature as an autonomous expression of a need of the spirit. In the poetry of Tate one feels the influence of the Latin poets, especially in his spirited and stinging satire, basically political, in the mode of Persius and Martial, no less than the influence of Dante and Donne, in his ability to sustain his verse upon a rich basis of thought. The return to the closed forms of sonnet and terza rima does not prevent him from experimenting in even more complex rhythms, in which the verses are linked stanza to stanza by recurrent rimes and the images are sustained by a coherent logical structure. But upon this passionately intellectual ground there developed in Tate another source of inspiration: the hallucinated world of the South, peopled with memories of his boyhood and with the phantasms of the Civil War. The warm and luxurious landscape alternates, in his poems, with evocations of ambiguous states of soul in which one seems to halt listening to catch the faint voices that swarm in a dusk filled with shades and specters. In this sense, Tate moves in the same sphere as other symbolist writers of the South, such as Faulkner and Poe. In "Mother and Son," for example, is represented with great dramatic force a troubled spirit's struggle for salvation on the brink of damnation and death. In "Ode to the Confederate Dead," a poem on the dead of the Civil War ("The people—people of my kind, my own / People but strange with a white light / In the face"), the prodigious formal virtuosity and the perfect accord of the images serve to focus a vision broken by infernal flashes and celestial lightnings, in which the paean of glory for the dead soldiers is linked with the sense of bodily decay and the realistic notation is made one with the metaphysical breath.

No less interesting than his poetry is Tate's vast body of critical work, which gathers into various volumes (among which the most important are *Reactionary Essays* and *On the Limits of Poetry*) essays on esthetics, critical studies, and historical depictions of culture and manners. Tate's theoretical position derives directly from that movement of thought, that in America has had its most authoritative representative in Henry James, for which literature has an autonomous validity as complete knowledge of the experience of man. This trend is clearly opposed to the other, that calls to mind Walt Whitman, which tends to see in literature above all a means of ideological propaganda: linked in part to Marxist tendencies, it has today its most brilliant exponents in the critic Edmund Wilson and the poet Archibald MacLeish.

But it should be noted that the autonomy of art is not defended by Tate upon the basis of a sterile estheticism, like that of a Wilde or a Mallarmé, and not even on the grounds of an abstract idealism, like that of Croce. Tate adheres on the contrary to that total conception of man of the classico-Christian tradition, which is traceable to Aristotle and St. Thomas, and which has been taken up again by the French philosopher Jacques Maritain, for whom the work of art is engrafted like an integral part in a vaster whole. Tate's polemic, extending beyond the strictly esthetic plane to that of philosophy in general, is in fact directed above all against that scientific positivism dominant now especially in the United States, which in placing man upon the purely biological plane of the instincts and stimuli, denies the spiritual world any independence of the physical. As in sociology we get then passive adaptation to environment, and in psychology reduction of individual actions to sheer physiological mechanism, so in art and history man becomes prisoner of a coarse utilitarianism, in terms of which he exists as mere Homo economicus, without any respite moral or religious. Scientific methods when applied to literature reveal, in fact, according to Tate, the insufficiency of a vision of life that looks upon everything from the practical angle of experimentation and of

results. Lacking a true faith in art and thought as values superior to
pure utility, even the historical and literary critic occupies himself
often in a mechanical and arbitrary research into origins and influences or in a cataloguing of facts without significance. Thus Tate
criticizes esthetic theories, like that of Richards, which see in poetry
only a resource of emotive experience serving to order and organize
the impulses for action, or of Morris, who distinguishing on the
schematic level between the word as designation, that is as mere pragmatical means of determining behavior, and the word as denotation,
that is as addition of extrinsic particulars to a thing already noted,
destroys the unity of language as form of complete knowledge.

These false theories were born, according to Tate, of the historic
breach that in the romantic period opened between science and poetry.
It is then that one encounters the phenomenon of the poet who,
deprived of a true cognitive function, puts himself into competition
with science and pretends to compensate, with intensity of sentiment
and willed affirmation of the individual self, for the loss of the total
vision of reality. Out of this situation there arose, in criticism also,
upon the one hand the cold determinism of science and upon the
other the emotional and verbal impressionism which reflect the divided
and distorted conceptions of art characteristic of the modern era. What
then is the criterion for making use of poetry, if not for producing it,
something which is a secret of genius and of history, at least for judging it and distinguishing it? Good poetry, Tate answers, is that in
which the texture of the imagery is coherent, the meanings, however
multiple and ambiguous, can always be related to the central motive,
and every phrase can bear the strictest logical examination, without,
however, any possibility of the whole being resolved into pure thought.
Experience emotional and cognitive at the same time, great poetry—
says Tate—whether ancient or modern, requires for its understanding
the cooperation, on the part of the reader, of all his intellectual
energies.

These esthetic ideas, in many ways close to those of Blackmur, Empson, and Eliot, are amply illustrated in Tate's critical essays. Particularly important is that on Hart Crane, in which he sees the typical
example of the modern romantic poet, whose sensibility without center and without object, not succeeding in localizing itself in the external world, encloses him in pure sensation, or, if he desires to escape

from it, falls into sentimentalism and into chaos. In this essay, as in the others on Donne, Keats, Emily Dickinson, and Thomas Hardy, Tate sees the author, with exemplary historical insight, as an inseparable part of the spiritual experience of the civilization in which he lives. Considering this approach, it is easy to understand how the esthetic problem became for him therefore also a political, social, and religious problem.

Modern art is in crisis, because commercialism has destroyed the spiritual unity of man, reducing his life, depleted of all moral and religious purpose, to a mere system of economic relations. Hence the artist suffers today only more intensely from the same sickness that afflicts other men too. Like the people of Eliot's Waste Land, he is still surrounded with the grandeur of the past, but it is only a dead tradition, in which he does not share and which does not sustain him. Having lost faith in anything greater than himself he is in danger of being only "a cruel animal without a soul . . . a congeries of possibilities without order and aim."

An Introduction to the Poetry of Allen Tate

by ALFREDO RIZZARDI

translated by Glauco Cambon

> DUCHESS: Thou speak'st, as if I lay upon my death bed. Gasping for breath: do'st thou perceive me sicke?
> BOSOLA: Yes, and the more dangerously since thy sicknesse is insensible.
>
> John Webster, *The Duchess of Malfi*

Emerging from the exuberant literary climate of the first postwar period, Allen Tate's poetry has had to face the dizzy changes of perspective that took place in the last three decades. These changes mirror the modern writer's endeavor to throw light on his spiritual predicament in a world beset by the demonic dynamism of the atomic age. An unquestionable vitality marks Tate's poetry when we set it beside so much of the derivative elegiac production that sprouted from Eliot's *Waste Land* only to wither shortly after at the first change of weather. Tate's poetry endured—thanks to its incisive language, its structural rigor, and its seminal authenticity.

Confronted by the difficult, exacting poet, by the subtle essayist who seemed to some "the most speculative mind of New Criticism," by the passionate biographer, by the novelist versed in the most advanced narrative techniques, the critic sometimes would just point out the his-

EDITOR'S NOTE: Reprinted from *Ode ai Caduti Confederati e Altre Poesie*, trans. Alfredo Rizzardi (Milan: Arnoldo Mondadori, 1970), by permission of the publisher.

torical importance of Tate's literary contribution to the awakening of
a non-provincial Southern poetry. Other critics, sensing the deeper
import of his poetry, would go so far as to admit that Allen Tate had
introduced in American poetry a dramatic element of social and spiritual *desengaño,* through the ironic force of a language scarified by
cultural awareness. Only today, after such a crowded time, the value
of his poetical work shows fully, and his contribution to twentieth-
century poetry is understood in its cognitive and ethical implications.
For his writing hovers in an interstellar emptiness, between a very
remote world of aristocratic culture where the individual had fulfilled
the supreme ambition of making himself the spiritual legislator of
reality, and a closer yet equally (for the artist) unattainable world
where the machine is king and levels out of existence whatever proves
irreducible to the standards of industrial use in a Babelic civilization.

Tate's authentic note rings out from the permanent structures of
his ironic vision. His knife-sharp paradox cuts into our consciousness.
He has filled the emptiness with a real anguish, with a tension of
suffering which bespeaks a dramatic perception of life. Intellectual
bewilderment at a dehumanized world wore very thin, and actually
evaporated, in the cosmic poetry of the "Wastelanders," whose prophetic attitude degenerated into a mannered posture of "metaphysical" cast and wailing tone. In Allen Tate's poetry the bitter awareness
of a hopeless split between past and present finds such graphic expressions as this line (from "The Mediterranean"): We've cracked the
hemispheres with careless hand!" It always implies the concrete experience of a place, of a time, of a history. Like William Faulkner's fiction, Allen Tate's vision is linked to the myth and reality of the South.
It is the South that looms behind both writers' work: a motherland
harboring darkness and splendor, haunted by images of heroism and
human misery, obsessed by the tragedy of slavery and by the yearning
for a lost tradition of spiritual freedom.

This is where both the poet and the novelist have erected the best
stage for the performance of that disinherited and divided character,
contemporary man. With them, the violent contrasts stirring in every
image of that land, the dream of integrity and human richness which
hovers over a defeated scene, do not result in local color or regional
melodrama of the facile sort pursued by the folklore hunters whom
Fiedler calls "feminizing Faulknerians." The local conflicts, to be

traced historically as far back as America's colonial origins, foment the poet's vision of an essentially universal predicament, for they actually underlie in whatever variant shape the seared consciousness of modern man, torn as he is between loss of faith in an impossible order and longing for the felicities and security of the tradition that imperfectly embodied that order.

Accordingly, the more closely our poet's range is circumscribed by blood ties to a family world, the more clearly individual chronicle becomes spiritual history; private drama is transfigured into the mystery play of a modern Calvary where the individual appears crucified to the skyless scaffoldings of his knowledge. This is the image at the still center of the historical vision where our poet translates figures and lineaments of his land. This is his myth of the vanquished Aeneades who turn out to be the frustrated dreamers of a new civilization in a new world—a world described with a mixture of irony and despair, yet almost in the same words that the first chroniclers of Virginia used:

> . . . the tired land where tasseling corn,
> Fat beans, grapes sweeter than muscadine
> Rot on the vine . . .

The image reaches its exemplary neatness in the manifold vision of the "Ode to the Confederate Dead." The rich past of the land, linked to the great European tradition as transplanted overseas by a society vowed to the splendors of an aristocratic culture, echoes to the Ode's persona like the broken blare of the horn which from afar hits the ear of dying Roland. The man standing at the gate of the weatherbeaten Southern war cemetery, that shadowy figure imprisoned in his impotent solipsism, can only grasp sparse fragments of it, windborne, like dead leaves. He can momently delude himself that he is relating again to the past, he can endeavor to re-enter that abolished world, when mere physical cues evoke a phantom heroic shape:

> In a tangle of willows without light
> The singular screech-owl's tight
> Invisible lyric seeds the mind
> With the furious murmur of their chivalry

The spell also arises from the mere sound of battle names, in a masterly Homeric catalogue:

> Stonewall, Stonewall, and the sunken fields of hemp,
> Shiloh, Antietam, Malvern Hill, Bull Run

Thus, among painful starts, there takes shape the epic celebration of
a world dedicated to the defense of its ideals, to the bitter end. That
world remains unattainable, because the South's "agrarian" culture
has been stifled forever by the "industrial" North, and now: "All are
born Yankees of the race of men," as the poem "To the Lacedaemon-
ians" says, with a pejorative connotation not to be missed when the
word "Yankee" rings on Southern lips. But the persona alone is the
real object of the complex exploration of the past enacted by the
"Ode": a grotesque and suffering figure brooding before the crumbling
graves, a stranger to himself, surrounded by a landscape which piti-
lessly reflects the traits of his own spiritual barrenness. This man is
present in every poem, and even when he is not portrayed against the
background of his land he carries the bitter awareness of a situation in
which he is painfully caught, namely, the clash between the spiritual
plenitude of the past (which the poet defines as "unity of being") and
the fragmentary perception of an inert existence devoid of meaning:
"Without will, as chalky cliffs by the sea," as "Last Days of Alice" has
it—one of Tate's tensest and most outspoken pieces. The agony of a
culture is personified in what was once a creature of wonderful imagination and is now reduced to mere eyesight: pathetic in her over-
blown logical knowledge, an actual "incest of spirit," she "stares at
the drowsy cubes of human dust." In the last lines, against the image
which positivist science gives of human nature, the poet advocates the
return to an ampler and more vital vision, whatever the cost of tor-
menting doubts. He propounds, in other words, the recovery of a
Christian conception of life, with good and evil as firm orientation:

> We too back to the world shall never pass
> Through the shattered door, a dumb shade-harried crowd
> Being all infinite, function depth and mass
> Without figure, a mathematical shroud
>
> Hurled at the air—blessèd without sin!
> O God of our flesh, return us to Your wrath,
> Let us be evil could we enter in
> Your grace, and falter on the stony path!

This integral vision of life indeed confers a unique cognitive value on
Allen Tate's poetry; he himself has said that in its highest forms literature offers us the only "complete" version of our experience, and
therefore the most "responsible." It is a religious poetry, as Donald

Davidson has seen, but well beyond theological speculation and the death of feeling it causes, "for abstraction is the death of religion no less than the death of everything else"; well beyond a denominational limitation, though the poet does eventually accept Catholic dogma in whose fusion with Humanism he has long seen the salvation of civilization. In the essay "Religion and the Intellectuals," published in a *Partisan Review* symposium in the very year of his conversion (1950), Allen Tate stated that all his poems had sprung from the suffering engendered by the lack of faith. And this can be felt not just in the frequent recurrence of religious clues in dramatic monologues which recall Gerard Manley Hopkins and (even more) John Donne's Holy Sonnets ("The Twelve," "The Cross," "Sonnets at Christmas"), but in the continuous underlying relationship between physical perception and metaphysical vision. This relationship, which at times manifests itself in the ironic portrayal of the quotidian world, postulates the need for such a broad perspective as a scientific outlook will never grant. It may be a question of the unattainable unity which has been reduced to illusory echo, as happens in the "Ode to the Confederate Dead," but more often it will have to do with the physical form of the world and its mechanical vitality which the poet renders with expressionist violence, so much so that reality becomes unrecognizable and frightening, as in "The Wolves," "Winter Mask," "Shadow and Shade," "The Subway," "The Eye," "The Traveller," etc. Mankind presses against the bars of these poems as a modern bestiary; it is not hard to extract a catalogue of this kind from practically all of Tate's lyrics, especially from the "Seasons of the Soul," which can be considered one of his most taut and lucid poems, fit to rank with the best of twentieth-century American poetry, and on a par with the most inspired pages of William Butler Yeats and Paul Valéry. In the solitude of the world the individual finds himself walled in by anguish, unable to recognize or express himself, passive like a Dantesque soul in a hell of horrid and flimsy transparences, as in the visions of Hieronymus Bosch:

> Beyond the undertow
> The gray sea-foliage
> Transpires a phosphor glow
> Into the circular miles:
> In the centre of his cage
> The pacing animal

> Surveys the jungle cove
> And slicks his slithering wiles
> To turn the venereal awl
> In the livid wound of love.

The tragic unreality of existence jailed in its rational finitude is portrayed by resorting to the Platonic myth of the cave: an ironic device, of course, for the myths which helped our classical forefathers to pierce the barrier of death serve today only to decorate "a cornice on the Third National Bank" ("Retroduction to American History"), and present mankind may well boast of the void gaping behind his visual power, as the bitter, grotesque speech of a guest clarifies at the end of a dinner ("The meaning of death"): "We are the eyelids of defeated caves." A sense of closeness to death emerges from every composition; a quick analysis of language would show the frequency of nouns, modifiers, and verbs, which tells us we are here in the thick of the Dance of Death that has engaged Western art between the two world wars. And as a great seventeenth-century poet of comparable disposition, John Webster, had discovered, "we grow phantasticall in our death bed"—hallucinatory images possess the mind, push it away from the control of reason, into wide darknesses never surveyed by logical activity. A surreal world of instinctual terror, witness the lines from "The Meaning of Life":

> . . . subterranean
> As a black river full of eyeless fish
> Heavy with spawn . . .

which the poet approaches with the intellectual violence of his "fierce Latinity" and his Blakean visionary power, emerges at the center of that reality which resigned, workaday habit seemed to have tamed. The consciousness of death alone can give us back balance, wake us to the vanity of pride and to the inadequacy of our ideals. A Stoical attitude such as the persona of "Ode to the Confederate Dead" took fails to solve the problem, for it founders too in the hamstringing patterns of logical knowledge when death intervenes with its "strict gesture." And the poet's irony shows that no consolation can come either from the acceptance of quotidian routine, from that "warm water of a yawn" where catharsis stifles in the "Horatian Epode to the Duchess of Malfi":

> The streetcars are still running however
> And the katharsis fades in the warm water of a yawn.

Elsewhere, the stultifying effect of routine is denounced:

> There is a calm for you where men and women
> Unroll the chill precision of moving feet

The poem from which this excerpt was taken, "Death of Little Boys," is perhaps the tenderest to come from a poet who never surrenders to feeling unless filtered through intellectual awareness; but it is easy to sense in the rush of lines (Hopkinsian as they are in their rhythmic urge, and Dickinsonian in their exotically lucid imagery, witness the much discussed "cliff of Norway") wide symbolical resonances which poetry, "its own knower," has yielded on the page as a perfect cognitive experience.

Poetry is identified with an autonomous vehicle of knowledge, thanks to the "creative spirit" operating well beyond the boundaries of intellectual logic (a conception quite similar to Jacques Maritain's, who beautifully translated into French, with the help of his wife Raissa, the "Ode to the Confederate Dead"). The creative act is antiromantically upheld in the full light of consciousness by the interpenetration of thought and feeling which bespeaks the will to reproduce in language the emotional basis of ideas. Thus the poet turns with paramount interest to the instruments of his art, so that the fullness of his vision may be entrusted to the word. Allen Tate's is an elaborate poetry: the "Ode" reached its final draft after ten years. It is difficult, locked in a form impervious to paraphrase and translation. The poet himself may have pointed out his two main modes of composition by an analogy with life as such, in "The Meaning of Life":

> Think about it as will: there is that
> Which is the commentary; there's that other,
> Which may be called the immaculate
> Conception of its essence in itself.
> It is necessary to distinguish the weights
> Of the two methods lest the first smother
> The second, the second be speechless (without the first).

There are poems in a quasi-discursive mode, where the poet employs a line modeled on Eliot's dramatic monologue (of the Prufrock type), and there are others where traditional meter combines with a strongly elliptical language, compressing the syntactic structure to the point—at times—of impenetrability. The main difficulty in Allen Tate's

poetry is not due to the very numerous cultural and literary references, to the fragments of his past which betray his constant preoccupation with the problem of tradition: "Poetry does not dispense with
tradition; it probes the deficiencies of a tradition. But it must have a
tradition to probe. . . . The poet in the true sense 'criticizes' his tradition, either as such, or indirectly by comparing it with something
that is about to replace it; he does what the root-meaning of the verb
implies—he *discerns* its real elements and thus establishes its value,
by putting it to the test of experience." Whether well known or esoteric, the references are totally assimilated into the language and thus
reshaped as a unique experience, like any other in poetry. The difficulty of his lines inheres in the intellectual quality of Tate's symbolic
language, which does not merely register an emotion but claims for
poetry, as he himself has written, ". . . it is very hard for people to
apply their minds to poetry, since it is one of our assumptions that
come down from the early nineteenth century that our intellects are
for mathematics and science, our emotions for poetry. . . . So it is not
'modern' poetry which is difficult; it is rather a certain kind of poetry
as old, in English, as the sixteenth century, and, in Italian, much
older than that. It is a kind of poetry that requires of the reader the
fullest cooperation of all his intellectual resources, all his knowledge
of the world, and all the persistence and alertness that he now thinks
only of giving to scientific studies."

A child of his time, Allen Tate had to claim the resources of metaphysical poetry, the only kind to offer him a model of total application of the mind to poetry, both to react against the tired *fin de siècle*
Decadentism so widespread in the early twentieth century and to
shape the tools for exploring a world seemingly inaccessible to any
other "strategy." The poet lucidly stated this problem when he said:
"It is significant that at the present time we get, from both scientist
and pure poet, a renunciation of poetry because it cannot compete
with the current version of our objective world, a version that is pre-
empted by the demands of the will with its certified scientific statements." Actually by subsuming sensuous imagery and musical verse
to an intense realization of intellectual values, Tate places himself
on the opposite side of Symbolism and pure poetry. These are just a
portion of the experiences absorbed by his poetry, which in the last
resort, as Herbert Read has seen, flaunts a paradoxical union of

romantic with classical elements, the former implied by the very concept of "tension," the latter by the necessity of a formal rigor. As a matter of fact, even while sharing the thrill of discovering metaphysical poetry, Tate was never completely imprisoned by a poetics which mirrored a time-worn mechanism of sensibility. In his eyes, Metaphysical conception represents one extreme, with the other extreme supplied by a Romantic or Symbolist conception: one tends toward the other, in the urge to occupy all the possible intervening space in this range of tensions. His poetics, thanks to the awareness of a last alternative, marks a step beyond a strictly metaphysical conception. It aims at an ultimate fusion of "extensive" and "intensive" values of experience and language, in the median point, so hard to reach nowadays, which our poet illustrates with a few lines of Dante's, the model he has chosen in his recent work characterized by terza rima. This median point would be where the harmony of verse in the individual poem becomes one with the recaptured harmony of a vaster order.

On Allen Tate

by DENIS DONOGHUE

There is a moment in Allen Tate's novel, *The Fathers*, when the narrator, Lacy Buchan, says that people living in formal societies "lacking the historical imagination, can imagine for themselves only a timeless existence: they themselves never had any origin anywhere and they can have no end, but will go on forever." This is one of many places in the novel where the narrator's voice, convincing in its own resonance, is joined by another voice, Mr. Tate's, and the effect is a notable unison of feeling. The novel is not harmed; novelist and narrator are two, not one, and they rarely sink their difference: when they do, the words on the page mark a sense of life which is simultaneously personal and historical. In the authority of the words the individual feeling, remaining human, has purged itself of eccentricity, of everything merely personal. Lacy Buchan testifies to his own experience, but he does not rest his case upon the quirks and turns of his personality. He respects idiosyncrasy, not least his own, but he lets it take its chance against the grand critique of history and eventually of life itself. If a quirk does not survive, well and good, it has had its day. The question is one of feeling: the relation between individual feeling, history, and form. It is my impression that Mr. Tate's mind, like Lacy Buchan's, may be understood in this relation.

To begin with, Mr. Tate was born in Kentucky and he is an American with that inflection. Wallace Stevens said, reading John Crowe Ransom's poems, that there were even more Ransoms in Tennessee than Tates in Kentucky, and that Ransom's poems were composed

EDITOR'S NOTE: Reprinted from *The Spectator*, 16 January 1971, pp. 88–89, by permission of the author.

287

of Tennessee. The condition of being a Tate in Kentucky is the first theme of "The Swimmers"; a theme as sturdy as, in *The Fathers*, the conditions of being a Buchan in Virginia. Mr. Tate has always spoken the speech of his place, and he has been sharp with those Yankee critics who, not content to see the defeated South at Appomattox, determined to complete the spectacle by seeing it in Hell. He has not forgotten "the immoderate past," or the moral heritage of "Shiloh, Antietam, Malvern Hill, Bull Run." But he is a man of letters, a scholar, a Southern gentleman. So the rhetorical tradition of the South brings him back beyond Fugitives and Agrarians to the ancient poets and rhetoricians. "The Mediterranean," the first and one of the finest poems in his collection, sends the spirit back to Virgil, Cicero, Longinus, as later poems invoke Dante's Christendom. Mr. Tate's history is "knowledge carried to the heart," and the civility of his style depends upon values brought from afar, tested by centuries of tribulation. Accustomed to historical defeat, he would scorn to win by virtuosity or personal stratagem. The Yankees won by such means, and look what happened. *The Fathers* was written, I believe, both to praise the Old South and to reveal that corruption in its source which made the New South inevitable. These are moral considerations, exacerbated by fact and history. So Mr. Tate has a subject, a theme, and a culture rich enough to sustain the meditation. Largely as a result of these possessions, he is also gifted with an answerable style.

As for the presence of form, completing the triad with history and feeling: it is enough if we take form as comprising poetry, fiction, and religion, making no priority in the sequence. Poetry is syntax, an executive relation among the parts; and prosody, the music of that relation; and diction, often making an impression of density and weight, marking the significance of the past, so far as it is acknowledged in the words. Religion is belief, ritual, worship, each a form of humility, an escape from the self. Mr. Tate has been a Catholic and, whatever his affiliation at this moment, he has Christendom in his veins. I think he has often envisaged a Rome greater than the pagan Rome or the Christian Rome, but compounded of both in their perfections. He would have his Christendom include much that the Christian Rome refuted or transcended: his translation of the *Pervigilium Veneris* speaks to me of such inclusions.

Such a great Rome would figure in Mr. Tate's mind like the imagined Rome celebrated by Henry James in *William Wetmore Story and His Friends*; where James contrasts Rome with London, Paris, and New York, to their disadvantage, "cities in which the spirit of the place has long since lost any advantage it may ever have practised over the spirit of the person." Mr. Tate has always wanted the spirit of the person, personal feeling, to live within the order of the greatest Romes one might conceive. Fiction speaks of that possibility, even while it shows disorder in the particular case; as in *The Fathers*, where George Posey is seen as "heightened vitality possessed by a man who knew no bounds."

The bounds which Mr. Tate knows are indicated by his essay on "the angelic imagination." Briefly, what he has in view is a possible harmony among the three classical faculties: feeling, will, and intellect. He describes a hypertrophy of the first as "the incapacity to represent the human condition in the central tradition of natural feeling." The second hypertrophy is "the thrust of the will beyond the human scale of action." The third is "the intellect moving in isolation from both love and the moral will, whereby it declares itself independent of the human situation in the quest of essential knowledge." That last adjective explains why such an imagination is described as angelic: it represents a claim upon essence without the mediation of existence, flesh, or history. Mr. Tate's text for all three forms of excess is Edgar Allan Poe, and it may be said that some of his most penetrating criticism arises from his engagement with "our cousin, Mr. Poe." The other imagination Mr. Tate calls "symbolic," and his text is Dante: it is a dramatic imagination "in the sense that its fullest image is an action in the shapes of this world: it does not reject, it includes: it sees not only with but through the natural world, to what may lie beyond it." To the symbolic imagination the world is a place of good and evil, "mandible world sharp as a broken tooth." In "Last Days of Alice" Mr. Tate writes:

> O God of our flesh, return us to Your wrath,
> Let us be evil could we enter in
> Your grace, and falter on the stony path.

The angelic imagination is Manichean or, in another idiom, abstract: what it refuses is direct engagement with image, discourse, person.

Mr. Tate's most sustained meditation on these matters is "The Hov-

ering Fly," a causerie on the imagination in its relation to the actual
world. The fly appears out of nowhere in the last scene of Dostoiev-
sky's *The Idiot*, settling upon the bed where Nastasya lies dead. I shall
not humiliate Mr. Tate's account of that great scene by paraphrasing
it—it is included in *Essays of Four Decades*—besides, it is one of the
grand occasions of modern criticism, and readers will want to have it
intact. I admire particularly its tact, its extraordinary power of implication, its style at once lofty and specific. Every reader of Mr. Tate's
criticism carries in his head certain passages which are so gorgeously
perceptive that they renew his faith in the relation between literature
and criticism. My own short list favours "Tension in Poetry," especially the pages in which Mr. Tate comments on a detail in the Paolo
and Francesca episode in the *Inferno*. These pages are included in
Essays of Four Decades, too, the best selection of Mr. Tate's criticism
because it is the largest.

The poems and the essays ought to be held together in the mind. I
came to the essays first, and for a long time I found the poems intrac-
table. Mr. Tate's sense of the relation between feeling, form, and history attends like a conscience upon the actual engagement with the
words of his poems. There is the bearing of one word upon another,
line by line, but there is also his response to the history of each word,
what it has had to bear. It is probably impossible to write with non-
chalance, given such a conscience. Mr. Tate's verses are rarely prepared to move freely, mostly they are restrained by his respect for the
awful history they inherit. Often the lines are so dense with history
that to move at all they need a push. The best poems are those in
which the push comes from a powerful feeling, and the words are not
intimidated by the ancestral burden they carry. I think of "The Mediterranean," "Causerie," "The Oath," "Mother and Son," "Ode to the
Confederate Dead," "Last Days of Alice," "The Meaning of Life," and
"The Cross."

There are some lovely moments in the *terza rima* of "The Swimmers," a poem of middle length which was planned, I think, as something longer still. I assume that the idea of a long poem appealed to
Mr. Tate as "conceit and motion to rehearse / Pastoral terrors of youth
still in the man, / Torsions of sleep, in emblematic verse / Rattling
like dice unless the verse shall scan / All chance away."

One collection of Mr. Tate's essays was called *The Man of Letters*

in the Modern World, and in two or three places the critic is willing
to speak of his work under this phrase: there is also an essay on "the
profession of letters in the South." It is clear that Mr. Tate's favourite
terms are deployed in that last essay, where he speaks of the relation
between a writer and his society. In his own behalf Mr. Tate speaks of
a code of manners, and of form, religion, family, land, class, Europe,
meaning especially England and France. The essay is perhaps the best
introduction to a body of work which seems to me, in its concern for
first and last things, heroic.

Allen Tate's Terzinas

by RADCLIFFE SQUIRES

It may well turn out that of Allen Tate's poems those which will
claim the greatest attention are those that today are the least read.
These include two poems written in 1952, "The Maimed Man"
and "The Swimmers," and one poem written in 1953, "The Buried
Lake." They must be approached from several different directions:
first, as logical developments in Tate's poetry as poetry; second, as
logical developments in Tate's thought; third, as a logical break on
Tate's part with certain aspects of T. S. Eliot's poetry.

The suggestion behind the phrase "logical developments in Tate's
poetry as poetry" is that a writer's poetry possesses a life of its own. It
may be affected by many externalities, yet it possesses a core immune
to influences. This is so because poetry exists in an alliance of rhythmic, imagistic, and linguistic forces. Any one or all of these powers

EDITOR'S NOTE: Reprinted from *Allen Tate: A Literary Biography* by Radcliffe Squires (Indianapolis: Bobbs-Merrill Co., 1971), pp. 197–214, by permission of the publisher.

can be magnetized by events or another poet's accomplishment, but
the alliance will adjust to a new balance, and the alliance will con-
tinue. Another reason that an individual's poetry has an autonomous
existence is that the compulsive images of a poet come from private
experience, and, even more importantly, that these images sometimes
beget, without extramural contact, further images by parthenogenesis.
To observe this process in operation we may ponder Tate's outburst of
creativity in 1942 and 1943, that culminated in "Seasons of the Soul,"
which in its phrase "make the eye secure" entreats a correction of
vision. This same fascination with the metaphoric eye continued in a
negative way in the poem "The Eye," written in 1947. In 1950 Tate
published in pamphlet form from the Cummington Press a poem,
"Two Conceits for the Eye to Sing, If Possible." The very title of this
poem suggests an aesthetic desperation. The poem itself is based
on parodic imitations of nursery rhymes—and nursery rhymes often
border on hysteria.

> Sing a song of 'sistence
>   Pocketfull of Eye

or

> Big, inside the tub,
>   Rubbed hey dub-a-dub,

and

> Mary quite contrary
> Light as a green fairy
> Dances, dances. Mary.

No disrespect to Tate is intended in saying that these formulations
are "fond and foolish." They are the kind of fatuity that is sometimes
necessary to move one's art to another plane. And Tate himself has not
thought enough of the poem to preserve it in later collections. The
point, however, is this: although the poem takes the image or symbol
of the eye—employed suggestively in the poems of 1942–1943, aus-
terely in "The Eye"—and reduces it momentarily to gibberish, two
significant extensions of the image emerge. First, the "eye" obtains a
ratiocinative twin (a "conceit") through a pun:

> When the I's were opened
>   They saw ne'er a thing . . .

Second, this poem, which is about the triumph of naturalism and science over humanity, terminates with the vision, quoted above, of Mary who is "green." To be brutal in paraphrase: the Mother of Christ is separated from the world of the positivist's eye and the egoistical "I," and in her greenness, growth, and life, she dwells only in an infantine world of mysterious doggerel. Now, in the poems of 1952 and 1953, the eye and the pastoral (green) world reassemble, but they do so seriously and importantly. All this is a way of saying that a poet must sometimes use up his failures before he can find his success. This development, at any rate, lay within the boundaries of the logic of Tate's poetry.

As to the second direction, the "logical developments in Tate's thought": we need to be able to weigh the effect of Jacques Maritain's views on Tate's own concepts. This is most difficult to do. Tate's ideas on religion and art were developed and similar to Maritain's before they met. One needs only to remark how early Tate had reacted against the secularity of twentieth-century neo-humanism to see that he and Maritain were intellectual allies. But doubtless Maritain stood as a confirming hero to Tate, and Maritain's book *The Dream of Descartes* (1944) gave support and vocabulary to him. This book, which was very fashionable reading after World War II, takes the position that Descartes, in giving form and direction to the rising rationalism, split man in two. Maritain speaks of Descartes as possessing "two precious truths—one that is old, the other new." The new is "the living truth of physico-mathematical science." The old is "that ancient truth, the Socratic and Christian precept: Go back into thyself and into the spiritual element which is within thee." Yet, according to Maritain, Descartes's famous solitude and introspection were not those of a man of prayer; the solitude and introspection served the creation of a cosmos, a very abstract one, within Descartes's intellect. It is a mechanical cosmos free from the senses. It accounts for what Maritain calls "the three great ruptures" of modern man: "the rupture of thought with being, [the rupture] of the movement of the soul toward wisdom, and [the rupture] of the human compound."

Tate incorporated some of this view in his incomparably fine essays on Edgar Allan Poe, "Our Cousin, Mr. Poe" (1949) and "The Angelic Imagination" (1951). Poe's "angelism" directs the creation of a world of absolute order, indeed of logic, but one which yields no true equivalent to the world as revealed by the senses. Poe's angelism is modern man's: "Poe as God sits silent in darkness. Here the movement of tragedy is reversed: there is no action. Man as angel becomes a demon who cannot initiate the first motion of love, and we can feel only compassion with his suffering, for it is potentially ours."

Against Poe's a-sensuous cosmogony in which Satan has triumphed over God—for it is the sin of intellectual pride Tate is talking about in "The Angelic Imagination"—Tate counterweighs the cosmos of Dante. In his great essay "The Symbolic Imagination" Tate's primary point is that Dante works from the common and sensual to the extraordinary and the suprasensual. Tate's word for it is not "suprasensual" but "anagogical," a word that appears frequently in the later essays, just as the word "failure" occurred frequently in the earlier essays. Indeed, the anagogical or mystical discovery became Tate's way of surmounting what he once thought to be inevitable failure. In his classes at Minnesota he taught that there are four levels to poetry, the historical, the substantive, the rhetorical, and the anagogical which gives us the spiritual meaning of a poem. The anagogical plane was forbidden to Poe, who in order to "discover" God can only become a god. The opposite, Tate came to believe, was true of Dante, who employs among his common analogies an analogy of mirrors, which allows him to *partake* of God rather than supplant him.

In these essays Tate is engrossed as always in the pursuit of wholeness, particularly the wholeness of the poet. Yet his concern has shifted from Eliot's "dissociation of sensibility," that split between feeling and intellect, to a dissociation of the self and outer nature. In 1964 Tate put it this way in "The Unliteral Imagination; Or I, Too, Dislike It": "But if we still find useful the idea of dissociation, I suggest that what was dissociated—whenever it may have been dissociated—was not thought from feeling, nor feeling from thought; what was dissociated was the external world which by analogy could become the interior world of the mind." The passage makes us think of "The Trout Map." It also contains the third direction, "a logical break on Tate's part with certain aspects of T. S. Eliot's poetry." It was a logical break because it was ordained by Tate's Catholicism.

We may put these directions together by considering his three late poems. "The Maimed Man," "The Swimmers," and "The Buried Lake" are autobiographical poems, constituting but three parts of one long poem. The original, though tentative, scheme was for nine parts, with "The Maimed Man" standing first. Later Tate altered the scheme to include only six poems, with "The Maimed Man" standing last. Other sections of the poem exist in various stages of completion, but they have not been published. We deal with the parts, then, not the whole. Just as the poems of 1942–1943 materialized through the medium of severe prosodic form, so these poems speak through the form most difficult to employ in English, *terza rima*. "The Swimmers" retells an experience from childhood; the other two poems also depend upon youthful experiences but they primarily develop from dreams or reveries reminiscent of the nightmare section of "Seasons of the Soul."

At the outset one may well ask why, if Tate wanted to bring into his poetry an external sensuous world after the model of Dante, he should attend to memories of childhood and the inner world of fantasy and dream. The place of childhood is obvious enough. The eye of the child is fierce and fresh. So we may see here that Tate's desire is like Wordsworth's desire to *see* in a visionary way. He wishes to recapture the poignancy of "fair seed time" when everything is seen as new, when nothing yet has lapsed into patterns. Hence in "The Swimmers" the voice goes forth crying in the deserts of middle age:

> O fountain, bosom source undying-dead
> Replenish me the spring of love and fear
>
> And give me back the eye that looked and fled
> When a thrush idling in the tulip tree
> Unwound the cold dream of the copperhead.

As to why Tate should have worked into these poems the irrational dream world, the answer must be more complex and less satisfactory. Childhood is held dumb and hidden (dead childhood is carried like the unborn child in the psyche) beneath adult consciousness except for times such as dream-states, when the terrors or fixations of the earlier state break forth. In this way the dream and the childhood experience are similar. We can find a stronger reason in a letter Tate wrote to Wallace Stevens on December 7, 1949:

I have been reading your ten new poems ["Things of August"] in *Poetry,* and I am very much moved by two of them. This is a letter to myself which you have picked up from the floor and read because it is about your poems. I take these two poems very much to myself as the occasion of stating certain differences from the work of an older contemporary whom I admire and have learned from. The poems are numbers 2 and 3. To attempt to formulate differences is to try to keep on learning.

When I was young I admired "Sunday Morning" more than any other poem of our time; and I still do, for what it taught me, and for its own magnificence. But I knew then that what you were doing was not for me: I could never reach it. The *angelisme* of the intelligence which defines "horizons that neither love nor hate" I could *believe* in as a human possibility but I could not possess it, or live inside it. It is perhaps a little presumptuous of me to take these two poems of yours as a profound insight, accidentally reached, into my own special limitations; if so, you will accept my apology. The "air within a grave or down a well" is almost the inevitable air for the man of our time who cannot be, like the woman in "Sunday Morning," alone in the world with the "thought of heaven."

That is my message to myself. The man who breathes the air of the well cannot breathe purer air unless it be the air of revelation: the angelic intellect is not within his reach. What I have learned, then, from these two poems is a new way of putting a dilemma of our time— and it my be *the* dilemma: either the revealed access to the world or the angelic mind looking down upon it.

Quite naturally, Tate, who in "Seasons of the Soul" had written "I was down a well," would be arrested by Stevens's phrase. More significantly, one can see that for Tate the avoidance of *angelisme* (in the sense Maritain uses the word, not quite in the sense Stevens uses it in his essays) derived from his looking out from his "well," his Plato's cave, his mind, rather than gazing gigantically down like Poe's Satan. In other words, Tate approaches vision through the self's confined space rather than the universe's isotropic vistas.

"The Maimed Man" is locally confined to the very common space of a street and a vacant lot. Nevertheless, it begins with an invocation to "didactic Laurel," who is asked to "assert your blade / Against the Morning Star, enlightening Thief / Of that first Mother who returned the Maid." The invocation cuts the human universe into three parts, that of the Laurel, that of the Morning Star, and that of the myrtle. The Laurel, sacred to Apollo, evokes a poetry located in reason; the myrtle, sacred to Aphrodite, evokes Pandemic love. Exactly what association of the Morning Star is intended cannot be so surely asserted, for the Morning Star can be a number of planets. But because of the reference to the "enlightening thief," one supposes with R. K. Meiners that the reference is to the planet Mercury, hence to Hermes. It is Hermes who is the son of Maia, which means "mother," and he does return Persephone to Demeter. In the Homeric "Hymn to Demeter," the goddesses Demeter and Kore (Persephone) are referred to as the "Mother" and the "Maid." Hence, the beginning of the poem sets Apollonian reason against passion and Hermetic knowledge. The associations of Hermes as the archetypal thief, the god who conducts shades to the underworld, as well as the scientist god of alchemy, emerge wittily and ultimately associate Hermes, through the one word "enlightening," with Cartesian Enlightenment.

> . . . because I am afraid
> Of him who says I have no need to fear,
> Return, Laurel!

The fear is of the scientifically "explained" universe. The poet continues then to sue for the help of Apollonian Laurel because the world of sense has failed him and he can no longer feel. His tear is "metal." Hence, his poetry must be realized through form and tradition.

After the invocation the poem veers suddenly to a scene, represented as a memory, where the poet walking in sunlight sees a young man who is headless and whose feet are bluegrass. The grotesque encounter reminds one of Shelley's encounter with Rousseau, ruined and gnarled like a tree root, in the beginning of "The Triumph of Life"—a poem that like Tate's is also Dantean. One suspects that the headless figure is based, like part II of "Seasons of the Soul," upon a recurrent dream. There is no evidence for the suspicion, but the suspicion is intensified by a late chapter in Caroline Gordon's novel *The Malefactors*. Here the hero dreams of pursuing two figures who hurl themselves over a precipice. He looks down to see that they are headless. He is prevented from following them by his father, who also threatens in the dream to remove his head. A bit later we discover that the abyss is in a cave entered by pushing aside a growth of laurel. It is perhaps of significance also that one of the headless figures in the dream is Horne Watts, who is obviously modeled on Hart Crane. Finally, in this context two lines are quoted from Tate's early poem "Homily" (1922):

> Tear out the close vermiculate crease
> Where death crawled angrily at bay.

All of this may be only coincidence, or, if it has any basis in fact, it may have been altered beyond relevance by the exigencies of fiction. In Tate's poem the headless and footless figure is offered as a premonitory symbol of a life without reason and a life—so one takes these bluegrass feet—incapable of movement, hence incapable of moral action. The speaker then observes that he ought to join his own head and feet with the maimed man's body by putting them together in the grave. But he goes on to ask how he could "know this friend without reproach." That very question is the one he says he will be asking "in the poor boy's curse, / Witching for water in a waste of shame." The reference to Shakespeare's sonnet reminds us that one pays for waste of shame by an "expense of spirit." Nevertheless, to these "pastoral terrors of youth, still in the man," Tate promises to devote "emblematic verse / Rattling like dice unless the verse shall scan / All chance away." The rest of the poem will not yield to paraphrase:

> Meanwhile the scarecrow, man all coat and stem,
>   Neither dead nor living, never in this world—
>   In what worlds, or in what has essenced them,
> I did not know until one day I whirled
>   Towards a suggesting presence in my room
>   And saw in the waving mirror (glass swirled
> By old blowers) a black trunk without bloom—
>   Body that once had moved my face and feet.
>   My secret was his father, I his tomb.
> (By *I* I mean iambics willed and neat;
>   I mean by *I* God's image made uncouth;
>   By eye I mean the busy, lurked, discrete
> Mandible world sharp as a broken tooth.)
>   And then rose in the man a small half-hell
>   Where love disordered, shade of pompous youth,
> Clutched shades forbearing in a family well;
>   Where the sleek senses of the simple child
>   Came back to rack spirit that could not tell
> Natural time: the eyes, recauled, enisled
>   In the dreamt cave by shadow womb of beam,
>   Had played swimmer of night—the moist and mild!
> Now take him, Virgin Muse, up the deeper stream:
>   As a lost bee returning to the hive,
>   Cell after honeyed cell of sounding dream—
> Swimmer of noonday, lean for the perfect dive
>   To the dead Mother's face, whose subtile down
>   You had not seen take amber light alive.

This is a parade of earlier poetic materials. The "shades forbearing in a family well" recalls "Sonnets of the Blood" and, more obviously, part II of "Seasons of the Soul." The play on the word "I" recalls "The Eye" and "Two Conceits for the Eye to Sing, If Possible." But the poem also looks forward to "The Swimmers" in the icon of the embryo-child whose senses shame the mature man who has lost the natural world. To this child beneath the skin the poet at the end turns. And the ending of "The Maimed Man" is as sublime poetry as the century has produced. Unfortunately, the rest of the poem does not come up to it. The puns and colloquialisms are embarrassingly embedded in the graver matrix of the poem. Some of the passages are incomprehensible; some are clumsy. And the end gives no certitude that the invocation to Apollonian reason at the beginning squares with the emphasis on "the sleek senses" at the end. It should square, for Tate had come to believe that true reason required tutoring by the senses. But the philosophic conviction behind a poem is a different matter from its demonstration. Although "The Maimed Man" was published in *The Partisan Review* in 1952, Tate did not choose to include it in *Poems* (1960). The two poems that followed "The Maimed Man" belong with his best.

"The Swimmers" did exactly what Tate hoped it would. The *terza rima* worked perfectly. The imagery presented thematic epiphanies. Furthermore, the poem is so lucid that any extended "interpretation" would constitute an insult. "The Swimmers" retells, with only a few facts altered, the experience Tate had of seeing when he was eleven the body of a lynched Negro dragged into the town of Mount Sterling, Kentucky. The lynching was not the standard "rape-case." The Negro had murdered his landlord after an altercation, but Tate does not specify any background to the lynching, for he wants the drama to remain a universal agony upon which he can affix his personal yet conforming specifics. There are visible specifics—even the names of his playmates are given. He goes so far as to make a joke at his own expense. His memory of his parents' apprehension that he suffered from hydrocephalus appears in his reference to "Tate, with water on the brain." A compound joke, philosophical, religious, as well as biographical.

The ending of "The Swimmers" is true to the important fact of the incident—the town never admitted to itself that the lynching had occurred:

> My breath crackled the dead air like a shotgun
> As, sheriff and the stranger disappearing,
> The faceless head lay still. I could not run

> Or walk, but stood. Alone in the public clearing
> This private thing was owned by all the town,
> Though never claimed by us within my hearing.

Unimportant facts were changed for dramatic purposes. Tate did not, as in the poem, follow the sheriff back into town, but cut through the fields and beat him into town. Nor, in the actual incident, did Tate's companions desert him. But the solitariness of the boy who followed the "cloudy hearse" was necessary to the full impact of the Jesus-Christers' ritual sacrifice of the Negro. The town itself had to be rendered as nearly deserted as possible so as to tune to a blinding sharpness the focus upon all humanity's desolation in evil. In that desolation we perceive that the evil must be "owned."

Robert Lowell wrote to Tate to say that "The Swimmers" was the best poem Allen had ever done, the finest *terza rima* in English. He found it better even than Shelley's use of the form. Yet Lowell was less sanguine about Tate's next poem, "The Buried Lake." He found the sound of it like "choking." And he objected to its similarities with "Seasons of the Soul," its "Allenisms" and contorted phrasing. In contrast, W. H. Auden wrote that he thought "The Buried Lake" might well be Tate's best single poem. Let Lowell and Auden both be right. "The Swimmers" is Tate's most nearly perfect poem. "The Buried Lake" is his richest.

It will be remembered that "The Maimed Man" begins with an invocation to the "didactic laurel," while "The Swimmers" begins with an invocation to the hypersensitivity of childhood. "The Buried Lake" trundles a vulgate epigraph from the Apocrypha: *"Ego mater pulchrae dilectionis, et timoris, et agnitionis, et sanctae spei."* ("I, mother of rare beauty, fear, knowledge, and divine hope.") This mother, as versatile as Robert Graves's White Goddess, serves to draw us into the invocation which this time is addressed to the lady of light or Santa Lucia. As others have pointed out, among this saint's virtues is her power to cure blindness—at once we understand her presence. She has been waiting for years for Tate to come to her with his optical problems. These words are not intended to be flippant. The poem, all

one hundred and twenty lines, is about a cure of the vision. The cure
requires an approach, a way, to Santa Lucia:

> The Way and the way back are long and rough
> Where Myrtle twines with Laurel . . .

And so the Heraclitean *odos* trodden by Eliot in the *Four Quartets*
combines here with the elements of laurel and myrtle which were kept
separate in "The Maimed Man." This twining of love and reason,
which is the cure for the failing vision, takes us for a time down in a
dream trance below the play and terrific babble of childhood toward
the buried lake of—shall we say—memory; we could say "salvation."
Finally, the poet enters a "pinched hotel" where a dog, like Cerberus,
welcomes him with "a sickly cark." Suddenly it is not really a hotel he
has entered. It is a deserted music room with benches ranged along the
walls. We are then informed that he exults in a secret plan: he has
come there to play his violin.

> I laid my top hat to one side; my chin
>   Was ready, I unsnapped the lyric case;
>   I had come there to play my violin.
>
> Erect and sinuous as Valence lace
>   Old ladies wore, the bow began to fill
>   The shining box—whence came a dreaming face,
>
> Small dancing girl who gave the smell of dill
>   In pelts of mordents on a minor third
>   From my cadenza for the Devil's Trill.
>
> No, no! her quick hand said in a soft surd.
>   She locked the fiddle up and was not there.
>   I mourned the death of youth without a word.

We can pinpoint one memory to which the poem has returned. Between October, 1916, and April, 1917, Tate studied violin at the Cin-
cinnati Conservatory of Music. At a student recital he played for his
teacher, Eugène Ysaÿe, Tartini's "Devil's Trill Sonata." Ysaÿe compli-
mented him on his left hand but said he had no talent for music. At
this time Tate abandoned his aspirations to a musical career. It would
seem, therefore, that the episode records a blighted hope. If this is so,
the dancing girl is not to be taken as a girl Tate knew, but only as the
face that appears in the sheen of the violin. Come to think of it, the

resin applied to violin bows smells, as does this girl, like dill. With
this failure, just as Tate returned to academic studies after giving up
music, the poet must seek for another, more capable existence, asking
if he could "go where air was not dead air." He is met, however, by
the enemy:

> And could I go where air was not dead air?
>   My friend Jack Locke, scholar and gentleman,
>   Gazed down upon me with a friendly glare,
>
> Flicking his nose as if about to scan
>   My verse; he plucked from his moustache one hair
>   Letting it fall like gravel in a pan . . .

Surely John Locke is really Descartes or Hermes. And how very nicely
Tate depicts his own exclusion from the world of "enlightenment" in
the ironic picture of the hair falling like gravel into one pan of the
scales. And how much this John Locke is like Zeus, who is fond of
weighing the fates of heroes in the scale pan. The encounter with John
Locke dramatizes another failure, this time a failure not of art but of
one of art's antipodes, the positivist's rationalism.

Then the poet sinks deeper into his dream, and a lost love comes to
him. She has come back to give him "all," she says. But as he reaches
her, her head becomes "another's searching skull whose drying teeth /
Crumbled me all night long and I was dead":

> Down, down below the wave that turned me round,
>   Head downwards where the Head of God had sped
>
> On the third day; where nature had unwound
>   And ravelled her green that she had softly laved—
>   The green reviving spray now slowly drowned
>
> Me, since the shuttling eye would not be saved.

The conception of the Head of God speeding down is very strange.
Literally it refers to the legend of Christ's going down to harrow hell
after His resurrection on the third day. But the image exceeds its literal basis. Perhaps it was originally intended to mate with the line in
"The Maimed Man" where we find "I mean by *I* God's image made
uncouth." It is also possible that Tate is thinking of one of Thomas
Hardy's poems he had admired for a long time, "Nature's Questioning,"
from which he quotes the following lines with approval:

> Or come we from an Automaton
>   Unconscious of our pains?
>   Or are we live remains
> Of Godhead dying downwards, brain and eye now gone?

In a final estimate, we need neither "The Maimed Man" nor Thomas Hardy. God has disappeared into a pastoral world that has become hidden under a covering of Cartesian science. That insight is William Blake's rather than Hardy's. Indeed, the image of the Head of God speeding down toward hell has much in common with the spatial energies of Blake's graphic art.

In any case the image takes us as deep as we can go into hell. Then from the dark night of the senses the dream begins to rise. And it seems significant that the poet must rehearse his own and history's failures, must go down to the ultimate dark of the self before he can bend his knees and receive the benison of Santa Lucia. He receives this benison or awareness exactly in the way that Tate observes that Dante receives his awareness—that is, through a mirror symbol. In his essay "The Symbolic Imagination" Tate quotes from the beginning of *Paradiso* XXVIII and comments as follows: "Beatrice's eyes are a mirror in which is reflected that 'sharp point,' to which Dante, still at a distance from it, now turns his direct gaze. As he looks at it he sees for the first time what its reflection in Beatrice's eyes could not convey: that it is the sensible world turned inside out. For the sensible world as well as her eyes is only a reflection of the light from the sharp point. Now he is looking at the thing-in-itself. *He has at last turned away from the mirror which is the world.*" Tate has further commentary upon the mirror symbol and Beatrice's laboratory demonstration of the symbol, but this much is sufficient to relate the poem with the essay. Once the poet's vision is corrected, "The Buried Lake" moves toward restorations of the sensuous world, promising that "all the sad eclogue . . . will soon be merry." The final lines are entirely beautiful:

> [I] knew that nature could not more refine
>   What it had given in a looking-glass
>   And held there, after the living body's line
>
> Has moved wherever it must move—wild grass
>   Inching the earth; and the quicksilver art
>   Throws back the invisible but lightning mass

To inhabit the room; for I have seen it part
The palpable air, the air close up above
And under you, light Lucy, light of heart—

Light choir upon my shoulder, speaking Dove,
The dream is over and the dark expired.
I knew that I had known enduring love.

With these confident lines Tate's published poetry ceases. Looking at the three late poems one sees that they belong to a pattern repeated throughout Tate's career. It is a pattern in which we are conscious of a ratio of relative failures to relative successes. "The Maimed Man," fine as it is in places, fragments, and the macabre elements will not stay with the rational. "The Buried Lake" *vibrates* continuously but does not *move* very far. "The Swimmers," perfectly attuned to Dante's form, moves through its journey-encounters and stands at last, as all fine poetry does, not as a set of symbols, but as an action which is *in toto* symbolic. Now, this same ratio may be observed in the summits of all of Tate's poetry. "Ode to the Confederate Dead" emerges from a context of several inferior poems that are thematically similar. "The Mediterranean" rises above the lesser poem "Aeneas at Washington"; "Seasons of the Soul" issues from the lesser poem "Winter Mask." But that is only part of the pattern. It remains to be observed that all of these poems are concerned with integrity or its absence. The visitor to the Confederate graveyard is locked in his sensibility; the picnicker at the Mediterranean cove has exchanged the telic search of Aeneas for a search for those spiritual roots which will give him a sense of wholeness; the man who looks at World War II and perceives that the world is a dead land, perceives also that the world could be restored by love—although he is not sure that love can be found; the man who sinks into the buried lake of the self is self-baptized, and his pastoral vision is restored. Tate was right, then, when he told his friends that he was always writing only one poem. But there are peaks in the one poem and these peaks obtained with the most severe effort throughout his career are the poems which make him one of the masters of a varied and brilliant epoch. But even if his superior poems had not come, he would still be an important poet, for we should have "Death of Little Boys" instead of "Ode to the Confederate Dead." We should have "The Buried Lake" instead of "The Swimmers." And we should pay them homage as examples of a poetry that strained, indeed wrenched, the language with bitter zeal. We should see, moreover, that that zeal was one that sprang from a refusal to tolerate falseness either in the self or in man in general. Tate's language is of that kind which wells forth when the poet presses with all his force for a victory which he knows he will not obtain.

Because he has been unable to lie to us about victory, his poems have never been very popular. For popular poetry is the kind that encourages people who are not poets to believe that they are. Tate's poetry cannot have that effect. But the effect it can and does have is that of reminding us that the heroic, the saintly act is a subjective, even a hidden, act of such private intensity that its public implementation is only an inevitable step, not a greater step. In this way Tate is entirely different from T. S. Eliot, whom he resembles in such obvious but superficial ways that some critics stopped digging for the treasure when they found a few coins in the topsoil. Eliot's poetry has no *private* morality. His figures are either public saints or paralyzed puppets, just as his cats are either practical or dead. But it is by reason of this very difference that Tate in his later poetry could achieve an optimism that never came to Eliot. One can after all save what can be saved if he does not try to save what cannot be saved.

A question remains as to why Tate has not finished or at least has not published the rest of the long poem of which "The Maimed Man," "The Swimmers," and "The Buried Lake" are parts. If the question cannot be answered it can be surrounded. It is noteworthy that "The Buried Lake" was written just at a time when the whole life of poetry underwent one of its periodic changes. "The Buried Lake," like Eliot's *Four Quartets* and Stevens's *Auroras of Autumn,* belongs in a category of poetry which brings a literary movement to an end. Though they are not weary poems, they are not poems written with either the bravura of beginnings or the impudence of revolt. "The Buried Lake" incorporates most of the devices of the great modernist period, all the effort at "concreteness," which as it becomes formula threatens to become abstraction; all the subtleties of symbol, which as it becomes décor threatens to become obvious. These and other devices of Modernism come up like slow, beautiful bubbles in the viscous element of "The Buried Lake." Yet "The Buried Lake" is a marvelous poem. After all, it takes as high a talent to finish an age as to begin one. But the phrase "to finish" applies only to "The Buried Lake." It does not apply to "The Swimmers," which contains so much organic life that it could be carbon-dated every day for the next century, and the reading would always come back: "Born today."

"The Buried Lake" appeared just as a new poetry began to rise in America. This new poetry's obsessions with oratory, romantic gesture, and exhibitionism have for nearly two decades altered the way poetry works in the modern world. Even some of Tate's friends shifted eventually toward the new mode, among them Robert Penn Warren, Robert Lowell, and John Berryman. Tate knew that this change had occurred sooner than the proponents of the new poetry did, for he wrote in 1955 to Brewster Ghiselin: "The long poem I am doing (at intervals) *is* difficult, and I fear that even when it's done—if it ever is—it will make little headway with even the 'literary' people. The drift today is all against this sort of thing." But would this knowledge keep Tate from completing his poem? Probably not. It is only part of the picture. In any case Tate has continued to work over other sections of the poem. As late as 1964, with his grandson for company, he made an automobile trip through Kentucky, visiting places he had not seen for forty years in order to acquire confidence in what he was writing.

It may be that Tate will publish the rest of the long poem soon and thereby render these words obsolete. That is an antiquation devoutly to be wished for. For one may be sure that new poems will not be given to the world until Tate is certain that the world is where they belong. It is because of this scrupulousness that one can say of Allen Tate, who has not been a prolific poet, what Dryden said of a very prolific poet: "Here is God's plenty."

BIBLIOGRAPHY

The Works of Allen Tate

BOOKS

The Golden Mean and Other Poems. With Ridley Wills. N.p., 1923.
  CONTENTS: "The Golden Mean"; "The Chaste Land (Continued)"; "Empathy"; "Tatian Episode to a Probable Duke of Malfi"; "Impatience"; "In Defense of Suicide"; "To the Classicists"; "To Ridley Wills: Stanzas Written in Circumspection"; "Tercets of the Triad"; "Oum"; "Tribrachs" (with Wills).
Fugitives: An Anthology of Verse. New York: Harcourt, Brace & Company, 1928.
  CONTENTS: "Ignis Fatuus"; "To a Romanticist"; "Mr. Pope"; "Death of Little Boys"; "Obituary"; "Idiot"; "Procession"; "Ode to the Confederate Dead"; "Causerie II."
Mr. Pope and Other Poems. New York: Minton, Balch & Company, 1928.
  CONTENTS: "Mr. Pope"; "Death of Little Boys"; "Idiot"; "Obituary"; "Long Fingers"; "Ditty"; "The Subway"; "Procession"; "Light"; "Resurgam"; "Shrine"; "Prayer to the Woman Mountain"; "Homily"; "A Pauper"; "Horation Epode to the Duchess of Malfi"; "Hitch Your Wagon to a Star"; "For a Dead Citizen"; "Touselled"; "Pastoral"; "Credo"; "Retroduction to American History"; "Ode to the Confederate Dead"; "Epistle"; "Sonnet to Beauty"; "The Screen"; "Reflections in an Old House"; "To a Romanticist"; "Art"; "The Progress of Œnia" (I. "Madrigale"; II. "In Wintertime"; III. "Vigil"; IV. "Divagation"; V. "Epilogue to Œnia"); "Translations" (I. "Correspondences" [Baudelaire]; II. "Farewell to Anactoria" [Sappho]); "Ignis Fatuus: *Epilogue.*"
Stonewall Jackson, the Good Soldier: A Narrative. (Biography.) New York: Minton, Balch & Company, 1928; London: Cassell & Co., Ltd., 1930; Ann Arbor Paperbacks, 1957.
Jefferson Davis, His Rise and Fall: A Biographical Narrative. (Biography.) New York: Minton, Balch & Company, 1929.
Three Poems: "Ode to the Confederate Dead," being the revised and final version of a poem previously published on several occasions; to which are added "Message from Abroad" and "The Cross." New York: Minton, Balch & Company, 1930.
I'll Take My Stand: The South and the Agrarian Tradition. By Twelve Southerners. New York and London: Harper and Bros., 1930.
  CONTENTS: "Remarks on the Southern Religion," pp. 155–75.
Poems: 1928–1931. New York: Charles Scribner's Sons, 1932; London: Charles Scribner's Sons, Ltd., 1932.
  CONTENTS: "Ignis Fatuus"; "Ode to Fear"; "The Traveller"; "The Cross"; "The Twelve"; "The Eagle"; "Last Days of Alice"; "Inside and Outside" (I. "Now twenty-four or maybe twenty-five"; II. "There is not anything to say to those");

"The Oath"; "The Paradigm"; "The Wolves"; "Emblems" (I. "Maryland Virginia Caroline"; II. "When it is all over and the blood"; III. "By the great river the forefathers to beguile"); "Records" (I. "A Dream"; II. "A Vision"); "Causerie"; "Message from Abroad" (I. "What years of the other times, what centuries"; II. "Wanderers to the east, wanderers west"; III. "I cannot see you"); "Elegy"; "Mother and Son"; "Sonnets of the Blood" (I. "What is this flesh and blood compounded of"; II. "Near to me as my flesh my flesh and blood"; III. "My brother you would never think me vain"; IV. "The times have changed, there is not left to us"; V. "These generations that have sealed your heart"; VI. "Our elder brother whom I had not seen"; VII. "The fire I praise was once perduring flame"; VIII. "This message hastens, lest we both go down"; IX. "Not power nor the storied hand of God"; X. "Captains of industry, your aimless power"); "Ode to the Confederate Dead."

Reactionary Essays on Poetry and Ideas. New York: Charles Scribner's Sons, 1936; London: Charles Scribner's Sons, Ltd., 1936; Ann Arbor Paperbacks, 1959.
    CONTENTS: "Four American Poets" (I. "Emily Dickinson"; II. "Hart Crane"; III. "Ezra Pound"; IV. "John Peale Bishop"); "A Note on Donne"; "A Note on Elizabethan Satire"; "Three Types of Poetry"; "Humanism and Naturalism"; "The Profession of Letters in the South"; "Religion and the Old South"; "Reviews"; "Edwin Arlington Robinson"; "MacLeish's *Conquistador*"; "T. S. Eliot"; "Edna St. Vincent Millay"; "E. E. Cummings."

The Mediterranean and Other Poems. New York: The Alcestis Press, 1936; twelve copies privately printed in 1936 exclusively for Benjamin Ethan Tate, designed and printed by Leu Ney with incunabula type set by hand.
    CONTENTS: "The Mediterranean"; "Aeneas at Washington"; "Sonnets at Christmas" (I. "This is the day His hour of life draws near"; II. "Ah, Christ, I love you rings to the wild sky"); "To the Romantic Traditionists"; "Fragment of a Meditation"; "Pastoral"; "Shadow and Shade"; "The Meaning of Life"; "The Meaning of Death"; "The Ancestors"; "To the Lacedemonians"; "The Anabasis"; "The Robber Bridegroom"; "Unnatural Love"; "The Ivory Tower."

Who Owns America?: A New Declaration of Independence. (Essays.) Ed. Herbert Agar and Allen Tate. Boston: Houghton Mifflin Co., 1936; Cambridge, Mass.: The Riverside Press, 1936.

Selected Poems. New York: Charles Scribner's Sons, 1937; London: Charles Scribner's Sons, Ltd., 1937.
    CONTENTS: "The Mediterranean"; "Aeneas at Washington"; "To the Lacedemonians"; "Message from Abroad" (I. "What years of the other times, what centuries"; II. "Wanderers to the east, wanderers west"; III. "I cannot see you"); "Idiot"; "To the Romantic Traditionists"; "Elegy"; "Ode to the Confederate Dead"; "Horation Epode to the Duchess of Malfi"; "Retroduction to American History"; "Causerie"; "Fragment of a Meditation"; "The Cross"; "The Twelve"; "Sonnets at Christmas" (I. "This is the day His hour of life draws near"; II. "Ah. Christ, I love you rings to the wild sky"); "Ode to Fear"; "The Ancestors"; "The Traveller"; "The Oath"; "Ditty"; "The Wolves"; "The Subway"; "Shadow and Shade"; "Pastoral"; "The Paradigm"; "The Robber Bridegroom"; "To a Romantic"; "Unnatural Love"; "Last Days of Alice"; "The Eagle"; "Epistle to Edmund Wilson"; "The Meaning of Life"; "The Meaning of Death"; "Inside and Outside" (I. "Now twenty-four or maybe twenty-five"; II. "There is not anything to say to those"); "Death of Little Boys"; "The Anabasis"; "Mr. Pope"; "Procession"; "Mother and Son"; "A Pauper"; "Obituary"; "Sonnets of the Blood" (I. "What is the flesh and blood compounded of"; II. "Near to me as perfection in the blood"; III. "Then, brother, you would never think me vain"; IV. "The times have changed. Why do you make a fuss"; V. "Our elder brother whom we had not seen"; VI. "The fire I praise was once perduring flame—"; VII. "This message

hastens lest we both go down"; VIII. "Not power nor the storied hand of God"; IX. "Captains of industry, your aimless power"); "Emblems" (I. "Maryland Virginia Caroline"; II. "When it is all over and the blood"; III. "By the great river the forefathers to beguile"); "Records" (I. "A Dream"; II. "A Vision"); "Ignis Fatuus."

America through the Essay: An Anthropology for English Courses. (Textbook.) By A. Theodore Johnson and Allen Tate. New York: Oxford University Press, 1938.

The Fathers. (Novel.) New York: G. P. Putnam's Sons, 1938; London: Eyre and Spottiswoode, Ltd., 1939; Denver: Alan Swallow, 1960, with an introduction by Arthur Mizener; London: Eyre and Spottiswoode, Ltd., 1960, with an introduction by Arthur Mizener. London: Penguin Books, 1969.

Reason in Madness: Critical Essays. New York: G. P. Putnam's Sons, 1941.
CONTENTS: "The Present Function of Criticism"; "Literature as Knowledge"; "Tension in Poetry"; "Understanding Modern Poetry"; "Miss Emily and the Bibliographer"; "Hardy's Philosophic Metaphors"; "Narcissus as Narcissus"; "Procrustes and the Poets"; "Nine Poets: 1937"; "The Function of the Critical Quarterly"; "Liberalism and Tradition"; "What Is a Traditional Society?"

Invitation to Learning. By Huntington Cairns, Allen Tate, and Mark Van Doren. New York: Random House, 1941.

Sonnets at Christmas. Cummington, Mass.: Cummington Press, 1941.
CONTENTS: "This is the day His hour of life draws near"; "Ah, Christ, I love you rings to the wild sky."

The Language of Poetry. By Philip Wheelwright, Cleanth Brooks, I. A. Richards, and Wallace Stevens. Ed. Allen Tate. Princeton: Princeton University Press, 1942; New York: Russell & Russell, 1960.

Princeton Verse between Two Wars: An Anthology. Ed. Allen Tate. Princeton: Princeton University Press, 1942.

American Harvest: Twenty Years of Creative Writing in the United States. (Anthology.) Ed. Allen Tate and John Peale Bishop. New York: L. B. Fischer, 1942; Garden City, N.Y.: Garden City Publishing Co., 1943.

Recent American Poetry and Poetic Criticism: A Selected List of References. (A checklist.) Compiled by Allen Tate. Washington, D.C.: Library of Congress, 1943.

The Vigil of Venus: Pervigilium Veneris. The Latin text with an introduction and English translation by Allen Tate. Cummington, Mass.: Cummington Press, 1943.

The Winter Sea: A Book of Poems. Cummington, Mass.: Cummington Press, 1944.
CONTENTS: "Seasons of the Soul" (I. "Summer"; II. "Autumn"; III. "Winter"; IV. "Spring"); "Jubilo"; "More Sonnets at Christmas" (I. "Again the native hour lets down the locks"; II. "The day's at end and there's nowhere to go"; III. "Give me this day a faith not personal"; IV. "Citizen, myself, or personal friend"); "Winter Mask to the Memory of W. B. Yeats"; "Ode to Our Young Pro-consuls of the Air"; "The Trout Map"; "Eclogue of the Liberal and the Poet"; "False Nightmare."

Sixty American Poets, 1896–1944. (A checklist.) Selected, with a preface and critical notes, by Allen Tate. Washington, D.C.: Library of Congress, 1945. Revised by Kenton Kilmer, 1954.

Poems, 1920–1945: A Selection. London: Eyre and Spottiswoode Ltd., 1947.
CONTENTS: "Seasons of the Soul" (I. "Summer"; II. "Autumn"; III. "Winter"; IV. "Spring"); "The Mediterranean"; "Aeneas at Washington"; "To the Romantic Traditionists"; "The Ancestors"; "To the Lacedemonians"; "Message from Abroad" (I. "What years of the other times, what centuries"; II. "Wanderers to the east, wanderers west"; III. "I cannot see you"); "Idiot"; "Ode to the Confederate Dead"; "Winter Mask to the Memory of W. B. Yeats"; "Jubilo"; "Horation Epode to the Duchess of Malfi"; "Retroduction to American History"; "Causerie"; "Fragment of a Meditation"; "Eclogue of the Liberal and the Poet"; "False Nightmare"; "The Twelve"; "Sonnets at Christmas" (I. "This is the day His hour of life draws

near"; II. "Ah, Christ, I love you rings to the wild sky"); "More Sonnets at Christmas" (I. "Again the native hour lets down the locks"; II. "The day's at end and there's nowhere to go"; III. "Give me this day a faith not personal"; IV. "Citizen, myself, or personal friend"); "Ode to Our Young Pro-consuls of the Air"; "Ode to Fear"; "Elegy"; "The Traveller"; "The Oath"; "Ditty"; "The Wolves"; "The Subway"; "The Eagle"; "Last Days of Alice"; "The Trout Map"; "The Meaning of Life"; "The Meaning of Death"; "The Cross"; "Inside and Outside" (I. "Now twenty-four and maybe twenty-five"; II. "There is not anything to say to those"); "Death of Little Boys"; "The Anabasis"; "Mr. Pope"; "To a Romantic"; "Procession"; "Unnatural Love"; "Epistle"; "The Progress of Œnia" (I. "Madrigale"; II. "In Wintertime"; III. "Vigil"; IV. "Divagation"; V. "Epilogue to Œnia"); "Shadow and Shade"; "Pastoral"; "The Paradigm"; "The Robber Bridegroom"; "Mother and Son"; "A Pauper"; "Obituary"; "Captains of Industry"; "Emblems" (I. "Maryland Virginia Caroline"; II. "When it is all over and the blood"; III. "By the great river the forefathers to beguile"); "Records" (I. "A Dream"; II. "A Vision"); "Ignis Fatuus"; "The Vigil of Venus."

A Southern Vanguard: The John Peale Bishop Memorial Volume. (Anthology.) Ed. Allen Tate. New York: Prentice-Hall, Inc., 1947.

Poems: 1922–1947. New York: Charles Scribner's Sons, 1948, 1949.

    CONTENTS: "The Mediterranean"; "Aeneas at Washington"; "To the Romantic Traditionists"; "The Ancestors"; "Message from Abroad" (I. "What years of the other times, what centuries"; II. "Wanderers to the east, wanderers west"; III. "I cannot see you"); "To the Lacedemonians"; "Ode to the Confederate Dead"; "Seasons of the Soul" (I. "Summer"; II. "Autumn"; III. "Winter"; IV. "Spring"); "Records" (I. "A Dream"; II. "A Vision"); "Mother and Son"; "The Paradigm"; "Sonnets at Christmas" (I. "This is the day His hour of life draws near"; II. "Ah, Christ, I love you rings to the wild sky"); "More Sonnets at Christmas" (I. "Again the native hour lets down the locks"; II. "The day's at end and there's nowhere to go"; III. "Give me this day a faith not personal"; IV. "Gay citizen, myself, and thoughtful friend"); "False Nightmare"; "Jubilo"; "Winter Mask to the Memory of W. B. Yeats"; "The Eye"; "Horation Epode to the Duchess of Malfi"; "Retroduction to American History"; "Causerie"; "Fragment of a Meditation"; "Elegy"; "Eclogue of the Liberal and the Poet"; "Ode to Our Young Pro-consuls of the Air"; "Ode to Fear"; "The Traveller"; "The Oath"; "Ditty"; "The Wolves"; "The Subway"; "The Eagle"; "Last Days of Alice"; "The Twelve"; "The Trout Map"; "The Meaning of Life"; "The Meaning of Death"; "The Cross"; "Inside and Outside"; "Death of Little Boys"; "The Anabasis"; "Shadow and Shade"; "Pastoral"; "Mr. Pope"; "To a Romantic"; "Unnatural Love"; "The Robber Bridegroom"; "The Progress of Œnia" (I. "Madrigale"; II. "In Wintertime"; III. "Vigil"; IV. "Divagation"; V. "Epilogue to Œnia"); "Sonnet to Beauty"; "Light"; "Homily"; "Art"; "Ignis Fatuus"; "Idiot"; "A Pauper"; "Obituary"; "Emblems" (I. "Maryland Virginia Caroline"; II. "When it is all over and the blood"; III. "By the great river the forefathers to beguile"); "Sonnets of the Blood" (I. "What is the flesh and blood compounded of"; II. "Near to me as perfection in the blood"; III. "Then, brother, you would never think me vain"; IV. "The times have changed. Why do you make a fuss"; V. "Our elder brother whom we had not seen"; VI. "The fire I praise was once perduring flame"; VII. "This message hastens lest we both go down"; VIII. "Not power nor the casual hand of God"; IX. "Captains of industry, your aimless power"); "The Vigil of Venus" (*Pervigilium Veneris*); "Farewell to Anactoria" (Sappho); "Adaptation of a Theme by Catullus"; "Correspondences" (Baudelaire); "A Carrion" (Baudelaire).

On the Limits of Poetry: Selected Essays, 1928–1948. New York: Alan Swallow, 1948; William Morrow & Company, 1948.

CONTENTS: "Preface to *Reactionary Essays on Poetry and Ideas*"; "Preface to *Reason in Madness*"; "The Present Function of Criticism"; "Literature as Knowledge"; "Miss Emily and the Bibliographer"; "The Function of the Critical Quarterly"; "Tension in Poetry"; "Three Types of Poetry"; "Understanding Modern Poetry"; "Techniques of Fiction"; "The Hovering Fly"; "A Reading of Keats"; "Hardy's Philosophic Metaphors"; "Emily Dickinson"; "Yeats's Romanticism"; "Hart Crane"; "John Peale Bishop"; "Narcissus as Narcissus"; "The Profession of Letters in the South"; "The New Provincialism"; "What Is a Traditional Society?"; "Religion and the Old South"; "A Note on Donne"; "A Note on Elizabethan Satire"; "T. S. Eliot"; "Ezra Pound"; "Edwin Arlington Robinson"; "MacLeish's *Conquistador*."

The Hovering Fly and Other Essays. Cummington, Mass.: Cummington Press, 1948; Freeport, N.Y.: Books for Libraries Press, 1968.
CONTENTS: "The Hovering Fly"; "The New Provincialism, with an Epilogue on the Southern Novel"; "Techniques of Fiction"; "A Reading of Keats"; "Stephen Spender's *Poems*"; "An Exegesis on Dr. Swift"; "Longinus"; "A Suppressed Preface to a Collection of Poems."

The Collected Poems of John Peale Bishop. Ed., with a preface and a personal memoir, by Allen Tate. New York: Charles Scribner's Sons, 1948; London: Charles Scribner's Sons, Ltd., 1948.

Two Conceits for the Eye to Sing, If Possible. Cummington, Mass.: Cummington Press, 1950.
CONTENTS: "Sing a song of sistence"; "Big, inside the tub."

The House of Fiction: An Anthology of the Short Story. Ed. Caroline Gordon and Allen Tate. New York: Charles Scribner's Sons, 1951, 1960.

The Forlorn Demon: Didactic and Critical Essays. Chicago: Regnery, 1953.
CONTENTS: "The Man of Letters in the Modern World"; "To Whom Is the Poet Responsible?"; "The Symbolic Imagination: The Mirrors of Dante"; "The Angelic Imagination: Poe as God"; "Our Cousin, Mr. Poe"; "Is Literary Criticism Possible?"; "Johnson on the Metaphysical Poets"; "Longinus and the 'New Criticism' "; "A Miscellany" ("Crane: The Poet as Hero"; "Ezra Pound and the Bollingen Prize"; "A Note on Critical 'Autotelism' "; "Modern Poets and Conventions"; "The Point of Dying: Donne's 'Virtuous Men' ").

The Man of Letters in the Modern World: Selected Essays, 1928–1955. New York: Meridian Books, Inc., 1955.
CONTENTS: "The Man of Letters in the Modern World"; "To Whom Is the Poet Responsible?"; "Literature as Knowledge"; "Tension in Poetry"; "Techniques of Fiction"; "The Symbolic Imagination"; "The Angelic Imagination"; "Our Cousin, Mr. Poe"; "The Hovering Fly"; "Is Literary Criticism Possible?"; "Longinus and the 'New Criticism' "; "A Reading of Keats"; "Emily Dickinson"; "Yeats' Romanticism"; "A Note on Donne"; "The Point of Dying: Donne's 'Virtuous Men' "; "A Note on Elizabethan Satire"; "Ezra Pound"; "Ezra Pound and the Bollingen Prize"; "John Peale Bishop"; "Edwin Arlington Robinson"; "Hart Crane"; "Crane: The Poet as Hero"; "MacLeish's *Conquistador*"; "The Profession of Letters in the South"; "The New Provincialism"; "Narcissus as Narcissus."

Modern Verse in English: 1900–1950. (Anthology.) Ed. David Cecil and Allen Tate. New York: Macmillan Co., 1958; London: Eyre and Spottiswoode, Ltd., 1958.

Collected Essays. Denver: Alan Swallow, 1959.
CONTENTS: Essays included in *On the Limits of Poetry* and *The Forlorn Demon*, plus one essay not previously collected: "A Southern Mode of the Imagination."

Poems. New York: Charles Scribner's Sons, 1960; Denver: Alan Swallow, 1961.
CONTENTS: Poems included in *Poems: 1922–1947*, plus two poems not previously collected: "The Swimmers" and "The Buried Lake."

Selected Poems of John Peale Bishop. Ed. Allen Tate. London: Chatto and Windus Ltd., 1960.

The Arts of Learning. (Textbook.) Ed. Ralph Ross, John Berryman, and Allen Tate.
New York: Thomas Y. Crowell, 1960.

Selected Poems by Denis Devlin. Ed. Allen Tate and Robert Penn Warren. New
York: Holt, Rinehart and Winston, 1963.

Christ and the Unicorn. An address delivered on 23 June 1954 at the Third International Congress for Peace and Christian Civilization held in Florence, Italy. West
Branch, Iowa: Cummington Press, 1966.

*T. S. Eliot, the Man and His Work: A Critical Evaluation by Twenty-Six Distin-
guished Writers.* Ed. Allen Tate. New York: Delacorte Press, 1966.

The Complete Poems and Selected Criticism of Edgar Allen Poe. Ed. Allen Tate.
New York: New American Library, 1968.

Essays of Four Decades. Chicago: Swallow Press, 1968; Oxford: Oxford University
Press, 1970; New York: Apollo Editions, Inc., 1970.

CONTENTS: "The Man of Letters in the Modern World"; "To Whom Is the Poet
Responsible?"; "Is Literary Criticism Possible?"; "The Function of the Critical
Quarterly"; "Tension in Poetry"; "Literature as Knowledge"; "The Hovering Fly";
"Techniques of Fiction"; "Miss Emily and the Bibliographer"; "Understanding
Modern Poetry"; "A Note on Critical 'Autotelism' "; "Three Types of Poetry";
"The Present Function of Criticism"; "Modern Poetry"; "Poetry Modern and Un-
modern"; "A Note on Donne"; "The Point of Dying: Donne's 'Virtuous Men' "; "A
Note on Elizabethan Satire"; "A Reading of Keats"; "Emily Dickinson"; "Yeats's
Romanticism"; "Hart Crane"; "Crane: The Poet as Hero"; "Hardy's Philosophic
Metaphors"; "Edwin Arlington Robinson"; "John Peale Bishop"; "MacLeish's
Conquistador"; "Ezra Pound"; "Herbert Read"; "Our Cousin, Mr. Poe"; "The
Angelic Imagination"; "The Symbolic Imagination"; "The Unliteral Imagination;
Or, I, Too, Dislike It"; "T. S. Eliot's *Ash Wednesday*"; "Longinus and the New
Criticism"; "Johnson on the Metaphysical Poets"; "Ezra Pound and the Bollingen
Prize"; "The Profession of Letters in the South"; "The New Provincialism"; "What
Is a Traditional Society?"; "Religion and the Old South"; "A Southern Mode of
the Imagination"; "Narcissus as Narcissus"; Prefaces ("To *Reactionary Essays on
Poetry and Ideas*"; "To *Reason in Madness*"; "To *On the Limits of Poetry*";
"To *The Forlorn Demon*"; "To *The Man of Letters in the Modern World*.")

The Swimmers and Other Selected Poems. London: Oxford University Press, 1970;
New York: Charles Scribner's Sons, 1971.

CONTENTS: "The Mediterranean"; "Aeneas at Washington"; "To the Romantic
Traditionists"; "The Ancestors"; "Message from Abroad"; "To the Lacedemonians";
"Ode to the Confederate Dead"; "Seasons of the Soul" (I. "Summer"; II. "Autumn";
III. "Winter"; IV. "Spring"); "The Maimed Man"; "The Swimmers"; "The Buried
Lake"; "Records" (I. "A Dream"; II. "A Vision"); "Mother and Son"; "The Para-
digm"; "Sonnets at Christmas"; "More Sonnets at Christmas"; "Sonnet"; "False
Nightmare"; "Jubilo"; "Two Conceits"; "Winter Mask"; "The Eye"; "Horation
Epode to the Duchess of Malfi"; "Retroduction to American History"; "Causerie";
"Fragment of a Meditation"; "Elegy"; "Epistle"; "Eclogue of the Liberal and the
Poet"; "Ode to our Young Pro-Consuls of the Air"; "Ode to Fear"; "The Trav-
eller"; "The Oath"; "Ditty"; "The Wolves"; "The Subway"; "The Eagle"; "Last
Days of Alice"; "The Twelve"; "The Trout Map"; "The Meaning of Life"; "The
Meaning of Death"; "The Cross"; "Inside and Outside"; "Death of Little Boys";
"The Anabasis"; "Shadow and Shade"; "Pastoral"; "Mr. Pope"; "To a Romantic";
"Unnatural Love"; "The Robber Bridegroom"; "Sonnet to Beauty"; "Light";
"Homily"; "Art"; "Ignis Fatuus"; "Idiot"; "A Pauper"; "Obituary"; "Emblems";
"Sonnets of the Blood"; "Red Stains"; "Credo in Intellectum Videntem"; "Non
Omnis Moriar"; "Intellectual Detachment"; "The Progress of Œnia" (I. "Madri-
gale"; II. "In Wintertime"; III. "Vigil"; IV. "Divagation"; V. "Epilogue to
Œnia"); "Nuptials"; "Hitch Your Wagon to a Star"; "Perimeters"; "Elegy for

Eugenesis"; "William Blake"; "For a Dead Citizen"; "Cold Pastoral"; "Reflections in an Old House." *Translations*: "The Vigil of Venus" (*Pervigilium Veneris*); "Farewell to Anactoria" (*Sappho*); "Adaptation of a Theme by Catullus"; "Correspondences" (*Baudelaire*); "A Carrion" (*Baudelaire*).

POEMS IN PERIODICALS

"Impossible," *American Poetry Magazine*, 2:5 (March 1920).

"Red Stains," *American Poetry Magazine*, 5:13 (Autumn 1921); *The Swimmers*.

"Battle of Murfreesboro," *Fugitive*, 1:84 (October 1922).

"Bored to Choresis," *Wave*, 1:48–49 (December 1922).

"Call On, Deep Voice," *Fugitive*, 1:59 (June 1922).

"Cul-de-Sac," *Fugitive*, 1:52–53 (June 1922).

"Elegy for Eugenesis," *Fugitive*, 1:92 (October 1922).

"Euthanasia," *Double Dealer*, 3:262 (May 1922). Reprinted, with revision, as "Elegy: Jefferson Davis, 1808–1889" in *New Republic*, 70:10 (17 February 1932); *Poems: 1928–1931*; *Selected Poems*; *Poems, 1920–1945: A Selection*; *Poems: 1922–1947*; *Poems*; *The Swimmers*.

"Farewell to Anactoria" (Sappho), *Fugitive*, 1:39 (June 1922); *Mr. Pope and Other Poems*; *Poems: 1922–1947*; *Poems*; *The Swimmers*.

"Hitch Your Wagon to a Star," *Double Dealer*, 4:270 (December 1922); *Mr. Pope and Other Poems*; *The Swimmers*.

"Horation Epode to the Duchess of Malfi," *Fugitive*, 1:76 (October 1922); *Mr. Pope and Other Poems*; *Selected Poems*; *Poems, 1920–1945: A Selection*; *Poems: 1922–1947*; *Poems*; *The Swimmers*.

"In Secret Valley," *Fugitive*, 1:57 (June 1922).

"Non Omnis Moriar," *Fugitive*, 1:96 (October 1922); *The Swimmers*.

"Nuptials (To J. C. R.)," *Fugitive*, 1:116–17 (December 1922); *The Swimmers*.

"Parthenia," *Double Dealer*, 4:46 (July 1922).

"A Scholar to His Lady," *Fugitive*, 1:64 (June 1922).

"Sinbad," *Fugitive*, 1:16 (April 1922).

"Stranger," *Double Dealer*, 4:231 (November 1922).

"These Deathy Leaves," *Fugitive*, 1:104 (December 1922).

"To Intellectual Detachment," *Fugitive*, 1:9 (April 1922).

"To Œnia in Wintertime," *Fugitive*, 1:71 (October 1922). Reprinted in the sequence "The Progress of Œnia" as "In Wintertime" in *Mr. Pope and Other Poems*; *Poems, 1920–1945: A Selection*; *Poems: 1922–1947*; *Poems*; *The Swimmers*.

"To a Prodigal Old Maid," *Wave*, 1:49 (December 1922).

"William Blake," *Double Dealer*, 4:28 (July 1922); *The Swimmers*.

"Calidus Juventa," *Double Dealer*, 5:77 (February 1923).

"The Date" (in the sequence "Perimeters"), *Fugitive*, 2:25 (February–March 1923); *The Swimmers*.

"First Epilogue to Œnia," *Fugitive*, 2:178–79 (December 1923). Reprinted in the sequence "The Progress of Œnia" as "Epilogue to Œnia" in *Mr. Pope and Other Poems*; *Poems, 1920–1945: A Selection*; *Poems: 1922–1947*; *Poems*; *The Swimmers*.

"From My Room," *Fugitive*, 2:132 (October 1923).

"The Happy Poet Remembers Death," *Fugitive*, 2:54 (April–May 1923). Reprinted as "Reflections in an Old House" in *Mr. Pope and Other Poems*; *The Swimmers*.

"In the cold morning the rested street stands up" (in the sequence "Perimeters"), *Fugitive*, 2:24 (February–March 1923); *The Swimmers*.

"Long Fingers," *Reviewer*, 3:914 (July 1923); *Mr. Pope and Other Poems*.

"Lycambes Talks to John," *Folio*, 1923. (Only one issue; pages not numbered; contributors arranged alphabetically.)

"Mary McDonald," *Fugitive*, 2:3 (February–March 1923).

"My house is banked with gardens overflowing" (in the sequence "Two Poems for Œnia"), *Fugitive*, 2:104 (August–September 1923).

"Perimeters," *Fugitive*, 2:24–25 (February–March 1923). Includes the following: I. "In the cold morning the rested street stands up"; II. "The Date." Reprinted in *The Swimmers.*

"Poem for Twilight," *Folio*, 1923. (Only one issue; pages not numbered; contributors arranged alphabetically.) Reprinted in the sequence "The Progress of Œnia" as "Divagation in *Mr. Pope and Other Poems*; *Poems, 1920–1945: A Selection*; *Poems: 1922–1947*; *Poems*; *The Swimmers.*

"Portent," *Double Dealer*, 5:123 (March–April 1923).

"Prayer for an Old Man," *Fugitive*, 2:188 (December 1923).

"Procession," *Fugitive*, 2:83 (June–July 1923); *Transition*, no. 7, p. 122 (October 1927); *Mr. Pope and Other Poems*; *Fugitives: An Anthology of Verse*; *Selected Poems*; *Poems, 1920–1945: A Selection.*

"Quality of Mercy," *Folio*, 1923. (Only one issue; pages not numbered; contributors arranged alphabetically.)

"Resurgam," *Modern Review*, 1:108 (April 1923); *Mr. Pope and Other Poems.*

"The Screen," *Fugitive*, 2:70–71 (June–July 1923); *Mr. Pope and Other Poems.*

"Sonnet: To a Portrait of Hart Crane," *Double Dealer*, 5:123 (March–April 1923).

"Teeth," *Fugitive*, 2:11 (February–March 1923).

"Two Poems for Œnia," *Fugitive*, 2:104 (August–September 1923). Includes I. "My house is banked with gardens overflowing"; II. "What questions you were asking, what answers got."

"Vision Beatific," *Folio*, 1923. (Only one issue; pages not numbered; contributors arranged alphabetically.)

"Voluntary: After a Conversation," *Fugitive*, 2:152 (October 1923).

"The Wedding," *Fugitive*, 2:170 (December 1923).

"You Left," *Fugitive*, 2:61 (April–May 1923).

"Art," *Fugitive*, 3:134 (December 1924). Includes I. "Brother, lest lonely beauty in the mind"; II. "When you are come by ways devoid of light." "When you are come by ways devoid of light" reprinted alone as "Art" in *Mr. Pope and Other Poems*; *Poems: 1922–1947*; *Poems*; *The Swimmers.*

"Brother, lest lonely beauty in the mind," *Fugitive*, 3:134 (December 1924).

"Correspondences" (Baudelaire), *Fugitive*, 3:133 (December 1924); *Mr. Pope and Other Poems*; *Poems: 1922–1947*; *Poems*; *The Swimmers.*

"Credo: An Aesthetic," *Fugitive*, 3:87 (June 1924). Reprinted as "Credo in Intellectum Videntum" in *Mr. Pope and Other Poems*; *The Swimmers.*

"Day," *Fugitive*, 3:126 (August 1924).

"Dusk," *Fugitive*, 3:126 (August 1924).

"Eager Youth to a Dead Girl," *Lyric*, 4:2 (November 1924).

"Fair Lady and False Knight," *Fugitive*, 3:132–33 (December 1924). (Listed in the table of contents as "Fair Lady to False Knight.")

"Light," *Reviewer*, 4:404 (October 1924); *Mr. Pope and Other Poems*; *Poems: 1922–1947*; *Poems*; *The Swimmers.*

"Lityerses," *Lyric*, 4:2 (June 1924).

"Poem for My Father," *Voices*, 3:47 (March–April 1924). Reprinted as "A Pauper" in *Mr. Pope and Other Poems*; *Selected Poems*; *Poems, 1920–1945: A Selection*; *Poems*; *The Swimmers.*

"Prothesis for Marriage," *Double Dealer*, 6:214 (August–September 1924).

"Shrine," *Guardian*, 1:5 (November 1924); *Mr. Pope and Other Poems.*

"To a Dead Citizen," *SAN*, no. 32, p. 38 (February 1924). Reprinted as "For a Dead Citizen" in *Transition*, no. 12, p. 129 (March 1928), and in *Mr. Pope and Other Poems.*

"Touselled," *Fugitive*, 3:8 (February 1924); *Mr. Pope and Other Poems.*

"Advice to a Young Romanticist," *Nation*, 120:45 (14 January 1925). Reprinted as
"To a Romantic" in *Mr. Pope and Other Poems*; *Fugitives: An Anthology of
Verse*; *Selected Poems*; *Poems, 1920–1945: A Selection*; *Poems: 1922–1947*; *Poems*;
The Swimmers.

"Death of Little Boys," *Nation*, 121:663 (9 December 1925); *Transition*, no. 3, p. 138
(June 1927); *Mr. Pope and Other Poems*; *Fugitives: An Anthology of Verse*; *Van-
derbilt Masquerader*, 10:13 (December 1933); *Selected Poems*; *Poems, 1920–1945: A
Selection*; *Poems: 1922–1947*; *Poems*; *The Swimmers*.

"Homily," *Fugitive*, 4:11 (March 1925); *Mr. Pope and Other Poems*; *Poems: 1922–
1947*; *Poems*; *The Swimmers*.

"Madness," *Guardian*, 1:235 (April 1925).

"The Metaphysical Fly," *Aesthete 1925*, 1:27 (February 1925).

"Mr. Pope," *Nation*, 121:258 (2 September 1925); *Transition*, no. 12, p. 130 (March
1928); *Mr. Pope and Other Poems*; *Fugitives: An Anthology of Verse*; *Selected
Poems*; *Poems, 1920–1945: A Selection*; *Poems: 1922–1947*; *Poems*; *The Swimmers*.

"Prayer to the Woman Mountain," *Fugitive*, 4:118 (December 1925); *Mr. Pope and
Other Poems*.

"To a Romantic Novelist," *Fugitive*, 4:82 (September 1925).

"Causerie," *Calendar of Modern Letters*, 3:205–6 (October 1926). Reprinted as
"Retroduction to American History" in *Mr. Pope and Other Poems*; *Selected
Poems*; *Poems, 1920–1945: A Selection*; *Poems: 1922–1947*; *Poems*; *The Swimmers*.

"Ditty," *Nation*, 122:669 (23 June 1926); *Mr. Pope and Other Poems*; *Selected Poems*;
Poems, 1920–1945: A Selection; *Poems: 1922–1947*; *Poems*; *The Swimmers*.

"Causerie," *Transition*, no. 3, pp. 139–42 (June 1927); *Fugitives: An Anthology of
Verse*; *Poems: 1928–1931*; *Selected Poems*; *Poems, 1920–1945: A Selection*; *Poems:
1922–1947*; *Poems*; *The Swimmers*. (This poem is entirely different from the one
of the same name published in *Calendar of Modern Letters*, 3:205–6 [October
1926], except for the epigraph.)

"Idiot," *Virginia Quarterly Review*, 3:395–96 (July 1927); *Mr. Pope and Other Poems*;
Fugitives: An Anthology of Verse; *Selected Poems*; *Poems, 1920–1945: A Selection*;
Poems: 1922–1947; *Poems*; *The Swimmers*. Translated as "L'Idiot," *Mesures*,
5:345–46 (July 1939).

"The Subway," *Nation*, 125:448 (26 October 1927); *Literary Digest*, 95:33 (26 November 1927); *Mr. Pope and Other Poems*; *Selected Poems*; *Poems, 1920–1945: A Selection*; *Poems: 1922–1947*; *Poems*; *The Swimmers*.

"Vigil," *Nation*, 125:18 (6 July 1927). Reprinted in the sequence "The Progress of
Œnia" in *Mr. Pope and Other Poems*; *Poems, 1920–1945: A Selection*; *Poems: 1922–
1947*; *Poems*; *The Swimmers*.

"Idyl," *Virginia Quarterly Review*, 4:381–82 (July 1928).

"The Eagle," *This Quarter*, 2:115–16 (July–August–September 1929); *Poems: 1928–
1931*; *Selected Poems*; *Poems, 1920–1945: A Selection*; *Poems: 1922–1947*; *Poems*;
The Swimmers.

"Adaptation of a Theme by Catullus: Carmen CI," *This Quarter*, 2:477 (January–
February–March 1930); *Poems: 1922–1947*; *Poems*; *The Swimmers*.

"The Cross," *Saturday Review of Literature*, 6:649 (18 January 1930); *Three Poems*;
Adelphi, n.s. 2:146 (May 1931); *Poems: 1928–1931*; *Selected Poems*; *Poems,
1920–1945: A Selection*; *Poems: 1922–1947*; *Poems*; *The Swimmers*.

"Historical Epitaphs," *Saturday Review of Literature*, 6:1021 (10 May 1930). Includes
I. "On the Martyr of Harper's Ferry"; II. "On the Founder of the Industrial
System"; III. "On the Sage of Monticello." (All previously published alone.)

"Mother and Son," *New Republic*, 64:42 (27 August 1930); *Poems: 1928–1931*;
Selected Poems; *Poems, 1920–1945: A Selection*; *Poems: 1922–1947*; *Poems*; *The
Swimmers*.

"On the Father of Liberty," *Sewanee Review*, 38:60 (January–March 1930). Reprinted in the sequence "Historical Epitaphs" as "On the Sage of Monticello," *Saturday Review of Literature*, 6:1021 (10 May 1930).

"On the Founder of the Industrial System in the United States," *Sewanee Review*, 38:49 (January–March 1930). Reprinted in the sequence "Historical Epitaphs," *Saturday Review of Literature*, 6:1021 (10 May 1930).

"On the Great Conciliator: Now Honored in the Old Dominion," *Sewanee Review*, 38:20 (January–March 1930).

"On the Martyr of Harper's Ferry," *Sewanee Review*, 38:29 (January–March 1930). Reprinted in the sequence "Historical Epitaphs," *Saturday Review of Literature*, 6:1021 (10 May 1930).

"Pioneers," *New Republic*, 64:152 (24 September 1930). Reprinted in the sequence "Emblems" as "By the great river the forefathers to beguile" in *Poems: 1928–1931*; *Selected Poems*; *Poems, 1920–1945: A Selection*; *Poems: 1922–1947*; *Poems*; *The Swimmers*.

"Captains of industry, your aimless power" (in the sequence "Sonnets of the Blood," which is in the group "The Rooftree"), *Poetry*, 39:65 (November 1931). Reprinted in the same sequence in *Poems: 1928–1931*; *Poetry*, 43:115 (November 1933); *Selected Poems*; *Poems: 1922–1947*; *Poems*; *The Swimmers*. Reprinted alone in *Poems, 1920–1945: A Selection*.

"A Dream," *Scribner's Monthly*, 90:400 (October 1931). Reprinted in the sequence "Records" in *Poems: 1928–1931*; *Selected Poems*; *Poems, 1920–1945: A Selection*; *Poems: 1922–1947*; *Poems*; *The Swimmers*.

"Emblems," *New Republic*, 68:182 (30 September 1931). Includes I. "Maryland Virginia Caroline"; II. "When it is all over and the blood." Reprinted, with the addition of III. "By the great river the forefathers to beguile" (previously printed as "Pioneers"), in *Poems: 1928–1931*; *Selected Poems*; *Poems, 1920–1945: A Selection*; *Poems: 1922–1947*; *Poems*; *The Swimmers*.

"The fire I praise was once perduring flame" (in the sequence "Sonnets of the Blood," which is in the group "The Rooftree"), *Poetry*, 39:63 (November 1931). Reprinted in the same sequence in *Poems: 1928–1931*; *Selected Poems*; *Poems: 1922–1947*; *Poems*; *The Swimmers*.

"I cannot see you" (in the sequence "Message from Paris," which is in the group "The Rooftree"), *Poetry*, 39:68 (November 1931). Reprinted in the sequence "Message from Abroad" in *Three Poems*; *Poems: 1928–1931*; *Selected Poems*; *Poems, 1920–1945: A Selection*; *Poems: 1922–1947*; *Poems*; *The Swimmers*.

"Last Days of Alice," *New Republic*, 66:354 (13 May 1931); *Poems: 1928–1931*; *Vanderbilt Masquerader*, 10:13 (December 1933); *Selected Poems*; *Southern Review*, 5:427 (Winter 1940); *Poems, 1920–1945: A Selection*; *Poems: 1922–1947*; *Poems*; *The Swimmers*.

"Maryland Virginia Caroline" (in the sequence "Emblems"), *New Republic*, 68:182 (30 September 1931). Reprinted in the same sequence in *Poems: 1928–1931*; *Selected Poems*; *Poems, 1920–1945: A Selection*; *Poems: 1922–1947*; *Poems*; *The Swimmers*.

"Message from Paris" (in the group "The Rooftree"), *Poetry*, 39:65–68 (November 1931). Includes I. "What years of the other times, what centuries"; II. "Wanderers east, wanderers west"; III. "I cannot see you." Reprinted in its entirety as "Message from Abroad" in *Three Poems*; *Poems: 1928–1931*; *Selected Poems*; *Poems, 1920–1945: A Selection*; *Poems: 1922–1947*; *Poems*; *The Swimmers*.

"My brother you would never think me vain" (in the sequence "Sonnets of the Blood," which is in the group "The Rooftree"), *Poetry*, 39:60–61 (November 1931). Reprinted in the same sequence in *Poems: 1928–1931*. Reprinted in the same sequence as "Then, brother, you would never think me vain" in *Selected Poems*; *Poems: 1922–1947*; *Poems*; *The Swimmers*.

"Near to me as my flesh, my flesh and blood" (in the sequence "Sonnets of the Blood," which is in the group "The Rooftree"), *Poetry*, 39:60 (November 1931). Reprinted in the same sequence in *Poems: 1928–1931* and *Poetry*, 43:114 (November 1933). Reprinted in the same sequence as "Near to me as perfection in the blood" in *Selected Poems*; *Poems: 1922–1947*; *Poems*; *The Swimmers*.

"Not power nor the storied hand of God" (in the sequence "Sonnets of the Blood," which is in the group "The Rooftree"), *Poetry*, 39:64 (November 1931). Reprinted in the same sequence in *Poems: 1928–1931* and *Selected Poems*. Reprinted in the same sequence as "Not power nor the casual hand of God" in *Poems: 1922–1947*; *Poems*; *The Swimmers*.

"The Oath," *Virginia Quarterly Review*, 7:228 (April 1931); *Poems: 1928–1931*; *Selected Poems*; *Poems, 1920–1945: A Selection*; *Poems: 1922–1947*; *Poems*.

"Our elder brother whom I had not seen" (in the sequence "Sonnets of the Blood," which is in the group "The Rooftree"), *Poetry*, 39:62–63 (November 1931). Reprinted in the same sequence in *Poems: 1928–1931*. Reprinted in the same sequence as "Our elder brother whom we had not seen" in *Selected Poems*; *Poems: 1922–1947*; *Poems*; *The Swimmers*.

"The Paradigm," *New Republic*, 68:45 (26 August 1931); *Poems: 1928–1931*; *Selected Poems*; *Poems, 1920–1945: A Selection*; *Poems: 1922–1947*; *Poems*; *The Swimmers*.

"The Rooftree," *Poetry*, 39:59–69 (November 1931). Includes I. "Sonnets of the Blood"; II. "Message from Paris"; III. "The Wolves." (See individual listings for subsequent publication.)

"Sonnets of the Blood" (in the group "The Rooftree"), *Poetry*, 39:59–65 (November 1931). Includes I. "What is this flesh and blood compounded of"; II. "Near to me as my flesh, my flesh and blood"; III. "My brother you would never think me vain"; IV. "The times have changed, there is not left to us"; V. "These generations that have sealed your heart"; VI. "Our elder brother whom I had not seen"; VII. "The fire I praise was once perduring flame"; VIII. "This message for you lest we both go down"; IX. "Not power nor the storied hand of God"; X. "Captains of Industry, your aimless power." Sonnets I–IV and VI–X reprinted in the same sequence, with varying revision, in *Poems: 1928–1931*; *Selected Poems*; *Poems: 1922–1947*; *Poems*; *The Swimmers*. Sonnets I, II, IV, and X reprinted in the same sequence in *Poetry*, 43:114–15 (November 1933). Sonnet X reprinted alone in *Poems, 1920–1945: A Selection*.

"These generations that have sealed your heart" (in the sequence "Sonnets of the Blood," which is in the group "The Rooftree"), *Poetry*, 39:62 (November 1931).

"This message for you, lest we both go down" (in the sequence "Sonnets of the Blood," which is in the group "The Rooftree"), *Poetry*, 39:63–64 (November 1931). Reprinted in the same sequence as "This message hastens, lest we both go down" in *Poems: 1928–1931*; *Selected Poems*; *Poems: 1922–1947*; *Poems*; *The Swimmers*.

"The times have changed, there is not left to us" (in the sequence "Sonnets of the Blood," which is in the group "The Rooftree"), *Poetry*, 39:61 (November 1931). Reprinted in the same sequence in *Poems: 1928–1931* and *Poetry*, 43:115 (November 1933). Reprinted in the same sequence as "The times have changed. Why do you make a fuss" in *Selected Poems*; *Poems: 1922–1947*; *Poems*; *The Swimmers*.

"The Twelve," *Adelphi*, n.s. 2:118 (May 1931); *Saturday Review of Literature*, 7:873 (6 June 1931); *Poems: 1928–1931*; *Selected Poems*; *Poems, 1920–1945: A Selection*; *Poems: 1922–1947*; *Poems*; *The Swimmers*.

"A Vision," *Nation*, 133:673 (16 December 1931). Reprinted in the sequence "Records" in *Poems: 1928–1931*; *Selected Poems*; *Poems, 1920–1945: A Selection*; *Poems: 1922–1947*; *Poems*; *The Swimmers*.

"Wanderers east, wanderers west" (in the sequence "Message from Paris," which is in the group "The Rooftree"), *Poetry*, 39:67 (November 1931). Reprinted in the sequence "Message from Abroad" in *Three Poems*; *Poems: 1928–1931*; *Selected Poems*; *Poems, 1920–1945: A Selection*; *Poems: 1922–1947*; *Poems*; *The Swimmers*.

"What is this flesh and blood compounded of" (in the sequence "Sonnets of the Blood," which is in the group "The Rooftree"), *Poetry*, 39:59–60 (November 1931). Reprinted in the same sequence in *Poems: 1928–1931* and *Poetry*, 43:114 (November 1933). Reprinted in the same sequence as "What is the flesh and blood compounded of" in *Selected Poems*; *Poems: 1922–1947*; *Poems*; *The Swimmers*.

"What years of the other times, what centuries" (in the sequence "Message from Paris," which is in the group "The Rooftree"), *Poetry*, 39:65–66 (November 1931). Reprinted in the sequence "Message from abroad" in *Three Poems*; *Poems: 1928–1931*; *Selected Poems*; *Poems, 1920–1945: A Selection*; *Poems: 1922–1947*; *Poems*; *The Swimmers*.

"When it is all over and the blood" (in the sequence "Emblems"), *New Republic*, 68:182 (30 September 1931). Reprinted in the same sequence in *Poems: 1928–1931*; *Selected Poems*; *Poems, 1920–1945: A Selection*; *Poems: 1922–1947*; *Poems*; *The Swimmers*.

"The Wolves" (in the group "The Rooftree"), *Poetry*, 39:68–69 (November 1931). Reprinted alone in *Poems: 1928–1931*; *Selected Poems*; *Poems, 1920–1945: A Selection*; *Poems: 1922–1947*; *Poems*; *The Swimmers*.

"Aeneas at New York: To Archibald MacLeish," *New Republic*, 73:125 (14 December 1932).

"The Anabasis" (in a group entitled "Two Poems"), *Poetry*, 40:74–75 (May 1932). Reprinted alone in *The Mediterranean and Other Poems*; *Selected Poems*; *Poems, 1920–1945: A Selection*; *Poems: 1922–1947*; *Poems*; *The Swimmers*.

"Brief Message" (in a group entitled "Two Poems"), *Poetry*, 40:75 (May 1932).

"Her Posture," *Saturday Review of Literature*, 8:486 (30 January 1932). Reprinted in the sequence "Inside and Outside" as "Now twenty-four or maybe twenty-five" in *Poems: 1928–1931*; *Selected Poems*; *Poems, 1920–1945: A Selection*; *Poems: 1922–1947*; *Poems*; *The Swimmers*.

"Ode to Fear: Variation on a Theme by Collins," *New Republic*, 70:10 (17 February 1932); *Poems: 1928–1931*; *Selected Poems*; *Poems, 1920–1945: A Selection*; *Poems: 1922–1947*; *Poems*; *The Swimmers*.

"To the Lacedemonians," Richmond (Virginia) *Times-Dispatch*, 21 June 1932; *New Republic*, 85:250 (8 January 1936); *The Mediterranean and Other Poems*; *Selected Poems*; *Poems, 1920–1945: A Selection*; *Poems: 1922–1947*; *Poems*; *The Swimmers*.

"The Traveller," *Yale Review*, 21:249–50 (Winter 1932); *Poems: 1928–1931*; *Selected Poems*; *Poems, 1920–1945: A Selection*; *Poems: 1922–1947*; *Poems*; *The Swimmers*.

"Two Poems," *Poetry*, 40:74–75 (May 1932). Includes I. "The Anabasis"; II. "Brief Message."

"Unnatural Love," *Nation*, 134:314 (16 March 1932); *The Mediterranean and Other Poems*; *Selected Poems*; *Poems, 1920–1945: A Selection*; *Poems: 1922–1947*; *Poems*; *The Swimmers*.

"Aeneas at Washington," *Hound and Horn*, 6:445–46 (April–June 1933); *New Verse*, no. 7, pp. 4–5 (February 1934); *Bozart-Westminster*, 24:34 (Spring–Summer 1935); *The Mediterranean and Other Poems*; *Selected Poems*; *Poems, 1920–1945: A Selection*; *Poems: 1922–1947*; *Poems*; *The Swimmers*.

"The Ancestors," *New Republic*, 76:331 (1 November 1933); *The Mediterranean and Other Poems*; *Selected Poems*; *Poems, 1920–1945: A Selection*; *Poems: 1922–1947*; *Poems*; *The Swimmers*.

"The Meaning of Life," *New Verse*, no. 2, pp. 9–10 (March 1933); *Hound and Horn*, 7:42 (October–December 1933); *The Mediterranean and Other Poems*; *Selected Poems*; *Poems, 1920–1945: A Selection*; *Poems: 1922–1947*; *Poems*; *The Swimmers*. Translated as "Le Sens de la Vie," *Mesures*, 5:356–57 (July 1939).

"The Mediterranean," *Yale Review*, 22:474–75 (Spring 1933); *New Verse*, no. 5, pp. 8–9 (October 1933); *The Mediterranean and Other Poems*; *Selected Poems*; *Poems, 1920–1945: A Selection*; *Poems: 1922–1947*; *Poems*; *The Swimmers*.

"Ode to the Confederate Dead," *Vanderbilt Masquerader*, 10:12 (December 1933); *Mr. Pope and Other Poems*; *Fugitives: An Anthology of Verse*; *Poems: 1928–1931*; *Poems, 1920–1945: A Selection*; *Poems: 1922–1947*; *Poems*; *The Swimmers*. Translated as "Ode aux Morts des Confédérés," *Mesures*, 5:346–56 (July 1939). A second translation in *Sewanee Review*, 60:512–17 (Summer 1952), and 68:598–603 (Fall 1959).

"Shadow and Shade," *New Republic*, 75:344 (9 August 1933); *The Mediterranean and Other Poems*; *Selected Poems*; *Poems, 1920–1945: A Selection*; *Poems: 1922–1947*; *Poems*; *The Swimmers*.

"Ah, Christ, I love you rings to the wild sky" (in the sequence "Sonnets at Christmas"), *New Republic*, 81:185–86 (26 December 1934). Reprinted in the same sequence in *The Mediterranean and Other Poems*; *Selected Poems*; *Sonnets at Christmas*; *Poems, 1920–1945: A Selection*; *Poems: 1922–1947*; *Poems*; *The Swimmers*.

"The Meaning of Death," *The Magazine*, 2:80–81 (September–October 1934); *The Mediterranean and Other Poems*; *Selected Poems*; *Poems, 1920–1945: A Selection*; *Poems: 1922–1947*; *Poems*; *The Swimmers*.

"Sonnets at Christmas," *New Republic*, 81:185–86 (26 December 1934). Includes I. "This is our day, His hour of life draws near"; II. "Ah, Christ, I love you rings to the wild sky." Reprinted, with revision, in *The Mediterranean and Other Poems*; *Selected Poems*; *Sonnets at Christmas*; *Poems, 1920–1945: A Selection*; *Poems: 1922–1947*; *Poems*; *The Swimmers*.

"This is our day, His hour of life draws near" (in the sequence "Sonnets at Christmas"), *New Republic*, 81:185 (26 December 1934). Reprinted in the same sequence as "This is the day, His hour of life draws near" in *The Mediterranean and Other Poems*; *Selected Poems*; *Sonnets at Christmas*; *Poems, 1920–1945: A Selection*; *Poems: 1922–1947*; *Poems*; *The Swimmers*.

"Fragment of a Meditation," *Southern Review*, 1:339–42 (Autumn 1935); *The Mediterranean and Other Poems*; *Selected Poems*; *Poems, 1920–1945: A Selection*; *Poems: 1922–1947*; *Poems*; *The Swimmers*.

"To the Romantic Traditionists," *Virginia Quarterly Review*, 11:254–55 (April 1935); *The Mediterranean and Other Poems*; *Selected Poems*; *Poems, 1920–1945: A Selection*; *Poems: 1922–1947*; *Poems*; *The Swimmers*.

"Light Interval," *Virginia Quarterly Review*, 12:58 (January 1936). Reprinted as "Pastoral" in *Mr. Pope and Other Poems*; *The Mediterranean and Other Poems*; *Selected Poems*; *Poems, 1920–1945: A Selection*; *Poems: 1922–1947*; *Poems*; *The Swimmers*.

"The Robber Bridegroom," *Southwestern Journal*, 15:36 (Spring 1936); *The Mediterranean and Other Poems*; *Selected Poems*; *Poems, 1920–1945: A Selection*; *Poems: 1922–1947*; *Poems*; *The Swimmers*.

"Eclogue of the Liberal and the Liberal Poet," *Twentieth Century Verse*, nos. 12–13, pp. 85–86 (September–October 1938); *Partisan Review*, 6:50–51 (Winter 1939). Reprinted as "Eclogue of the Liberal and the Poet" in *The Winter Sea*; *Poems, 1920–1945: A Selection*; *Poems: 1922–1947*; *Poems*; *The Swimmers*.

"The Trout Map," *Kenyon Review*, 1:404–5 (Autumn 1939); *The Winter Sea*; *Poems, 1920–1945: A Selection*; *Poems: 1922–1947*; *Poems*; *The Swimmers*.

"False Nightmare," *New Republic*, 104:399 (24 March 1941); *The Winter Sea*; *Poems, 1920–1945: A Selection*; *Poems: 1922–1947*; *Poems*; *The Swimmers*.

"Again the native hour lets down the locks" (in the sequence "More Sonnets at Christmas"). *Kenyon Review*, 5:186 (Spring 1943). Reprinted in the same sequence in *The Winter Sea*; *Poems, 1920–1945: A Selection*; *Poems: 1922–1947*; *Poems*; *The Swimmers*.

"Citizens, myself, or personal friend" (in the sequence "More Sonnets at Christmas"), *Kenyon Review*, 5:188 (Spring 1943). Reprinted in the same sequence in *The Winter Sea* and *Poems, 1920–1945: A Selection*. Reprinted in the same sequence as "Gay citizen, myself, and thoughtful friend" in *Poems: 1922–1947*; *Poems*; *The Swimmers*.

"The day's at end and there's nowhere to go" (in the sequence "More Sonnets at Christmas"), *Kenyon Review*, 5:187 (Spring 1943). Reprinted in the same sequence in *The Winter Sea*; *Poems, 1920–1945: A Selection*; *Poems: 1922–1947*; *Poems*; *The Swimmers*.

"Give me this day a faith not personal" (in the sequence "More Sonnets at Christmas"), *Kenyon Review*, 5:187 (Spring 1943). Reprinted in the same sequence in *The Winter Sea*; *Poems, 1920–1945: A Selection*; *Poems: 1922–1947*; *Poems*; *The Swimmers*.

"Jubilo," *Kenyon Review*, 5:184–86 (Spring 1943); *Horizon*, 9:86–87 (February 1944); *The Winter Sea*; *Poems, 1920–1945: A Selection*; *Poems: 1922–1947*; *Poems*; *The Swimmers*.

"More Sonnets at Christmas," *Kenyon Review*, 5:186–88 (Spring 1943). Includes I. "Again the native hour lets down the locks"; II. "The day's at end and there's nowhere to go"; III. "Give me this day a faith not personal"; IV. "Citizens, myself, or personal friend." Reprinted in its entirety, with varying revisions, in *The Winter Sea*; *Poems, 1920–1945: A Selection*; *Poems: 1922–1947*; *Poems*; *The Swimmers*.

"Ode: To Our Young Pro-consuls of the Air," *Partisan Review*, 10:129–32 (March–April 1943); *The Winter Sea*; *Poems, 1920–1945: A Selection*; *Poems: 1922–1947*; *Poems*; *The Swimmers*.

"Winter Mask: To the Memory of W. B. Yeats," *Chimera*, 1:2–3 (Spring 1943); *The Winter Sea*; *Poems, 1920–1945: A Selection*; *Poems: 1922–1947*; *Poems*; *The Swimmers*.

"Air" (in the sequence "Seasons of the Soul"), *Kenyon Review*, 6:1–3 (Winter 1944). Reprinted in the same sequence as "Summer" in *The Winter Sea*; *Poems, 1920–1945: A Selection*; *Poems: 1922–1947*; *Poems*; *The Swimmers*.

"Earth" (in the sequence "Seasons of the Soul"), *Kenyon Review*, 6:3–5 (Winter 1944). Reprinted in the same sequence as "Autumn" in *The Winter Sea*; *Poems, 1920–1945: A Selection*; *Poems: 1922–1947*; *Poems*; *The Swimmers*.

"Fire" (in the sequence "Seasons of the Soul"), *Kenyon Review*, 6:7–9 (Winter 1944). Reprinted in the same sequence as "Spring" in *The Winter Sea*; *Poems, 1920–1945: A Selection*; *Poems: 1922–1947*; *Poems*; *The Swimmers*.

"Seasons of the Soul," *Kenyon Review*, 6:1–9 (Winter 1944). Includes I. "Air"; II. "Earth"; III. "Water"; IV. "Fire." Reprinted in its entirety with revisions of titles (I. "Summer"; II. "Autumn"; III. "Winter"; IV. "Spring") in *The Winter Sea*; *Poems, 1920–1945: A Selection*; *Poems: 1922–1947*; *Poems*; *The Swimmers*.

"Water" (in the sequence "Seasons of the Soul"), *Kenyon Review*, 6:5–7 (Winter 1944). Reprinted in the same sequence as "Winter" in *The Winter Sea*; *Poems, 1920–1945: A Selection*; *Poems: 1922–1947*; *Poems*; *The Swimmers*.

"The Eye," *Partisan Review*, 15:40–41 (January 1948); *Poems: 1922–1947*; *Poems*; *The Swimmers*.

"The Maimed Man," *Partisan Review*, 19:265–67 (May–June 1952). Reprinted with revisions in *The Swimmers*.

"The Buried Lake," *Sewanee Review*, 61:177–80 (Spring 1953); *Poems*; *The Swimmers*.

"Sulpicia to Corinthus," *Western Review*, 18:49 (Autumn 1953).

"The Swimmers," *Hudson Review*, 5:471–73 (Winter 1953); *Poems*; *The Swimmers*.

ESSAYS IN PERIODICALS

"Whose Ox," *Fugitive*, 1:99–100 (December 1922).

"One Escape from the Dilemma," *Fugitive*, 3:34–36 (April 1924).

"A Polite Protest," *Poetry*, 25:169–70 (December 1924).

"Last Days of the Charming Lady," *Nation*, 121:485–86 (28 October 1925).

"On Critics and Poets," *Saturday Review of Literature*, 1:886 (4 July 1925).

"Poetry and the Absolute," *Sewanee Review*, 35:41–52 (January 1927).

"The Revolt against Literature," *New Republic*, 49:329–30 (9 February 1927).

"Emily Dickinson," *Outlook*, 149:621–23 (15 August 1928). Reprinted, with extensive revision, as "New England Culture and Emily Dickinson," *Symposium*, 3:206–26 (April 1932). This revised version reprinted as "Emily Dickinson" in *Reactionary Essays on Poetry and Ideas* (in the group "Four American Poets"); *On the Limits of Poetry*; *The Man of Letters in the Modern World*; *Collected Essays*; *Essays of Four Decades.*

"The Passing of the 'Christmas Number,'" *Brentano's Book Chat*, 7:35–37 (January–February 1928).

"American Poetry since 1920," *Bookman*, 68:503–8 (January 1929).

"The Fallacy of Humanism," *Criterion*, 8:661–81 (July 1929); *Hound and Horn*, 3:234–57 (January–March 1930). Reprinted as "Humanism and Naturalism" in *Reactionary Essays on Poetry and Ideas.*

"The Bi-Millennium of Vergil," *New Republic*, 64:296–98 (29 October 1930).

"Confusion and Poetry," *Sewanee Review*, 38:133–49 (April–June 1930).

"A Distinguished Poet," *Hound and Horn*, 3:580–85 (July–September 1930). Later forms part of the essay "Hart Crane" in *Reactionary Essays on Poetry and Ideas* (in the group "Four American Poets"); *On the Limits of Poetry*; *The Man of Letters in the Modern World*; *Collected Essays*; *Essays of Four Decades.* See also "Hart Crane and the American Mind" and "In Memoriam: Hart Crane."

"The Same Fallacy of Humanism: A Reply to Mr. Robert Shafer," *Bookman*, 71:31–36 (March 1930).

"An Exegesis on Dr. Swift," *This Quarter*, 3:475–83 (March 1931); *The Hovering Fly and Other Essays.*

"Ezra Pound's Golden Ass," *Nation*, 132:632–34 (10 June 1931). Reprinted as "Ezra Pound" in *Reactionary Essays on Poetry and Ideas* (in the group "Four American Poets"); *On the Limits of Poetry*; *The Man of Letters in the Modern World*; *Collected Essays*; *Essays of Four Decades.*

"Irony and Humility," *Hound and Horn*, 4:290–97 (January–March 1931). Reprinted as "T. S. Eliot" in *Reactionary Essays on Poetry and Ideas*; *On the Limits of Poetry*; *Collected Essays.* Reprinted as "T. S. Eliot, Ash Wednesday" in *Essays of Four Decades.*

"Miss Millay's Sonnets," *New Republic*, 66:335–36 (6 May 1931). Reprinted, with revision, as "Edna St. Vincent Millay," in *Reactionary Essays on Poetry and Ideas.*

"Regionalism and Sectionalism," *New Republic*, 69:158–61 (23 December 1931).

"The Aesthetic Emotion as Useful," *This Quarter*, 5:292–303 (December 1932).

"The American Language," *New English Weekly*, 2:157–58 (1 December 1932).

"Editorial Note," *Poetry*, 40:90–94 (May 1932).

"Hart Crane and the American Mind," *Poetry*, 40:210–16 (July 1932). Later forms part of the essay "Hart Crane" in *Reactionary Essays on Poetry and Ideas* (in the group "Four American Poets"); *On the Limits of Poetry*; *The Man of Letters in the Modern World*; *Collected Essays*; *Essays of Four Decades.* See also "A Distinguished Poet" and "In Memoriam: Hart Crane."

"In Memoriam: Hart Crane," *Hound and Horn*, 5:612–19 (July–September 1932). Later forms part of the essay "Hart Crane" in *Reactionary Essays on Poetry and Ideas* (in the group "Four American Poets"); *On the Limits of Poetry*; *The Man of*

Letters in the Modern World; Collected Essays; Essays of Four Decades. See also "A Distinguished Poet" and "Hart Crane and the American Mind."

"Not Fear of God," *New Republic,* 71:77–78 (1 June 1932). Reprinted, with revision, as "MacLeish's *Conquistador*" in *Reactionary Essays on Poetry and Ideas; On the Limits of Poetry; The Man of Letters in the Modern World; Collected Essays.*

"A Note on Donne," *New Republic,* 70:212–13 (16 April 1932); *Reactionary Essays on Poetry and Ideas; On the Limits of Poetry; The Man of Letters in the Modern World; Collected Essays; Essays of Four Decades.*

"Personal Convention," *Poetry,* 39:332–37 (March 1932). Reprinted as "E. E. Cummings" in *Reactionary Essays on Poetry and Ideas.*

" 'There Ought to Be a Law,' " *New Republic,* 70:326–27 (4 May 1932).

"Again, O Ye Laurels," *New Republic,* 76:312–13 (25 October 1933). Reprinted, with revision, as "Edwin Arlington Robinson" in *Reactionary Essays on Poetry and Ideas; On the Limits of Poetry; The Man of Letters in the Modern World; Collected Essays; Essays of Four Decades.*

"A New Artist," *New Verse,* no. 3, pp. 21–23 (May 1933). Reprinted as "Stephen Spender's *Poems*" in *The Hovering Fly and Other Essays.*

"A Note on Elizabethan Satire," *New Republic,* 74:128–30 (15 March 1933); *Reactionary Essays on Poetry and Ideas; On the Limits of Poetry; The Man of Letters in the Modern World; Collected Essays; Essays of Four Decades.*

"Poetry and Politics," *New Republic,* 75:308–11 (2 August 1933).

"The Problem of the Unemployed: A Modest Proposal," *American Review,* 1:129–49 (May 1933).

"Three Types of Poetry," *New Republic,* 78:126–28 (14 March 1934); 78:180–82 (28 March 1934); 78:237–40 (11 April 1934). Reprinted, as a whole, in *Reactionary Essays on Poetry and Ideas; On the Limits of Poetry; Collected Essays; Essays of Four Decades.*

"A Note on Bishop's Poetry," *Southern Review,* 1:357–64 (Autumn 1935). Reprinted as "John Peale Bishop" in *Reactionary Essays on Poetry and Ideas* (in the group "Four American Poets"); *On the Limits of Poetry; The Man of Letters in the Modern World; Collected Essays; Essays of Four Decades.*

"The Profession of Letters in the South," *Virginia Quarterly Review,* 9:161–76 (April 1935); *Reactionary Essays on Poetry and Ideas; On the Limits of Poetry; The Man of Letters in the Modern World; Collected Essays; Essays of Four Decades.*

"The Function of the Critical Quarterly," *Southern Review,* 1:551–59 (Winter 1936); *Reason in Madness; On the Limits of Poetry; Collected Essays; Essays of Four Decades.*

"Mr. Kenneth Burke and the Historical Environment," *Southern Review,* 2:363–72 (Autumn 1936); *Purpose,* 7:75–83 (April–June 1937).

"Notes on Liberty and Property," *American Review,* 6:596–611 (March 1936); *Who Owns America?*

"What Is a Traditional Society?" *American Review,* 7:376–87 (September 1963); *Reason in Madness; On the Limits of Poetry; Collected Essays; Essays of Four Decades.* (Originally Phi Beta Kappa Address, University of Virginia, June 1936.)

"Modern Poets and Conventions," *American Review,* 8:427–35 (February 1937). Reprinted in the group "A Miscellany" in *The Forlorn Demon* and *Collected Essays.*

"R. P. Blackmur and Others," *Southern Review,* 3:183–98 (Summer 1937). Reprinted as "Nine Poets: 1937" in *Reason in Madness.*

"A Traditionist Looks at Liberalism," *Southern Review,* 1:731–44 (Spring 1936); *Purpose,* 9:158–67 (July–September 1937). Reprinted as "Liberalism and Tradition" in *Reason in Madness.*

"Homage to T. S. Eliot," *Harvard Advocate,* 125:41–42 (December 1938).

"Narcissus as Narcissus," *Virginia Quarterly Review,* 14:108–22 (Winter 1938);

Reason in Madness; *On the Limits of Poetry*; *The Man of Letters in the Modern World*; *Collected Essays*; *Essays of Four Decades.*

"The Reading of Modern Poetry," *Purpose*, 10:31–41 (January–March 1938).

"Tension in Poetry," *Southern Review*, 4:101–15 (Summer 1938); *Reason in Madness*; *On the Limits of Poetry*; *The Man of Letters in the Modern World*; *Collected Essays*; *Essays of Four Decades.*

"Edmund Wilson," *Gotham Book Mart Catalogue (We Moderns)*, no. 42, p. 71 (1940).

"Hardy's Philosophic Metaphors," *Southern Review*, 6:99–108 (Summer 1940); *Reason in Madness*; *On the Limits of Poetry*; *Collected Essays*; *Essays of Four Decades.*

"Miss Emily and the Bibliographer," *American Scholar*, 9:449–60 (Autumn 1940); *Reason in Madness*; *On the Limits of Poetry*; *Collected Essays*; *Essays of Four Decades.*

"The Present Function of Criticism," *Southern Review*, 6:236–46 (Autumn 1940); *Reason in Madness*; *On the Limits of Poetry*; *Collected Essays*; *Essays of Four Decades.*

"Statements" (an appreciation of Wallace Stevens), *Harvard Advocate*, 127:31 (December 1940).

"Understanding Modern Poetry," *English Journal*, 19:263–74 (April 1940); *Reason in Madness*; *On the Limits of Poetry*; *Collected Essays*; *Essays of Four Decades.*

"We Read as Writers," *Princeton Alumni Weekly*, 40:505–6 (8 March 1940).

"Literature as Knowledge: Comment and Comparison," *Southern Review*, 6:629–57 (Spring 1941); *Reason in Madness*; *On the Limits of Poetry*; *The Man of Letters in the Modern World*; *Collected Essays*; *Essays of Four Decades.*

"Literature in the South," *Saturday Review of Literature*, 23:11 (11 January 1941).

"Procrustes and the Poets," *New Republic*, 104:25–26 (6 January 1941); *Reason in Madness.*

"Yeats's Romanticism: Notes and Suggestions," *Southern Review*, 7:591–600 (Winter 1941); *On the Limits of Poetry*; *The Man of Letters in the Modern World*; *Collected Essays*; *Essays of Four Decades.*

"The Fugitive, 1922–1925: A Personal Recollection," *Princeton University Library Chronicle*, 3:75–84 (April 1942).

"On the 'Brooks-MacLeish Thesis,'" *Partisan Review*, 9:38–39 (January–February 1942).

"To Ford Madox Ford," *Chimera*, 1:19–20 (Spring 1942).

"Dostoevsky's Hovering Fly: A Causerie on the Imagination and the Actual World," *Sewanee Review*, 51:353–69 (Summer 1943). Reprinted as "The Hovering Fly" in *On the Limits of Poetry*; *The Hovering Fly and Other Essays*; *The Man of Letters in the Modern World*; *Collected Essays*; *Essays of Four Decades.*

"The Post of Observation in Fiction," *Maryland Quarterly*, 2:61–64 (1944).

"The State of Letters," *Sewanee Review*, 52:608–14 (Autumn 1944); 53:165–66 (Spring 1945); 53:504–6 (Summer 1945).

"Techniques of Fiction," *Sewanee Review*, 52:210–25 (Spring 1944); *On the Limits of Poetry*; *The Hovering Fly and Other Essays*; *The Man of Letters in the Modern World*; *Collected Essays*; *Essays of Four Decades.*

"Mr. Davidson and the Race Problem," *Sewanee Review*, 53:659–60 (Winter 1945).

"The New Provincialism, with an Epilogue on the Southern Novel," *Virginia Quarterly Review*, 21:262–72 (Spring 1945); *On the Limits of Poetry*; *The Hovering Fly and Other Essays*; *The Man of Letters in the Modern World*; *Collected Essays*; *Essays of Four Decades.*

"Prefazione inedita e piccola antologia lirica," *Inventario*, 1:69–77 (Autumn–Winter 1946–1947).

"A Reading of Keats," *American Scholar*, 15:55–63 (Winter 1946); 15:189–97 (Spring 1946). Reprinted, as a whole, in *On the Limits of Poetry*; *The Hovering Fly and*

Other Essays; *The Man of Letters in the Modern World*; *Collected Essays*; *Essays of Four Decades*.

"John Peale Bishop: A Personal Memoir," *Western Review*, 12:67–71 (Winter 1948).

"Longinus," *Hudson Review*, 1:344–61 (Autumn 1948). Reprinted as "Longinus and the 'New Criticism' " in *The Hovering Fly and Other Essays*; *The Forlorn Demon*; *The Man of Letters in the Modern World*; *Collected Essays*; *Essays of Four Decades*.

"Further Remarks on the Pound Award," *Partisan Review*, 16:666–68 (June 1949). Reprinted as "Ezra Pound and the Bollingen Prize" in *The Forlorn Demon* (in the group "A Miscellany"); *The Man of Letters in the Modern World*; *Collected Essays* (in the group "A Miscellany").

"Johnson on the Metaphysical Poets," *Kenyon Review*, 11:379–94 (Summer 1949); *The Forlorn Demon*; *Collected Essays*; *Essays of Four Decades*.

"A Note on Autotelism," *Kenyon Review*, 11:13–16 (Winter 1949). Reprinted as "A Note on Critical 'Autotelism' " in the group "A Miscellany" in *The Forlorn Demon* and *Collected Essays*. Reprinted alone in *Essays of Four Decades*.

"Our Cousin, Mr. Poe," *Partisan Review*, 16:1207–19 (December 1949); *The Forlorn Demon*; *The Man of Letters in the Modern World*; *Collected Essays*; *Essays of Four Decades*.

"Homage to St.-John Perse," *Poetry*, 75:213–16 (January 1950).

"Preface to *Libretto for the Republic of Liberia*," *Poetry*, 76:216–18 (July 1950). Reprinted as preface to Melvin B. Tolson, *Libretto for the Republic of Liberia*, 1953.

"Religion and the Intellectuals," *Partisan Review*, 17:250–53 (March 1950).

"The Teaching and Study of Writing," *Western Review*, 14:165–67 (Spring 1950).

"Three Commentaries: Poe, James, and Joyce," *Sewanee Review*, 58:1–15 (Winter 1950).

"To Whom Is the Poet Responsible?" *Hudson Review*, 4:325–34 (Autumn 1951); *The Forlorn Demon*; *The Man of Letters in the Modern World*; *Collected Essays*; *Essays of Four Decades*.

"The Angelic Imagination: Poe and the Power of Words," *Kenyon Review*, 14:455–75 (Summer 1952). Reprinted as "The Angelic Imagination: Poe as God" in *The Forlorn Demon*; *The Man of Letters in the Modern World*; *Collected Essays*. Reprinted as "The Angelic Imagination" in *Essays of Four Decades*.

"Crane: The Poet as Hero," *New Republic*, 127:25–26 (17 November 1952); *The Forlorn Demon* (in the group "A Miscellany"); *The Man of Letters in the Modern World*; *Collected Essays* (in the group "A Miscellany"); *Essays of Four Decades*.

"Is Literary Criticism Possible?" *Partisan Review*, 19:546–57 (September–October 1952); *The Forlorn Demon*; *The Man of Letters in the Modern World*; *Collected Essays*; *Essays of Four Decades*.

"The Man of Letters in the Modern World," *Hudson Review*, 5:335–45 (Autumn 1952); *The Forlorn Demon*; *The Man of Letters in the Modern World*; *Collected Essays*; *Essays of Four Decades*. (Originally Phi Beta Kappa Address, University of Minnesota, 1 May 1952.)

"The Symbolic Imagination: A Meditation on Dante's Three Mirrors," *Kenyon Review*, 14:256–77 (Spring 1952).

"Orthodoxy and the Standard of Literature," *New Republic*, 128:24–25 (5 January 1953).

"The Point of Dying: Donne's 'Virtuous Men,' " *Sewanee Review*, 61:76–81 (Winter 1953); *The Forlorn Demon* (in the group "A Miscellany"); *The Man of Letters in the Modern World*; *Collected Essays* (in the group "A Miscellany"); *Essays of Four Decades*.

"The Self-Made Angel," *New Republic*, 129:17, 21 (31 August 1953).

"Christ and the Unicorn," *Sewanee Review*, 63:175–81 (Spring 1955).
"Reflections on American Poetry: 1900–1950," *Sewanee Review*, 64:59–70 (Winter 1956). Reprinted as "Introduction," *Modern Verse in English: 1900–1950*.
"Twenty Years of *Western Review*," *Western Review*, 20:99 (Winter 1956).
"The Novel in the American South," *New Statesman*, 57:831–32 (13 June 1959).
"Random Thoughts on the 1920's," *Minnesota Review*, 1:46–56 (Fall 1960).
"A Southern Mode of the Imagination: Circa 1918 to the Present," *Carleton Miscellany*, 1:9–23 (Winter 1960); *Collected Essays*; *Essays of Four Decades*.
"A Great Stylist: The Prophet as Critic," *Sewanee Review*, 69:314–17 (Spring 1961). (On Edward Dahlberg.)
"Homage to Yvor Winters," *Sequoia*, 6:2–3 (Winter 1961).
"The Gaze Past, the Glance Present," *Sewanee Review*, 70:671–73 (Autumn 1962). (On Donald Davidson.)
"Memories of Sylvia Beach," *Mercure de France*, 349:n.p. (August–September 1962).
"William Faulkner," *New Statesman*, 64:408 (28 September 1962); *Sewanee Review*, 71:160–64 (Winter 1963).
"The Battle of Gettysburg: Why It Was Fought," *Carleton Miscellany*, 4:32–45 (Summer 1963).
"For John Ransom at Seventy-Five," *Shenandoah*, 14:5–8 (Spring 1963).
"Shadow: A Parable and a Polemic," *Carleton Miscellany*, 4:61–64 (Winter 1963).
"What Is Creative Writing?" *Wisconsin Studies in Contemporary Literature*, 5:181–84 (Autumn 1964).
"Appomattox, April 9, 1865: A Peroration a Hundred Years After," *Spectator*, 9:467–68 (April 1965).
"Eat and/or Die," *Minneapolis Tribune*, 17 April 1966, sec. E, p. 1.
"The Unliteral Imagination; Or, I, Too, Dislike It," *Southern Review*, n.s. 1:530–42 (Summer 1965); *Essays of Four Decades*.
"Postscript by the Guest Editor," *Sewanee Review*, 74:383–87 (Winter 1966). Reprinted in *T. S. Eliot, the Man and His Work*.
"Subsidized Publication," *The Little Magazine and Contemporary Literature: A Symposium Held at the Library of Congress, 2 and 3 April 1965*. Washington, D.C., 1966, pp. 42–47.
"Several Thousand Books," *Sewanee Review*, 75:377–84 (Summer 1967). (Originally Commencement Address, University of Minnesota, 18 March 1967.)
"Faulkner's *Sanctuary* and the Southern Myth," *Virginia Quarterly Review*, 44:418–27 (Summer 1968). Reprinted as the introduction to *Sanctuary*, New American Library, 1968.
"The Poetry of Edgar Allen Poe," *Sewanee Review*, 76:214–25 (Spring 1968).
"More Literature and Lost Traveller." Nashville: The Peabody Library School, 1969. (Brochure.)

COMMENTARY

"Waste Lands" (Correspondence), *Literary Review of the New York Evening Post*, 3:886 (4 August 1923).
"A Polite Protest," *Poetry*, 25:169–70 (December 1924).
"Dear Mr. Hankel," *Aesthete 1925*, no. 1, pp. 10–11 (February 1925).
"On Critics and Poets," *Saturday Review of Literature*, 1:886 (4 July 1925).
"Editorial on *The Criterion*," *Nation*, 123:259 (22 September 1926).
"Literary Criticism in America," *New Republic*, 47:283 (28 July 1926).
(Correspondence), *New Republic*, 55:149 (27 June 1928).
"An Open Letter to Mr. Howard Mumford Jones," *Archive*, 41:4–5 (May 1929).
(Correspondence), *Hound and Horn*, 4:117 (October–December 1930).
(Correspondence), *New Republic*, 62:103 (12 March 1930).

(Editorial), *Lyric*, 11:14 (Winter 1932).

(Editorial Note), *Poetry*, 40:90–94 (May 1932).

"More about Lanier," *New Republic*, 76:338 (1 November 1933).

"Correspondence in *re* Paul Engle's *American Song*," *New Republic*, 80:245 (10 October 1934).

"An Enquiry" (with nineteen other contributors), *New Verse*, no. 11, pp. 20–22 (October 1934).

"Correspondence: Fascism and the Southern Agrarians," *New Republic*, 87:75–76 (27 May 1936).

"How They Are Voting IV," *New Republic*, 88:304–5 (21 October 1936).

"Sixteen Comments on Auden" (with fifteen other contributors), *New Verse*, nos. 26–27, p. 27, (November 1937).

"Enquiry" (answers by six contributors), *Twentieth Century Verse*, nos. 12–13, p. 112 (September–October 1938).

"Allen Tate on 'The Fathers,'" *Partisan Review*, 6:125–26 (Winter 1939).

"America and the Next War," *New Republic*, 99:148 (14 June 1939).

"The Situation in American Writing" (with ten other contributors), *Partisan Review*, 6:28–30 (Summer 1939).

"Apology," *New Republic*, 104:309 (3 March 1941).

"Literature in the South" (Comment on W. J. Cash's essay of that title in *Saturday Review of Literature*, 28 December 1940), *Saturday Review of Literature*, 23:11 (11 January 1941).

"What Is Poetry?" *New Republic*, 104:183 (6 January 1941).

BOOK REVIEWS

Abercrombie, Lascelles. *The Theory of Poetry*. In *New Republic*, 46:281 (21 April 1926).

Adams, Léonie. *Those Not Elect*. In *Nation*, 122:237–38 (3 March 1926).

Æ. *Voices of Stones*. In *New Republic*, 44:209–10 (14 October 1925).

Agar, Herbert. *The People's Choice*. In *American Review*, 2:231–37 (December 1933).

_____. *Pursuit of Happiness: The Story of American Democracy*. In *Free America*, 2:16–18 (October 1938).

Aiken, Conrad. *Priapus and the Pool*. In *Nation*, 122:38–39 (13 January 1926).

_____. *Senlin: A Biography*. In *Nation*, 122:38–39 (13 January 1926).

An Anthology of Negro Poetry. In *Nashville Tennessean*, 3 August 1924.

Anderson, Maxwell. *You Who Have Dreams*. In *Nation*, 121:680 (9 December 1925).

Auden, W. H. *The Double Man*. In *Accent*, 2:118–19 (Winter 1942).

Beale, H. K. *The Critical Year: A Study of Andrew Johnson and Reconstruction*. In *New Republic*, 63:376–77 (13 August 1930).

Belgion, Montgomery. *The Human Parrot and Other Essays*. In *New Republic*, 70:133 (16 March 1932).

Benét, Stephen Vincent. *John Brown's Body*. In *Nation*, 127:274 (19 September 1928).

_____. *Tiger Joy*. In *Nation*, 121:680 (9 December 1925).

Berl, Immanuel. *The Nature of Love*. In *Nashville Tennessean*, 10 August 1924.

Bishop, John Peale. *Now With His Love*. In *New Republic*, 78:52–53 (21 February 1934).

Blackmur, R. P. *The Expense of Greatness*. In *Partisan Review*, 8:67–69 (January–February 1941).

_____. *From Jordan's Delight*. In *Southern Review*, 3:192–98 (Summer 1937). Later forms part of the essay "Nine Poets: 1937" in *Reason in Madness*.

Blunden, Edmund. *English Poems*. In *New York Herald Tribune Books*, 28 March 1926, p. 1.

Bogan, Louise. *The Sleeping Fury.* In *Southern Review,* 3:190–92 (Summer 1937). Later forms part of the essay "Nine Poets: 1937" in *Reason in Madness.*

Braithwaite, W. S., ed. *Anthology of Magazine Verse for 1925.* In *New York Herald Tribune Books,* 14 February 1926, p. 18.

Bronowski, J. *The Poet's Defense.* In *New Republic,* 100:52–53 (16 August 1939).

Brooks, Van Wyck, and others, eds. *The American Caravan,* vol. 1. In *Bookman,* 68:353–55 (November 1928).

Burdett, Osbert. *Critical Essays.* In *New Republic,* 51:79–80 (8 June 1927).

Bynner, Witter. *Caravan.* In *Nation,* 121:680 (9 December 1935).

Cabell, James Branch. *The High Place.* In *Nashville Tennessean,* 16 March 1924.

———. *The Way of Ecben.* In *New Republic,* 61:201–2 (8 January 1930).

Calverton, V. F. *Sex Expression in Literature.* In *Nation,* 123:694 (29 December 1926).

Campbell, Roy. *Adamastor.* In *New Republic,* 66:133 (18 March 1931).

———. *The Flaming Terrapin.* In *New Republic,* 66:133 (18 March 1931).

Cheney, E. Ralph, ed. *The Independent Poetry Anthology.* In *Guardian,* 2:463 (October 1925).

Coatsworth, Elizabeth J. *Atlas and Beyond.* In *Nashville Tennessean,* 3 August 1924.

Coffin, R. P. T. *Salt Water Ballads.* In *Southern Review,* 3:184 (Summer 1937). Later forms part of the essay "Nine Poets: 1937" in *Reason in Madness.*

Couch, W. T., ed. *Culture in the South.* In *American Review,* 2:411–32 (February 1934)

———. *These Are Our Lives.* In *Free America,* 3:18–20 (November 1939).

Cournos, John. *The New Candide.* In *Nashville Tennessean,* 25 May 1924.

Cowley, Malcolm. *Blue Juniata: Poems.* In *New Republic,* 60:51–52 (28 August 1929).

Crane, Hart. *The Bridge.* In *Hound and Horn,* 3:580–85 (July–September 1930). Later forms part of the essay "Hart Crane" in *Reactionary Essays on Poetry and Ideas; On the Limits of Poetry; The Man of Letters in the Modern World; Collected Essays; Essays of Four Decades.*

Craven, Avery. *Edmund Ruffin: Southerner.* In *New Republic,* 72:25–26 (17 August 1932).

Cummings, E. E. *50 Poems.* In *Partisan Review,* 8:242–43 (May–June 1941).

———. *Tulips and Chimneys.* In *Nashville Tennessean,* 23 March 1924.

———. *Viva.* In *Poetry,* 39:332–37 (March 1932). Reprinted as "E. E. Cummings" in *Reactionary Essays on Poetry and Ideas.*

Dahlberg, Edward. *Can These Bones Live.* In *Sewanee Review,* 69:314–17 (Spring 1961).

Daiches, David. *Poetry and the Modern World.* In *New Republic,* 104:25–26 (6 January 1941). Reprinted as "Procrustes and the Poets" in *Reason in Madness.*

Damon, S. Foster. *Thomas Holley Chivers: Friend of Poe.* In *New Republic,* 63:294–95 (23 July 1930).

Davidson, Donald. *The Long Street.* In *Sewanee Review,* 70:671–73 (Autumn 1962).

Dell, Floyd. *Janet March.* In *Nashville Tennessean,* 17 February 1924.

Deutsch, Babette. *Epistle to Prometheus.* In *New York Herald Tribune Books,* 26 April 1931, p. 4.

Dillon, George, and Edna St. Vincent Millay, trans. *Flowers of Evil.* In *Nation,* 143:22–23 (4 July 1936).

Dodd, W. E. *Lincoln or Lee.* In *New Republic,* 55:75–76 (6 June 1928).

Dos Passos, John. *Manhattan Transfer.* In *Nation,* 122:160–62 (10 February 1926).

Dow, Dorothy. *Black Babylon.* In *Nashville Tennessean,* 8 June 1924.

Dowdey, Clifford. *Bugles Blow No More.* In *Atlantic Monthly,* 160:n.p. (August 1937).

Doyle, Camilla. *Poems.* In *Nashville Tennessean,* 13 April 1924.

Edman, Irwin. *The Contemporary and His Soul.* In *New York Herald Tribune Books,* 24 May 1931, p. 7.

———. *Poems.* In *Nation,* 121:680 (9 December 1925).

Eliot, T. S. *Ash Wednesday.* In *Hound and Horn,* 4:290–97 (January–March 1931). Reprinted as "T. S. Eliot" in *Reactionary Essays on Poetry and Ideas; On the Limits of Poetry; Collected Essays; Essays of Four Decades.*
_____, ed. *London: A Poem.* In *New Republic,* 68:23–34 (19 August 1931).
_____. *Poems: 1909–1925.* In *New Republic,* 47:172–73 (30 June 1926).
Fernandez, Ramon. *Messayges.* In *New Republic,* 51:339–40 (17 August 1927).
Field, Sara Bard. *Darkling Plain.* In *Southern Review,* 3:187–88 (Summer 1937). Later forms part of the essay "Nine Poets: 1937" in *Reason in Madness.*
Five Young American Poets: An Anthology (New Directions). In *Partisan Review,* 8:243–44 (May–June 1941).
Fletcher, John Gould. *The Two Frontiers: A Study in Historical Psychology.* In *New Republic,* 62:132 (19 March 1930).
Frank, Waldo. *Chalk Face.* In *Nashville Tennessean,* 23 November 1924.
Freeman, Douglas Southall. *Lee's Lieutenants: A Study in Command.* In *New Republic,* 108:644 (10 May 1943).
_____. *R. E. Lee.* Vols. 1 and 2, in *New Republic,* 81:171–72 (19 December 1934); vols. 3 and 4, in *New Republic,* 82:255 (10 April 1935).
Fuller, J. F. C. *The Generalship of Ulysses S. Grant.* In *New Republic,* 62:277–78 (23 April 1930).
Garrod, H. W. *Keats.* In *New Republic,* 51:154–55 (29 June 1927).
Gottschalk, Laura Riding. *The Close Chaplet.* In *New Republic,* 50:76 (9 March 1927).
Graves, Robert. *Contemporary Techniques of Poetry.* In *New Republic,* 44:263 (28 October 1925).
Gregory, Horace. *No Retreat.* In *New Republic,* 74:255–56 (12 April 1933).
_____. *Poems: 1930–1940.* In *Partisan Review,* 8:241–42 (May–June 1941).
Guthrie, Ramon. *Trobar Clus.* In *Nashville Tennessean,* 27 April 1924.
Hackett, Florence. *With Benefit of Clergy.* In *Nashville Tennessean,* 27 April 1924.
Harris, Julia C. *Joel Chandler Harris: Editor and Essayist.* In *New Republic,* 71:320–21 (23 April 1930).
Hart, B. H. L. *Sherman: Soldier, Realist, American.* In *New Republic,* 62:277–78 (23 April 1930).
Hemingway, Ernest. *In Our Time.* In *Nation,* 122:160–62 (10 February 1926).
_____. *The Sun Also Rises.* In *Nation,* 123:642, 644 (15 December 1926).
_____. *The Torrents of Spring.* In *Nation,* 123:89–90 (28 July 1926).
Hendrick, Burton J. *The Lees of Virginia.* In *New Republic,* 85:233–34 (1 January 1936).
Hergesheimer, Joseph. *Swords and Roses.* In *New Republic,* 59:50–51 (29 May 1929).
Heyward, DuBose. *Skylines and Horizons.* In *Nashville Tennessean,* 20 April 1924.
Hibbard, Addison, ed. *The Lyric South: An Anthology of Recent Poetry from the South.* In *New York Herald Tribune Books,* 16 September 1928, p. 13.
Holmes, John. *Address to the Living.* In *Southern Review,* 3:184 (Summer 1937). Later forms part of the essay "Nine Poets: 1937" in *Reason in Madness.*
Horton, Philip. *Hart Crane: The Life of an American Poet.* In *Poetry,* 50:219–24 (July 1937).
Housman, Lawrence. *Echo De Paris.* In *Nashville Tennessean,* 6 April 1924.
Humphries, Rolfe. *Europa and Other Sonnets.* In *New Republic,* 62:25–26 (19 February 1930).
Huxley, Aldous. *The Cicadas and Other Poems.* In *Poetry,* 39:285–87 (February 1932).
Johnson, Stanley. *Professor.* In *New York Herald Tribune Books,* 5 April 1925, p. 11.
Jones, H. M. *They Say the Forties.* In *Southern Review,* 3:184–85 (Summer 1937). Later forms part of the essay "Nine Poets: 1937" in *Reason in Madness.*
Kallen, Horace M. *Culture and Democracy.* In *Nashville Tennessean,* 21 September 1924.

Kantor, MacKinlay. *Long Remember*. In *Nation*, 138:420–41 (11 April 1934); *New York Herald Tribune Books*, 8 April 1934, pp. 1–2.

Kreymborg, Alfred. *Our Singing Strength*. In *New Republic*, 62:51–52 (26 February 1930).

————. *Scarlet and Mellow*. In *New York Herald Tribune Books*, 18 July 1926, p. 3.

Kroll, Harry Harrison. *The Cabin in the Cotton*. In *Nation*, 133:614–15 (2 December 1931).

Langner, Lawrence. *Moses: A Play, a Protest, and a Proposal*. In *Nashville Tennessean*, 7 December 1924.

Leavis, F. R. *How to Teach Reading: A Primer for Ezra Pound*. In *Poetry*, 44:53–55 (April 1934).

Lee, Lawrence. *Monticello and Other Poems*. In *Southern Review*, 3:189–90 (Summer 1937). Later forms part of the essay "Nine Poets: 1937" in *Reason in Madness*.

Ludwig, Emil. *Lincoln*. In *Nation*, 130:185–86 (12 February 1930).

Lutoslawski, Wicenty. *The World of Souls*. In *Nation*, 119:549 (19 November 1924).

Lytle, Andrew. *The Long Night*. In *New York Herald Tribune Books*, 6 September 1936, p. 3.

MacIntyre, C. F. *Poems*. In *Southern Review*, 3:188–89 (Summer 1937). Later forms part of the essay "Nine Poets: 1937" in *Reason in Madness*.

Mackail, J. W. *Studies of English Poets*. In *New York Herald Tribune Books*, 28 May 1926, p. 12.

MacKaye, James. *The Logic of Conduct*. In *Nashville Tennessean*, 13 July 1924.

MacLeish, Archibald. *Conquistador*. In *New Republic*, 71:77–78 (1 June 1932). Reprinted as "MacLeish's *Conquistador*" in *Reactionary Essays on Poetry and Ideas*; *On the Limits of Poetry*; *The Man of Letters in the Modern World*; *Collected Essays*; *Essays of Four Decades*.

————. *The Happy Marriage*. In *Nation*, 124:185–86 (16 February 1927).

————. *Streets in the Moon*. In *Nation*, 124:185–86 (16 February 1927).

MacNeice, Louis. *Modern Poetry: A Personal Essay*. In *New Republic*, 100:52–53 (16 August 1939).

MacVeagh, Lincoln, ed. *Poetry From the Bible*. In *New York Herald Tribune Books*, 16 August 1925, p. 12.

Masters, Edgar Lee. *The New Spoon River*. In *Guardian*, 2:334 (May–June 1925).

————. *Whitman*. In *Poetry*, 50:350–53 (September 1937).

Millay, Edna St. Vincent. *Fatal Interview*. In *New Republic*, 56:335–36 (6 May 1931). Reprinted as "Edna St. Vincent Millay" in *Reactionary Essays on Poetry and Ideas*.

————. *The Harp-Weaver and Other Poems*. In *Nashville Tennessean*, 10 February 1924.

Milton, G. F. *The Age of Hate: Andrew Johnson and the Radicals*. In *New Republic*, 66:24–25 (18 February 1931).

Morand, Paul. *Green Shoots*. In *Nashville Tennessean*, 18 May 1924.

More, P. E. *The Demon of the Absolute*, vol. 1. In *New Republic*, 57:116–17 (12 December 1928).

Morrow, H. W. *Mary Todd Lincoln*. In *New Republic*, 55:127 (20 June 1928).

Morton, David. *The Sonnet Today and Yesterday*. In *New York Herald Tribune Books*, 14 March 1926, p. 18.

Muir, Edwin. *Transition*. In *Nation*, 123:509 (17 November 1926).

Munson, Gorham B. *Destinations: A Canvass of American Literature Since 1900*. In *New Republic*, 54:395–96 (16 May 1928).

Murry, John Middleton. *Keats and Shakespeare*. In *New Republic*, 51:154–55 (29 June 1927).

Nicolson, J. V. *The King of the Black Isles*. In *Nashville Tennessean*, 6 April 1924.

Parks, Edd Winfield. *Segments of Southern Thought*. In *Free America*, 3:18 (March 1939).

Patterson, F. A., ed. *The Works of John Milton* (Columbia edition). Vols. 1 and 2, in *New Republic*, 68:266–68 (21 October 1931); vols. 8–18, in *New Republic*, 99:23 (10 May 1939).
Peterson, Houston. *The Melody of Chaos*. In *New Republic*, 67:265–66 (22 July 1931).
Petronius. *The Satyricon*. In *Nashville Tennessean*, 2 March 1924.
Phillips, Ulrich B. *Life and Labor in the Old South*. In *New Republic*, 59:211–12 (10 July 1929).
Porter, Katherine Anne. *Flowering Judas*. In *Nation*, 131:352–53 (1 October 1930).
Pound, Ezra. *Cantos LII–LXXI*. In *Partisan Review*, 8:241–44 (May–June 1941).
_____. *A Draft of XXX Cantos*. In *Nation*, 132:632–34 (10 June 1931).
_____. *How to Read*. In *Poetry*, 41:107–12 (November 1932).
_____. ed. *Profile: An Anthology Collected in MCMXXXI*. In *Poetry*, 41:107–12 (November 1932).
Putnam, Phelps. *The Five Seasons*. In *Hound and Horn*, 6:345–49 (January–March 1933).
_____. *Trinc*. In *New Republic*, 53:75–76 (7 December 1927).
Ransom, John Crowe. *Chills and Fever*. In *Guardian*, 1:25 (November 1924).
_____. *Two Gentlemen in Bonds*. In *Nation*, 124:346 (30 March 1927).
Read, Herbert. *Poetry and Anarchism*. In *New Republic*, 100:52–53 (16 August 1939).
Richards, I. A. *Practical Criticsm*. In *New Republic*, 61:111–13 (18 December 1929).
Rickert, Edith. *New Methods for the Study of Literature*. In *New Republic*, 50:281–82 (27 April 1927).
Robinson, Edwin Arlington. *The Man Who Died Twice*. In *Nashville Tennessean*, 4 May 1924.
_____. *Talifer*. In *New Republic*, 76:312–13 (25 October 1933). Reprinted, with revision, as "Edwin·Arlington Robinson" in *Reactionary Essays on Poetry and Ideas*; *On the Limits of Poetry*; *The Man of Letters in the Modern World*; *Collected Essays*; *Essays of Four Decades*.
Rosenberg, James N. *Punchinello: A Ballett*. In *Nashville Tennessean*, 30 March 1924.
Rowland, Eron. *Varina Howell: Wife of Jefferson Davis*. In *New Republic*, 55:127 (20 June 1928).
Santayana, George. *Dialogues in Limbo*. In *Nation*, 122:416, 418 (14 April 1926).
Shapiro, Karl Jay. *Person, Place and Thing*. In *Common Sense*, 12:67–68 (February 1944).
Sheppard, Eric William. *Bedford Forrest*. In *Virginia Quarterly Review*, 7:134–38 (January 1931).
Sitwell, Edith. *Bucolic Comedies*. In *Nashville Tennessean*, 10 February 1924.
Sitwell, Osbert. *Out of the Flame*. In *New Republic*, 43:270–71 (29 July 1925).
Sitwell, Sacheverell. *The Thirteenth Caesar*. In *New Republic*, 43:270–71 (29 July 1925).
Spencer, Theodore, ed. *A Garland for John Donne*. In *New Republic*, 70:212–13 (6 April 1932). Reprinted as "A Note on Donne" in *Reactionary Essays on Poetry and Ideas*; *On the Limits of Poetry*; *The Man of Letters in the Modern World*; *Collected Essays*; *Essays of Four Decades*.
Spender, Stephen. *Poems*. In *New Verse*, no. 3, pp. 21–23 (May 1933). Reprinted as "Stephen Spender's *Poems*" in *The Hovering Fly and Other Essays*.
Spengler, Oswald. *The Decline of the West*. Vol. 1, in *Nation*, 122:532, 534 (12 May 1926).
_____. *The Hour of Decision*. In *American Review*, 3:41–47 (April 1934).
Spingarn, J. E. *Poems*. In *Nashville Tennessean*, 11 May 1924.
Starke, A. H. *Sidney Lanier*. In *New Republic*, 76:67–70 (30 August 1933).
Stevens, Wallace. *Harmonium*. In *Nashville Tennessean*, 10 February 1924.
Stribling, T. S. *Unfinished Cathedral*. In *Nation*, 138:709–10 (20 June 1934).

Strong, L. A. G. *The Lowery Road.* In *Nashville Tennessean,* 15 June 1924.

Taggard, Genevieve. *Words for the Chisel.* In *Nation,* 122:481–42 (28 April 1926).

Thomason, John W., Jr. *Jeb Stuart.* In *Virginia Quarterly Review,* 7:134–38 (January 1931).

Thorpe, C. D. *The Mind of John Keats.* In *New Republic,* 51:154–55 (29 June 1927).

Toomer, Jean. *Cane.* In *Nashville Tennessean,* 24 February 1924.

Turbyfill, Mark, and Samuel Putnam. *Evaporation.* In *Double Dealer,* 6:32–33 (January 1924).

Turner, F. McD. C. *The Element of Irony in English Literature.* In *New York Herald Tribune Books,* 27 June 1926, p. 9.

Untermeyer, Louis. *The Forms of Poetry.* In *New York Herald Tribune Books,* 1 August 1926, p. 10.

Van Doren, Mark. *Now the Sky and Other Poems.* In *Nation,* 127:691–92 (19 December 1928).

————. *The Private Reader.* In *New Republic,* 106:506, 508 (13 April 1942).

————. *7 P.M. and Other Poems.* In *Nation,* 124:482–83 (27 April 1927).

————. *A Winter Diary and Other Poems.* In *Nation,* 140:339–40 (20 March 1935).

Wade, John Donald. *John Wesley.* In *New Republic,* 65:113 (10 December 1930).

Weber, Brom, ed. *The Letters of Hart Crane: 1916–1932.* In *New Republic,* 127: 25–26 (17 November 1952). Reprinted as "Crane: The Poet as Hero" in *The Forlorn Demon; The Man of Letters in the Modern World; Collected Essays; Essays of Four Decades.*

Whicher, George F. *This Was a Poet.* In *Kenyon Review,* 1:200–3 (Spring 1939).

Whistler, Laurence. *The Emperor Heart.* In *Southern Review,* 3:186–87 (Summer 1937). Later forms part of the essay "Nine Poets: 1937" in *Reason in Madness.*

Williams, Charles. *Windows of Night.* In *New Republic,* 44:209–10 (14 October 1925).

Williams, Oscar, ed. *New Poems: 1942.* In *Nation,* 154:688 (13 June 1942).

Wilson, Edmund. *Axel's Castle.* In *Hound and Horn,* 4:619–24 (July–September 1931).

Winston, R. W. *Robert E. Lee.* In *Nation,* 138:512 (2 May 1934).

Winters, Yvor. *The Bare Hills.* In *New Republic,* 54:165–66 (21 March 1928).

————. *Collected Poems.* In *New Republic,* 128:17–18 (2 March 1953).

Wood, Clement. *Poets of America.* In *Guardian,* 2:462–63 (October 1925).

Woods, Margaret L. *A Poet's Youth.* In *Nashville Tennessean,* 13 April 1924.

Wylie, Elinor. *Collected Poems of Elinor Wylie,* ed. William Rose Benét. In *New Republic,* 72:107 (7 September 1932).

Yeats, W. B. *Letters on Poetry from W. B. Yeats to Dorothy Wellesley.* In *New Republic,* 103:730, 732 (25 November 1940).

Young, James C. *Marse Robert: Knight of the Confederacy.* In *New Republic,* 62:277–78 (23 April 1930).

SELECTED TRANSLATIONS
Books

COLLECTED ESSAYS: *Dirasat fi-l-nqd.* Trans. Abdul Rhaman Yaghi. Beirut: Maktabat Al-Maaref, 1962. *Hyundae Moonhak Ui Yungyuk.* Trans. Chu Young Kim and Sang Ok Lee. Seoul: Chungang Moonhwa Sa, 1962.

FATHERS, THE: *Die Väter.* Trans. Gerhart M. Hotop, Munich: Rütten and Leoning, 1967. *I nostri patri.* Trans. Marcella Bonsanti. Milan: Feltrinelli, 1964. *Les ancêtres.* Trans. Marie Canavaggia. Intro. Frank Kermode. Paris: Gallimard, 1948.

ODE TO THE CONFEDERATE DEAD AND OTHER POEMS: *Ode ai Caduti Confederati e Altre Posie.* Trans. and intro. Alfredo Rizzardi. Milan: Arnoldo Mondadori, 1970.

ON THE LIMITS OF POETRY. *Gendaishi no ryōiki.* Trans. Rikutaro Fukuda. Tokyo: Nan'undo, 1961. *Saggi.* (Selections from *On the Limits of Poetry* and *The Forlorn Demon.*) Trans. Nemi D'Agostino. Rome: Edizioni di Storia e Litteratura, 1957.

Essays

"Fuôkunâ no Sankuchûari to nanbu shinwa" ("Faulkner's 'Sanctuary' and the South-
ern Myth"), *Nichibei Forum*, 15:57–65 (August 1969). Tokyo: U.S. Information
Agency.
"L'Imagination angélique, ou de la divinité de Poe" ("The Angelic Imagination").
Trans. Didiez Coupage, in *Configuration Critique de Edgar Allan Poe, La Revue
des Lettres Modernes*, no. 12, pp. 191–213 (1969).
"O Poezji Nowoczesnej i Nienowczesnej" ("Poetry: Modern and Unmodern"). Trans.
Zofia Kozarynowa, in *Temafy*, 7:70–85 (Spring–Summer 1969).

MISCELLANEA

"Foreword," *White Buildings: Poems by Hart Crane*. New York: Horace Liveright.
1926.
"The Tower of Babel" (by Noel Gordon, pseud.), *Brentano's Book Chat*, 5:58–62
(September–October 1926); 5:58–61 (November–December 1926); 6:59–75 (May–
June 1927); 6:59–62 (July–August 1927); 6:59–62 (September–October 1927); 7:67–70
(January–February 1928); 7:59–62 (March–April 1928); 7:59–62 (July–August 1928).
"The Immortal Woman" (a short story), *Hound and Horn*, 6:592–609 (July–Septem-
ber 1933).
"The Migration" (a short story), *Yale Review*, 24:83–111 (Autumn 1934).
"Preface," *Poems by Samuel Greenberg*. Ed. and intro. Harold Holden and Jack
McManis. New York: H. Holt and Company, 1947.
"The Question of the Pound Award" (comment on William Barrett's "A Prize for
Ezra Pound"), *Partisan Review*, 16:520 (May 1949).
"Preface," *Libretto for the Republic of Liberia*, by Melvin B. Jolson. New York:
Twayne, 1953.
"Introduction," *In the Deepest Aquarium*, by Hy Sobiloff. New York: The Dial Press,
1959.
"Foreword," *Selected Writings: Poetry and Criticism*, by Herbert Read. London:
Faber and Faber, 1963; New York: Horizon Press, 1964.
"Foreword," *The Hero with the Private Parts*, by Andrew Lytle. Baton Rouge:
Louisiana State University Press, 1966.
"Memoir," *Selected Essays*, by William Troy. Ed. and intro. Stanley Edgar Hyman.
New Brunswick: Rutgers University Press, 1967.

Works about Allen Tate

Abel, Darrell. "Intellectual Criticism," *American Scholar*, 12:414–28 (Autumn 1943).

Allen, Charles. "The Fugitive," *South Atlantic Quarterly*, 43:382–89 (October 1944).

Amacher, Anne W. "Myths and Consequences: Calhoun and Some Nashville Agrarians," *South Atlantic Quarterly*, 59:251–64 (Spring 1960).

"American Writing Today, Its Independence and Vigor," *Times Literary Supplement*, special number, 17 September 1954.

Amyx, Clifford. "The Aesthetics of Allen Tate," *Western Review*, 8:135–45 (1949).

Arnold, Willard B. *The Social Ideas of Allen Tate*. Boston: Bruce Humphries, 1955.

Beatty, Richmond C. "Allen Tate as a Man of Letters," *South Atlantic Quarterly*, 47:226–41 (April 1943).

———. "Allen Tate at Princeton," *Vanderbilt Alumnus*, 25:24 (June 1940).

Bennett, Fleming. "The Forlorn Demon," *Arizona Quarterly*, 9:276–77 (Autumn 1953).

Benson, Lewis. "Correspondence," *New Republic*, 55:149 (27 June 1928).

Bentley, Eric Russell. "To Baudelaire via Allen Tate," *Nation*, 160:78–79 (20 January 1945).

Berland, Alwyn. "Violence in the Poetry of Allen Tate," *Accent*, 11:161–71 (Summer 1951).

Bernetta, Sister Mary. "Allen Tate's Inferno," *Renascence*, 3:113–19 (Spring 1971).

Bishop, Ferman. *Allen Tate*. New York: Twayne, 1967.

Blackmur, R. P. *Language as Gesture*, New York: Harcourt, Brace and Co., 1952.

——— "San Giovanni in Venere: Allen Tate as Man of Letters," *Sewanee Review*, 67:614–31 (Autumn 1959).

Blum, Margaret Morton. "Allen Tate's 'Mr. Pope': A Reading," *Modern Language Notes*, 74:706–8 (December 1959).

Bradbury, John M. *The Fugitives: A Critical Account*. Chapel Hill: University of North Carolina Press, 1958.

———. *Renaissance in the South*. Chapel Hill: University of North Carolina Press, 1963.

Bradford, M. E. *Rumors of Mortality: An Introduction to Allen Tate*. Dallas: Argus Academic Press, 1969.

Brégy, Katherine. "Allen Tate: Paradoxical Pilgrim," *Catholic World*, 180:121–25 (November 1954).

Brickell, Herschel. "Allen Tate's Picture of the South," *New York Times Book Review*, 25 September 1938, p. 2.

Brilli, Attilio. "Le ferite degli emisferi," *Galleria*, 20:238–40 (September–December 1970).

Brooks, Cleanth. "Allen Tate," *Poetry*, 66:324–29 (September 1945).

_____. *Modern Poetry and the Tradition.* Chapel Hill: University of North Carolina Press, 1939; New York: Oxford University Press, 1965.

_____. "The Modern Southern Poet," *Virginia Quarterly Review,* 11:304–20 (April 1935).

_____. "On the Poetry of Allen Tate," *Michigan Quarterly Review,* 10:225–28 (Fall 1971).

_____. (Untitled essay.) Jacket of the record of Allen Tate reading, *Yale Series of Recorded Poets,* ed. Cleanth Brooks. New Haven: Carillon Records, 1960 (Record number: YP300).

_____, and Mark Van Doren. "Modern Poetry: A Symposium," *American Review,* 8:427–56 (February 1937).

Brynes, Oscar. "The Poet as Political Animal," *New Republic,* 76:104–5 (6 September 1933).

Burke, Kenneth. "Tentative Proposal," *Poetry,* 50:96–100 (May 1937).

Burnham, James. "The Unreconstructed Allen Tate," *Partisan Review,* 16:198–202 (February 1949).

Burnshaw, Stanley. "In Defense of Mr. Kreymborg," *New Republic,* 62:103 (12 March 1930).

Campbell, Harry M. "Tate on Hardy: The Critic as Moralist," *CEA Critic,* 29:8–9 (1967).

Carruth, Hayden. "A Debt to Allen Tate," *Poetry,* 99:123 (November 1961).

Chapin, Katherine G. "The Courage of Irony: The Poetry of Allen Tate," *New Republic,* 153:4–5, 22–24 (24 July 1965).

Clark, Axton. "Poetry without Purpose," *New Republic,* 79:148–50 (20 June 1934).

Collins, Seward. "Criticism in America, II: The Revival of the Anti-Humanist Myth," *Bookman,* 71:400–15 (July 1930).

Colum, M. M. "The Double Men of Criticism," *American Mercury,* 52:762–68 (June 1941).

Connelly, T. L. "The Vanderbilt Agrarians: Time and Place in Southern Tradition," *Tennessee Historical Quarterly,* 22:22–37 (1963).

Core, George. "A Metaphysical Athlete: Allen Tate as Critic," *Southern Literary Journal,* 2:138–47 (Autumn 1969).

Couch, W. T., ed. *Culture in the South.* Chapel Hill: University of North Carolina Press, 1934.

Cowan, Louise. *The Fugitive Group: A Literary History.* Baton Rouge: Louisiana State University Press, 1959.

Cowley, Malcolm. "The Merriwether Connection," *Southern Review,* n.s., 1:46–56 (January 1965).

_____. "Two Winters with Hart Crane," *Sewanee Review,* 67:547–56 (Autumn 1959).

Crane, R. S. "Cleanth Brooks: Or, the Bankruptcy of Critical Monism," *Modern Philology,* 45:226–45 (May 1948).

Craven, Avery. "Not Writ Sarcastick," *New Republic,* 72:156 (21 September 1932).

Cunningham, J. V. "The New Books," *Bookman,* 75:83–85 (April 1932).

Dahlberg, Edward. *Alms for Oblivion.* Minneapolis: University of Minnesota Press, 1964.

Daiches, David. "Notes for a Reply to Mr. Tate," *Southern Review,* 6:843–46 (Spring 1941).

Daniel, Robert. "The Critics of Nashville," *Tennessee Studies in Literature,* 1:19–25 (1956).

Daniels, Earl. *The Art of Reading Poetry.* New York: Rinehart and Co., Inc., 1941, pp. 312–14.

Davidson, Donald. "'I'll Take My Stand': A History," *American Review,* 5:301–21 (Summer 1935).

_____. "Lines Written for Allen Tate on His Sixtieth Anniversary," *Sewanee Review*, 67:540–41 (Autumn 1959). Reprinted in *The Long Street*. Nashville: Vanderbilt University Press, 1961.

_____. "The Meaning of War: A Note on Allen Tate's 'To the Lacedemonians,'" *Southern Review*, n.s., 1:720–30 (Summer 1965).

_____. "The Mystery of the Agrarians," *Saturday Review of Literature*, 26:6–7 (23 January 1943).

_____. *Southern Writers in the Modern World*. Athens: University of Georgia Press, 1958.

_____. "The Thankless Muse and Her Fugitive Poets," *Sewanee Review*, 66:201–28 (Spring 1958).

Davis, Robert Gorham. "The New Criticism and the Democratic Tradition," *American Scholar*, 19:9–19 (Winter 1950).

Deutsch, Babette. "Wit as the Wall," in *Poetry in Our Time*. New York: Henry Holt and Co., 1952, pp. 195–202.

Donahoe, Wade. "Allen Tate and the Idea of Culture," *Hopkins Review*, 6:116–31 (Spring–Summer 1953).

Donoghue, Denis. "On Allen Tate," *Spectator*, 16 January 1971, pp. 88–89.

Dupee, F. W. "Frost and Tate," *Nation*, 160:464–66 (21 April 1945).

Eder, Ursula E. "The Poetry of Allen Tate," Ph.D. dissertation, Wisconsin, 1956.

Eliot, T. S., "A Note," *Sewanee Review*, 67:576 (Autumn 1959).

Feder, Lillian. "Allen Tate's Use of Classical Literature," *The Centennial Review* 4:89–114 (Winter 1960).

Fergusson, Francis. "A Note on the Vitality of Allen Tate's Prose," *Sewanee Review*, 67:579–81 (Autumn 1959).

Fitzell, Lincoln. "Sword and Dragon," *South Atlantic Quarterly*, 50:214–32 (April 1951).

Fitzgerald, Robert. "The Poetic Responsibility," *New Republic*, 118:31–33 (26 April 1948).

_____. "Poetry and Perfection," *Sewanee Review*, 56:685–97 (Autumn 1948).

Fleming, Rudd. "Dramatic Involution: Tate, Husserl, and Joyce," *Sewanee Review*, 60:445–64 (Summer 1952).

Fletcher, John Gould. "The Modern Southern Poets," *The Westminster Magazine*, 23:229–51 (Winter 1935).

Flint, F. Cudworth. "Five Poets," *Southern Review*, 1:650–74 (Winter 1936).

_____. "*Poems, 1928–1931*," *Symposium 3*, pp. 407–14 (July 1932).

Foster, Richard J. "Allen Tate: From the Old South to Catholic Orthodoxy," in *The New Romantics: A Reappraisal of the New Criticism*. Bloomington: Indiana University Press, 1962.

_____. "Narcissus as Pilgrim: Allen Tate," *Accent*, 17:158–71 (Summer 1957).

_____. "The Romanticism of the New Criticism," *Hudson Review*, 12:232–46 (Summer 1959).

Friedman, Norman. "Point of View in Fiction: The Development of a Critical Concept," *PMLA*, 70:1160–84 (1955).

Gerlach, Lee Florian. "The Poetry and 'Strategies' of Allen Tate." Ph.D. dissertation, Michigan, 1955.

Ghiselin, Brewster. "The Burden of Proof," *Sewanee Review*, 74:527–40 (Spring 1966).

_____. "A Dove," *Michigan Quarterly Review*, 10:229–30 (Fall 1971).

Glicksberg, Charles I. "Allen Tate and Mother Earth," *Sewanee Review*, 45:284–95 (Summer 1937).

Grattan, C. Hartley. "The Present Situation in American Literary Criticism," *Sewanee Review*, 40:11–23 (Spring 1932).

Greenbaum, Leonard Aaron. "The *Hound and Horn*: Episodes in American Literary History, 1927–34." Ph.D. dissertation, Michigan, 1963.

Greenhut, Morris. "Sources of Obscurity in Modern Poetry: The Examples of Eliot, Stevens and Tate," *The Centennial Review* (Michigan State), 7:171–90 (Spring 1963).

Handy, William J. *Kant and the Southern New Critics.* Austin: University of Texas Press, 1963.

————. "The Ontological Theory of the Ransom Critics," *Texas Studies in English,* 25:32–50 (1956).

Hartsock, E. "Roses in the Desert: A View of Contemporary Southern Verse," *Sewanee Review,* 37:328–35 (Autumn 1929).

Hayakawa, S. I. "The Linguistic Approach to Poetry," *Poetry,* 60:89–94 (May 1942).

Hecht, Anthony. "A Few Green Leaves," *Sewanee Review,* 67:568–71 (Autumn 1959).

Hemphill, George. *Allen Tate.* Minneapolis: University of Minnesota Press, 1964. University of Minnesota Pamphlets on American Writers, no. 39. Reprinted in *Seven Modern American Poets,* ed. Leonard Unger. Minneapolis: University of Minnesota Press, 1967.

Hodges, Jerry Whitfield. "The Religious Aspects of the Agrarian Movement." Ph.D. dissertation, Ottawa, 1959.

"Homage to Allen Tate" Issue, *Sewanee Review,* 67:528–631 (Autumn 1959).

Hook, Sidney. "Late Mr. Tate and the Positivist Critics," *Southern Review,* 6:840–43 (Spring 1941).

Horrell, Joe. "Some Notes on Conversion in Poetry," *Southern Review,* 7:117–31 (Summer 1941).

Howard, Richard. "Tate's Essays," *Poetry,* 116:43–45 (April 1970).

"Il nostro male é il vostro," *La Fiera Litteraria,* no. 17, pp 1–2 (26 April 1953).

Jack, Peter Monro. "Allen Tate's Critical Integrity," *New York Times Book Review,* 12 April 1936, pp. 4, 11.

Jacobs, Robert D. "An Irrepressible Conflict: Allen Tate's *The Fathers,*" *Critique,* 10:9–17 (Summer 1968).

————. "Poe and the Agrarian Critics," *Hopkins Review,* 5:43–54 (Spring 1932).

Janet, Sister Mary. "Poetry as Knowledge in the New Criticism," *Western Humanities Review,* 16:199–210 (Summer 1962).

Janssens, Marcel. "Robert Weimann, 'New Criticism,' und die entwicklung der burgerlichen litteraturwissenschaft," *Leuvense Bijoragen,* 53:181–83 (1964).

Jarrell, Randall. "Fifty Years of American Poetry," *Prairie Schooner,* 37:1–27 (1963).

Johnson, Carol H. "The Heroism of the Rational: The Poetry of Allen Tate," *Renascence,* 17:89–96 (Winter 1964). Reprinted in *Reason's Double Agents.* Chapel Hill: University of North Carolina Press, 1966.

Jones, Howard Mumford. "Is There a Southern Renaissance?" *Virginia Quarterly Review,* 6:184–97 (1930).

Jury, John G. "Mr. Jury on Pegasus," *New Republic,* 68:129 (16 September 1931).

Kane, Patricia. "Allen Tate's *The Fathers* and R. K. Meiners' *The Last Alternatives: A Study of the Works of Allen Tate,*" *Critique,* 7:112–18 (Spring 1964).

————. "An Irrepressible Conflict: Allen Tate's *The Fathers,*" *Critique,* 10:9–16 (Summer 1968).

Karanikas, Alexander. "John Crowe Ransom and Allen Tate: A Study of the Southern Agrarian Theory of Literature." Ph.D. dissertation, Northwestern, 1953.

————. *Tillers of a Myth.* Madison: University of Wisconsin Press, 1965.

Kazin, Alfred. "Criticism at the Poles," *New Republic,* 107:492–95 (19 October 1942).

Kermode, Frank. "Contemplation and Method," *Sewanee Review,* 72:124–31 (Winter 1964).

————. "The Dissociation of Sensibility," *Kenyon Review,* 19:169–94 (Spring 1957).

————. "Old Orders Changing," *Encounter,* 15:72–76 (August 1960).

_____. *Puzzles and Epiphanies*. New York: Chilmark Press, 1962; London: Routledge, 1962.

_____. *Romantic Image*. New York: Macmillan Co., 1957.

Kewasaki, Toshihiro. "John Donne's Religious Poetry and the New Criticism." Ph.D. dissertation, Wisconsin, 1958.

Kliewer, Warren. "Allen Tate as a Teacher," *Descant*, 7:41–48 (Autumn 1962).

Knickerbocker, William S. "Fiction of Powder-Puffs: Latian Esoterics," *Sewanee Review*, 48:315–21 (Summer 1940).

_____. "The Return of the Native," *Sewanee Review*, 38:479–83 (Autumn 1930).

Koch, Vivienne. "The Poetry of Allen Tate," *Kenyon Review*, 11:355–78 (Summer 1949). Reprinted in *The Kenyon Critics*, ed. John Crowe Ransom. Port Washington, N.Y.: Kennikat Press, 1951.

Korges, James. "Allen Tate: A Checklist Continued," *Critique*, 10:35–52 (Summer 1968).

Krieger, Murray. *The New Apologists for Poetry*. Minneapolis: University of Minnesota Press, 1956.

_____. " 'Recent Criticism,' 'Thematics,' and the 'Existential Dilemma,' " *The Centennial Review*, 4:32–50 (Winter 1960).

Kunitz, Stanley J., ed. *Twentieth Century Authors, First Supplement*. New York: Wilson, 1955.

Link, Frank H. "Das Verhältnis der dichtung zur wirklichkeit bei Allen Tate und anderen 'New Critics,' " *Deutsche Vierteljahrschrift für Litteraturwissenschaft*, 34:554–80 (December 1960).

Lively, Robert. *Fiction Fights the Civil War*. Chapel Hill: University of North Carolina Press, 1957.

Lombardo, Agostino. "L'errore simbolistico," *Mondo*, 13:39 (26 September 1961).

Lowell, Robert "Visiting the Tates," *Sewanee Review*, 67:557–59 (Autumn 1959).

Lytle, Andrew. "Allen Tate: Upon the Occasion of His Sixtieth Birthday," *Sewanee Review*, 67:542–44 (Autumn 1959).

McCormick, Virginia T. "Is Poetry a Live Issue in the South?" *Sewanee Review*, 37:399–406 (Fall 1929).

McDonald, James L. "The Literary Theory of a Modern Man of Letters: The Critical Principles of Allen Tate." Ph.D. dissertation, Northwestern, 1965.

McLuhan, Herbert Marshall. "The Southern Quality," *Sewanee Review*, 55:357–83 (Summer 1947).

Maritain, Jacques. *Creative Intuition in Art and Poetry*. New York: Pantheon Books, 1953.

Mason, August H. "Tate's 'Again the Native Hour,' " *Explicator*, vol. 7, item 23 (December 1948).

Mather, Frank J., Jr. "The Babbittiad," *New Republic*, 63:156–59 (25 June 1930).

Matthews, Jackson. "A Note on the French Version ('Ode to the Confederate Dead')," *Sewanee Review*, 60:518–21 (Summer 1952).

Matthiessen, F. O. "American Poetry, 1920–40," *Sewanee Review*, 55:24–55 (Winter 1947).

_____. "Fragmentary and Whole," *New Republic*, 112:232 (12 February 1945). Reprinted in *The Responsibilities of the Critic*. New York: Oxford University Press, 1952.

Meiners, R. K. "The Art of Allen Tate: A Reading of 'The Mediterranean,' " *University of Kansas City Review*, 27:155–59 (December 1960).

_____. "The Center: Unity and Dissociation," *Twentieth Century Literature*, 9:54–79 (April 1963). A chapter from *The Last Alternatives*.

_____. "The End of History: Allen Tate's 'Seasons of the Soul,' " *Sewanee Review*, 70:34–74 (Winter 1962).

————. *The Last Alternatives: A Study of the Works of Allen Tate*. Denver: Swallow Press, 1962.

————. "Tate's 'The Meaning of Life,'" *Explicator*, vol. 19, item 62 (June 1961).

Miller, Vincent. "Over a Sinful Abyss," *National Review*, 9:282–83 (5 November 1960).

Millgate, Michael. "An Interview with Allen Tate," *Shenandoah*, 12:27–34 (Spring 1961).

Mizener, Arthur. "Among the Shabby Lucifers," *New Republic*, 128:18–19 (13 April 1953).

————. "*The Fathers* and Realistic Fiction," *Accent*, 7:101–9 (Winter 1947). Reprinted in *Sewanee Review*, 67:604–13 (Autumn 1959). This essay is also the introduction to the 1960 edition of *The Fathers*. Also reprinted in *The Sense of Life in the Modern Novel*. Boston: Houghton Mifflin, 1964.

Monk, Samuel Holt. "Tate's 'Again the Native Hour,'" *Explicator*, vol. 7, item 58 (June 1948).

Montgomery, Marion. "Bells for John Stewart's Burden: A Sermon upon the Desirable Death of the 'New Provincialism' Here Typified," *Georgia Review*, 20:145–81 (Summer 1966).

Moore, Edward M. "The Nineteen-Thirty Agararians," *Sewanee Review*, 71:133–42 (Winter 1963).

Morgan, Frederick. "Recent Verse," *Hudson Review*, 1:258–66 (Summer 1948).

Morse, Samuel F. "Second Reading," *Poetry*, 51:262–66 (February 1938).

Muir, Edwin, "Crucial Questions," *The Observer*, 9 December 1956, p. 13.

————. "New Novels," *The Listener*, 16 March 1939, p. 597.

Munson, Gorham B. "Correspondence," *New Republic*, 55:149 (27 June 1928).

Nemerov, Howard. "The Current of the Frozen Stream: An Essay on the Poetry of Allen Tate," *Furioso*, 3:50–61 (February 1948). Reprinted in *Sewanee Review*, 67:585–97 (Autumn 1959). Also reprinted in *Poetry and Fiction: Essays*. New Brunswick: Rutgers University Press, 1963.

"New Jersey Writers Conference," *Publisher's Weekly*, 139:19–26 (10 May 1941).

Nyren, Dorothy. "Allen Tate," *A Library of Literary Criticism*. New York: Ungar, 1960, pp. 476–80.

O'Dea, Richard J. "Allen Tate's 'The Cross,'" *Renascence*, 18:156–60 (Spring 1966).

————. "*The Fathers*, a Revaluation," *Twentieth Century Literature*, 12:87–95 (July 1966).

————. "The Poetry of Allen Tate," in *Nine Essays in Modern Literature*, ed. Donald E. Stanford. Baton Rouge: Louisiana State University Press, 1965, pp. 145–58.

————. "To Make the Eye Secure: The Criticism, Fiction, and Poetry of Allen Tate." Ph.D. dissertation, Stanford, 1964.

Pearce, Roy Harvey. "A Small Crux in Allen Tate's 'Death of Little Boys,'" *Modern Language Notes*, 73:419–21 (June 1958).

————. "A Small Crux: Postscript." *Modern Language Notes*, 75:213–14 (March 1960).

Porter, Katherine Anne. "A Sprig of Mint for Allen," *Sewanee Review*, 67:545–46 (Autumn 1959). Reprinted in *Collected Essays*. New York: Delacorte, 1970.

Pressly, T. J. "Agrarianism: An Autopsy," *Sewanee Review*, 49:145–63 (Spring 1941).

Pritchard, J. P. *Criticism in America*. Norman: University of Oklahoma Press, 1956, pp. 246–50.

Purdy, Rob Roy, ed. *Fugitives' Reunion: Conversations at Vanderbilt*. Nashville: Vanderbilt University Press, 1959.

Rackin, P. R. F. "Poetry without Paradox: The Limitations of the New Criticism of the Lyric." Ph.D. dissertation, Illinois, 1963.

Raleigh, John H. "The New Criticism as an Historical Phenomenon," *Comparative Literature*, 11:21–28 (Winter 1959).

Ramsey, Paul. *The Lively and the Just: An Argument for Propriety.* Tuscaloosa: University of Alabama Press, 1962.

Ransom, John Crowe. "In Amicitia," *Sewanee Review*, 67:528–39 (Autumn 1959).

_____. "Mr. Tate and the Professors," *Kenyon Review*, 2:348–50 (Summer 1940).

_____. *The New Criticism.* Norfolk, Conn.: New Directions, 1941, pp. 222–25.

_____. *The World's Body.* Baton Rouge: Louisiana State University Press, 1968.

Read, Herbert. "Our Cousin, Mr. Tate," *Sewanee Review*, 67:572–75 (Autumn 1959).

Rock, Virginia Jean. "The Making and Meaning of *I'll Take My Stand*: A Study of Utopian Conservatism, 1925–39." Ph.D. dissertation, Minnesota, 1964.

Roellinger, Francis X., Jr. "Two Theories of Poetry as Knowledge," *Southern Review*, 7:690–705 (Summer 1942).

Rubin, Louis D., Jr. "The Concept of Nature in Modern Southern Poetry," *American Quarterly*, 9:63–71 (Spring 1957).

_____. "Four Southerners," in *American Poetry*, ed. Irvin Ehrenpreis. New York: St. Martin's Press, 1965.

_____. "The Poetry of Agrarianism," in *The Faraway Country: Writers of the Modern South.* Seattle: University of Washington Press, 1965.

_____. "The Serpent in the Mulberry Bush," *Hopkins Review*, 6:132–47 (Spring-Summer 1953). Reprinted in *Southern Renascence: The Literature of the Modern South*, ed. Rubin. Baltimore: The Johns Hopkins Press, 1953.

_____. "The South and the Faraway Country," *Virginia Quarterly Review*, 38:444–59 (1962). Reprinted in *The Faraway Country: Writers of the Modern South.* Seattle: University of Washington Press, 1963.

_____. "The Southern Muse: Two Poetry Societies," *American Quarterly*, 13:365–75 (Fall 1961).

_____ and R. D. Jacobs. "Allen Tate: The Arrogant Circumstance," in *South: Modern Southern Literature in Its Cultural Setting*, ed. Rubin and Jacobs. Garden City, N.Y.: Doubleday, 1961.

Russell, Peter. "A Note on the Poetry of Allen Tate," *Nine*, 3:89–91 (May 1950).

Schoeck, R. J. "The Ordered Insight Which Is Earned," *Commonweal*, 58:205 (29 May 1953).

Schwartz, Delmore. "The Poetry of Allen Tate," *Southern Review*, 5:419–38 (Winter 1940).

Scott, Nathan A., Jr. "Tate's Collected Essays," *Chicago Review*, 15:113–19 (Summer 1961).

Shafer, Robert. "Humanism and Impudence," *Bookman*, 70:489–98 (January 1930).

_____. "In Wandering Mazes Lost: A Final Note," *Bookman*, 71:37–39 (March 1930).

Smith, Janet Adam. "The End of the Old Dominion," *New Statesman*, 59:718–19 (14 May 1960).

"Southern Gentleman of Letters," *London Times Literary Supplement*, 19 March 1971, p. 320.

"Southern Style," *London Times Literary Supplement*, 59:496 (5 August 1960).

Spears, Monroe K. "The Criticism of Allen Tate," *Sewanee Review*, 57:317–34 (Spring 1949).

_____. "Homage to Allen Tate: Essays, Notes and Verses in Honor of His Sixtieth Birthday," *Sewanee Review*, 67:527 (Autumn 1959).

_____. "Poems of Permanent Value," *Nashville Banner*, 17 February 1948, p. 26.

Speight, Thomas, et al. "Allen Tate Interview," *Rebel Magazine*, 9:3–17 (Winter 1966).

Squires, Radcliffe. *Allen Tate: A Literary Biography.* New York: Bobbs-Merrill, 1971.

_____. "Allen Tate: A Season at Monteagle," *Michigan Quarterly Review*, 10:57–65 (Winter 1971).

_____. "Allen Tate's *The Fathers*," *Virginia Quarterly Review*, 46:629–49 (Autumn 1970).

_____. "Mr. Tate: Whose Wreath Should Be a Moral," in *Aspects of Modern Poetry*, ed. Richard M. Ludwig. Columbus: Ohio State University Press, 1962.

_____. "The Temperate Manichee," *Voices: A Quarterly of Poetry*, no. 134, pp. 49–51 (1948).

_____. "Will and Vision: Allen Tate's *Terza Rima* Poems," *Sewanee Review*, 78:543–62 (Autumn 1970).

Stallman, Robert W. "The New Criticism and the Southern Critics," in *A Southern Vanguard*, ed. Allen Tate. New York: Prentice-Hall, Inc., 1947.

_____. "The New Critics," in *Critiques and Essays in Criticism*, ed. R. W. Stallman. New York: The Ronald Press 1939, pp. 488–506.

Stanford, Derek. "Allen Tate," *Critic*, 18:70–73 (June–July 1959).

_____. "Tradition and Mr. Allen Tate," *Month*, 208:39–45 (July 1959).

Starke, Aubrey. "Agrarians Deny a Leader," *American Review*, 2:534–53 (March 1934).

_____. "More about Lanier," *New Republic*, 76:337–38 (1 November 1933).

Stewart, John Lincoln. *The Burden of Time: The Fugitives and Agrarians*. Princeton: Princeton University Press, 1965.

Stiehl, Harry. "Achievement in American Catholic Poetry," *Ramparts*, 1:26–38 (November 1962).

Stocking, Fred H. "Poetry as Knowledge: The Critical Theory of John Crowe Ransom and Allen Tate." Ph.D. dissertation, Michigan, 1946.

Stuart, Jesse. "What Vanderbilt University Meant to Me," *Vanderbilt Alumnus*, 53:18 (November–December 1967).

Sullivan, Walter. "Southern Novelists and the Civil War," *Hopkins Review*, 6:133–46 (Winter 1953).

Swallow, Alan. "Preface," in *An Editor's Essays of Two Decades*. Seattle and Denver: Experiment Press, 1962.

Thompson, John. "Allen Tate 1961," *Poetry*, 99:120–22 (November 1961).

Thorp, Willard. "Allen Tate: A Checklist," *Princeton University Library Chronicle*, 3:85–98 (April 1942). Reprinted in *Critique*, 10:17–34 (Summer 1968).

Tobin, James Edward. "Tate's 'Mr. Pope,'" *Explicator*, 15:35 (March 1957).

Troy, William. "Tradition for Tradition's Sake," *Nation*, 142:747–48 (10 June 1936).

Unger, Leonard. *The Man in the Name*. Minneapolis: University of Minnesota Press, 1956.

Van Deusen, Marshall. "Criticism in the Thirties: The Marxists and the New Critics," *Western Humanities Review*, 17:75–85 (1963).

Van Doren, Mark. "A Note," *Sewanee Review*, 67:567 (Autumn 1959).

Viereck, Peter. "Five Good Poets in a Bad Year," *Atlantic Monthly*, 182:95–96 (November 1948).

Vivas, Eliseo. "Allen Tate as Man of Letters," *Sewanee Review*, 62:131–43 (Winter 1954). Reprinted in Vivas, *Creation and Discovery*. New York: Noonday Press, 1955, Henry Regnery Co., 1966.

_____. "Mi ritrovai per una selva oscura," *Sewanee Review*, 67:560–66 (Autumn 1959).

Walcutt, Charles C. "Tate's 'The Cross,'" *Explicator*, vol. 6, item 6 (April 1948).

Ward, C. A. "The Good Myth," *University of Kansas City Review*, 24:272–76 (June 1958).

_____. "Myths: Further Vanderbilt Agrarian Views," *University of Kansas City Review*, 25:53–56 (October 1958).

Weaver, Richard M. "The Southern Phoenix," *Georgia Review*, 17:6–17 (1963).

Weber, Brom, ed. *The Letters of Hart Crane*. New York: Hermitage House, 1952.

Wedde, Ian. "The Passing of the South," *London Magazine*, n.s. 11:171–78 (April–May 1971).

Westbrook, John T. "The Fugitives Overhauled," *Southern Review*, 44:340–43 (Autumn 1959).

Wheelock, John Hall. "Allen Tate," *Sewanee Review*, 67:577–78 (Autumn 1959).

Whittemore, Reed. "Mr. Tate and Mr. Adams," *Sewanee Review*, 67:582–84 (Autumn 1959).

Wilson, Edmund. *The Shores of Light: A Literary Chronicle of the Twenties and Thirties.* New York: Farrar, Straus and Young, Inc., 1952.

———. "The Tennessee Poets," *New Republic*, 54:103–4 (7 March 1928).

Wimsatt, W. K., Jr. *The Verbal Icon.* New York: Noonday Press, 1958, pp. 146–49.

Winters, Yvor. *Forms of Discovery.* Chicago: Swallow Press, 1967.

———. *The Function of Criticism: Problems and Exercises.* Denver: Alan Swallow, 1957.

———. *In Defense of Reason.* Denver: Alan Swallow, 1947, 1960.

———. "In Vindication of Poetry," *New Republic*, 56:255–56 (17 October 1928).

———. "Poets and Others," *Hound and Horn*, 5:675–86 (July–September 1932).

———. *Primitivism and Decadence.* New York: Arrow Editions, 1937.

Wohl, Sam. "A View of Allen Tate," *Hopkins Review*, 2:28–35 (Spring 1949).

Wysgod, Vera. "Allen Tate e Roma," *Fiera Litteraria*, 161:34–39 (28 May 1961).

Zabel, Morton D. "The Creed of Memory," *Poetry*, 40:34–39 (April 1932).

———. "A Critic's Poetry," *Poetry*, 33:281–84 (February 1929).

———. "Reactionary Poems," *New Republic*, 92:315–16 (20 October 1937).

INDEX

Index